"Like the host of a television documentary, Kaniut sets up the story, teasing you, daring you not to continue reading. He then lets the participants in the events tell the story in the first person."
--Jay Barrett, *The Bristol Bay Times*, June 9, 1994

"You have that rare gift which transports a reader and immerses him into the story so that he actually feels the emotions of the minute. Possibly you are the PAGEMASTER. I also read *Alaska Bear Tales* and *More Alaska Bear Tales* with equal enjoyment. Continue to produce these books as they will become a treasured storehouse of Alaska lore."
--P.K. Willis, FAA examiner, Anchorage, Alaska, April 1995

"My wife and I were seated at a banquet on Saturday night with two couples who used to live in Anchorage. They went on-and-on about the Alaska experience and I mentioned (quite proudly) that one of my clients is Alaska's most prestigious writer and author of the well-known classic *Alaska Bear Tales*. In response, one of them exclaimed, "Larry Kaniut coached my son's wrestling team in high school!""

--Bert Krages, Attorney at Law, Portland, OR

"People recognize he's preserving their stories."
--Stephany Evans, FinePrint Literary Management, *Business News Alaska*

"I am a big fan of your books, they are fascinating. Why don't you have them as audio books for everybody to enjoy? The added suspense with changing tones of the narrator amplifies the thrill."
--Hisham Younis, Ph.D, C.R.E.

"You have compiled the best bear research I've ever seen. I wish I were writing the book."(1978)
--Jim Rearden, *Alaska Bear Tales* editor (outdoor editor for *Alaska Magazine* and author of numerous books)

"The author of *Alaska Bear Tales*—one of my all time favorites. I'd love to contribute to your new book." (P.S. If you are interested in some akro dual, let me know if you are coming to Florida and we can make that happen.)
--Patty Wagstaff, USA and International Aerobatic Champion, Inductee, Air Show Hall of Fame

"You have a corner on the market for telling bear stories. All the accounts are excellent and you are fast becoming the best chronicler of bear escapades in the world."
--Dalton Carr, 41-year predator controller Yakima Indian Reservation in Washington, marshal of Red River in Colorado, author *Tales of a Bear Hunter*

"This book may save your life! I simply COULD NOT put this book down. It's chilling, bold and a bit nauseating, but well worth the read! Larry Kaniut pulls no punches in this book...I highly recommend this book to anyone who plans to poke around in bear country. **Stephen King, eat your heart out!"**
--Amazon reviewer zakmartin@yahoo.com, Seattle, WA March 7, 1999

SAFE with Bears

Stay Alive From Encounters

Bear Conflict
Survival

Larry Kaniut

Paper Talk

Anchorage, Alaska

ISBN 978-1-955728-06-5 (Paperback, 3rd edition 2023)

978-1-955728-07-2 (ebook)

ACKNOWLEDGMENTS

Photographer Phil Schofield allowed me the use of the cover photo, taken in the mid-1990's.

Jody Winquist at Northern Printing for her invaluable, extraordinary expertise.

Sarah Risch, our awesome granddaughter, has faithfully worked toward the promotion and publication-distribution of our books. We greatly appreciate her and her efforts.

Grandson Logan Kaniut for editing help.

COVER PHOTO

Phil Schofield took the photograph. It is NOT photo-shopped. After I saw the photo in *PEOPLE Magazine*, I contacted Phil in hopes of using it for the cover of this book. I'm grateful that Phil permitted me to do so. See Phil's comments about his experience with Timothy in chapter 1.

DEDICATION

I dedicate this book to Tom Smith and Gary Shelton—two dedicated bear "studiers"…who have contributed greatly to public safety. And honorable mention to all who place the safety of mankind before that of beasts.

AUTHOR CONTACT INFORMATION

Larry Kaniut, 4800 Natrona, Anchorage, AK 99516
Email: kaniut@alaska.net
Web site: www.kaniut.com

TABLE OF CONTENTS

DISCLAIMER

This book is NOT politically correct. We are living in a PC world where those politically incorrect folk are scorned. Whether they are acceptable or not to the politically correct crowd, I provide facts. If there are errors in the text, I apologize; however I've tried to document everything correctly. And this book's contents are no guarantee of your safety with bears.

If you want safety with bears, the choice is yours—you can read touchy-feely books by authors who want bear safety...or you can read books where authors promote public safety—YOURS. Books of this nature are James Gary Shelton's, Tom Hron's, Ted Gorsline's and, of course, mine.

Unfortunately, many authors portray bears as our coexistent pals. I disagree. Bears can live with people but we can't live with bears. They habituate to us then monopolize us. Man should make the rules, not bears.

Because we probably have more bears on the planet than ever AND because we have a NEW bear, I promote a new motto—instead of "a fed bear is a dead bear," how about "a city bear is a dead bear"? Because I refuse to wallow in political correctness, I confront it in order to deal with reality.

Some may find this book voluminous however I chose to include as much material as possible so that the reader could select—highlight, underscore, study—what is most relevant to his needs.

PREFACE

In January 1998 Dr. Tom Smith, USGS bear ecologist of Anchorage, Alaska, phoned me to compliment me on my book *Some Bears Kill* and to comment on pepper spray. I was humbled and gratified to learn that not all fish and game biologists were opposed to my bear books. Tom kindly supported and defended me before his colleagues. Obviously he believed in my findings because he asked me to co-author a bear book with him.

I told him I'd be happy to help him but that he didn't need my name on his book. We kicked around some ideas. Within a short time I got excited about the book, worked up an outline and contacted Tom, who told me that he'd learned since our earlier discussion that he couldn't profit from his research since it had been done on government time.

I kept hoping that we could figure a way for Tom to realize his dream. But all that passed was time so I chose to do the book myself. As of October 1, 2017, it's been percolating nineteen years and it's time to provide the best available information on staying out of a bear's mouth

Besides Tom's initial offer, my impetus for writing this book was to provide people the most viable solutions for safety in bear country, time tested and proven solutions.

Although I am the author, the contributors and their stories deserve the lion's share of the credit--this is their book.

INTRODUCTION

After completing my first book, I thought I was finished writing. However, publishers requested more. This is my fifth bear book, hopefully the last one providing bear safety information. I provide general bear information, multiple bear-human scenarios, advice for eliminating contact with bears, attack stories and attendant effects of a bear encounter gone bad, effective ways to deal with bears and a plea for public safety regarding "city" bears.

In order to survive a bear encounter gone bad, you must respect yourself, your companions, your family and the animal enough to prepare yourself for a possible encounter. Although it is highly unlikely that you will have a bear encounter, a couple of factors remain tantamount to your safety.

What happens when man meets bear? What value do you place on each species? Are bears more important than man? Do you choose to protect yourself and/or others? How do you intend to do so? Your regard for the contents of this book will determine this book's effect upon you.

Perhaps you know that bears can be both dangerous and deadly. However maybe you **do not know how** to avoid a bear mauling. If you do it right, you come back. If you goof, you may get help or rescue… or…you may NOT come back.

Knowledge about bears, their nature, behavior and characteristics and proper safety practices in proximity with bears provide both bears and people a greater chance of avoiding an injurious encounter. As is always true with knowledge, sometimes a little is better than a lot. **The two most important things that you need to know** about a bear are 1) whether the animal is in your space and 2) what you're prepared to do about it.

If you travel the backcountry and follow the formula presented in this book, you WILL avoid bear injury. But like any other endeavor, the "safe" journey requires a map or plan and diligent adherence to its directions. If you hope to be safe with bruin, you must master the message—apply the information.

It is both desirable and hopeful to coexist with bears. The reality, however, may be harder to implement. I have experienced no serious bear conflict since arriving in Alaska in 1966 nor have I had to kill a bear. I hope that never changes. If man accepts the responsibility of learning about bears and practices "proper protocol" in bear country, that takes a heap of pressure off bears to "do the right thing."

People have used many means to protect themselves from bears, but which works best? If you were advising your closest friend about safety in bear country, what would you tell him? If you are called upon to save someone from injury, are you capable of doing it? If you're given responsibility for your party's safety, how can you assure that they will be SAFE with Bears?

FORWARD - WHY THIS BOOK?

What, do we need another bear book? Not if the information is sugar-coated malarkey. But if you want truthful remedies to bear problems—not a politically correct manifesto of nonsense—but a book geared for public safety, yes. It's time to give backcountry users the country back and to provide hope for safety and the latest-best information. It's time to replace the feel-good ideas with personal power. If we cannot provide viable options for people safety or better information than is already in bear mauling avoidance manuals, we should NOT write yet another bear book!

Let's start with the difference between this and most bear safety books. The good news is that this book will show you how to escape injury from a bear. I present anecdotal information such as the "new" bear that Gary Shelton addresses—an animal that we have created by our inaction. I present the causes of bear attacks upon humans, deterrents, advice and bear stoppers. I provide both general and specific tested or experiential information about the bear, its characteristics, body language in a confrontational situation with man and advice to assist your safety in a close encounter (close encounter and bear safety are somewhat oxymoronic—you shouldn't have a close encounter if you're practicing good visibility).

My job is to present information that gives you the best means of staying out of a bear's mouth…to provide you the most up to date and effective method of safe travel in bear country—to advise you to the best of my ability. Your job is to select what works best for you.

After researching countless books and websites, I've come to the conclusion that we can do better. For instance when I input "bear safety" into the World Wide Web on January 23, 2006, I checked out http://www.dnr.state.ak.us/parks/safety/bears.htm (Division of Parks and Outdoor Recreation). The site proclaimed, "Nothing will guarantee your safety in bear country, but knowledge of bears and proper behavior greatly reduce your risk."

Nothing will guarantee safety? Say, what! You can greatly reduce the risk EVEN if you know nothing about bears…but have a weapon that will stop one.

My perception is that nearly every bear book printed since 1995 was published for the bears. The authors favor giving the bear all the breaks. I challenge you to conduct your own research. What percentage of bear books published since 2000 were written for the bears as opposed to those written for the people? Bear books dealing with human safety should uphold mankind and not relegate man to a lower rung on the food chain. What bear life is more valuable than a human life? (One I read in April of 2006 seemed like a 221-page commercial for pepper spray. It is filled with grand sensationalism and misinformation which will likely get people mauled or killed.)

Numerous books suggest REDUCING injuries from bear encounters. I recommend ELIMINATING injury to humans. This is not a bear mauling survival book but rather a bear mauling AVOIDANCE book.

The implication of *SAFE with Bears* is NOT that we can carelessly and recklessly tip-toe willy-nilly through the timber with no concerns about bruin, the cuddly critter that "won't bother you if you don't bother him"…the "animal that is more scared of you than you are of it." *SAFE with Bears* is not a declaration of safe passage, an endorsement of inconsequence to injury nor a guarantee of safety in bear country. SAFE is an acronym—Stay Alive From Encounters.

Paul Hogan (Crocodile Dundee) wrote on Pg. ix of the Foreword in *Crocodile Attack*,

"I can also guarantee you one thing: once you've read it, you'll think twice before you go swimming in croc country."

I hope that your reading this book will cause you to question bears and to learn more about them and your safety around them. For instance, perhaps you don't know that a crocodile can "leap" from the water or that a polar bear can porpoise eight feet out of the water. What other information can you learn about bears?

The contents of this book will challenge you to consider the value of man as juxtaposed to the value of bruin; it will apprise you of the need for **preparation** before entering bear country and the importance of **practicing** for a safe return.

Bear mauling's are avoidable. If the backcountry sojourner follows the formula presented in this book, he WILL be *SAFE with Bears*. This book's for you.

Should You Continue?

Originally I planned to put these two sections—Should You Read This Book and Humbling Endorsements—in the appendices. However, in order to be fair to the readers, I decided they would fit better at the beginning of the book so that you could determine immediately whether or not to buy and/or read farther.

Should You Read This Book?

While perusing Amazon.com for an ISBN number February 2, 2011, I read some reader comments regarding four of our books. I rarely visit reviews of my books but I'm glad I did. I randomly selected and listed some for your perusal. As you will discover, people have views from 1 to 5, kind of like those who responded in letters to the editor regarding me—the evil, gun happy guy who wants to kill all the bears in town (Appendix 11).

I've listed the "ratings" verbatim from Amazon's website. What is the best means of ascertaining the validity of reviewer comments? Enjoy.

I tried unsuccessfully to find a publisher to compile an anthology of adventures in the North I could use for my high school literature of the North class. Six years later a publisher stated he thought I could do a bear book. After I completed the bestselling *Alaska Bear Tales*, four other publishers asked me to write books. Following are some "reviews" of our bear books.

Alaska Bear Tales

I live in Alaska and spent the summer camping with brown bears in Katmai National Park. I can say from experience that everything in this book is myth, grotesque fantasy, made up nonsense and lore. These types of book feed the false stereotype that bears are man eaters, which they are not. For example, hundreds of tourists a day walk with bears in Katmai National Park. The only fatal bear attack in Katmai, since it was opened in the 1920's, was Timothy Treadwell - and he was mentally ill. When bears are treated without violence, they are peaceful. This book is nothing more than propaganda by the hunting establishment. If people knew that children and the elderly walk safely with bears every summer, it would seem really pathetic to go out and shoot them. Read *Grizzly Heart* by Charlie Russell if you want to read a book about real bears.

1.0 out of 5 stars **One of the worst books on bears ever written**, October 16, 2007 By Jessica Teel (Hawaii) [Author's note: She also bad mouthed my *More Alaska Bear Tales*]

The author of this book, Larry Kaniut, is standing in front of my high school English class right now telling the students how he researches his books and how he writes. About myself: I was a journalist for 15 years before becoming a teacher; much of that career was spent in Alaska. I now teach in Bush Alaska. Most of my students are Native Alaskans. Reviewers who have stated that the author is inventing his stories are wrong. Period. Bear-lovers who say that the author is demonizing bears sound as if they have no real-life, consistent, up-close experience with bears. True, most bears leave you alone. Also, true, bears are unpredictable and they will attack, maul, and kill you, without provocation or apparent reason. Kaniut is explaining right now to the students how he interviews the victims (or survivors), uses police and fish and game documents, and essentially "writes a research paper." His research is good. I happen to know some of the same people in his stories, and their stories match the stories in the book. It's a good read. You won't want to walk into the Alaskan Bush without a good firearm, though. Amazon reader, J. Paul Apfelbeck "redpoll", 5.0 out of 5 stars, April 14, 2006, Alaska

More Alaska Bear Tales

The Stuff of Nightmares. I still have nightmares after reading this book. I go to Alaska every couple of years, and you better believe I never go anywhere unarmed while I'm in bear country. This book will make you understand why.   Amazon reader Criss Morgan, 5.0 out of 5 stars, September 3, 2010

Some Bears Kill

Great book from a great story teller. This is a great book by one of the best authors on the subject. Mr. Kaniut is an authority on the subject of bear attacks. He has devoted many hours, days and trips across Alaska to bring firsthand accounts, when possible, not only by the victims but by tracking down witnesses to the attacks. I have read several of his books and never been disappointed. This is a must read for the outdoor and wildlife enthusiast. A book that will stay in your bookcase for a re-read.
Amazon reader Randy Chapman, Sept. 13, 2001, 5 of 5 stars

So Real! Cannot tear away from this book.
Amazon reader, JIM, November 8, 2014

"You don't know me…I just finished *Some Bears Kill* and read it in a few evenings. Your books are better than anything on TV… FASCINATING. You do a good job balancing the graphic-sensationalism with reality. I'm one of your biggest fans…just keep 'em coming if you can…I've enjoyed talking to you, sir."
--Spencer Ward, September 26, 1997 phone call from Maryland

Bear Tales for the Ages

"Reality TV can't hold a candle to the reality described in *Bear Tales for the Ages*." -Richard Simms. www.chatanooga.com/outdoors

HUMBLING ENDORSEMENTS

DALTON CARR

Several years ago Dalton Carr called me to discuss bears. He wanted to meet in person so I drove an hour north to his daughter's where he enthralled me for three hours with his bear stories. We communicated over the years while he worked on his *Tales of a Bear Hunter* book.

Dalton was an expert outdoorsman, professional bear hunter and lawman. His forty-one years getting to know bears, being a predator control agent on the Yakima Indian Reservation and marshal of Red River in New Mexico prepared him to write about bears and weaponry. I am happy to say that he finished his outstanding book *Tales of a Bear Hunter* which I highly recommend.

Dalton was a gamer. I'm saddened to say that his Parkinson's took him much too soon. It was my privilege to know him.

During the winter-spring of 1999-2000 Dalton and I were on the telly discussing his manuscript of bear-man stories, and I told him I thought the best bear books ever written were Frank Dufresne's *No Room for Bears* and Andy Russell's *Grizzly Country*. Dalton disagreed and said that my three bear books were in the top five on his list. A short time later I received an e-mail addressing this subject.

"I was asked a question recently about what I thought the best bear books were and if I could come up with the top ten. They are as follows:

1.	*No Room for Bears*	Frank Dufresne
2.	*Some Bears Kill*	Larry Kaniut
3.	*The Grizzly Bear*	Will Wright
4.	*Alaska Bear Tales*	Larry Kaniut
5.	*More Alaska Bear Tales*	Larry Kaniut
6.	*Grizzly*	Enos Mills
7.	*Kodiak Bear*	Jim Woodworth
8.	*Grizzly Country*	Andy Russell
9.	*Bear Attacks 1 & 2*	Kathy Etling
10.	*Game Trails* (game guide)	Charles Keim

"I think only Dufresne and Kaniut gave the black bear the credit they deserve, since a black can be as deadly as any grizzly once he is committed. If you want to learn about bear habits, read Dufresne and Russell. If you are interested in bear attacks and how very dangerous they can be, just read Kaniut's 3 books and Etling's 2 volumes on bad bears. They are very informative and well written."

--Dalton Carr, July 18, 1999

(Author: I was quite humbled to be in the company of Dufresne, Wright, Mills, Woodworth and Russell.)

DONALD HILL

During 2007 I began email communication with Donald Hill of Ronan, Montana, and have listed a couple of his emails:

Dec. 5, 2007 Re: list above

You are in pretty heady company, but You deserve to be there! Very few authors write books that can be read over and over again, but yours are that. Noticed that of the top five books on the list that three of them are yours. I would include *Bear Tales for the Ages* in that list of top ten books and I am sure that had the list been made after it was published it would have made it also. Congratulations on your recognition as an author of the best bear books!

I also noted the absence of McMillion and Herrero in the list. Both books had been published at the time of the Carr's email.   Sept. 25, 2007

I have long been a reader of Peter Hathaway Capstick's books on Africa. Even have some of his series on the old ivory hunters. His books have always been my favorite adventure books, until I started reading yours. You have a way of putting you right into the action and always give the reader a good story, but also give sage advice to people that venture into grizzly country.

You may use any of my emails to you in your book.

JACK OLSEN

Jack Olsen is a former bureau chief for *Time Magazine*, author of 32 books published in 17 languages. I've been a fan of Jack's ever since the late 1960's when I read his incredible investigative bear book *Night of the Grizzlies*. I began email correspondence with him in the early 2000's, about a year prior to his death. I sent him a copy of *Bear Tales for the Ages* (From Alaska and Beyond). Before his untimely death he kindly responded with some emails...some of which I've listed:

May 5, 2001

Hi Larry --

That was a great tonic -- unfortunately it arrived just before bedtime when I need to be settling down like a tired old grizzly! Good luck! And tnx for a nice bedtime present.

Wed., June 27, 2001

Great stuff, Larry! I thought I was bored with bears, but you revive my interest. Tnx pal.

Sat. June 30, 2001

Damn, man, you kept me awake till 3 AM!

Sat. July 21, 2001

I read your last bear story on a one-week vacation in the San Juan Islands and I'm just damn glad they got no bears there. Great stuff, man.

Sat. Dec. 1, 2001

Good going on your book, Larry. You deserve it. Keep in touch, pal.
Jack Olsen   http://www.jackolsen.com

CHAPTER 1
WHAT'S WRONG WITH THIS PICTURE?

Sometimes we gain a misleading perspective from information and/ or images. In the case of the book cover, I'm wondering if Timothy Treadwell read my first book or if he held it merely as a prop. His activities in Katmai National Park generated considerable concern, even more so after he was killed by a bear.

The following four incidents address "what's wrong with this picture"—Timothy Treadwell, a sportsman, Brian Knowlton and an Idaho aunt.

TIMOTHY TREADWELL

When I requested photographer Phil Schofield to comment about the cover photo, he wrote:

The photo shoot of Timothy Treadwell was for a *People Magazine* feature they assigned me after Tim was on the David Letterman's show. We flew from Kodiak Island on a Uyak Air Beaver on floats. I was accompanied by a staff writer, who I would guess had never been anywhere there weren't paved streets and sidewalks.

We spent three days at Tim's camp on the Katmai Peninsula. We flew in at high tide up a small creek mouth right to his camp. The next morning the tide was out, WAY OUT, at least 1/4 mile farther from the camp then when we landed. One of the most amazing things I saw that trip was that morning the beach was covered with maybe 15 bears (brown bears, AKA griz), all lying on their stomachs digging razor clams like little kids playing at the beach! The camp had two resident red foxes that were never more than 2 feet from whatever you were doing, especially if it involved food, really a very entertaining pair of comedians.

We spent the next 2½ days following Tim around this sedge grass plain before the mountains checking on his bear friends. They seemed oblivious to us, just concentrating on the salad bar portion of their annual feast before they made their way up to Brooks Falls and the fresh salmon entre. Many times the BIG brown bears would walk right thru our camp, with no interest in us. I think they thought we were some other form of resident wildlife, which Tim definitely was!

I was stunned by how poorly equipped Tim was for the ever-changing weather of coastal Alaska. No good tent, poor outdoor clothing, cotton long johns. We actually had him join us in my backcountry tent the last night. That night while Tim was boiling some water for his dinner, he knocked over the pot and scalded his leg bad enough that we took him back with us on your return flight to Kodiak to get some medical attention.

He was a very charming and likable guy. I don't know if you knew that he just missed his big show biz chance. He came in second place for the part on the TV Comedy *Cheers* as the bartender, Woody Harrelson won that gig and that was a major turning point in Tim's life.

Phil

When our neighbor Carole Miller gave us a copy of *People Magazine* (October 3, 1994) with the article "Bears Fan" and accompanying picture (this book's cover) of Timothy (Dexter) Treadwell sitting on the beach holding a copy of my first book, I told my wife, "It's just a matter of time. It's not if, but when."

Nine years and two days later, it happened. Our son's father-in-law Dave Hemry and I returned to Anchorage later that week after our failed Anchorage-Tucson flight via the Alaska Highway in his Cessna 180. That night in 2003 while visiting my wife Pam, daughter Jill and me, our family friend Joanna Dicarlo mentioned that "the guy who wrote about bears was killed by a bear." I was shocked and responded, "Do you mean Timothy Treadwell?" I tried to describe him, found the *People Magazine* and showed it to her. Joanna readily recognized him.

When asked my opinion of him my response was that "he had the wrong message and the wrong method. You don't tell people that you can bond with bears and become one of them."

Then Joanna related that he and his girlfriend were killed...and partially consumed. I was shocked and saddened. *Why would anyone expose another to that kind of danger?*

Early on Timothy Treadwell struck a blow for saving bears from poachers. He anthropomorphized bears and bandied the idea of becoming one of them. Treadwell figuratively stole a line from Rodney King suggesting "can't we all get along." But what are the facts…not the emotions but the rationale?

Unfortunately, Treadwell was paid to present his bear experiences with audiences that often included small children, telling them that he was protecting the bears from extinction. Also, unfortunately, Timothy took a friend who died with him. And, perhaps as unfortunate, he had the means of saving himself—did he read the book pictured on this book's cover?

Before long my friend Lew Freedman, formerly of *Anchorage Daily News* and then of the *Chicago Tribune*, called me. I jokingly suggested, "So you must want a good quote for a piece on Timothy?" Lew affirmed his desire and wrote a piece which I've included below (with permission of the *Chicago Tribune*, "Scary truth about bears," Nov. 2, 2003):

They are not the kind, cute animals of Disney, but fierce creatures worthy of extreme caution.

Bears are not humans. Bears are not cuddly. Bears do not speak English. Bears are not pets. Bears are not play-date friends.

Timothy Treadwell never seemed to understand this. Disney apparently doesn't understand this.

Bears are animals. Bears have sharp teeth. Bears have sharp claws. Bears may kill people. Bears may eat people.

And now Timothy Treadwell—and his girlfriend Amie Huguenard—are dead, and Disney is showing kids how warm and cuddly bears can be.

Treadwell, 46, and Huguenard, 37, of Malibu, Calif., were killed by bears in Katmai National Park and Preserve in Alaska in early October. This was an unfortunate though not surprising incident. For years, Treadwell, who wrote a book titled *Among Grizzlies*, spent months at a time in the wild living in a tent observing grizzly bears.

While such actions in pursuit of science can be laudable, Treadwell had aroused park ranger concern and attention for treating the risks of his wanderings—documented thoroughly in print and on nature TV specials—too cavalierly. Treadwell frequently tread well inside the safety margin of bears' space, sang to bears, talked to them, apparently petted them and named them. He was both dedicated and foolish.

His thesis was that man and bears could coexist in the same environment and that the bears wouldn't harm him once they got used to him. Some people were impressed. Others thought he was nuts. Eventually, Huguenard joined him on the sojourns.

Both the TV specials and the book were entertaining. There was a certain element of low key daring underlying Treadwell's campouts. But anyone who has lived where big bears roam, brings a certain amount of skepticism to such viewing or reading. In those places it is not about bears in the abstract, or bears in the zoo. Not when there may be bears in the backyard.

People who live in bear country believe in common-sense protection, carrying guns, pepper spray or both, and they do not ascribe anthropomorphic characteristics to bears. Treadwell argued that unprovoked bears are not dangerous. In the end, Treadwell set up his camp along a frequently used bear path, and bears killed and partially ate him and Huguenard.

It was not as if Treadwell failed to recognize the power of a 1,000-pound grizzly. On the very first Pg. of his book, he wrote, "The grizzly bear is one of a very few animals remaining on Earth that can kill a human in physical combat. It can decapitate with a single swipe, or grotesquely disfigure a person in rapid order. Within the last wilderness areas where they dwell, they are the undisputed kings of all beasts. I know this all very well. My name is Timothy Treadwell."

Not anymore.

"What a sad, sad thing," said Larry Kaniut, an Anchorage-based author who has written four books about bear attacks on humans, including the best-selling *Alaska Bear Tales*.

Five years ago, Kaniut saw a magazine story about Treadwell that was accompanied by a photo of Treadwell sitting down, holding one of Kaniut's books as a bear sauntered past.

"This is not a matter of if, it's a matter of when," Kaniut decided at the time.

Kaniut has studied every bear attack on a human in Alaska since 1895 and he said there have been more than 50 fatalities. Treadwell, he said, set a bad example for the average person.

"You can want to study and be around bears, but you can't play with them," Kaniut said, summarizing the Treadwell mentality as "'don't bother them and they won't bother me and I'm going to bond with them and I want them to be my friend.' That's the danger."

There's no telling what type of danger the new Disney cartoon movie *Brother Bear* will create if it convinces youngsters that bears are cute animals with human traits rather than the majestic, powerful impressive beasts without consciences or complex vocabularies that they really are.

The plot of the movie revolves around one bear cub trying to find its mother and the magical transformation of one young hunter into a bear who helps protect the cub. Larger issues of family tolerance and interspecies understanding are involved as well. There's nothing new about Disney portraying animals as chatty creatures, but it is important for young people to understand what is fact and what is fiction.

In the real world, a large, adult, male bear would be more likely to devour a cub for snack food than protect it. Grisly, but true.

Brother Bear might be a wonderful film for children, but if kids walk away without comprehension of how bears really live and behave, they might become future Treadwells.

If so, as Kaniut noted, "I can write bear books forever."

Scary, but true.

As a result of the deaths of Timothy Treadwell and his friend Amie Huguenard near Kaflia Lake in Katmai National Park and Preserve a panel convened to review park camping and bear management policies. They also considered the circumstances surrounding the deaths of the couple. Both were killed and partially consumed by a 28-year-old 1000-pound boar brown bear.

It was a poor year for berries and bears sought salmon at the last locale available which stressed them and limited their tolerance for people. One of the panel members, Larry Van Deale, state wildlife biologist, acknowledged that Treadwell was "an unconventional person with unconventional behavior towards bears, camped in the middle of a very dangerous situation with an older male bear that's even less tolerant."

The panel felt that the location of their tent contributed to the attack and that they would have had a greater chance to survive had they been half a mile away.

(Source: Panel wraps bear attack review, TREADWELL: Board recommends a review of camping, other policies, RACHEL D'ORO, The Associated Press, December 18, 2003)

On the same *Anchorage Daily News* web page above was the caption "Map: Tracking Anchorage grizzlies." Yes, we're not only having bears in our cities, we're also promoting them! Or at least some folks are.

BEARS GALORE

What's Wrong with This Picture/Soldotna man attacked 2009

Picture this: Bears in the streets and yards. Bear numbers on the increase. Conveniently habituated to man. Game managers blame attractants such as garbage, chickens, pet and livestock food, curing fish eggs, bird seed and fish smokers. Meanwhile many citizens' eyes turn toward game managers for allowing a growing population of brown bears.

> "We have a LOT of brown bears around Soldotna and we've never had them here in such numbers before. The reason for all these DLP shootings is simply an over population of browns within OUR territory. In my 31 years living here, I've never seen a brown bear anywhere close to Soldotna until 2 years ago. Then we suddenly had several of them wandering all around town. Last year there were 3 by the airport, 1 by the college, 3 more back between Gaswell & Poppy lane, and a couple around Mackey Lake (where the shooting in question occurred) that I know of. That's way to many brown bears within a very small urban/suburban area."
>
> (JOAT, Aug. 21, 2009, www.forums.outdoorsdirectory.com)

Picture this: A mile from downtown Soldotna, Alaska, on the morning of August 2009, a man left his home accompanied by his three dogs. It was a nice day, time to relax after coffee and checking emails. His Ruger .454 Casul pistol hung from a holster on his hip. Having seen thirteen bears in his yard the previous summer as well as those this year which had walked his driveway, rumbled by his kid's trampoline, chewed on his house siding and startled his wife ten feet from her front door, he was all too familiar with bears in the neighborhood.

Picture this: A 9-foot boar brown bear, emaciated and hungry, a couple of blocks down the road from the dog walker's yard. The animal is lurking in the shadows, ready to consume anything that's edible and handy. And then…

Emanating from the trees a snap and low guttural *woof* caught the outdoorsman's attention. On full alert, he looked in the direction of the noise. Bounding with blinding speed toward him, jaws popping, head low, ears pinned back, full out bear attack. No fire breathing dragon could have presented a greater survival situation.

Melt down.

Mr. Dog Walker instinctively pulled his cannon from its holster and, running backward down the road, fired from the hip as fast as he could pull the trigger. He had no time to aim, merely pointed and fired.

Boom! A clean miss. He did not hear the muzzle blast.

Boom! Boom! He felt no recoil.

He continued backpedaling and the fourth shot dropped the beast. The man sidestepped the bear and fell to the ground onto his derriere, hyperventilating. Even though the 350 grain bullet effectively stopped the animal, it's momentum carried it past him, gouging a groove in the gravel road shoulder.

The groaning bear was within ten feet of him when the shooter rose to his feet and fired a finishing shot into the brownie. After that fifth bullet, he discovered bullet number six jumped the crimp and locked up the pistol.

The scrawny bear was fifteen to twenty years old and in poor condition. Several scars covered its heavy, huge head. The hide measured 9-foot 6-inches from nose to tail and 10-foot 6- inches from claws to claws over the front shoulders. The carcass weighed between 900 and 1000 pounds and should have weighed an additional 400 pounds, had it been eating its normal diet of salmon, moose calves or carrion. Instead it was eating grass and was starving to death.

> "This is the third bear attack on that road in two years. The houses down that road report bears all the time now. If that would have been any of the kids who live down that road they would be dead. And I dont think its due to people building houses in bear habitat as there never were bears in that area in the past. I think there are just a lot more bears around now as even moose hunters and black bear baiters are having a lot more brown bear encounters on the Kenai. I think the woman attacked in the paved parking lot of the Princess Lodge pretty much exemplifies this. The permit hunting seasons are a joke and need to be greatly increased to keep bear populations to a more reasonable level... "
> Sollybug (www.forums.outdoorsdirectory.com)

This brown bear shooting brought the total number of defense of life and property kills to four through August in the area: one at a bear baiting station, second killed near Sunrise on the Hope road and a third at the end of Denise Lake Drive, off Mackey Lake Road.

Whereas 31 brown bears in the area resulted in death from DLP's in 2008, only four were DLP kills in 2009 (through August).

The Alaska Department of Fish and Game has restricted hunting for browns in order to keep the populations viable since they view brown bear habitat is threatened by human encroachment in the form of recreational, residential and commercial developments.

Jeff Selinger, ADFG biologist, suggested even though education is helping and people are coming around by helping minimize attractants, Kenai Peninsula residents are not out of the woods. It appears the bear management on the Kenai Peninsula is improving and reducing human-bear casualties. Hopefully their efforts will spread statewide. What a positive step that would be; we could experience less bear-man conflicts.

Bestul, Scott, *Field & Stream*, "Charging Bear Killed in Alaska," August, 17, 2009

Gresham, Tom, Gun Talk (radio show), August 23, 2009

www.outdoordirectory.com

Robertia, Joseph, joseph.robertia@peninsulaclarion.com

BRIAN KNOWLTON

Brian Knowlton shot and killed a large black bear IN HIS HOUSE

When I read about Brian Knowlton and his bear, I contacted his father Stan via the phone book requesting Brian contact me if he chose. He did. I visited him and his wife, mother and father and brother June 10, 2006, when they shared his story which follows.

My wife and I slept soundly in our hillside home in Anchorage, Alaska at 2:30 AM Friday June 2nd, 2006 until our dog Baby, sleeping beside the bed barked agitatedly. I told her to shut up. My wife sat up and said, "She's really barking like she's worried!" I saw my wife's silhouette by the little bit of moonlight in the room as she continued, "Maybe you should check."

I said, "Nah, it's just a moose outside, just go back to sleep."

Baby continued barking at a real high pitch. Then we heard two sounds like something falling in the kitchen. From my nightstand I grabbed a Sure Fire 6P tactical combat light (so bright it disorients you if shined in your eyes).

Assuming that it was our cat on the counter, I determined to shine the light in her eyes to teach her not to get onto the counter. I reluctantly climbed out of bed and quickly swung the door open to surprise the cat. But I got the surprise!

Less than two feet from me was a large black bear standing sideways, facing to my right. Standing on all fours his back was as high as my belly button, and I'm six feet tall. I got a real good look at his head. If you measured from his nose to his ears, it was about two-thirds the width of my doorway.

I slammed the bedroom door shut and put my foot against it to hold tight. I looked at my wife and yelled in a half terrified-half disbelieving tone, "There's a bear in the house!"

She looked at me and said, "What? There's a bear?"

I said, "There's a bear in our kitchen."

My wife asked, "Where's your gun?"

I normally have a pistol by our bed just in case something crazy like this happens.

In anticipation of emergency self-defense situations I have taken a Concealed Carry course —CCW—and have competed in IDPA— International Defensive Pistol Association events to hone my skills, knowing that the TRUE "first responder" is always the VICTIM and the police comprise the cleanup crew. I quickly assessed the situation and realized that I had a flashlight and no phone and no gun. I'd left the phone and my carry gun in the other room. I'd carried the gun with me as my CCW and when I emptied my pockets at the end of the day, I left my gun in my office. I knew right where it was…in the next room—a million miles away.

Because the bear didn't have the dished face of a grizzly, I knew that it was a black bear. Within seconds of slamming the door, I realized that we would have to make him leave. I immediately started banging on the door with my fist as hard as I could to make as much racket as possible "Bam! Bam! Bam!" and yelled (my wife said that I sounded more aggressive than she'd ever heard me), "Get out of my house! Get out of here bear! GIT!!!" What else could I do?!

As I listened, I heard him retreat. *Pom, pom, pom* through the living room or down the stairs. I knew there was no way I could hold the door shut if he wanted to come into the bedroom. If the bear felt trapped in our home or wanted to defend his new food source, he would be real trouble. I determined to take the fight to him. I remembered reading in *Alaska Bear Tales* about people fighting back against black bears and winning. If I was NOT going to be a victim, I would have to fight back! (This was my mindset and why I did what I did)

I opened the door quickly and hit the flashlight, but I didn't see anything. I reached around with my hand and flipped on the light to the kitchen and the living room, which is a split hallway—we can see the kitchen and the living room from our bedroom. I hit both lights at the same time and I shined my flashlight at the bathroom, which is at an angle to the right and I could see he wasn't in any of those areas. I've done the "slice the pie" drills for defensive use of your house and have figured the angles of my house in case I had to defend or search the house. The "slice the pie" term is a method that one may employ to carefully search an area while not revealing himself to an adversary. People usually don't believe they will use their training while learning skills like those.

We didn't know if he'd left the house. I looked around the corner and didn't see him by the top of the stairwell, the only way out of the house. I didn't see any danger.

Our only other option was the second story window. Do we climb out a window and drop to the ground? What if he's outside and we break our legs falling off the roof? That was not really an option.

I made a mad dash for my office, another bedroom right next to our bedroom. I had my wife stay in the bedroom and hold the door shut while I ran to grab my concealed carry pistol, a Glock M27, the only one easily accessible. It carries 9 rounds in the magazine and one in the chamber (While I would have rather had a different gun, the gun you have beats the one locked up in your safe. I have other more capable bear guns, but they were all downstairs in my gun safe. That's the only one I remembered the location of coming out of a dead sleep.). It was loaded with 10 rounds of Winchester Silvertip hollow point 155 grain, very capable rounds.

We didn't know how the bear got in or if he knew how to get back out. All I knew was that I wanted that bear out of my house—right now! And I never wanted him to come back. I knew if this guy came in once, he could come in again.

I moved into the living room toward the stairwell and used our couch as a "barricade" to slow a possible rush from the bear. The lights were on but I took my flashlight and pistol and "sliced the pie" to check the noise on the dark stairway. Holding the light in my left hand and the pistol in my right, I "sliced the pie" from left to right, aiming the pistol at the center of the light. As I illuminated the stairwell with my flashlight, I saw him halfway up the stairs, maybe five or six steps away from me. Knowing a bear has the ability to move quickly, realizing that I had no time to get a better shooting stance and knowing that I had to make my decision instantly, I opened fire.

I don't know how I had the presence of mind, but I said to my wife, "Cover your ears, Honey."

I raised my pistol: "*bang, bang, bang, bang, bang…*" and fired ten rounds at him.

Everything happened very fast. At first the bear was facing me but turned and ran down the stairs bawling loudly as my rounds hit him. I did my best to keep the front sight on his center of mass while holding the flashlight on him to be sure of my target. I remember seeing a lot of fur and gun smoke as I emptied my gun into him. Some might question why I kept firing as the bear fled—I learned in my training that if you are defending your life with a firearm, you *shoot until the cessation of hostilities*—or rather, you shoot to kill or don't shoot at all.

I aimed the flashlight at the steps and saw big pools of blood so I knew I got some good vital hits. I learned later that I'd hit him in the jugular even though I had aimed for center of mass for as much central nervous system shock as I could get.

I ran back to my office looking for my spare 15 round magazines (for my full size Glock M22, also in .40 caliber) but I had my spare magazines in my backpack, *downstairs where the bear went* (I wasn't too excited to go after them).

While I searched for my Glock hi-capacity magazines, I opened up my cabinet because sometimes I have some spare gun stuff there from a trip to the range. I looked at a variety of rifle magazines, fully loaded but worthless in my Glock. As I opened up the door to the office, I realized I had an AK that I'd been cleaning and hadn't put back in the safe (a buddy had introduced me to collecting semi-automatic military arms for fun). Now I had a gun and ammo combination that would be real bear medicine! I got that sucker and put an AK magazine in it and chambered a live round. At the same time I grabbed the cell phone. The local newspaper (who never interviewed me at all) completely misrepresented my actions—stating that I stood at the top of my stairwell with an empty gun while calling 9-1-1. Not in this lifetime! Priority one was keeping that bear down!

I went back to the stairwell and covered it with the flashlight and the rifle, a .30 caliber (7.62x39), kind of like a .308 short. With 30 rounds of rifle ammo, if he came back up the stairs, he was going to be Swiss cheese. I balanced the rifle over the top of the couch and kept my light aimed at the stairs and then dialed 9-1-1 and said, "Hey, I just shot a bear in my house."

The dispatcher did a great job. It seemed like it took about a half an hour but it was probably fifteen minutes for Anchorage Police Department to respond. The dispatch stayed on the line with me and was a real nice guy. He was not anti-gun in any way. I was impressed with this guy because he said, "You just keep your gun on the stairwell. When we get there we just don't want you to shoot through the house. Then we'll ask you to maneuver with us to avoid any danger." They did ask me to disarm when they were going through the property and into the house. As an afterthought, my wife and I realized that this may be safer for them, but what about us if the bear ran from them and came back upstairs? We would be defenseless and trapped against an enraged bear!

They coordinated with us when they got there. They took their time checking the perimeter to see if the bear had left a blood trail and may be outside.

By this time my father, who lives next door, had appeared outside our home which we rent from them.

I wanted to make sure I cooperated with APD to keep them safe and not to upset them since I'd shot a bear—I've heard horror stories about guys who have shot a bear in self-defense and then ended up in the hoosegow. I left my AK in the living room. As I think back, I should have just carried it into the kitchen with me when they asked me to move to the kitchen. They were very sympathetic and exercised extremely good muzzle discipline. They were very professional.

We had the front door dead bolted so I had to throw the police officers my keys through the upstairs window and then we gathered in the kitchen (directly above the front entry of the house) in case they had to shoot at the bear…two officers had 12 gauge shotguns and one officer had an AR 15 or M4 type rifle. One officer asked my father, "What does he have up there?"

My dad said, "Oh, he's got an AK 47."

The officer said, "He's got more heat than I've got." At least that guy knew what his limitations were. A .223 rifle wouldn't be the best fight stopper on a bear and over penetration could be a huge problem.

They weren't sure where the bear was and asked, "Is there another way we can come in?" My father showed the officers a side door between his house and ours. After entering they were nervous about how dark the house was and with their unfamiliarity with where light switches were. They staged one guy by the front door in case the bear came out that way. They worked their way in slowly. I heard them moving and talking when they saw the bear's muzzle, "I see his muzzle. He's not moving."

This was a very clever bear. He had entered through the side door, which opens inward. Then he went through an interior door that he had to unlatch and open towards him. He was actually able to shut the doors behind him. He left no marks on either door. He knew doors and had learned how to operate them!

The *Anchorage Daily News* quoted Fish & Game's Rick Sinnott stating that the door latch was faulty. *Well, it is now that the bear broke it!*

My wife and I were still in the kitchen and our dog was in the office behind the closed door.

While I talked with dispatch, our cat appeared on the stairway sniffing at the blood. I called the cat to come up and my wife now held it.

The bear was downstairs in the bathroom directly below the position I'd shot from. He ran down the stairs and made a 180 degree turn left and went down the hallway towards his entry point. I don't know if he ran out of blood by then or if he ran out of life (did the jugular hit kill him or did the three center of mass shots cause sufficient shock to his central nervous system—or both?). He went into the bathroom on his right, turned around and faced back out. I've read most of the *Alaska Bear Tales* books and I've read just about every article I could ever find on bears because we like to play in the outdoors and we want to know what we're up against. You hear how hunters talk about when they shoot a bear and it's wounded, they go to track it and it circled back onto them. I think he went into that bathroom and was defending himself by circling back, because he was facing out. He hit the bathroom door jamb hard enough to break it. He left a two-foot long crack in it.

We finally went downstairs and saw how large he really was! His head covered most of the doorway. The officers stood in awe of the size of the bear. One officer said it was the largest black bear he had ever seen in the Anchorage area. The F&G guy said it was very large for our area as well. It took four guys (six feet tall each) to lift the bear into the F&G truck. When we lifted him so that his paws were above the tailgate of the Ford Super Duty truck, the bear's back was still on the ground. We later learned that he was 275 pounds. We could see that he would easily stand up to around six feet tall on his hind legs.

At the time we weren't really concerned with taking a lot of pictures of the bear or digging around in him to discern where I hit him. We just wanted him gone and were very happy that the F&G was not taking an unkindly approach to this shooting. The police officers were great guys and assured me that I was completely within my rights to shoot the bear (some comments: "good shooting," "your golden" and "that's the cheapest bear hunt you'll ever go on!"). I appreciated their levity as I was still coming down from the adrenaline and my wife was very distraught at the situation. They also made comforting comments to my wife.

After the officials were gone, we began to look around the property to inspect for damages from the bear and the shooting. We found no evidence of the exterior door being broken, *only that it wouldn't latch anymore*. He caused little damage inside the house. He did meander through our entryway looking for food and our living room where he ate some candy in a bowl by the couch and into our kitchen where he found dishes from our dinner. The most damage resulted from my shooting him in self-defense—he bled all over the carpet, the walls and the bathroom. He left a nasty pile of bear poop in the bathroom. And the smell just won't go away! *Note: It has been nearly two months since he broke in and we still have a sweet sick smell like a bad perfume in the downstairs hallway. It's faint, but even after shampooing the carpet we still can't escape it!*

When we first examined the house where I shot at the bear, we wondered how many times I'd hit him. At first we believed that I had an incredible 90% hit rate. The newspaper quoted Sinnott saying that I had "four vital hits, one of them being in the jugular," and my brother

Phil, who helped us pack the bear out, remembers seeing one hit in each rear lower leg. Later, while cleaning all the blood up, we found a bullet hole in the stairs that penetrated one step, one riser and lodged in the next step down. We removed our coats from the downstairs coat hanger (on the right side wall) and found two more misses – I shot both Angie's coat and my Carhartt coveralls – the bullets penetrated at a steep angle and did not exit the wall. There is of course the most expensive miss of all: Clearly visible at the end of the stairwell in the end wall was a small bullet hole about 10" up from the lower landing. We went outside to check if it exited and sure enough, it did... right into a paving stone, which it skipped off of and into the passenger door of my new work car!

A few folks asked why I didn't use a bigger gun on a bear or why I didn't have a gun in my bedroom with me, and perhaps funniest (in a bad way) of all, why I didn't try to just "shoo" the bear out of my house or use pepper spray or just stay in my room! Here are my answers to why I did what I did, and used what tools I did:

1. Why did you use a .40 Glock? If I had access to a bigger gun, I would have used it (which would have been a bad thing as you will see in a moment). I woke up from a dead sleep, facing an aggressive bear and used the only sufficient caliber gun I had access to. The .40 S&W round has over a decade of proof showing its effectiveness—it is and will be sufficient to take out a black bear at extremely close quarters. A guy shot and killed a brown bear sow with a .40 S&W Glock pistol last year or the year before as it charged him. Put the bullet where it belongs and let it work (sure, I'd rather have a Ma Deuce .50 BMG, too! You use what you have.). I always carry my baby Glock, even if I carry my .44 Magnum and my Benelli 12 gauge shotgun.

2. Why didn't I have the gun in my bedroom? Good question, I ALWAYS do have a pistol with me in the bedroom. Not this night. Another peculiar thing—I just happened to park my car facing in the opposite direction that night. If I had shot at the bear from the bedroom and over penetrated him or missed him, I would have shot directly at my neighbor's house—in direct line with several of their bedrooms! As it turned out, the delay of retrieving my pistol caused me to meet the bear on the stairwell, the safest direction I could have shot at him—there was nothing in line with him (no gas lines, no electrical breaker boxes, no people!). The only negative thing was that I shot through the exterior wall and hit my work car. But if it had been facing the other direction, it would have suffered a whole lot more damage. We do not believe that these facts are mere coincidence. My wife and I are Christians as are our neighbors (my parents, my grandmother and younger brother). We believe that God protected us. If I'd grabbed the AK-47, I would have destroyed the car. If I had the rifle in the bedroom, there would have been far worse danger of over penetration! *If I had used my .44 Magnum (S&W Alaska Backpacker with a 3" barrel), I would have had to hit the bear with my first or second bullet. The recoil would have prevented me from getting as many shots into him as I did and if I missed he would have been alive and able to come back—not an acceptable solution!* If the bear had entered my parents' home, it would have been a far worse story—they had no guns at hand! They do now. I keep a handgun of at least .40 caliber with me everywhere I go in the house now—I don't care what whiny liberals say—once you experience a bear in your house, you'll understand! It's only paranoia until you're the victim.

3. Why not just "shoo" the bear away, or use pepper spray or stay in your room (a lady actually asked me that last one!)? Well, we did yell and bang on our door. The bear wasn't in a hurry to leave, as evidenced by the fact that he was still on the stairs when I met him the second time. He obviously had no fear of people or my 93 pound Rottweiler which is no sissy. "Shooing" him away was a very temporary solution. So, how about pepper spray? Pepper spray is a one shot deal—you better not miss—and with all the adrenaline you experience, you'll miss at least once! The pepper spray would easily have blasted off my walls in the narrow stairway and floated back up to my wife and me! *Then we would have an angry bear in the house, no more pepper spray, and we would be disabled by our own weapon.* Okay, so just stay in your room and call 9-1-1, right? Well, we would have if we had a phone in the bedroom. It's best that we didn't. It took at least 15 to 20 minutes for the police to get there (again no complaint on APD, it takes time to find a caller's home and we live on a twisty gravel road with few road signs to lead the way—they did a great job). If the bear wanted in the bedroom while APD was rushing to our rescue, how would my wife and I stop him from clawing his way through our flimsy door? What if the police did arrive with the bear in the house and had to take a shot at it? Would their shots over penetrate or miss the bear and hit us or a gas line or the 220 volt line to our upstairs kitchen stove? You—not the police—are responsible for your life.

4. Why didn't you shoot with both hands/ or shoot more accurately? This is one that bothered me at first when I learned of my hits and misses. My answer to this question is simple: *imagine you have just been awakened at 2:30 AM and your eyes are heavy and you could sleep through World War Three. In just a moment you find yourself about one foot from a large black bear inside your dark house. What do you* *do?* I'm a civilian not a Navy Seal. I practice, but not that much! The F.B.I. states that most self-defense pistol shootings occur in low light, at less than 21 feet against a moving, aggressive opponent, and that you will miss with several of your shots. I'm satisfied with the outcome, but I am going back for more practice with I.D.P.A. and I plan to attend a GunSite course soon. Training is critical, even for civilians.

From my understanding, most police officers are fortunate to report a hit count of 30% to 40% on an attacker in close quarters in the dark when they are wide awake and have way more training than I do. We know I scored at least 6 hits out of 10 for a 60% hit rate. I am satisfied but a little humbled that I didn't actually get all 10 into him. It happened within the space of a heartbeat. I hardly heard the gunshots (a phenomenon I've heard of – auditory exclusion under stress) and have no hearing loss from the shots. My wife said she didn't hear the shots, either. My father DID. He also heard the bear "bawl"clear over in his house! I've often worried that my little Glock .40 would be too much recoil in a life and death encounter—I don't even remember feeling the recoil of the potent 155 grain rounds (they kick kind of sharp and make recovering the front sight more difficult). I had tunnel vision on that bear and my front sight. All I can say about all that is: Practice as much as you can (as realistically as you can) and get training from those who know more than you— challenge yourself. And join the National Rifle Association. *My wife and I could've been mauled to death in our bed if we lived in an anti-gun "utopia"!*

My boss was most concerned about my safety and took care of the door repairs ($400!) and wouldn't allow me to pay any of the costs—I have the best boss in the world! We were fortunate that it did not over penetrate the car door due to the bullet's deflection off an interior brace. The body shop guy said I was fortunate it wasn't off ¼ inch either way— it would've been over a thousand dollars!

My wife and I are very grateful to God for our neighbor's and our safety. We don't ignore our dog's warning barking anymore and we are now constantly armed where legal (where we are not infringed upon), especially in our house. *We still keep a firearm with us inside and outside of the house. I mean—right with us! ALWAYS.*

My wife and I have learned another lesson from this ordeal—the newspaper likely won't get your story correct. The *Anchorage Daily News* stated in their story that I did not want to be interviewed (*rule number one in defensive shootings is don't talk to the press, but that's beside the point…*). I had to work that day from 9 AM to 9 PM I would not be able to talk to them in their unrealistic timeline. They stated that

32

I stood at the top of the stairs with an empty gun—now anybody who knows me, knows that I would do better than that! There were other glaring problems, but the point is—they won't get it right, and you will be too pumped full of adrenaline at the time to see all the little details to really tell things well, too.

AUNT TO THE RESCUE

What's wrong with this picture? While you're cogitating, I'll provide more food for thought.

Would the result have been different for Lisa and Ian Dunbar if Lisa had been given the warning and the weapon that the lady in the following story had? (see Lisa Dunbar, predatory attack stories) This story illustrates the importance of adult awareness to the dangers of predatory animals and the need for an appropriate bear stopper.

Brooklyn, Charles and Cleo Henslee played in their Porthill, Idaho, back yard. Their babysitting aunt was nearby. The twin boys were a year younger than their 3-year-old sister Brooklyn. Amidst the play, auntie was alerted when Brooklyn suddenly shouted, "Bear! Bear!"

When auntie looked up and saw a black bear running into the yard from the adjoining woods, she grabbed the children and hightailed it for the house. Aunt, niece and nephews reached the sliding glass door just ahead of the 422-pound bear. Slamming the door behind them, auntie turned to see the bear pounding at the door, damaging the screen door and window frame.

Securing the children in a back bedroom, she grabbed a 7 mm rifle, loaded it and returned to the glass door. Momentarily distracted, the bear looked down.

Auntie quickly slid the door open a foot and with the rifle at waist level fired two rounds into the bear, only three feet distant. The animal dropped dead on the step.

Officials passed the attack off as human error—in their minds some food attractant caused the bear to charge! (Source: "Area babysitter kills black bear," Posted: Thursday, Oct 12, 2006, By ROBERT JAMES, Hagadone News Network, BonnerCountyDailyBee.com, Sandpoint, Idaho)

Here we have another prime example of blaming man. It's always his fault.

The BonnerCountyDailyBee.com web site permitted me to include some of their blogged comments in return for crediting them. You might be surprised by some of the following which I selected. FYI, I did not select all so some responses to unselected posts should be obvious. The following (verbatim) posts illustrate the people's extreme philosophies.

Nancy, October 12, 2006 8:20 PM: "For once an intelligent babysitter! She's hired!"

Dave A., October 12, 2006 8:44 PM: "If the bear was attracted to smells from a barbecue grill on the back porch, why did it make such an early attempt on the house? A black bear is more predatory than a grizzly, probably only second to a mountain lion."

Chuck, October 13, 2006 12:39 PM: "Did officers talk to the lady to find out if the gun used in the killing of the bear was under lock and key so the small children could not get it? Seems to me that with a pair of twins & 3 year old in and around the house the gun would be secured and the ammunition put up...this all happened so quickly that the bear stood as much chance as getting shot as the children finding easy access to the gun and ammo. I wonder what possible harm could happen to those 3 little children if that gun is not secured? Think about it."

Dynahog, October 13, 2006 3:11 PM: "That's about the dumbest thing I ever heard. The family needs counseling on what to do if you sight a bear near the house...My guess is that the "mother" probably started screaming (that caught the bear's attention), and then picking up the kids ran to the house. Too late, the bear was challenged and went for them... NEVER EVER RUN FROM A BEAR. That is the sign of you challenging the bear. NEVER EVER LOOK AT A BEAR IF HE'S APPROACHING AT CLOSE DISTANCE... ALSO GET A STRONGER / TALLER FENCE. Glass sliding doors? Not a very safe house to be in."

Mr Noble, October 13, 2006 3:17 PM: "MOVE YOUR a hole OUT OF THE BEAR'S BACKYARD"

BT, October 13, 2006 10:41 PM: "I know a guy that lost a kid to a bear. Enough of the armchair-bear lovers. You should have grabbed some pots and pans my keester. City-fied crackheads! I bet the dumb half of the posters here don't even know where food comes from. Where does the grocery store get it? If you live in the city, please don't try to theorize how folks should live outside cities!!"

Herman from Texas, October 14, 2006 2:23 AM: "This is what has happened to our safety when moronic, know-nothing, condo dwelling animal rights A-Holes are allowed to tell people they can no longer threaten animals. From joggers and bikers being killed and eaten by big cats and bears chasing kids for an afternoon meal these predators are no longer afraid of people…and that's dangerous. Years ago just the smell of humans was enough to keep a broad border between us and them, now however, because of idiots who know little to nothing about survival around animals…like the moron that stated you should NOT run or look at the very thing that is about to eat you…guns have become necessary to preserve life. Doesn't that make the animal rights idiot responsible for the death of this hungry animal??? LOL"

Chris, October 14, 2006 6:01 AM: "You can read these comments and see which liberal nut jobs value a bear more than human life. That bear needed to die and I am glad this brave woman killed it before it could maul her or worse, one of the children. "

Gronad, October 14, 2006 6:23 AM: "Babysitters - 1 Bears - 0"

eddd7, October 14, 2006 6:58 AM: "That's it Dynahog......blame the children! And "Paul".....yeah, with a 422 pound bear trying to get through the slider, the first thing I'd go for is the pots and pans. And, as for Mr. Noble".....what animals lived where you lived, before YOU lived there? None? Jeeeeesh. Where do we get these people??"

Lawrence Robinson, October 14, 2006 7:11 AM: "A bear came charging out of the woods, hell bent on mayhem, because there was a barbeque on the back porch? How bloody stupid do these government types think we are? Why didn't the bear stop and give some attention to the barbeque then? Those fuzzy little bears. Ya just gotta love our government officials!"

Scott wrote on October 14, 2006 7:43 AM: "Okay, are there really agressive brown Bears where this happened? I've never heard of a bear that was unprovoked chasing people. They're generally pretty timid creatures. These boneheads have been watching too many movies. Did the stupid babysitter think that it was going to break in through the sliding glass door and eat them? I say that her story doesn't make sense." (Author's comment: Yo, Scotty. Keep reading. One reason I wrote this book is to educate people like you. Read about Lisa Dunbar, the mother who tried to save her son from a black that came through the opened sliding door for her! And, the bear at Teslin Lake, Yukon Territory that came into the house in 2014. Yes, Scotty. And killed the lady. Guess what? Bears pretty much go where they want.)

Topekan, October 14, 2006 8:29 AM: "Dynahog says it's the family's fault that they hadn't taken Bruin Defense 101? As far as needing counseling (sic.) goes, that's "about the dumbest thing I've ever heard." I suppose Dynahog would have preferred that the bear had enjoyed a four-course repast of homo sapiens and then gone back to the wild. Animal rights activists are the ones who need counseling."

Smoki in Washington, October 14, 2006 9:47 AM: "Good for her. I hate to hear of animals shot because of people's stupidity, but in this case, she was right on target in more ways than one. And for the comment about locking guns up - my daughter was taught at age 2 what a gun would do, has had her own rifle (a 22) since age 4. Don't lock up the guns, educate the kids. A locked up rifle would have gotten someone killed that day."

Tom, October 14, 2006 9:47 AM: "As I live in bear country, a full grown bear on two legs, pounding on your sliding glass door with small children and women inside is a serious threat. Only self-proclaimed "idiots" would advocate rattling a few pots and pans (yes, make the bear mad and maybe it might just knock the door completely down and enjoy a smorgasbord of whatever it wants), or worrying about whether or not anyone had a "bear tag", or trying to run away from the bear in the first place with little children in your arms (sometimes running is the only option, especially when you have safe cover nearby). Then there are those who think we should all move out of bear territory. These are the same ones whose knowledge has completely abandoned them when it comes to understanding that, except for the deserts, the whole country was bear territory before civilization moved in. So, retreat for the sake of "bear territory" means for civilization to move to the tallest mountains or the desert. Such knowledge and perfect wisdom—ain't the kind the women used. Theirs was a good dose of common sense—and the desire to live."

Nancy Woods, October 14, 2006 10:16 AM: "Thank God the babysitter kept her cool and did the right thing! It's sad to say but Greg Johnson's response is all too common.....trying to defend and make excuses for the bear...these kinds of comments from an official might cause someone else to hesitate just a little too long before defending themselves and lose their life."

Gary In Sacramento, October 14, 2006 11:47 AM: "98% of the people think like normal. Then here comes the Liberal Tree Huggers with all of their stupid garbage about how "we the people" are the problem. Give me a break. I love animals as much as anyone BUT when the animal is out of control and crosses the line, they have to be controlled and the emergency of the moment determines the outcome."

Rae wrote on October 14, 2006 1:12 PM: "This is what happens when morons who live in bear country don't properly secure food sources. Poor bear." (Author's comment: Rae, I refer you to Lisa Dunbar—no mention of food here, and she lost her most precious child. Do you have children?)

Gene Gray, October 14, 2006 2:22 PM: "I am 89 years old grew up in North woods of Wisconsin and now live in Southern California. I have hiked and hunted most of my life-until 5 years ago. I recommend all animals dangerous to humans-bear, mountain lions, and snakes be eliminated." (Author's comment: thin the herd!)

Mike Kuhn wrote on October 14, 2006 8:30 PM: "What does it matter if she had a bear hunting permit? Would she have been CHARGED had she not had one? I suppose she would have been CHARGED had she not, from the gyst of this story. In the first sentence, eighth paragraph, the article mentioned that she had a "bear tag". I suppose that means that had she not had a government permit, that CHARGES would be PENDING. I'm surprised that other CHARGES weren't brought, such as shooting near an occupied dwelling (there were CHILDREN inside, for pity's sake!), animal cruelty, and endangering the welfare of an animal. Add to that endangering the welfare of a child (by virtue of having a firearm in the house), which would be three CHARGES, since there were three kids. She probably should have been CHARGED with criminal negligence as well, and further CHARGED with reckless endangerment. Following these FELONY CHARGES (all of them, since nothing is a misdemeanor anymore), she should have to attend ANIMAL SENSITIVITY TRAINING…

alee Ess, October 14, 2006 9:30 PM: "This summer there was one bear story every week where black bears were coming into the yards of the LA suburbs (Claremont, Pasadena, etc). I visited my son in Wisconsin and parents in Michigan this summer and am astonished to hear coyotes in their yards every night! This was unheard of just a few years ago. There are also sightings of cougars throughout Michigan. It was disputed by authorities until the cougars started killing horses on farms. Locals have caught animal rights activists releasing coyotes on private property, where they are ruining many farmers in lower Michigan. How many children need to be attacked and killed before people wise up and say ENOUGH ANIMAL RIGHTS BS!"

Joe Siegl, October 15, 2006 5:01 AM: "Can't help wonder what one of them Animal lovers would have done if one of them was the Baby sitter or their loved ones would have been attacked? Call Fish and Game while the bear was running away with one of the kids hanging from its Snout?"

Wyoming Skye, October 15, 2006 9:27 AM: "In Canada they have taken away the right to bear arms when hiking and working in the woods and only duly licensed government officials can kill a predatory animal. The animals have obviously figured this out because predation on children, hikers, campers, and forest workers has skyrocketed since the law change. This has been shown for grizzlies, black bears and mountain lions who are learning to prey on defenseless people. Nature is the law of the strongest. People without guns are not the strongest. In Wyoming grizzlies will come running now at the sound of a rifle. They have learned it means dead elk. I like to have the wild spaces and the animals, but we must be able to protect ourselves around them to gain their respect. The only thing that will really save nature is human birth control. We are overpopulating the earth."

Mountain girl, October 15, 2006 1:46 PM: "Banging pots and pans is NOT effective—I tried it, and also some really obnoxious rock music played very loudly, on a 2-year old cub who kept coming to our yard looking for a litter of baby kittens a stray mother had hidden somewhere on our property. The bear was not impressed and did not leave until it was good and ready. All I have to show for my efforts is some mangled pan lids It is a shame that our 300 million population means loss of bear territory, but co-existence doesn't always work and bears ARE dangerous, wild and unpredictable. Tell ya what—you bear lovers out there take up a collection to build a huge bear-proof fence and a few million acres of forest land to enclose the hairy dears in and we'll ALL be happy."

Hey, now. Bears were here first! Never ceases to amaze me.

Why is it so difficult for some people to value humans over bears? Why is it necessary to take a position placing human value above that of bear's?

And for those of you who claim the great silvertip is endangered, I invite you to read Appendix 8.

In the featured stories above, bears targeted each person. What's wrong with this picture?

CHAPTER 2
READER CONFUSION

With the abundance of contradictory information about bears and how to deal effectively with them, it's no wonder that readers are confused about proper protocol in bear country. While wading through the piles of information, the reader faces two problems: 1) determining whether the author (or agency) is more interested in protecting him or the bear and 2) discovering which author(s) provide(s) the most workable advice for being safe in bear country.

Knowledge of bears and their nature, including causes for bear attacks, is essential to a safer outing. Although it is good to learn as much as is reasonably possible, most woods frequenters know little about bears—folks are there for the brief adventure and really don't have much time for cramming up on bears, taking the test or graduating Magna Cum Bruin before their visit. They have neither the interest nor the time to earn a B.S. in bear language, a B.A. in bear behavior or a Ph. D in "ursusology."

Because I am more interested in seeing people protected than bears, the bulk of *SAFE with Bears* is to help people avoid physical contact with bears. I exhort people to respect bears in order to reduce injury to either creature, however I unwaveringly promote mankind's health above the health of the bear clan. I don't blame people for being injured by bears. Even though a person may trigger a bear attack, the person's "bad" behavior does not justify that person's living through life with disfigurement or permanent injuries of a physical or emotional nature. Nor does that behavior deserve a person's death sentence.

It makes me angry when I read about people going into the woods and suffering at the claws and jaws of a bear. Angry because too many of those people are ignorant of bears and their nature. Angry because even those who are competent in regards to confronting a bear on its turf, are hindered from self-protection by government rules and/or the eco-nuts. Angry because too many authors recommend inadequate weapons for personal protection—their interest tends to either favor the bear or their understanding of bear attacks is incomplete.

One author who is cited as the world's expert and who has studied and documented numerous bear attacks uses as his case studies bears that are "park" animals. By their very nature, these animals are either habituated to people or in close enough contact that they have knowledge of people activities. My concern with this scene is that wild bears are a different animal from habituated ones. And the aforementioned author has given advice which can seriously endanger people in a bear confrontation.

Unfortunately, a husband and wife couple took advice provided by this author and lay on the ground when a punk adolescent grizzly approached then mauled, killed and partially consumed the wife. I'd bet my life she'd have hers in that situation if they'd had pepper spray or a firearm…or even a knife with a long enough blade (at least 5-inches)… or read a bear safety book providing better information.

It bothers me when I think a person elevates a bear's safety status above a human's. For instance, at least one author touts carrying pepper spray instead of a firearm into bear country (his is about a 200 page commercial for pepper spray). He writes that people are safer in the woods without a weapon. What kind of advice is that to a person unfamiliar with woods travel and the outdoors? It's the kind of advice that will expose the traveler to serious danger, limited safety and possibly death.

Going into the forest without a firearm puts you face to face with any dangers that may arise. Are there any cougars about? Coyotes? Wolves? Snakes? Is there any danger from a rabid animal? Are there human sickos out there?

And what about your getting lost. Would a firearm be beneficial in procuring food? *Let's see, now…I think I can bag a bunny with my pepper spray.*

It is incumbent upon outdoor travelers to know their environment and the creatures that inhabit it. How intelligent is it for me to go into snake country with no knowledge of them? Or to go swimming in an alligator or shark infested body of water? Or to hike onto Alaska's mudflats where "quicksand" and/or rising tide could end my existence? How can the outdoor traveler enjoy his experience and return safely?

The primary purpose of this book is to **eliminate** human injury. The secondary purpose is to reduce bear deaths resulting from human misbehavior. It's your right and your responsibility to question information. How can the reader—especially one unfamiliar with bears—discern the truth about behavior in the woods? You need to question an author's reason for writing and his statements. Is he more interested in protecting bears? Or is he more interested in staving off injury to mankind? Is his motive to sell his products—pepper spray, book, firearm, tent, electric fence, alarm system, etc.? Or is he attempting to provide helpful information? When you read authors' comments, don't take them at face value. Ask questions. Get the facts.

Please question my statements. Some are merely theories—like eye contact. The bear "experts" tell you to never make eye contact because it can be a threat to the bear's ego…a sign of aggression…a challenge. However, I say, if it IS a sign of aggression, I'm going to make eye contact every time to let the bear know that I own the woods. And if he wants to call my bluff, I'll be ready with a full house.

Some authors tell the reader that a bear will NOT charge outside of 50 yards. My records indicate over half dozen bears charging or "investigating" from 50 yards and up to one mile. (APPENDIX 1)

One author states that the best response to a defensive or surprise attack by a grizzly bear is to play dead. In the first place how do you know it's a grizzly. Secondly, is it a defensive attack? Third, why would you play dead and, more than likely, be chewed on when you have better options? For instance, if you were carrying pepper spray, a flare gun, a high caliber pistol, shotgun or rifle capable of stopping a grizzly, why would you lie down and allow any bear to chew on you?

Another author offers a hypothetical bear accompanied by cubs climbing through a kitchen window and awakening the homeowner who dispatches the bear and leaves two orphaned cubs. The man is blamed. What homeowner wouldn't try to protect his domicile, his family, himself? Are we NOT entitled to the safety of ourselves and our homes?

Books of this nature impair man's safety and totally mislead people as to the nature of bears and to man's self-defense actions. Make sure that you have the facts and act correctly upon them.

To further complicate the novice's knowledge in bear country, how do you know what's correct? As an illustration of mixed messages and confusion, I've listed below some contradictory comments from a few selected and supposed bear expert-authors' books.

Statistics (Hit by Lightning)

"Statistically, you're quite safe from bears…Auto accidents…claim thousands of lives every year…(Pg. 7) Domestic dogs kill more people than bears. So do bees, Hereford bulls, and lightning. Walking the streets of Washington, D.C., or Detroit is much more hazardous than walking in bear country. Central Park is more dangerous than Yellowstone Park." (*Be Bear Aware*, Pg. 8)

"One of the most important things I tell people who take my training is they must not believe the misleading statistical statements made by some biologists about the risk of bear attacks—like the comparison of bear attacks to bee stings, traffic accidents, or lightning strikes. I've heard many similar claims, and they all apply to the average North American and do not take into account the different statistical frequencies of risk for different categories of people.

"What these people don't tell you is that about 90 % of all North Americans are exposed to bee stings, traffic accidents, and lightning strikes, but less than 5 % are exposed to bear attacks in a given year. The preceding categories of risk cannot be statistically compared to the latter, because the numbers of people exposed are vastly different. In other words, these statistical statements pertain to someone who lives in New York City and once in their life goes to Yellowstone Park and hikes around in bear country." (*Bear Attacks: The Deadly Truth*, Pp. 203-204)

Ninny

According to one author you need not worry about being rushed by a black bear unless you are "a biologist working closely with bears or a ninny feeding roadside bears in a national park." (*Backcountry Bear Basics*, Pg. 58)

If I knew nothing about bears, I'd feel safe anywhere they live—just as long as I wasn't a biologist and I didn't feed bears. However I DO know something about bears. In fact several black bear maulings from my books come to mind— (*Alaska Bear Tales*) Robert McGregor, killed and partially devoured; Cynthia Dusel-Bacon lost both arms; (*Some Bears Kill*) Cynthia's friend Marty Miller was stalked in a copy-cat incident; pilot Stephen Routh and Will Atkinson punch out blacks; Colorado guide Jim Heine; Art LeGault berry picker and Larry Reimer fisherman.

Other black attacks—all resulting in fatal injuries to the people— come from multiple sources and include the fishing young brothers George and Mark Halfkenny and their friend William Rhindress of Ontario, Canada; Lee Randal Morris, Carol Ann Marshall and Marty

Ellis in Alberta, Canada; and Carol Ann Pomerankey.

Of course I address other black maulings in this book. NOTE: not one of these victims (or those above) was a biologist or a roadside ninny! (APPENDIX 2)

Carrying a firearm

"Carrying a gun can create an air of overconfidence that can lead to trouble." (*Bears of the World*, Pg. 174)

"Guns, I am convinced, do more harm than good for most people, unless you are willing to start shooting as soon as you see a bear, before it even charges..." (*Mark of the Grizzly*, Pg. xvi Introduction)

"I use the following statistics in my training program regarding potential success (no injury or death) against bear attacks: Firearms 95 percent; spray 70 percent; and play dead/fight back 45 percent. But the 95 percent firearms defense success rate is based on B.C. field workers only and doesn't include B.C. hunter defense against grizzly bears." (*Bear Attacks II Myth & Reality*, Pg. 243)

Pepper spray

"Pepper spray makes more sense to me" (than carrying a firearm)... "Spray it in a violent thug's face and he finds it hard to see and breathe. The throat constricts, the eyes gush tears, the skin burns like fire. In most cases, it brings a man to his knees as effectively as a nightstick or a gun, lawmen say, and the perpetrator heals up a lot faster. After a couple hours of misery, he's fine...

"The same theory is applied to bears, although you need bigger doses of spray. Grizzlies have twice the muscle density of humans, making them twice as strong, pound for pound, as a well-toned man. Plus they're a lot bigger so it takes more spray to divert them. The better brands of pepper spray are designed to spew a cloud of pepper gas a dozen feet wide, to create a barrier between you and a charging bear. Plus, as in police work, the spray doesn't kill anybody. The bear goes away upset and in pain, but at least it goes away. That's the theory anyway." (*Mark of the Grizzly*, Pg. xvi Introduction)

Gary Shelton tells about four B.C. timber cruisers working a cut block in May 1996 when a black bear approached them. Trevor Stephen's dog Chessie intervened and while the bear bit her, Trevor kicked it and hacked at it with a hatchet until two companions "could move in with their bear mace. The stinging spray did absolutely no good." (*Bear Attacks II Myth and Reality*, Pg. 137)

Predictability

Are bears predictable? Some say yes; some say no.

One author suggests that labeling grizzlies unpredictable "means that the observer is ignorant." (Dave Smith, *Backcountry Bear Basics*, Pg. 20).

Another author and brown bear guide suggests, "The single factor that makes the Alaskan brown bear so dangerous to hunt is the complete unpredictability of its behavior." (*Grizzlies Don't Come Easy*, Pg. 82)

"All bears think they own the world, and they often act that way. Their actions are completely unpredictable when you get in their way, especially if you upset their normal behavior patterns." (Bud Cheff, 32-year hunting guide, "Bears I Have Known," *Outdoor Life*, February 1969, Pg. 50)

Yelling, screaming, waving arms

"When confronting a bear, do not scream or wave your arms, as these actions will only provoke it. Do not make any sudden movements or imitate any of the bear's aggressive sounds or postures…In any case, try to avoid direct eye contact with the animal. Staring can be interpreted as an aggressive signal." (*Bears of the World*, Pg. 170)

"The 'Bear Man' of Admiralty Island, Allen Hasselborg, advocated talking bears down. He believed that it didn't do any good to bluff a bear because it was too intelligent. Hasselborg advocated getting firm with the animal and telling it to back off; and others witnessed him telling bears to go away, which they did." (*Alaska Bear Tales*, Pg. 269)

Making eye contact

"…never look a bear in the eyes, and, if you are attacked, don't try to fight."   (*Mark of the Grizzly*, Pg. xv Introduction)

"It is extremely important to face a predatory bear and to maintain eye contact."   (*Bear Encounter Survival Guide*, Pg. 88)

"When he turned back, the bear was lunging at him, but when he made eye contact, the grizzly again hesitated." (*Bear Attacks: The Deadly Truth*, Pg. 42)

"The grizzly was charging at him in full gallop only 25 yards away. When their eyes met, the bear turned 90 degrees and ran into the trees at the shoreline." (*Bear Attacks: The Deadly Truth*, Pg. 207)

The animal here is not a bear, but a crocodile, and the following quote is offered as a survival strategy: "…never take your eyes off their eyes…You can often 'eyeball' a dangerous animal into backing away. If you appear confident and aggressive, the animal's own doubt grows. You can use the crocodile's natural caution against it…Most big predators in unfamiliar situations—and man is unfamiliar prey—tend to err on the side of caution. When in doubt they back out…Everyone has met…an aggressive dog…But if you hold your ground, talk to the dog calmly and firmly, he will most often back off, though he still growls and barks at a distance. Saving face is important even in the animal world." (*Crocodile Attack*, Pg. 157)

Backing away, talking calmly

"Bear experts generally recommend standing still until the bear stops and then **slowly backing away**." http://usparks.about.com/cs/natlparkbasics/a/beartips.htm

"If the bear has seen you, speak softly and back away slowly while facing the bear." --www.mountmagazinestatepark.com

"Just as backing away shows fear, standing confidently means something to a bear," Smith says. "It's very difficult to stand down a menacingly curious bear, but no matter what, it is imperative that people **not back away**." (Source: "Bear Attacks!" Outdoor Life.com website, by Christopher Batin, December 2005, quoting Tom Smith, Anchorage USGS)

Playing dead

"Playing dead, I believe, is the best response once contact is inevitable. Until that point, it is best to stand your ground, offering the bear your profile and avoiding direct eye contact." (*Mark of the Grizzly*, Pg. xvi Introduction)

"Never play dead with any bear; always defend yourself…If your defense system fails, or if you are foolish enough to believe that it's not necessary to defend yourself against bears, you have no choice but to play dead in a defensive-aggressive attack, and fight back in a predatory attack—that is, if you are lucky enough to experience an attack that clearly falls into one of these two categories." (*Bear Encounter Survival Guide*, Pg. 125)

Misinformation about safety from bear injury abounds. For instance, I discovered during months of searching the Internet from June 2003 through March 2006 many sites proclaim that spraying and playing are the primary defense mechanisms against bear attacks (on April 20, 2003 I Googled 38 Internet sites and all but two suggested pepper spray as the primary [and only] defensive weapon against a charging bear. Only two of the sites mentioned using a firearm for personal protection).

Polar bears

"They (polar bears) are gentle giants, playful and inquisitive, not the aggressive killers that their reputation demands." (*White Bear*, Pg. 143— Hugh Miles, co-author of *Kingdom of the Ice Bear* and BBC filmmaker)

"…white bears…are life-threatening menaces…On the ice we carried weapons or went with armed guards. Polar bears were enemies to be feared." (Pg. 143, *White Bear*, Charles T. Feazel, Houston geologist and veteran of arctic expeditions)

I would be the first to admit that bears are not interested in people…

that bears are mostly "passing through" while looking for food, a mate or a place to sleep…

that bears rarely hurt people…

that, for the most part, bears and people can co-exist.

However, I would also be the first to admit that bears are wild animals. Even "tame" bears go off. It is wise to have the knowledge of the situation and to be able to react accordingly…and to provide your safety. Don't be confused by misinformation. Get the facts. Save yourself from bear-related injury. If you don't know bears, know your bear "expert"!

CHAPTER 3
BEAR ENCOUNTER OVERVIEW

ANATOMY OF A BEAR ATTACK,
20 Seconds and MORE

Prelude to an attack

A bear attacks a person with the intent of either disabling or devouring him.

Bruin tries to knock the person to the ground where he can utilize his teeth and claws to accomplish his work more efficiently.

Many mauling victims describe the initial body contact "like being hit by a truck" which is the result of the bear's running intentionally into the victim, hitting him with its head, chest, shoulder or forepaw. For those who've never seen a bear and have no concept what the charging animal can do on contact, imagine a 300 pound man running at you full speed, intent on injuring you or taking your life. He slams into you. In the case of a bear charge, however, the bear weighs more, has all four legs propelling it in your direction and is much more powerful and substantially faster than the man…and armed to the teeth, so to speak.

Once the person is on the ground, the bear bites the closest body part, which is usually an arm or leg. The animal normally proceeds from the appendage to the back of the neck or the head, the theory being that if the bear can get the person's head into its mouth, it crushes the skull to kill. Sometimes bruin holds the person down with front paws and bites the head in an effort to pull it off. Commonly the bear grabs the victim by the head, back or neck with its mouth, picks him up and shakes him from side to side.

The bear's biting is a hasty chomping, not a slow, methodical bite here, bite there but rather a staccato action.

If the attacking bear is a sow grizzly attempting to protect her cubs, she normally mauls the person then steps back to watch for movement. If the person moves, so does she...often mauling the person three or more times before leaving, and only when the victim ceases to move, which indicates that the threat to her cubs has ended.

Bear attack

Most bear mauling victims believe their attack lasted twenty to thirty seconds from start to finish—quicker than you can open the refrigerator, remove a quart of milk, reach down a glass from the cupboard, fill it with milk and return the container to the fridge.

Because the majority of people have no clue as to the speed, agility, ferocity and power of an attacking bear, I wanted to give the reader an idea of what happens when man meets bear. I've reviewed dozens of mauling victims' stories and created a simulated grizzly bear situation below, attempting to break down the attack by the second.

Let's say that you're in bear country with a partner. It's 10:00 AM on a clear, sunny mid-August morning. Neither of you carries a firearm, however you have a canister of pepper spray in a hip holster. And, of course, you're wearing bear bells...that is, they are tied to your pack, tinkling a melodic tune as you travel the trail.

You're in the lead by ten yards, thumping along the well-worn path through the timber and talking with your companion when suddenly you hear a sound. You look up and spot three bears, a mother grizzly and two cubs. They're thirty yards ahead and walking the path your way. Your eyes and the sow's lock. Suddenly you're at ground zero and the second hand is ticking. The meltdown begins:

10:00.1   An earth shaking roar fills the air. She's coming.
You stiffen in shock, disbelief and denial..."*it's not a bear... it's a dog.*" You have just enough time to be in denial, reach for your spray and shout "bear!"

You see a wall of brown-beige fur in a full attack, paws barely touching the earth as she claws her way toward you. Her ground-eating gallop covers the space between you in a blur…6, maybe 7 jumps…at a rate of 40 miles an hour…or 30 yards in 1.6 to 1.8 seconds.

00.25   You're unable to un-holster the spray. Making no effort to slow down, the 350-pound sow slams into you like a runaway VW, ramming into you at mid-thigh to waist level with her chest and sending you flying…the force so great it feels like your guts might come out your mouth.

00.35   You land ten feet away on your stomach in the grass and vegetation. Almost before you hit the ground, she's on top of you, biting. You try to convince yourself that this isn't happening. And even if it were, *it's not happening to me!* You don't know it now, but your upper thighs will bruise and you'll feel the pain of mashed muscles for days.

You shout to your buddy, "Help! Get her offa me!" You wonder if you'll survive. You wonder if she'll go after your partner. Then what?

00.4   While holding you down with her right front paw, she bites your left leg, lower teeth penetrating the calf, her top canines ripping your pants, breaking the skin, scraping across the shin bone and leaving twin parallel groves. You hear her teeth rip cloth and flesh. The lower canines leave two puncture wounds 2-inches apart and 2½-inches deep.

Your buddy is looking frantically for a weapon. Trees. All he sees is trees! Then he spots a football-sized rock protruding from the ground at his feet. He drops to his knees and starts prying and digging at it.

00.5   She bites your left thigh three times in rapid succession, like semi-automatic pistol fire—*chomp, chomp, chomp,* leaving four puncture wounds each time.

00.6   Her right paw reaches under you and lifts you off the ground, her 3-inch dagger-like claws, ripping open your clothing and your right side and back. She leaves you a souvenir of 5 claw marks 2-inches apart, 4-inches long nearly half an inch deep. You hope that your pack will protect most of your back. Instantly she clamps onto the back of your neck with her canines.

00.7-10   Her mouth spans your neck which she bites repeatedly. Your partner can't free the rock but keeps trying. It's his only weapon. He's baffled and fearful, unclear why she hasn't come for him too.

She opens her jaws as wide as she can and bites onto

your head. The pressure's so great that you think your eye balls will pop out. You see a bright light in your head. Her lower canines find purchase in the skin above your right ear as her top teeth rake over the skull from mid-left ear to the right-top side of your head, ripping off the top half of your left ear and scraping loose that portion of your scalp.

You wonder if she's going to crush your skull. It sounds like she's grinding one 40-pound boulder across another.

Then she bites your face and her upper canines enter your left cheek, one just below the eye bone, the other beside your right nostril; her lower canines enter the soft tissue beneath your jaw on either side of your chin. She closes her jaws and your facial bones break. She releases her grip without pulling your face off and turns her attention to the top of your head.

She tries to bite the skull again, three times in all. But she can't get your head into her mouth to crush your skull.

You've heard that a bear's breath reeks if they've been feeding on carrion—a cached moose or an elk kill. But her breath smells almost sweet. *Maybe she's been eating grass and berries.*

00:10-12   She looks around for her cubs. They are standing twenty yards away, gazing at their mother, a look of bewilderment on their first year faces.

00.13-16   She returns to your neck. Bites once, looks away then bites your lower back. Then she grabs your upper right thigh in her teeth and lifts you off the ground and shakes you before dropping you. She swats at your torso then goes for your right leg.

00.17   Your companion has freed the rock and rises, 13 yards away. But just as he starts to step forward, the sow looks around again to assess the location and the condition of her cubs. They've started to move away, glancing back over their shoulders. Your partner freezes in fear, hopeful that she'll follow after her cubs.

00.18-19   She bites your right leg at mid-thigh leaving 4 puncture wounds over 2-inches deep then bites the right calf. Again, her lower canines puncture the calf muscle but the upper ones slide across the shin bone.

00.20   Content that you're no longer a threat and aware that her cubs are confused, perhaps frightened, she spins away from you, catches a glimpse of your friend from her peripheral vision, chooses not to harm him and sprints after her cubs.

Now what? How severe is the damage? How far from medical help are you? Can you walk? Have you a cell phone, radio, Emergency Locator Transmitter, Personal Locator Beacon or a SPOT GPS? What have you in the way of First Aid supplies?

Are you bleeding heavily? Spurting blood?

You've heard some people say they heard the bear when it mauled them, but you don't remember whether she growled, roared or popped her teeth.

Injuries and rescue

Although your injuries are many, no arteries were severed. Your facial wounds include puncture wounds, gashes up to half-inch wide and an inch and a half long, broken facial bones and a broken jaw. Fortunately, your eyes remained in their sockets and there is no damage to your vision.

Your scalp is ripped from the crown of your head but still attached like a hinged toupee and hanging from the right side of your head.

The top of your left ear lies on the ground. Can it be re-attached?

Your legs are riddled with puncture wounds. The good news is that they're oozing, not pouring blood. You're just now conscious of pain in your legs and back.

Your back gashes seep blood. You feel a bit of a chill.

You suffered three cracked ribs and your breathing is extremely painful.

Considering the power of the grizzly, your injuries are minimal. It could have been much worse.

This attack lasted only twenty seconds. One third of a minute. Faster than you can put on your training shoes and tie them! About a twelfth of the time you've been reading this chapter.

And people consider bears harmless, giving little consideration to the dangers with bears and making little preparation for such an encounter. Even those who do prepare, are sometimes caught off guard.

What portion of your life do you wish to give a bear? If 20 seconds of the mauling is enough, how much more including hospitalization, therapy, healing and/or loss of the use of a limb, eye or your life are you willing to risk/surrender? I refer you to Kathy Dunagan, who fears entering the woods after her encounter with a grizzly mama (Defensive Attack chapter).

EFFECTS (aftermath) OF A MAULING

Chances are good that you may never see a bear in the woods. That being said, your expectations of seeing one and your expectations of being safe with one should never cease. Few people are mauled by a bear and fewer still have been killed by a bear. Nevertheless, even one person injured by a bear is too many.

Avoiding injury afield should be a priority. However, some people either do not focus on that or they fail to discern environmental dangers. Consider, for instance, the Australian sailor who sought adventure and never returned.

The Royal Australian Navy vessel HMS *Geranium* arrived in Vansittart Bay in September 1920. The crew was excited to go ashore at Freemantle for R&R. One of them was eager to explore, thinking of his upcoming wedding. In fact, his bride-to-be was aboard a passenger liner en route to meet him.

The sailor left the safety of the city and ventured into the bush, failing to take notice of any landmarks that would assure his safe return. In his travels he first encountered darkness, then thirst and sore-injured feet, then a creek. Thinking that he could swim to the bay where his boat lay at anchor and be safe, he was overjoyed and hit the water.

When he did not return, a search revealed his tracks leading into—but not out of—the creek. Found were his belt and various body parts. (*Crocodile Attacks*)

His decision to explore an unfamiliar area caused him to become lost, resulting in his death and cancelling his wedding.

No, it wasn't a bear attack. But there is a striking similarity between crocs and bears. Both predators can be deadly, depending upon their size and motivation.

I've stated for many years that in spite of all the people I've interviewed who were in a bear's mouth, I can't imagine what it was like. Thus, I was impressed when I read long time outdoorsman and bear researcher Gary Shelton's comments that run along the same line, "I couldn't help wondering what it felt like to have a bear get hold of you. I've had some bad injuries in my life, but none could compare with the ripping and tearing that takes place as a bear sinks its canine teeth into you, then proceeds to violently shake you." (*Bear Attacks: The Deadly Truth*, Pg. 24)

What if, by chance, a bear does get hold of you? What can you anticipate? What will be the extent of your physical and emotional injuries? You might get by with a claw mark which heals and barely shows. You might. Or you could experience a life altering mauling. You might harbor hatred for bears for your lifetime—some I've interviewed want to kill every bear they see. Bear mauling victims react in different ways. I've listed a few effects to injuries caused by bears.

Lee Hagemeier and Daniel Bigley were blinded in their youth. Several victims spent months in hospitals or rehabilitation and/or incurred thousands of dollars in medical expenses including reconstructive surgery. Many had recurring nightmares. Knut Peterson endured four months of intense headaches and thought he'd be better off dead. Cynthia Dusel-Bacon regretted the loss of her arms to a black bear and said, "I don't think I'll ever completely get over being without arms." (*Alaska Bear Tales*, Pg. 234) But Cynthia did not allow her accident to curb her zest for life. She is one of the most courageous people I know. Forest Young and Ron Cole contemplated suicide. After a lifetime of physical and emotional pain one lady took her life, as did others such as King Thurmond.

Teenaged Lee Hagemeier, who was blinded by a bear near Juneau, Alaska, July 1959, adjusted to his impairment and graduated *summa cum laude* from the University of Washington. Daniel Bigley seems to have the same kind of attitude, bouncing back with a very positive outlook from his attack on Alaska's Russian River in 2004. The sow blinded him. It seems like the difference between some people is their choice to overcome obstacles in a positive manner.

Kind of like Johan Otter. After he and his daughter Jenna ran into a Montana grizzly with cubs he decided that he couldn't let a grizzly attack keep him down.

One man was mauled so severely that he couldn't call for help because the bear had bitten off his lips. More than one person had his face bitten or clawed off.

A powerful fear of the woods often paralyzes people who've had a bad experience with a bear. One lady underwent months of therapy and feared returning to the woods.

A grizzly paw swiped Patricia Whiting-O'Keefe in the Arctic National Wildlife Refuge in August 1979, removing her right eye and nose, damaging her left eye and requiring reconstructive surgery.

A black bear knocked one woman onto her back where her backpack cushioned her somewhat from a log that she landed on. After the couple's dog intervened and the couple returned safely to their car, Tanya De Groot of British Columbia said, "…I didn't realize I had a serious back injury. Several months later I had to have surgery to remove a crushed disc.

I now suffer from nerve damage and have constant back pain." (*Bear Attacks II Myth & Reality*, Pg. 135)

Ben Moore endured nightmares for six months and suffers constant "cold" from membrane swelling in cold weather.

Diane Nelson experienced follow up neurosurgery and ophthalmology from a bear's tooth embedded in her skull, 2000 stitches and permanent double vision.

Don Kluting mentioned that he made the mistake of looking directly at the remains of a victim whom a bear had killed and fed upon.

Ralph Borders, who shared his story with me for *Some Bears Kill*, stated later that he wasn't changed inside and he wanted to get on with his life.

Malcolm Aspelet and his girlfriend were attacked in British Columbia's Glacier National Park in 1971. He underwent three to four dozen operations and costs surmounting his ability to pay. And the government took no responsibility. He was to undergo more surgeries in order to restore sight in his right eye.

In 1921 a sow mauled two prospectors, one later went insane from a tooth wound that penetrated his skull.

Paul Kissner tumbled 100 yards down an avalanche chute in 1967 on Admiralty Island and spent three weeks in the hospital and a year in therapy.

In September 1994 Wyoming elk hunter Clay Peterson endured a grizzly attack and underwent $158,000 to have his face put back on!

One person I interviewed indicated his medical expenses to that point in his life approached $990,000.00.

Professional hunters James A. Moore and his partner hunted meat in 1893 for soldiers at Ft. Bayard. One morning James left camp along the Gila River in New Mexico and ran into a large grizzly which he promptly wounded. Thinking he'd killed it, he started around the log it was behind only to meet it coming for him, fully aroused. Late that night James' partner found him grievously injured—heart exposed and still beating. The bear lay dead nearby. James underwent medical treatment. Although half his face was missing and his neck terribly scarred, he eventually returned to the outdoors. However, in an effort to hide his disfigurement at the Charles Rathburn Ranch, he grew his hair long and grew a beard. Later in life he moved to the mountains where he lived as a recluse.

In 1998 Glacier County Sheriff/Coroner, Gary Racine, Jr. investigated his first grizzly attack death, a young man who'd been mauled and devoured by three grizzlies in Glacier National Park. When he approached the scene of the body, Racine found only larger bones, skull, a small piece of skin, torn remnants of clothing and two hiking boots containing the victim's feet.

Patricia Anne Van Tighem (in this book) contemplated suicide. She and her husband Trevor Janz encountered a grizzly in 1983 and endured 22 years of physical and emotional anguish— pain, concern, doubt, nightmares, inability to see and requiring constant nursing care—before taking her life in December 2005. Would you exchange this physical and emotional pain for no injury—even if it meant a dead bear?

Effects of bear inflicted injuries can include 40-inches of scars, double vision, blindness, scalping, ribs ripped out, 2,000-4,000 stitches, major lacerations, broken bones, nightmares and mental anguish (often for years), death and/or suicide.

Juxtapose those results with saving the bear! If a single person a year could be saved by killing one bear, what is wrong with liquidating the bear?!

And these effects do not fully cover the emotional trauma of being assaulted by the media or others opposed to the taking of an animal life— that growing list of goobers who live in a fantasy world.

No person should suffer a bear injury—a bite, a scratch, broken or displaced ribs, blindness or death!

The point of all this is to ask you what you're prepared to do about an ugly encounter with a bear. If you are responsible for a group of people going into bear country and you realize that any of the foregoing results could be experienced by one or more in your group, what kind of weapon do you choose to carry to insure their safety? How can you bring reality into the lives of those who suggest that man deserves what animals do to him?

You have a right to your life. You have every right to return from your outing unscathed by either paw or jaw of a bear. You have more right to exterminate the animal than its right to destroy you. You can achieve that result by incorporating good information and practicing the use of a proven plan (which, of necessity, includes a weapon to stop or immobilize a bear—be it a flare, flame thrower or firearm…whatever it takes). There are numerous weapons from which to choose. The key is to select the one(s) that guarantee(s) your non-injury from a bear.

ASSESSING BEARS

Are North America's bears cute, cuddly critters or marauding killers? What are the facts? Depending upon their age or their activity, they can be cute or killer. But by in large they tend to be one of the neighboring scoundrels scrounging a living, content to let others do the same.

Of the eight bears (including the European brown with its grizzly cousin) inhabiting planet earth, three (grizzly, black and polar) roam North America and seem to be thriving. The other five bears—Giant Panda, Asiatic black, sun, sloth and speckled—are either endangered or in a state of decline.

All who enter bear country must know and consider carefully these traits in order that both man and beast may safely utilize the same territory

Pecking Order

To know about bears is to understand them better. From birth to death bears seek food, a mate, a place to sleep or safety. They grow up into a society of animals that has a pecking order, where their adaptation to their physical contact with other bears determines their place in that order where size, strength and dominance prevail. Dominant bears hold the higher position; the others fall somewhere in the chain of command... if, of course, they survive.

James Gary Shelton states in his *Bear Encounter Survival Guide* (Pg. 39), "Each bear must try to jockey its way up the hierarchy so that it can spend more time eating than running away."

When the mother leads her offspring from their birth den, she teaches them and attempts to protect them from danger. In the early stages of their lives cubs learn their place as they associate with others of their kind in bear society. Sows are nurturing and/or keep cubs in line. Thus, by nature they are protective—they must fight to protect their turf, their offspring, their space and their food. If they are unable to protect that range, they may be forced out of it and, often, onto another bear's range.

Cubs are sponge like—absorbing behavioral traits instilled by mom as well as environmental-societal situations in relation to other animals from their birth, learning daily from their mother and their experience and developing into individuals. In general cubs are inquisitive, carefree, fearful of mother's wrath and eager. Adolescents recently sent packing by mother need to prove themselves, the adolescent boars being more aggressive.

One of the greatest threats to their wellbeing includes boars that would just as soon kill and eat them so their mother comes into estrous. The big, old, bad boars are wired to take no prisoners; they're fiercely protective of their territory, space, food source and mate.

Although mother bears have been praised for protecting-to-the-death their cubs, that is a myth. It is true that generally mothers protect their cubs—have even fought to the death to do so; however I know many instances where black and grizzly sows cut and ran, leaving cubs behind to fend for themselves. In Ben East's *Bears* he quotes Michigan wildlife biologist El Harger, "Almost every outdoorsman believes that a female bear with cubs adds up to a risky combination…yet only four times in trapping and handling more than three hundred bears have I encountered sows that actually ran us off while we were trying to remove cubs from a live trap." (Pg. 67)

The personalities and behavior of North America's bears run the gamut. They can be curious, playful, cute, comical, nuisances and dangerous…or all of these. Who hasn't observed rollicking bear cubs, wrestling and goofing off? Or most recently in the news and on the internet a good sized black bear treed by a house cat—twice?

Stressing their penchant for mischievousness, storied outdoor writer Ben East quoted Wisconsin conservation warden Ralph Richardson, "No other animal in the country can hold a candle to a black bear for troublemaking…They hunt for deviltry every chance they get, whether they need to or not…They kill stock…The havoc they wreak is beyond description." (*Bears*, Pg. 45)

Cubs grow up wrestling, mock fighting, sparring on hind feet. They develop a sense of what the other animal is going to do and anticipate its movement. So when they engage a human in a battle, they transfer to man the learned or instinctive behavior they've acquired and expressed to their species and other animals. They seem to know what a person is going to do before he does it—swatting him and pouncing on him as he hits the ground or attacking him before he stops rolling. They beat him up and show him who is boss.

Their reactions are lightning fast. Fast beyond belief. I watched a medium sized black bear near Trail Lake, Alaska, swat at a plant with its forepaws three times in the blink of an eye, *right, left, right. Bam.* Maybe more than three swats, but I saw three. The animal was irritated by people's presence and sent the message, "back off."

Some of the behavior these animals learn and the body language they acquire includes various utterances, ground swatting, posturing (body positioning), bouncing on forelegs, bluff charges and actual contact.

Experience

Bear attacks are tempered (in part) by their experience. If he's never experienced man, the bear may not know proper etiquette around man. If he has experienced man, this smart animal will respond to its conditioning and either avoid man or engage man. Under normal circumstances a surprised wild bear at close range will either flee or attack man on discovery of his presence.

Personal space

Bears have a home range, an area that they occupy from one end to the other—they sleep, hunt, mate and/or die there; they protect that area and tolerate what is necessary in order for them to survive—including being rooted out of that range if they are incapable of combating their foe. (Gary Shelton says: "Bears pack their exclusive territory around with them; it is a varying, invisible, elastic space they don't want trespassed." *Bear Encounter Survival Guide*, Pg. 48)

In addition to a home range bears have a personal space which is determined by their individual nature, the particular situation and their experience. When that personal space is violated, the bear reacts. Sometimes it retreats; sometimes it attacks.

The defense of their home range as well as its curiosity get the bear into most of its conflicts with man.

Curiosity and Reputation

Curiosity is perhaps a bear's most noticeable characteristic. It usually propels him toward a food source. Thus he investigates nearly every smell or sound that suggests a meal. The bear wanders around the campsite sniffing and wondering about the smells or other things. It approaches the tent, boat or plane, perhaps attracted by food aroma. But man doesn't know that bruin is not interested in him.

According to W.P. Hubbard, "The grizzly, with few exceptions, is a very curious, intelligent, courageous, and dignified animal, and not the ferocious and dangerous one he is often portrayed to be. His curiosity drives him to do impulsive things which frequently have involved him in trouble. The results cause him to be falsely accused of many things of which he is guiltless, or had no intention of doing...

"...if he fails to see clearly, his curiosity will be aroused all the more...he will advance toward the point in question to investigate. About that time a nervous hunter will shoot. He tells how he was the victim of an unprovoked charge by a ferocious grizzly. The thing he fails to realize is that the bear, in almost every case, was merely trying to satisfy his insatiable curiosity and was handicapped by his poor eyesight." (*Notorious Grizzly Bears*, Pg. 38, Sage Books, Denver, 1960).

Gary Shelton takes the bear's food need and curiosity a step farther in *Bear Attacks II* (Pg. 85), "A grizzly enters a camp at night in its normal exploratory food search behavior. It becomes aware of something in a tent and starts to paw or bite the tent. Next it discovers an animal moving inside the tent, emitting high-pitched screams, and proceeds to bite and test it. Once the bear has blood in its mouth and the normal predatory instinct is aroused, it escalates the biting of the head and neck area until movement stops." (It's interesting that the bear's curiosity escalates into a possible fatality with the taste of blood.)

Bears are interested in two things, and people aren't one of them. They search for food and they procreate. They do whatever is necessary to protect their food and their procreation. That's it.

All too many people have little, if any, experience with bears. Therefore when a person encounters a bear, he normally overreacts, usually in panic. It has no interest in the person but the man thinks that because a bear showed up in his presence it is going to eat him.

Having spent fifty years in the northern Saskatchewan bush convinced trapper and homesteader Ted Updike that "every mature bear has a superiority complex...The instant something doesn't go his way he flies into a red-eyed rage." ("Bears Don't Always Run," Pg. 142, *Outdoor Life*, August 1970)

Just because a bear is curious and plops himself in man's pathway, is no reason to blame him for man's lack of proper bear etiquette.

Foods of black and grizzly

Bears eat just about anything they can acquire such as grubs, ants, bees and other insects; acorns and nuts; berries; birds; carrion; crayfish; caribou, deer, elk, moose; domestic animals and fowl; dog food; eggs; fish; frogs; fruits; grasses (rye, parsnip, wild iris, marsh marigold); herbs; honey; rabbits; rodents; human garbage; mushrooms; roots; seeds; sedges; skunk cabbage and squirrels.

(Polar bear food includes: seal, whales, narwhal carrion, birds and their eggs, caribou or muskoxen, seaweed, lichens, mosses, sorrel, sedges and grasses, human food [bacon, cheese, tea, fruit], engine oil, rope, rubber boats, tents, skidoo seats and nearly everything else associated with camp life)

Eyesight and Hearing

Bears have taken a bad rap for their eyesight and hearing, however, "Their hearing is four or five times better than ours..." (*Bear Encounter*

Survival Guide," Pg. 74). And their eyesight is equivalent to man's, say up to about a quarter of a mile.

Nearly every time I leave my yard on my mountain bike onto our gravel road, I am amazed at the number of neighborhood dogs that begin barking…for distances up to a quarter mile or so. If a dog's hearing is that good, how good is a bear's?

I'd like to have a good bear dog in my camp to warn me of dangers as did Slasher, Bruce Johnstone's loyal canine that saved him from Old Groaner (THE classic Alaska bear story).

Smell

"A bear that knows a man is near can become as allusive as a ghost. Hunters who tramp the hills and valleys seeking bears leave their scent with every move, spooking every bear that crosses their trail." (Pg. 396, Carl Williams, "My 40 Years With Bears," *Outdoor Life,* February 1980)

Over the years of my research I have heard that bears can smell food from twelve to fifty miles distant.

Size

North American bears range in size from under 100 pounds to over 1200, depending upon the species. Any bear—black, grizzly or polar—is capable of seriously injuring or killing man, even a hundred pound bear.

Strength and stamina

Bears possess incredible power—they kill adult moose or bovines with a single swat and carry 900-pound carcasses in their jaws. While telling me his story (*Bear Tales for the Ages*) Gene Moe said that he reached his arm around a 750-pound grizzly's neck and tried to toss it to the ground. Astonished that his efforts were inconsequential, he said, "You don't have any concept how strong they are." (Pg. 33)

In their anger and/or intensity to reach an assailant, bears commonly rip through or break 3 to 4-inch thick live trees. Gary Shelton shares a story in his *Bear Attacks II* about a man who nearly became the victim of a male grizzly that measured 6-foot 7-inches from snout to tail and weighed only 500 pounds…"When the bullet struck the bear in the left side of the neck, its right paw shot out and swiped a four-inch lodge pole pine, snapping it off." (Pg. 56)

One person witnessed a black bear cub weighing a little over 100 pounds lift a rock weighing over three times its weight with a paw. The 225 pound black bear that killed two people at Liard Hot Springs was extremely powerful.

Because of a bear's muscle density and lifetime climbing around in the woods, how much more powerful than a man is a bear? If a pet kitten can fight its way from a small cardboard box while a person holds the top, how hard would it be to contain a quicker, feistier and stronger bear cub of twenty pounds? Are its teeth and claws as sharp? Then multiply that cub's weight, size and strength by twenty, forty or eighty.

Following a tiger attack at San Francisco's zoo in December 2007 animal behavior specialist Diana Guerero told FOX News that, "Wild animals have about seven times the strength per pound than humans do." (FOXNews.com)

I cannot attest to their actual strength.

Alaskan guide Clark Engle addressed the brown bear's stamina in "Elusive Trophy, (*Alaska Sportsman*, October 1968, pg. 9): "Though mortally wounded, the big brown bear had traveled over rolling terrain for about fifteen miles from where he was first hit." And Clark commented on a bear's instinct to plaster mud or moss on a wound to stop the blood flow. Clark found a gut shot sow nine miles from where it had sustained 220 grain bullets from a .338: three bullet holes in the intestines "were completely plugged by its own hair…Most likely she licked the wounds and swallowed the hair either accidentally or instinctively."

Speed/agility/endurance

In spite of their waddling, slothful meanderings, bears are extremely agile, adroit and athletic. People don't realize 1) how fast bears are, 2) how much ground they can cover, 3) their agility, 4) how they can tear through the alders and 5) that one shot—unless vitally placed in a killing or paralyzing spot—will not likely stop an aroused bear. The waddling "Teddy" bear stereotype vastly belies its very athletic nature.

Dalton Carr talks about bear speed in his *Tales of a Bear Hunter*, "I have personally clocked a long, lean black bear running flat out on a logging road at forty-three miles per hour over a distance of a hundred fifty yards. Simply put, a bear can cover a hundred yards in four to five seconds and fifty yards in about two and a half to three seconds. So, if you intend to outrun one of these boys, you'd better be jet propelled and have on your best pair of Nike's!" (Pg. 52)

Ormond told about G.C.F. Dalziel of British Columbia. Dalziel happened onto a bear food source and said, "I knew bruin was there. But he'd winded me. I saw his mound, but he'd slipped off strategically to one side. But I guessed wrong, and he sprang from the right. A man shooting all the time gets to be pretty fast with a rifle. But here's something the average chap won't believe. Grizzly can make three jumps at you before you can swing a rifle and shoot from the hip. The human eye can't follow a grizzly's movement." (*The Grizzly Book*, Pg. 49)

Interestingly enough, a person armed against a charging bear, especially a grizzly, has a micro-second to respond. Consider a bear running full speed at you, covers 30 yards in less than three seconds. That equates to 10 yards in less than a second. So if the bear is 20 feet away (within pepper spray range), figure it's going to cover that distance in 3 to 5 **tenths** of a second. That means, if you spray it at 20 feet (or closer), you have **less than half a second** to stop it before it reaches you.

A grizzly surprised Harvey Cardinal, bushwhacked him from behind and crushed his skull with a single swat. The dead man did not have enough time to release his rifle's safety.

While visiting my guide friend John Graybill at his Peter's Creek, Alaska, home, he shared some of his adventures with me, including a picture of a good sized grizzly and a red dog on the tundra. He explained, "Right here is a picture of a long legged Irish setter and a grizzly. That grizzly caught that dog so quick."

I asked John, "Did he actually catch him?"

And he responded, "Oh, yeh. Caught it and ate it." The fellow with me thought he'd sic his dog on the bear. I said, 'I don't think I'd do that.'

"He said, 'Oh, no. He can outrun a bear.'

"I said, 'Ohhhhh…maybe.' As you can see by the picture, it was all open tundra, just ideal runnin' but it was just as ideal for the bear as it was for the dog.

"A friend of mine went down last spring to Afognak hunting. He's got film of those brown bears catchin' elk. Beautiful films! And they're killin' elk after elk. They had no trouble at all runnin' down those elk. A bear is fast. There are certain bears that aren't, big old boars. They have trouble getting' around anywhere. These bears looked to be seven, eight foot. They were catchin' elk quick. And had no trouble pullin'one down." (John Graybill interview at his Peters Creek home, Tuesday, May 2, 2000)

At the 2000 Great Alaska Sportsman's Show in April Ronne Richter told me about an experience he had which demonstrated the speed and sagacity of the incredible grizzly. Ronne is one of the cross-country runners, a solid athlete, who ran for A.J. Dimond High School in Anchorage in the 1960's when I was coaching the team. I asked him if he'd mind writing it so that I could use it in a future book. On June 27, 2000 I received the following e-mail from him.

Hi Coach,

I'll get an F on this assignment if I wait too much longer. Thanks for the prod.

In 1969 after graduating from high school, I took a job as a cook for a group of geologists on the south slope of the Brooks Range in northern Alaska.

As the cook for the group of 8 (5 geologists, 1 helicopter pilot, 1 mechanic, and 1 cook) I was able to take afternoons off to do whatever fishing or exploring I cared to.

One afternoon the pilot had a short pickup to make with an empty seat both directions and asked me if I'd like to fill it. I was delighted and accepted.

This pilot was not fond of bears for whatever reason, and this day we came across a nice big grizzly as we flew along the gently rolling foothills. He immediately slowed the chopper down and tucked it right above and behind the bear, who by now was running quite fast. I noted where we were and glanced at the airspeed indicator. For the next seven miles that bear kept up a steady 35 miles per hour down gullies, up hills, through alder patches that were so thick they were difficult to see through, until we got to a river that was 40 to 50 feet across. There the bear had to swim and the chopper flew on by but the pilot banked around and kept the bear in the river until it was visibly exhausted.

We flew away then and I was left pondering all the inaccuracies in my thoughts regarding bears and my ability to get away from them. This was strength and endurance beyond my wildest dreams.

Ron Richter

My friend Jay Massey wrote a piece describing the extreme speed of wild game animals ("Animals are faster than you think," *Anchorage Daily News*, March 18, 1982 Pg. B-2). A herd bull moose and a youngster were five "moose lengths" apart, probably 35-40 feet. The master didn't want the kid around and assaulted him. Through the study of film that took 1 second to complete 24 frames George Lukens noted that the big bull covered the 35 to 40 feet in 1 second, beginning with a 20 foot jump. Forty feet in one second. If you touched a pencil at the top of an 11x8 ½ sheet of paper and scribed a line to the bottom as straight and as fast as possible, that indicates the time it takes a bear running full speed to cover 10 to 20 yards, about one second.

Then Jay compared the moose attack with a grizzly charge in Mt. McKinley Park (so named in those days). The sow grizzly covered 40 feet in less than one second—19 frames, or roughly 3/4ths of a second.

Double the distance and the time and you get 80 feet or 27 yards and 1.5 seconds. And people think bears are slow!?

Jay ended his article with an anecdote about his friend Howard Terry of Kachemak Bay and an incident near his Fox River homestead. Terry had a habit of carrying his .30-30 lever action over his left shoulder, gripped at the butt below the lever and resting the magazine on his shoulder, iron sights down with the barrel pointing backward. If he needed it in a jiffy, Terry thrust his left hand down bringing the business end of the rifle into play. One day while walking through tall grass near his cabin, Terry was charged by a sow grizzly and had just enough time to un-shoulder the piece and cock the hammer with his thumb as the tube came into play. He fired into the animal's chest, diverting her charge. He assumed she died as he saw her cub alone later that summer.

A charging bear moving close to 40 miles per hour covers 100 yards in just over 5 seconds—that's about .5 to .6 seconds per every 10 yards. That leaves you little time to unlimber your weapon (100 yards = 5.3-5.6 seconds; 60 yards= 3.2-3.6 seconds; 30 yards=1.6-1.8 seconds). The bear will cover 30 yards in 1.6 to 1.8 seconds; you take .8 second to grasp the situation; while you're processing the situation, the bear's covered 15 yards in 3-4 jumps, leaving you 1 second to react…if you're depending upon pepper spray or a firearm, how accessible is either?

You have only so much time. Are you ready?

Stealth

Although bears have been known to make a lot of noise in the woods, they can travel through thick brush as silently as a shadow. If you're relying on your "listeners" as a trusty sentinel, you may find them ill prepared for detecting an approaching bear.

Dalton Carr related the aftermath of another grizzly encounter, "What still astounds me is how quietly the bear had charged. No woof, no snap of its jaws—it was as absolutely silent as a five-hundred pound ghost!" (*Tales of a Bear Hunter*, Pg. 45)

My friend Marty Niemi, who lives in Juneau, told me during a phone call in April 2006 (later re-confirming it with the following email) about an experience he's had on Admiralty Island…

"My experience with the stealth of bears took place at Pack Creek near Stan Price's cabin. We had flown in to observe and photograph the bears while the Humpies were running strong in the creek. We hiked about 3/4 of a mile to a nice platform especially built for watching the bears while they fished. We saw many bears. My first observation was that there was quite a variation in the skill level of the fishing bears. Some of the smaller bears showed their frustration while repeatedly missing the fish. They would charge the water, telegraphing their intentions, splashing wildly, and most often just scaring the fish. One old boar who fished well downstream from the viewing platforms never missed a fish. Every time he went into the water, he came out with a fish and then retreated well up the bank, out of sight, and feasted on his catch. He must have caught eight or nine fish and eaten every one of them out of our sight.

"The most astounding thing that I learned about bears that day was how silently a bear can move through the brush. I spotted an old bow-legged sow ambling along near the creek about 50 yards from the platform. She wasn't fishing at all but she was moving in our direction. These Pack Creek bears are pretty well habituated as they are observed by tourists all summer long so she showed no fear nor did she make any effort to go around the platform. She made us kind of nervous but we had taken the precautions that are allowed by the Alaska Fish and Game Department and we were armed. We knew full well that the use of a firearm was the last resort but having one along was a comfort. That bear passed almost directly beneath the platform through some very thick brush. I heard absolutely nothing—I repeat, I heard absolutely nothing! I repeatedly tried to hone in on what sound she might be making. Again, I heard nothing. She was pushing her way through some very thick brush and she was very close to where we were standing. I will admit there was some competing noise of the slow running creek (a rather soft and soothing sound). I asked everyone who was with me on the platform whether they had heard any sound that the bear had made. No one heard the bear. My hearing at my current age is much worse than it was then and I am still thankful for never having met a coastal grizzly in the thick, brushy Admiralty Island cover."

Best,

M Niemi

Individuals

Like people, bears exhibit individual personalities and characteristics. Some are happy go lucky while others are grumpy, often depending upon what they've experienced that day. A bear may respond in numerous ways depending upon different stimuli. Say, one day a bear protects his meat cache to the death from man; but on another day, the animal may allow the man to trespass because the bear is full or the meat supply may be nearly exhausted.

Noted journalist Mike Cramond stated, "...bears are all different. Each one has as definite a personality as each human being does: some shy, some brash, some vicious, some insane. I had close to thirty fights in my day, most of them brawls outside a ring. I didn't at any time seek a fight; I simply took on what was offered or couldn't be avoided. Some men just go looking for trouble. They are *mustachi*, or *macho*, or just plain bullying bastards; you name it. It is a quirk of their nature to dominate you if they can. Among the thousands of people you meet in a lifetime, you're bound to run afoul of such persons

"...I think you could meet 50, perhaps 1,000 bears and 49 or 999 of them would take off, perhaps stand curiously and examine you or even make a bluff rush at you. The 50th or the 1,0000th would, or will, take after you! And it might kill you. That goes for black or grizzly." (*Killer Bears*, Pp. 78 and 79).

Predictable/unpredictable

One of the critical aspects of man-bear encounters is to determine the bear's intention. If a person could read a bear's mind, it would eliminate a lot of indecision on the part of both. How can man know a bear's intent? Even though bears demonstrate their intent to a degree, even bear experts have problems determining what it is. At least one old time Alaskan stated, "If a man knows what a bear's going to do next, he knows more than the bear does."

For those who say that the bear is totally predictable and his body language tells the trespasser what he is about to do, the following anecdote may be revealing.

A black bear visited a family's camp while they were fishing on a lake. One of their sons, nine-year-old David Cremins, volunteered to stay behind to babysit his 7-month-old brother Charles. David placed Charles on a blanket just prior to a black bear's arrival in camp. The bear walked over to the blanket and scooped up Charles in its right forepaw and headed into the woods on three legs. About that time David threw rocks at the bear as he heard the motor of an approaching boat returning some family members. Charles began crying. Yelling frantically David chased the bear which ran about 15 to 20 feet before dropping the child and ambling into the woods. Later the bear returned and paced back and forth for an hour without bothering anything in camp before leaving for good. (*Bears*, Pp. 109-110)

Others insist that the bear is totally unpredictable. Mike Cramond states in his outstanding *Killer Bears* (Pg. 299), "There is no sure way of gauging how an individual bear will react in a given situation." And again Mike says, "Nobody, perhaps not even God, or whatever powers be, knows what a bear will do under any set of circumstances." (*Of Bears and Man*, Pg. 206)

An old hunter told Ben East, "Nobody knows one minute what a bear is going to do the next. Most of the time the bear himself doesn't know." (*Bears*, Pg. 75)

And Ralph W. Young adds "The longer I study brown bears the more amazed I am at their complete unpredictability. They are highly intelligent animals, and everyone is an individualist. There isn't a year that I don't see bears do things that I have never seen one do previously." (*Outdoor Life Bear Book*, "More Brown Bears," June 1960 *Outdoor Life*, Pg. 260)

Young further states, "…brown bears are unpredictable, have a way of appearing seemingly out of nowhere when least expected, and under certain conditions are extremely dangerous and prone to attack." (*Grizzlies Don't Come Easy*, Pg. 76)

One of of Alaska's best known big game guides on the Kenai Peninsula H.E. "Colonel" Revelle stated, "No man living can tell what a 'brownie' is going to do— 'till he does it…a 'brownie' is not afraid of anything that walks." (*Hunting the Alaska Brown Bear*, Pg. 203)

Of the grizzly Ben East wrote, "Like all bears, he is completely unpredictable. One day, under a given set of conditions, he may stand his ground or even carry the fight to his human enemy. The next day his only thought may be to get away."   ("The Hunter and the Hunted," *The Grizzly Book*, Pp. 73-74)

An American forester gave his version of bear behavior in1934: "Boys, whenever anybody refers to bears as dear little creatures that mind their own business if you mind yours, they stutter. All th' people that write in th' papers 'bout how you can tickle 'em under th' chin an' scratch their fleas fer 'em is plumb loco." (Pg. 70, The *Only Good Bear is a Dead Bear*)

Bear's M.O.

Normally a bear charges on all four legs, not the classically depicted animal walking on hind legs. This bear intends to dominate or destroy. It is fully capable of winning the day. A determined bear in full possession of its armament will not stop its human attack until it is satisfied that the threat has ended. Outsized physical dimensions include 1 ½ inch canines, 4-inch claws, and 2200 pounds. It fights to the end, until its goal is reached or unless driven away or stopped from its action by an efficient weapon.

Bad bear types

I refer to two types of bear in this book—wild or tame. I consider the wild bear one that knows nothing or little of man. My definition of "tame" bear is the animal that has become accustomed to man by association with him, like the bears in Yellowstone, Glacier and Yosemite, or has been habituated to man over time to the degree that it is greatly dependent upon man for its food or frequents man "places" in search of a handout (for instance, a river where people raft-camp and a bear has learned to associate that camp site with campers and food).

Veteran Alaskan guide Ralph Young said, "The two types of bears most likely to step out of character are immature boars, and sows with cubs.

"A young brownie of either sex is usually unstable, but the boar particularly is likely to consider himself a tough guy. He loves to strut and swagger, and has the instincts of a hoodlum. He's also a great bluffer, but you can never be sure when he's bluffing and when he isn't. Whenever I meet one at close range, I treat him with deference and respect, always keeping my rifle at the ready." (*Outdoor Life Bear Book*, Pg. 183)

Whereas most bear books tout the mama bear with cubs as the most dangerous, I agree with Gary Shelton—the big, old boars are by far the most likely to punch your time clock. They're the biggest and the baddest and get the best of whatever's available. They own the pecking order AND are at the top of that food chain. For the others it's survival by any means, kind of catch as catch can.

Grizzlies

Grizzlies have a special place among bears. An adult grizzly has a running stride of nearly 20 feet. Predatory animals usually do not make a sound—they stalk or sneak, often lowering their bodies close to the ground or utilizing ground cover, bushes or trees. Their intent is to surprise and kill their victim. They live in the woods—it's their territory where they grew up in the stealth mode. They're silent, stealthy and deadly. Man is at their mercy. When it comes to their nature, don't take my word for it, here is what a real bear man has to say.

On page 82 of his *Grizzlies Don't Come Easy* old time Alaska bear guide Ralph W. Young makes several observations about grizzlies, including a bear charge, "...no animal is more dangerous to hunt or to photograph…. Though a brownie attains about twice the size of a tiger or an African lion, it is just as quick and agile as either. A brownie in full possession of all its faculties and making a determined attack can cover 100 feet in something like two seconds…An attacking Alaskan brown bear is as chilling and awesome a spectacle as nature has to offer. Once I witnessed a bear attacking a deer. It leaped out of the forest like a huge cat, seized the deer in its jaws and tore the animal's head off! As often as not, bears start their attacks with no preliminary warning and at close range. If the man isn't ready to shoot—and shoot straight—he's a goner…The brownie charges on all four feet in great leaping bounds, very reminiscent of a huge, eager dog chasing a cat. When a brown bear charges, the beast kills you, or you kill it. On the several occasions I have faced charging brownies, I have rarely been able to get in more than one hastily aimed shot, and the only thing I've seen through my sights is blurred hair…"

False charge to contact--Charging brownie

Although grizzlies commonly false charge—running to within yards, retreating and repeating the process…most often breaking off the "attack," the target of a "charge" must be prepared to do battle.

Dalton Carr comments in his *Tales of a Bear Hunter* on bluff charges, "I've experienced so many bluff charges that it is almost anticlimactic to see a real charge in progress because the bluff is a lot more entertaining. When a bear bluffs, it will run at you snapping its jaws and woofing. Its hair is erect all the way down its back, and it charges as though it really means business. But the telltale clues that the charge is a bluff are the erect ears, high-head position, and absence of protruding lips…the bluffing bear will run full speed to within five yards, put on its brakes, and stand there trying to intimidate." (Pg. 51)

Then Dalton addresses the real thing, "When preparing to charge, the bear's head is low and its ears back, its lips protrude, and it will often be making very little noise unless it is wounded. The ears are rolled back so that they are not damaged by fang or claw, and its lips protrude and flare out slightly on the sides so it can bare its teeth for action." (Pp. 49-52)

Grizzly nature manifests a certain M.O. or pattern. A grizzly generally attacks on four legs and knocks down the victim where he can more readily engage his teeth and claws. A man staying upright enhances his survival. The bear tends to disarm his victim—knocking away a weapon. The animal goes for the head or neck with its teeth, biting rapidly and trying to turn the victim belly up. He holds the victim down with forepaw(s) and sometimes gets purchase of the head with its mouth and tries to pull the head off. Or he picks up the victim in its mouth and shakes him violently, side to side. The bear waits-watches for movement in order to determine whether or not to continue the (defensive) attack. They're determined to complete their mission.

Grizzlies can be deceptive—a couple of bears have dug holes and hid in them in ambush with only their ears showing.

Trees for safety

Even though both black and grizzly bears can climb trees, the large grizzlies are less apt or able to. Nevertheless, both bears have pulled people from trees.

Alaska guide Ralph Young has spent over 25 years with bears. He relates what he and hunter Jay Bromme watched a medium-size brownie in August 1954, "Whether it was our scent, or the near presence of another bear that frightened it, we'll never know. But with an explosive snort, it dropped the fish and crashed into the woods. A moment later we saw it rapidly climbing a tall spruce tree. The bear climbed easily and didn't stop until it reached a stout limb 40 feet above the ground." ("The Bear Nobody Knows," *Outdoor Life*, August 1957, Ralph W. Young)

In his books James Gary Shelton describes numerous grizzlies aloft.

Polar bear body language

About the late spring of 1999 I received a call from London and the British Broadcasting Service inquiring whether or not I could provide them a list of polar mauling victims they might be able to interview. I told them that Polar bears do not maul—they eat. In general a polar bear investigates anything that moves as its next meal, and it's not likely that a person mauled by one would be around for an interview.

Bear bonding

Some people approach bear-man relations as though they'd gone to college with ursus and were frat brothers or sorority sisters. It's almost like the people think they can reason with the beast, I won't bother you and you won't bother me. That's fine and dandy, but the bears don't know man's philosophy or his rules. And the sad part is that most people don't know the bear's.

Bears survive and exist because they have a certain tolerance for other creatures, including man, and they are protective of their space, range or territory. James Gary Shelton makes the point (*Bear Encounter Survival Guide*, Pg. 48) that "…grizzly bears cannot distinguish the level of danger an intruder poses…They do not know whether you want to end their life or wish them well."

Shelton also states, "A good portion of the predacious black bear encounters I have heard about in the last few years, where the bear was killed, have involved three-year-old males. These young bears were probably under considerable competitive stress, and very hungry." (*Bear Encounter Survival Guide*, Pg. 38)

So, where does man fit into this scenario? Do we compete with bears for their food? Not in the strictest sense. We do catch fish that they may have an interest in and we may shoot an animal that bears claim or try to claim.

The bottom line here is survival—yours! If that means killing a bear, too bad for the bear.

Intentions

Some experts say that man can co-exist better with bears if he knew the bear's intentions. Although man doesn't know a bear's intent, knowledge of bear nature and body language could help in understanding them and help eliminate a lot of pain on the part of both.

Predatory intent

Too often people think of a black bear as "harmless as a dog." Not so. Blacks do attack and do kill. Does an approaching black bear mean business?

These are very determined animals and once they've made a decision to press their attack, it will take some serious personal protection to stop one.

Are its ears pinned back, head low, making eye contact, not vocalizing?

If it displays any of these behaviors, the animal means business and intends to complete its mission or consummate the stalk or attack. You must be prepared to stop it.

It would probably amaze and benefit you to view some of the many video clips regarding bear characteristics such as speed, power, strength and so forth.

Assessing you

It is not only important to assess bears, but also it is imperative to assess you. What are your aptitudes? Know **your health** and physical condition before entering the woods. Many outdoorsmen lose their hearing of high frequency sounds with age and more than one has been mauled because he didn't hear a bear in time to react. Some have not known that the bear was close until they felt the ground shake. Do you need or wear a hearing aid? How are your vision and sense of smell? When moose hunting with my daughter Jill on Six Mile Creek in 1998 she brought my attention to noises that I hadn't heard, like water swishing against a moose's body as it crossed the creek.

On the other hand a few owe their safety to hearing a branch break from a stalking bruin, otherwise the bear probably would have made contact.

How strong are you? Are you capable of keeping someone from injury? What about your emotional stability, what can you handle?

Your appraisal of the bear's value shapes your approach to your outing. If you feel that the bear is more valuable than those in your group, you will prepare differently than if you place the welfare of your group ahead of the bruin. It's great to love the bear, to consider its physical and spiritual value. However, if it comes to a life and death showdown, what is your attitude regarding your survival and/or the survival of those in your group? What is your responsibility to people at that point? You may be liable for the results of the bear's actions (which could include a wounded animal and/or errant bullets). What is the value of your (group's) safety and to what extent are you willing to protect it?

In March 2007 my daughter Jill said, "As much as I know about bears and their speed, I wouldn't have time to use a pistol or rifle anyway. I'd just let them chew on me." I said, "That's where you're wrong. You have several options. First, your attitude needs to tell the bear that you own him. Second, you need visibility. If you don't have it, you need to make lots of noise. Third, you need to be prepared and have a weapon ready. Fourth if you can't hit a bear at 12 feet, you need to give him your arm and kill him while he's chewing on you."

Our humanity demands that we take a stand for people. We do this best by asserting our humanity and allowing a bear no quarter to his bluff. A new bear is emerging—one that does not fear man because we hunt him less and tolerate him more. This bear is learning that people are harmless because we don't threaten it. Although they usually clear out at the scent or sound of man if they are not protecting something, the new bear shows little, if any, fear, no respect, no tolerance and appears even in mid-day, viewing man disdainfully (see Chapter 7, New Bear).

It is incumbent upon you to have the necessary first aid materials and a means of communication with health facilitators.

SAFE with Bears is really all about you. On a scale of 1-10 where would you rate yourself on the following:

1. What do you know about bears, their nature, characteristics, behavior?

2. What do you know about causes of bear attacks?

3. Do you know how to avoid a bear attack?

4. What do you know about yourself?

5. What are your weaknesses?

6. Your capabilities?

7. What can you carry on your person—easily accessible and powerful—that will provide you the greatest margin of safety in bear country?

8. What can you do to stop a determined bear?

9. Are you capable of shooting one?

10. What are your qualifications for stopping an aggressive bear?

11. Do you possess first aid and communications items?

Chart yourself. What percentile are you in…top or bottom 10th percentile or somewhere in between. The bottom line is still 1) how close to the bear are you and 2) what are you prepared to do about it?

BEAR ENCOUNTER SEMINAR

Interestingly enough, bear appearances among humans are becoming less surprising. In the past few years North America has seen an increase in wild bears, yard bears, garage bears and house bears. I thought it would be both educational and mentally stimulating for those unfamiliar with bear-man encounters to review the following situations and to conjecture what action you'd take. Many of these scenarios occurred; others are entirely possible. Information following the scenarios is a summation which either presents the actual scenario or some suggestions (different font). The suggestions for action do not guarantee your safety.

1 A sow grizzly protecting her cubs and a food source knocks down your archery partner. You're 20 feet away, armed with pepper spray. What do you do?

Archery hunters Mark Matheny and friend Dr. Fred Bahnson mixed it up with a grizzly sow near Bozeman, Montana. She attacked, knocking Mark to the ground. Fred rushed the bear with his canister of pepper spray. She left Mark and attacked Fred who sprayed directly into her face from 5 to 6 feet before she knocked him to the ground and returned to Mark. Again, Fred engaged her and sprayed her for 2 seconds, emptying the canister. She knocked him down and bit him then fled. He had emptied the canister.

2 You're riding your mountain bike on a dirt trail, 50 yards ahead of your partner who's pedaling to catch you. It's a bright sunny day with no wind, no noise, you're listening to your headset when you see a brown colored bear and two smaller bears 50 yards up the trail walking your way.

Immediately and quietly, stop! Turn and follow your back trail. Keep riding, looking back often to ascertain that the bear has not seen nor followed you. In May 2006 a Banff employee encountered a predatory black bear in poor condition. Bruin chased him until it successfully separated him from his bike. Dragging him into the woods, it continued chewing on him until two ensuing bikers happened across his broken helmet, heard his cries for help and approached him. He warned them that the bear was in the neighborhood and while one stayed to comfort him the other rode for help, returning with an RCMP officer. The bear was shot and killed and the biker was expected to undergo weeks of reconstructive surgery to his damaged arm. (see Flaaten, predatory attack section this volume)

ALSO, more recently... ("Bike collision with grizzly cause of fatal encounter," Sarah Dettmer, sdettmer@greatfallstribune.com. March 6, 2017)

Customarily Forest Service law enforcement officer Brad Treat and his wife jogged trails from their home nearly every morning and he mountain biked 4 to 5 times a week. Between 1:30 and 2:00 PM on June 29, 2016, Brad mountain biked with a friend on the Green Gate Trails in the Flathead National Forest. Cruising 20-25 miles per hour and leading his friend, Treat rounded a curve and collided with a grizzly. His companion heard an "injured" bear sound, rode around the curve and observed a very large brownish-black bear with its hair bristled standing over Treat. Having no firearm, pepper spray nor cell phone, the companion left to seek help.

Later investigation confirmed after spotting the bear, Treat had between one and two seconds to respond. There were no skid marks or signs of evasive steering, indicating Treat slammed into the bear at full speed, likely flying over the handlebars and onto or over the bear. Both wrists and clavicle were broken as Treat tried to break his fall with his hands.

Treat's helmet was beside his body and was reported to be bitten to pieces by the bear.

Hair and swab samples indicated the bear had been captured in May 2006 in Glacier National Park, was an 18- to 20-year-old male grizzly weighing 370 pounds. Though this is the first incident where someone in Montana has been killed by a bear while mountain biking, bikers would be well advised to constantly make noise in low visibility areas and to carry some form of protection—firearm, pepper spray, flare—and personal communication device like a PLB (personal locator beacon), cell phone, etc.

3 You're dead—you just don't know it. One hundred yards ahead in the brush lies a boar grizzly protecting his food cache. You're in a direct line with him. Within moments he will smell and hear you. He guards his kill with his life. What could you have done to avoid this situation?

What could you have done? For starters, you could have given yourself the visibility factor. Could you see 30 yards in every direction? Did you have a partner or a pet? Were you armed?

4 You and your partner see a bear with two smaller ones on the hillside about 100 yards away eating berries—the larger one is black, one of the smaller ones is brown the other is black. The bears don't know your presence. What do you do?

Back off. Keep the bear unaware of your presence. Either retrace your steps or make a circle around and beyond the animals. If possible, keep the bears in sight until you are safely away from them.

5 You're hiking with a partner above timberline. Some scattered, climbable trees are thirty feet away. You spot a 4-foot tall bear walking towards you on all fours 100 yards distant on your trail. It sees you.

Do you know what type bear it is? It's four feet tall, so it's undoubtedly a medium-sized or larger grizzly. It may not be much of a climber and you might be able to out climb it. If there are trees available, start climbing, knowing that it can be at the foot of the tree in 6 seconds or less. Second, if there are no trees, you and your partner can make noise and stand as tall as possible, raising your hands, hold coats or shirts aloft, stare it in the eyes and maintain a confident attitude while talking authoritatively to it. Do not turn your backs to it. Back away slowly with dignity and determination.

6   You're on the city bike trail on the edge of town, rollerblading solo clad only in socks, shorts and tank top. You're armed with your car keys. A bear ambles toward you on the asphalt track fifty yards distant.

Have you practiced climbing with your roller blades? Are there any other people around? Is it possible to join them and do a group bear stand? How far away are the nearest vehicles or buildings...perhaps you could reach one.

7   You're fishing on a noisy stream when you sense a presence. You turn around and see a large black bear walking towards you, only ten yards away.

Is this stream heavily fished by people? Are they close enough for you to summon? If you're unarmed, stand your ground. Present your best boss of the woods attitude while making eye contact and talking authoritatively to the bear. Try to make yourself appear larger than the bear by spreading your arms, raising something above your head.

8   You're in a tent with two others at night. Three other people share a tent next to yours. It's dark and all are asleep. You hear tearing nylon. Then a bear is in your tent.

Each person should have a working flashlight and a canister of pepper spray or a firearm. And each person should be relegated a task: one holds the light, one unzips the tent, one sprays/shoots the bear. Exit the tent. Summon help from others.

9   Three family joggers run a mountain trail south of town running uphill through forested lands. One jogger screams. You don't know what's up.

Art Abel and his grandmother Marcie Trent jogged McHugh Creek trail in July 1995. His Uncle Larry was probably somewhere up ahead.

Art made out something running through the moving bushes and heard his grandmother scream. He dived into the bushes and rolled into a shallow gully then scampered up a tree where he remained forty-five minutes until he saw a hiker coming his way. Hoping that it was his uncle, Art called out. It was not his uncle, however help arrived in the form of other hikers, officials were notified and within hours the tragedy unfolded. Both Art's grandmother and uncle died as the result of a bear attack. (*Some Bears Kill*)

10 Two parents and two children, 8 and 10, are on the trail in heavy brush. You can't see more than 30 feet. Suddenly a bear jumps out of the brush 15 feet away and races in your direction. How much time do you have?

If you're unarmed, why are you in a low visibility area, especially with kids?! You   better summon forces, gather in as large group presentation as you can make and hope the bear's one of those that tolerates goofballs.

11 You're in a visqueen lean-to and realize the presence of something in camp. You whisper to that effect to warn your wife. All of a sudden a huge brown bear drops onto the lean-to with its forepaws, trying to tear your wife from her sleeping bag. How do you respond?

Joyce noticed a huge brown bear leg near her head just before the beast rose on hind legs and smashed down upon the barrier with its front paws. Al reached an arm around its neck and punched it in the head with his other fist. It clamped its teeth into Al's head, pulled him from his sleeping bag and shook him before running into the woods on three legs, one foreleg wrapped around Al's body. Wondering what became of Al and whether the bear might return, Joyce climbed a tree. After the bear dropped Al and he returned to camp, Joyce tended his injuries and at dawn both hiked 15 miles out. (*Alaska Bear Tales*)

12 You're anticipating a pleasant soak in a hot spring along the Alaska Highway. Should you be concerned about bears? You and your children encounter a bear which attacks you. A man comes to your rescue.

I suggest you check out the history of Liard Hot springs on the World Wide Web. There seem to be an overabundance of black bears habituated to people that are allowed free reign in the park. Why are bears allowed this proximity with people?

One man punched out a black bear in 1994 at Liard Hot Springs and escaped from its curious or predatory attempts to get closer. (*Some Bears Kill*) More tragically in 1997 a lady was fatally mauled as was her rescuer. (see Patti Reed McConnell, predatory attack section herein)

13 You're playing in the yard with your infant son, kicking a soccer ball when the phone rings just beyond the deck and the sliding glass door. You pick up the phone and notice a black lab approaching. Then you realize the dog is a BLACK BEAR! You run to your child and reach him just as the bear does.

One of the saddest stories I've ever read involved Lisa and her young son. In 1994 a black bear grabbed Ian. Lisa and the bear tugged on the child, the animal determined to win this battle. At length a neighbor drove to her rescue and she took the child into his pickup, rushing to the hospital. But he succumbed en route. (see Ian Dunlap, predatory attack section herein)

14 You're walking a wilderness trail collecting rock samples. You hear a noise and look up to see a black bear 20 feet down the trail, standing on all fours and looking at you. You have a rock hammer and wonder what you should do.

Cynthia wanted to "do the right thing." But for her hammer, she was unarmed as her supervisor had instructed workers of the dangers of wounding a bear with a firearm. Cyn spoke to the bear and raised the hammer above her head. She thought she'd be "bigger" by ascending the rock outcropping and turned to do so. Before she knew it, the bear attacked and knocked her to the ground and began chewing on her, literally eating her alive. Before she was rescued the damage done by the bear resulted in the loss of both her arms. (*Alaska Bear Tales*)

15 You're collecting rock samples when spotting a black bear stalking you from a half mile. You're armed with a rifle. The bear approaches within 100 feet. What do you do?

Years later, Cynthia's friend Marti Miller underwent weapons training in conjunction with her job, choosing her .30-06 rifle. She was dropped at a work site in remote Alaska and proceeded up a ridge. When she looked down the ridge, she observed a black bear, nose to the ground, following her every step. After some minutes she realized that it was stalking her and she took appropriate action. (this volume and *Some Bears Kill*)

16 You're a cattleman in the timber rounding up cattle—every day in bear country increases your chances of an encounter. You grew up in the cattle business and in the woods. As a youth you killed bears on two occasions, once to protect a companion, once in self-defense. You've returned to your roots not knowing that in your absence that government policies and bears have changed dramatically. You must qualify for a firearm in a distant city and don't have time to do so.

A black bear killed and partially devoured Sven. Is there anything he could have done to prevent this tragedy? How can your community prevent a repeat of this event which occurred in a country that does not allow firearms in the woods unless it's hunting season? This is another sad story about a man who was killed by a bear. Had his government's bear policy been different, he'd likely be alive. (see Denise Satre, predatory attacks this volume)

17 You're hunting solo, sneaking through the woods on a heavily used trail which the animals use as much as humans. Suddenly in the dim dawn a brown bear lunges from a short distance ahead of you. Then you see another…and another…and still another. Your rifle carries four bullets. And there are four bears!

Cool-headed Coogle killed every bear. He was a hunter and he was prepared. Reacting coolly, he took care of the problem. Four less bears. Better they than he. End of story. As a perp pulls a weapon on a cop and gets smoked, I see the same parallel with a bear…you mess with man and man has the right to mess you over. (*Some Bears Kill*)

18 You see a mother grizzly with cubs. You decide to follow and to get closer for a better photo. This is the chance of a lifetime. You approach to within 40 yards, focusing on the lens for a tight close up. But then you realize that the sow is sprinting toward you. (*Mark of the Grizzly*)

William Tesinsky wasn't as fortunate as Al Johnson. Tesinsky was on the ground and was killed and partially eaten; Al was in a tree when the grizzly pulled him from it. Although she bit and partially scalped him, the bear was more interested in her three cubs and left Al who had attempted to avoid injury by climbing 15-feet up the tree. (*Alaska Bear Tales*)

19 Planning to harvest a large grizzly, you are guiding a friend to a bear den which you'd last observed while scouting from the air. You approach the empty den on snowshoes only to discover that you have been ambushed by the waiting bear.

Lloyd Pennington and Everett Kendall were either ambushed or surprised at the den and both killed in 1956 (*Alaska Bear Tales*).

20 You've land on a lake in your float plane, heel the plane into the bank and walk up the bank looking for a place to tie the tail rope. You look one way, the other, something catches your peripheral vision and you look back…into the face of a black bear standing on hind legs. You're nose to nose.

You're waiting for your husband to tie the tail rope before exiting the plane. You hear him scream and see him tumble down the bank with a black bear clutching him.

Stephen Routh took on a large black bear unarmed. He chose to fight and to figure a way to kill the bear. He offered it his left arm, ripped a switch from a log and switched its face, putting it on the defensive. His wife Joanie exited the plane, stood on a float and screamed at the bear, diverting it from Stephen to her. When it rushed her, she entered the plane's cabin and the bear scratched at the windows while Stephen swam into deeper water. When the bear returned to him, he splashed water into its mouth, repelling it while his wife started the plane's engine. He was ultimately rescued. (*Some Bears Kill*)

21 You and your partner are following the blood spoor of a wounded black bear that you've shot. You've split up. Suddenly you hear a scream and look ahead to see a large brown colored bear charging your partner. It knocks him down and starts clawing and biting him.

You discover that it wasn't a black but a brown bear. It's killing your partner. You shoot it with your rifle, then your pistol. You administer first aid and try to carry your partner to camp. You're in unfamiliar territory. You make your partner comfortable and go for help. Radio communication is made and a helicopter arrives but you're not sure where your partner is. When you find him, it's too late. (*Some Bears Kill*)

22 You and your wife are hiking in a national park when a grizzly approaches you. Together you decide to play dead and lie on the ground. The bear knocks you down and attacks your wife. It returns to you then goes back to her. She screams for you to go for help— two hours away one way; what do you do while it's chewing on her?

Here's a case where a woman would be alive if the couple had better information or a weapon or both. So sad. (Paul and Christine Courtney, predatory attacks this volume)

23 You've downed a moose and a few days later return to the site. There is a grizzly on the remains and your guide moves upwind of the bear to scare it from the thick brush so you can get a shot. The bear is actually leaving your guide and the area when you start shooting, wound it and it returns to kill your guide.

Your shot at the bear causes it to turn on the closest moving object, your guide. The grizzly picks him up in its jaws and thrashes him around, splintering ribs into his heart and lungs. You shoot and kill the bear, run to the guide who instructs you on the proper use of his plane radio then you run a couple of miles to the plane and radio for help. Officials arrive but the guide's injuries are fatal. (*Alaska Bear Tales*)

24 You're dead. While trying to shoot a bear which was mauling you, your 12-year-old son shot you by mistake. What could you have done to prevent your death, your child's possible injury and his grief? How could you have prepared your child from a lifetime of anguish?

How many rescuers have accidentally shot the person instead of the bear? How difficult is it to avoid hitting the person in this situation? What would you want the shooter to do if you were the victim of a mauling?

25 You're vacationing in a national park with two young children. A black bear steps from the woods and grabs your infant in its jaws, igniting you into action. You attack the animal, pummeling it with sticks and your fists. In the melee your other child, grade school aged, runs in fear into the woods. You and your infant are in critical condition but people scare the bear from you. Searchers look for and later find your older child's body at the feet of the bear.

Why would a parent have to be concerned about a child within arm's length in a public park? What needs to be done to see that this doesn't happen again? (Elora Petrasek, predatory attacks this book)

26 You're enjoying a hike in the Great Smoky Mountains with your ex-husband when you encounter a small black bear and its cub. You're in a national park, unarmed. What's the best thing to do? Or, if you're the ex-husband, what can you do to see that your ex-wife is safe? The bears kill and feed upon the lady. (Glenda Ann Bradley, predatory attacks this book)

Pepper spray or a firearm probably would have saved her. Hopefully laws will allow every law-abiding citizen the right to protect himself against harm.

27 You're taking a neighborhood walk with your four children, ages 6, 4, 2 and 6 months, pushing the younger two in a bike chariot. You spot a bear across the street and halfway up the block. How can you be safe?

Is there anyone nearby...whom you can hail for help or whose home/garage you can enter? Is there a vehicle close enough to provide safety? Your only alternative may be getting your children under or on top of a vehicle and following them.

28 You're in Yosemite with a black bear in your car. Why is it there and how can you remove it?

Hopefully you know about Yosemite's bears. They represent the ultimate panhandlers, breaking into cars, often destroying part of it in the process. It will continue its activity until it finds something to eat or wearies of the process. You could be next. How are you prepared to defend yourself? You could evacuate your campground for a safer place...someone's camper or motor home.

29 You, your friend Chester Meeks and former student Louie Jensen hiked up Resurrection Creek south of Hope, Alaska, to search for a raft full of moose meat you'd lost. Part way up the creek while nearing the area of the raft's last sighting, you leave Louie unarmed to await your return—no need to have him straggle along. You and Chester find the raft and the soured meat, dump it into the creek, deflate the 2-man raft and start back down the trail.

You reach Louie, surprised to see him surrounded by stacks of boned out moose meat that he had rescued from the stream. That was a definite set up for a bear baited attack. Were we naïve, stupid or what?

30 You're 6-years-old, walking the sidewalk near home, a bear appears across the street.

How does a 6-year-old respond to this situation? More bears are invading our neighborhoods. What's the message for parents? How can children enjoy childhood in safety, without the restraints of being (s) "mothered"?

31 You're in a mountain race with a number of juniors, reached the turnaround point and are heading for the finish line near the highway below. You spot a bear and text with your cell phone that it is following you.

The most recent tragic death to bear in such an event involved 16-year-old Patrick Cooper of Anchorage, Alaska. On Father's Day, June 18, 2017, he was killed by a black bear. Running mountain trails arouses greater concern with bears in the vicinity.

Create your own scenario. What type bear experience are you likely to have? For instance, what if your neighbor elementary children await the school bus when a bear approaches them? Do you see yourself or others in these scenarios? What do you do?

CHAPTER 4
BEARS ABOUT

READ THE SIGNS

If you want to avoid bear problems, avoid "beary" situations—know bears and anticipate bear signs. These "signs" are not installed by the road department and do not consist of a metal warning attached to posts.

Know and be on the lookout for signs indicating the presence or recent passing of a bear, an attractant such as a berry patch or signs of people activity.

When reading the signs, do not focus only on sight but include your senses of smell and hearing. It's possible to smell the bear or carrion and it's possible to hear noises indicating a bear may be near—squealing cub or other bear sounds, birds around a kill site, sloshing water or crunching brush.

Signs include things that bears leave behind, that they do to the environment or that the environment entices them with...or indications of people. Both bear and people signs indicate the likelihood of a bear's presence. Listed under the two subjects are numerous signs the backcountry traveler needs to observe in order to avoid an encounter with a bear.

Bear signs include...

Tracks—could vary in size from an inch or so in diameter to 11 inches wide, depending upon the age and type of bear. The hind track is similar to a human foot print. The front paw is rounded with toe pads (sometimes claw prints are visible in front of them).

Scat—similar in size to large canine scat, may be concentrated with berries or grass, segments of fish bones, particles of hair or fur, bone, fruit such as apples or plumbs or wood. Depending upon digested food, the scat can also resemble a "cow pie," round pile of doo doo. The absence of scat, tracks and other signs does NOT mean the absence of bears!

Rubbed trees—these trees usually have rubbed spots (in some cases the bark on the rub is missing) and bear hair of various colors from blonde to black (often in little bunches) is evidenced on the tree from near ground level upwards of 8-feet. Sign posts or a bear tree may be a myth in the sense that bears mark their spot—Ralph Young comments that a "bear tree" is merely a place where bears find it convenient to rub, not a "sign post" where they demonstrate their size in an attempt to leave their sign or calling card.

Game drag trails—where a hunter may have dragged a deer or packed out game which dripped body fluids

Birds gathering in a certain area—in the sky or in trees or on the ground, may be seen and/or heard

Carrion—gut pile or mounded carrion, fish remains (heads, skeletons, tails)

Excavated areas—may resemble a pasture hogs have "plowed up"—indicate bear's digging for bulbs, tubers or roots, acorns, ground squirrels, squirrel caches, foxes and so on. Also includes shifted or overturned boulders or rocks

Shredded refuse or logs—a campsite may have strewn garbage; torn or shredded logs—bears digging for grubs

Overturned boulders, rocks or logs

Bitten (off) or missing objects like trees (missing bark—bears strip bark, eat it and/or lick the sap from trees); "grazed" grasses, skunk cabbage, flowers, dandelion, clover, spring beauty, horsetail, fireweed; park benches, coolers, beverage containers; partially eaten pine cones and/or scat with pine nuts in it

Berries include huckleberry, blackberry, strawberry, salmonberry, blueberry, cranberry, chokecherries, mountain ash berries

Bear hair

Trails and/or day beds

Smooshed down grass, ferns or other vegetation—bear beds. Some of the "real nice" trails that people credit the park or forest service for providing are actually bear trails!

Gut piles—watch and smell for gut piles; listen for crunching bones or predators arguing for the pickings

People signs

There are all kinds of "signs" that people create, all of which should be noted by the prospective bear country participant.

Parks and campgrounds are in and of their nature attractive to bears. Most are located in timbered areas adjacent to or in bear country. People participants hike, camp or eat on site and accrue garbage. The camper needs to assess the park or campground environment and have a bear avoidance strategy. In July 2000 my son-in-law Brad Risch and I journeyed to fish the Copper River with his father Fred and in the process camped at a site that overflowed with garbage, attracting at least one brown bear.

Some campgrounds have become noted for bear visits. One such dangerous area is Liard River Hot Springs in British Columbia, a favorite stopping off spot for Alaska Highway travelers. Unfortunately the resort has attracted numerous black bears which have created problems for the users, killing some people. What is the nature of your recreational site?

Two other areas of consideration include waterways and land use, which might be separate or combined. For instance, floating a stream and using the bank for a picnic. How heavily used are these areas? Heavy usage could attract animals because of litter, noise or other factors—especially high pitched children's voices or dogs. Many streams and lakes are used recreationally or commercially by boaters, canoers, kayakers and floaters for day or overnight use. In such cases if the boater encounters a bear, it behooves the person to evaluate the situation and to assess the site. Is the land site "contaminated" by previous users—is the site messy; has anyone left fish offal or other attractive objects? Is this a suitable place to spend the night? Land use could include fishing, hunting or camping areas where numerous outdoorsmen spend time. What is the nature of the area? What kind of fish or game may be hanging or in coolers? Is the game properly secured from bear thievery—in a cache above the ground, on meat poles or racks out of reach? Are the people properly prepared for a possible bear confrontation?

Air taxis drop off a lot of people in Alaska's bush, as well as Canada's. What is the nature of the drop site? Has the area been used numerous times? How have the previous users left the area? Some Alaskan hunters are challenged at government cabins (such as Forest Service dwellings) where previous users may have left attractants such as game remains.

Other people signs include:

Work related sites such as logging camps and oil facilities have with garbage pits

Livestock ranches

Orchards, vineyards, berry patches (in the wild) or grain fields such as corn

Homebrew or still action wherein alcoholic beverages are produced (fermented mash)

Fishing sites where people harvest and store their catch. Fish racks often attract bears.

Fish canneries have also been known to interest bears

Some cities abutting bear country are bear magnets—Juneau, Cold Bay, Girdwood, Tok, Ketchikan. Girdwood and Larsen Bay, Alaska for instance.

Conveyances—boats and airplanes used in hauling fish and game or berries attract bears. In some cases where the pilot sprayed the rubber bumpers of his plane's floats with pepper spray, brown bears ate the "seasoned" bumpers.

Home sites adjacent to bear country may contain attractants like smoke houses, livestock or feathered critters, dogs (dog food) or cats, bird feeders, bee hives, barbeque facilities.

Campfire cooking (especially bacon) or grilling

Maple or birch trees where maple syrup fixins are harvested

Transportation corridors—rights of way trails where animals choose to travel

Food in vehicles (Yosemite)

ATTRACTANTS and DETERRENTS

Attractants include:	Suggested action:
Cosmetics and deodorants	Leave at home
Food sources	
Fish	Store in cooler or in stream
Prepared goods	Secure in tents or packs
Snacks (granola and candy bars and tail mix)	Place well out of reach of bears - in trees or cache.
Tooth paste/ sensory items	Store in air tight containers
Food and drink containers	Elevate food and/or pack like coolers, fish creels
Animal foods—horse (grains)	Keep away from camp and dog
Firearms report	A shot is a dinner bell for some conditioned bears.

Some first aid items

Soaps

Pepper spray is loved by Alaska brown bears on the Alaska Peninsula

Motor oil, oil based products such as snow sled seats

Insect repellents

Dog—determine whether your dog is a bear stopper or a "retriever"…

Some people question the value of a dog in the woods. One advantage is that it will nearly always let you know when something is around. One advantage of a dog is that of its nose and ears. It should go without saying that a dog's nose and hearing is better than man's and should prove helpful in apprising you of impending danger within a few hundred yards. An exception, however, would hinge on the wind and whether the dog could catch the bear's scent or noise.

A decided disadvantage is that the frightened dog often "retrieves" bears to the dog's master. However, many a dog has saved his master. Therefore it may be that you have or would like to have a good bear dog, one that does not fear a bear and one that will keep you posted as to the presence of wild animals. It may benefit you to investigate the Karelian bear dogs.

Big game calling:	While hunting moose, elk or deer, you could attract a bear with a game call. Be prepared for such an event by being in a position from which you can see in 360 degrees and be able to defend yourself
Women	Reduce odors—no perfume, deodorant, hair spray, seal used tampons

Although olfactory studies have been done to determine bear's attraction to human menstruation, the controversy remains. Are women at greater risk in bear country during their monthly menstruation cycle?

I choose to err on the side of prudence and agree with Gary Shelton: "Most bears would be attracted to any blood or food smell; bears who are afraid of people would be repelled by a human smell; habituated park bears, or wild predatory bears, would probably be attracted by any smell." (*Bear Encounter Survival Guide*, Pg. 78)

Where there's smoke, there's fire. If I were a woman, I'd heighten my cautionary levels were I in the woods during my menstrual cycle. "Bears hunt by smell, and if very hungry, become frenzied as they get closer to the target." (*Bear Encounter Survival Guide*, Pg. 85)

I encourage extreme caution by those in your group for the safety of women who may be incurring their menstrual cycle.

DETERRENTS

Some of the deterrents are known to deter bears. Some are marginal if not questionable. Some—like Charl Fourie's Handi-Blaster—were available, but no longer on the market (to my knowledge as of January 2015).

Ammonia, human urine and ammonia mixed with human urine

I do not tout urine as a cure-all, however the following examples should provide food for thought.

1. Website www.bearsmart.com: "Urine: Human male urine can be used to effectively deter bears and other animals from specific locations. Female urine is ineffective. Simply deposit urine in areas where bears are not welcome or around the perimeter of your property. Effectiveness will lessen over time."

2. My friend Pete Sainsbury urinated around his USGS tent sites on Alaska's Seward Peninsula for 30-plus years, using a distant warning system (100-200 feet) and an early warning system (30-50 feet) diameter. He never had a bear in camp under those circumstances.

3. Pete called me on Nov. 6th, 1993, to relate an experience from his previous summer on the Alaska Highway. Around Burwash Landing he exited his truck and hiked up a dry creek bed until he spotted a grizzly 300-400 yards away. Pete reversed his trek for the safety of his rig since he did not have a firearm. Realizing that he would not reach his truck in time, Pete climbed a tree and urinated down the trunk. Pete said, "When the bear got close enough to smell the urine, it lit out."

On another note, I read or heard that human urine incenses male brown bears and they take it as a challenge. So…may not want to use as deterrent? (see Ken Cates story, mysterious attack section herein)

These examples may not be solid enough evidence for those "scientifically minded" of you, however I've used Pete Sainsbury's formula around my camps and (as stated earlier) have never had a bear problem in 40 years in Alaska's "outback." Of the five closest encounters (of which I'm aware), the score is Kaniut 5, Bears 0—with no injury to either party.

Audio: sounds that deter an attack?

Bear bells announce yourself

Air horn

Bear banger

Making noise—can the bear hear you?

Clap your hands, announce your presence.

Maybe play a boom box or some noise maker besides bear bells

Some new audio gizmos have come onto the market; may be worth checking out

Tree

Back pack

Laser: is there a laser that will turn a bear?

Scent Being "smellable"…or smelly—can the bear smell you? One of the most acute senses of the bear is its sense of smell.

Visible—can the bear see you?

Helmet—motorcycle or snowmachine would cover chin and lower neck; maybe kevlar neck collar and/or vest? Because bears tend to go for the head or neck to debilitate or kill. One problem is that a tight helmet could give bear purchase, causing neck or spine damage—perhaps easier for the bear to break the neck.

Moth balls

Flare (gun)

Bear flare—Check out the bear flare.

Flame thrower/propane bottle

Taser/ Stun gun

*Vibrations and/or Audio that deters bears? (Pg. 168, *White Bear*)

Tear gas

Water Pressurized water (fire hoses at zoos)

Pepper spray…or, perhaps, wasp spray

Knife—what brand/type is conducive to "survival"?

Axe

Fingers (in eye, ear, nose)

Pistol

Rifle

Shotgun

Club

Electric   electric fences work on polar bears (167 White Bear)

Tiring of losing fish to bears for over fifteen years, Dillingham residents Anuska and Hjalmar Olson turned the tables on the four-legged thieves. They agreed with the Alaska Department of Fish and Game to test an electric fence. Wildlife biologist Jim Woolington installed the fence which is powered by a solar panel about the size of a three-ring binder. Bears no longer bother the Olson's smokehouse. (Source: Solar-powered fence thwarts bears. Erik Hillstrom, *Bristol Bay Times*, July 15, 2002)

Margosupplies.com

BEAR ALERT ALARM SYSTEM

Maximize the effectiveness of your bear proof electric fencing system. The alarm system is activated when the bear touches the hot wire. The bear receives a shock which causes a short on the fence wire, simultaneously tripping the siren. The audio stimulation frightens the bear and, more importantly, alerts camp personnel of the bear's presence. This system comes complete with alarm control box and siren. It can be rigged with any alarm device (ie. lights, security monitors, etc.) that is triggered by a switch closure. Also ideal for monitoring the perimeter of game (deer/elk) fencing.

TRIP WIRE FENCE SYSTEM

The trip wire fence system is effective in detecting intruding bears or other wildlife. This compact system is simple to set up and operate. It is the most practical solution for fly camps and other situations which preclude the use of electric fencing. This lightweight (16 pounds) system comes complete with 10 fibreglas posts, wire hangers, 200 m of trip wire, alarm controller, siren and 12-volt power supply.

PACKALARM (by Tom Hron)

I strongly suggest you purchase and read Tom's excellent book *Fighting For Your Life (Maneater Bears)*. Another possible deterrent is Tom's PackAlarm. You can Google www.PackAlarm.net and look at the video explanation as well the testimonials).

CRITTER GITTER

Using passive infrared, body heat and motion detection, Critter Gitter detects animals moving into its protected area. It then makes ear piercing sounds (and flashing lights) to send them fleeing. Once the animal has cleared the area, Critter Gitter automatically resets itself. This detector changes its sound and light patterns with each intrusion and protects a diagonal area of up to 40' (depending on the size of the animal). It comes complete with a 9-volt alkaline battery and a protective weather bag.

The strobe siren enhancer is an auxiliary and separate source of light and sound greatly augmenting the effect of the device.

October 5, 2017 my friend Norm sent me the following email, endorsing some electric devices:

Larry:

Our home is somewhat remote; we are about 3 miles south of Pelican on Lisianski Inlet. We are set back in a cove; it is about 600 yards wide.

There are 7 houses in our cove; one other neighbor is here most of the year; the rest are recreational houses, occupied on the average 3 to 4 weeks per season. Three of these buildings were broken into by a brown bear about 4 years ago. After that time we began increasing our bear protective measures. I monitor 5 of these other buildings, not counting our own. Since that last set of break ins we have not had a re-occurence. Here are the measures we have employed:

• All of the buildings but one are guarded by Critter Gitter units made by AMTEK. These units are about the size of a pack of cigarettes and powered by one 9 volt battery. They are positioned to view a doorway or porch area. If motion is detected they emit a shrill modulating sound and red lights flash on the face of the unit. None of the buildings with these units activated have been broken into. I put them in a point of entry area where there is no background motion to set them off; like a bush wavering in the wind. I have four of these units around our house. I activate them only in the spring and fall when the bears are most likely to be roaming about, once the salmon are in the streams we have no issues and I bring the units inside. These units are available on the internet.

• Nite Guard Predator Lights. These solar powered lights come on at dusk and go off at dawn. They flash a bright red light continually. Impervious to wet weather I must have about 8 of these mounted around the outside of the house and on posts in the yard. These lights are available on the internet.

• Battery powered motion lights. I have bought the weather proof lights to put on the entrances to the house. These lights are mounted in such a manner to shine directly at the eye level of a bear. The lights have an extremely long life; have one up that is on year 4. These lights are available on the internet.

Bear deterrence:

We discourage bears from coming close to our home and getting comfortable. I used to shoot pop bottle rockets at them; moderately successful. I discovered a product by Tru Flare that shoots a variety of noise makers from a pen gun. The pen gun I carry in my pocket when walking around our lot if unarmed. The unit allows the operator to screw on a variety of projectiles to shoot from the pen gun. The orange colored projectile shoots out about 40 to 50 yards and emits a loud explosion similar to a 12 ga shotgun only louder. The blue projectile screams out of the unit trailing an immense amount of black smoke and emitting a loud noise; this works best on bears that wander too close. Any bear getting within 20 yards of our home is ushered off with one of the "blue screamers," kind of a miniature scud missile.

We take the normal precautions with food and trash; none left out. I believe the "break in bear" of a few years ago was trained by someone leaving cat food inside their house with a pet door. The bear smelled the food and knocked down the entire door to find all sorts of treats inside; from then on it was a constant menace. I am quite certain that bear was eventually shot. This year we have been visited by a pair of three or four year old bears and a single larger bear; the two parties are never present at the same time. These bear have wandered close to our home and received a warning from a "blue screamer." One of these projectiles went off underneath the bear causing a two foot levitation on part of the bear and a mad dash down the beach. I have not found a source for Tru Flare products in Southeast Alaska; they are available in Canada.
So that is our bear situation; so far we all respect our boundaries and get along.

Norm

Kevlar In an effort to learn more about Kevlar as a protectant from bear injury, I emailed srprace@aol.com:

Sir, I'm curious as to the reduction of such things as animal bites via kevlar clothes. Have you done any studies, can you point to effectiveness or suggest probabilities of reduced injury in a bear attack? I'm hopeful that Kevlar clothes will be a plus for hikers confronting bears and would like to pass on such information. Thanks.

Larry Kaniut

Sept. 3, 2001

The next day I received this response (9/4/01):

We don't think it wouldn't work as something comfortable for the hiker.
Kevlar is hot and kinda stiff material that is not comfortable to wear for long periods of time. It would also rub on the skin and irritate it. Plus the cost of the material people wouldn't buy it, too expensive.

Thank you

SRP

Weapon

CHAPTER 5
BEAR ATTACKS

In the contingent USA, where park animals have existed with people (perhaps becoming habituated to them) it is far more likely to see bears. However, in Alaska many people have never seen a bear in the wilds, even those who venture into the bush every year. There are something like three bear maulings a year in Alaska and a human death every two years, so your odds of seeing a bear are very minimal. In general unless you are on a salmon stream, flying or spotting above timberline (or, unfortunately, living in town where bears are becoming more predominant), you're probably not going to see a bear.

And your chances of being mauled are even fewer.

My father-in-law Howard J. Timmons used to say, "My mother always told me 'there would be days like this,' but I didn't know they'd come in bunches like bananas." It is pretty rare to read about many maulings in Alaska. However, there are times when they appear, in bunches like bananas. For instance, during one week in 2002 the *Anchorage Daily News* reported bear-man situations three days running: August 16, August 17 and August 18.

On Tuesday, August 13, Gene Trumbo encountered two black bears in East Anchorage in Campbell Tract (later, herein). Friday afternoon, August 16, Justin Dunagan and his mother Kathy hiked a few miles east of Cooper Landing on the Resurrection Pass Trail when a brown bear sow with a cub attacked and made contact with them both (Defensive attack chapter, herein). And on Saturday, August 17, Garen Brenner and two friends fished the Russian River near Cooper Landing when they were confronted by a brown bear sow and a cub (pistol section, herein).

A 15-year-old Barrow, Alaska, youngster on a group campout awakened during the night to discover the camp counselor shaking his tent on Deer Island in southeast Alaska. The "counselor" turned out to be a 400-pound brown bear.

When the lad realized it was a bear, he tried to wiggle free from the tent but the bear caught on. As he shielded himself with his right arm from the bear's jaws, she bit his forearm. Then the youngster punched the bear a half dozen times with his left hand, causing the bear to release him. The boy rose and tried to run but the bear bit him on the right side of his body, wounding his back. He hit the bear again and she let him go. Then he dodged behind some trees, trying to stay away from her. At length he remembered an air horn in his gear, grabbed it and blew it in the bear's face, awakening camp director Steve Prysunka.

Steve and counselor Willy Hollett stood between the bear and the boy and gave her a shot of pepper spray. She reared and got another shot of spray, twice. Another counselor fired a flare at her feet, scaring her away.

The boy's wounds were attended at a nearby barge serving as a floating camp, then the young man was transported to Ketchikan General Hospital by a medical crew and treated, released and sent home to recuperate. ("Teen camper fights off brown bear," SOUTHEAST: Rice-A-Roni in tent may have sparked attack, MARY PEMBERTON, The Associated Press, April 27, 2004)

The grizzly bear's arsenal has been stated previously, "An animal with three-inch, razor sharp claws, inch-and-a-half canines and boundless muscles with enough strength to break the neck of a barnyard bull with a single swat is an ominous beast." (*More Alaska Bear Tales*, Pg. 250).

Most maulings are non-fatal, though grievous injury results from the bear's teeth and paws. One-third of maulings in Alaska occurred while people were hunting; and 36% of the hunters were saved when their partner shot the animal off them.

So many people have told me "I'm afraid to go into the woods because I read your book" that I have come up with a standard response. First, your chances of even seeing a bear in the woods are minimal. Bears aren't interested in people and generally make every effort to avoid man. Second, Alaska has 2.5 bear maulings a year and a fatality every other year; whereas we lost 32 or so snow machine riders in 2001. I wonder, are you safer hiking the woods or riding a snow machine?

Upwards of six dozen people have had fatal encounters with bears in North America since 1900 (APPENDIX 3).

I write bear books to enable people to stay out of a bear's mouth. You don't quit driving when you see an accident, so why fear the woods and refuse to enter them just because someone was mauled?

Bears attack for two reasons: protection or predation. Either they want to protect something (defensive) or they want to eat something (predatory). It's that simple. To put it another way, you represent a threat or a treat—trouble or table fare.

Slice it any way you want, bears attack because they're defending a cub, mate, food source or personal space (this could include a surprise encounter or an adolescent bear with something to prove); or they plan to eat their intended victim.

A third "cause" for bear attacks which escapes explanation might be pigeon holed under the title mysterious.

DEFENSIVE ATTACKS

In the case of a defensive attack, the bear's behavior is to defuse the situation or counter the threat the human interloper presents. The bear tries to neutralize the threat by attacking or, possibly, false charging the human. If it's a defensive attack, the bear usually backs off, waits and watches for movement.

Normally the bear will try to down the person, knocking his weapon from his hands. With a singleness of purpose it focuses on the victim, though others may be present.

SOWS and CUBS

Rumor on the street has it that sows protect their cubs, however that is not totally accurate. Too many examples exist wherein mother bruin fled the scene in deference to the safety of her offspring. It is common for grizzlies to fight for their cubs, thus the defensive advice is to play dead in such an event. But, here again, grizzly sows do not always measure up to the maternal test.

KEN RADACH

I met Ken Radach at the 2006 Great Alaska Sportsman Show in Anchorage and he shared his story with me. I told him I'd like to use it in my upcoming book and a couple of weeks later I received the following email from him, followed by his story. For space purposes, I've included only the bear event.

April 25, 2006

Hey Larry,

Here is the story—half of it concerns the bear attack and the other half is about the ensuing moose hunt—had it published in a couple outdoor mags.

No thank you on extra scratches—I have no illusions about my luck in walking away with a few punctures—most don't get the chance to walk away relatively unscathed. Thanks again for the stories...kr

BROKEN ARROW BULL

It has been my obsession to get a brown bear with my bow for the past two years. A bow hunt on Kodiak Island a couple years ago for the big brownies left an empty spot in my Pope and Young list for North America. After hunting hard for 12 days and getting within 50 yards of a 9 ½ footer, I ended our hunt by taking that brownie with Chris' backup rifle. It was a great hunt, but I still want one with my bow and Cordova is a great place to fill that empty spot with lots of salmon-fattened brownies prowling around.

There is a heavily-used game corridor close to work that showed lots of promising brown bear tracks with at least two large boars using that corridor. Checking this corridor at least three times per week had only produced one actual sighting of one of the big boars, a beautiful dark chocolate with blonde guard hairs running down his back. Juvenile bears and sow sightings were a regular occurrence, but I was looking for those large boars that were leaving those large prints.

On September 8th, I was making my way back to my four-wheeler in near darkness, after searching in vain for one of the big bruins, when I heard something behind me coming out of the brush. It was a bear, but not the kind you want to see in the darkness and only 20 yards away. It was a brown bear cub, not a cute little fuzzy one, but a 200 pound two year old. The sounds that were coming from behind him let me know that he wasn't alone, so I dropped my bow to the ground and started reaching for my shotgun that was slung over my back. The cub heard, saw or smelled me—stood up on his hind legs, let out a "huff" and disappeared back into the brush.

Immediately, the sow appeared about 40 yards out and was on a dead run toward me. At this point, everything seemed to go into slow motion. The shotgun seemed to be stuck to my back. Getting a shell into the chamber seemed a cumbersome task as well, but finally the gun was pointed in the right direction and the 12 gauge slug was on its way. The flash from the barrel lit the angry sow up as she was only 5 feet away. She veered to my left, but kept coming.

The next few moments happened as a blur and the rest of the story has been pieced together through evidence left behind and brief glimpses retained in my memory. Next thing I can remember, I am lying on my back trying to jack another shell in while kicking her in the face and pushing her away from my torso with my legs. She kept trying to get to my upper body, but I was able to spin on my back and keep her from accomplishing her goal while trying to pump another shell in. I took the second shot with the shotgun between my legs while she was holding onto my left calf.

At the shot, she reared back and bit at the new wound in the center of her chest. This gave me a moment to get the third shell into the chamber and into her.

At the third shot, she took off and went back into the brush. Keeping a vigilant eye on the brush, I assessed the damage and realized that the wounds were not life-threatening, but that I needed to get some medical attention for the punctures in my leg. I walked a long mile back to my four-wheeler, looking over my shoulder the whole way, afraid that the sow may not be dead or the cub may be following me. That four-wheeler was a welcome sight, but I still had a 5 mile ride back to camp and a 50 mile drive to town. Some punctures and some minor muscle tears were treated and I was released.

The next day, while on crutches, I went to the Alaska State Troopers office and was informed that I had to go out to the scene accompanied by a trooper to skin the bear and turn the hide and head over to them. We made our way out to the attack site and found the sow dead about fifteen yards from where the struggle took place. She was an average sow weighing an estimated 450 pounds and maybe 7½ feet long. Skinning the bear showed that the first two slugs had entered on either side of the breastbone and that one had broken her shoulder. My bow lay close by where I had left it the night before, but apparently the cub came back and paid me his revenge by ravaging my bow. The quiver and arrows were broken as well as some rips in the string and cables. The bow was rebuilt within days and the broken arrows were replaced, but my leg wasn't healing right. One week after the attack, the local hospital sent me to Anchorage for an overnight stay at Providence Hospital for some blood clots, swelling, infection and a stiffer cast. Things were looking bleak for an October 6th departure for the moose hunt, but I still had hope that things were going to change in the next two and a half weeks.

I received this 4/25/06 from Ken and today (4/26) I found the following on Outdoorsdirectory.com: My bear attack Posted by Ken R on Jan 20 2006

I had a sow come right through a slug from my shotgun at 5 feet and ended up on top of me. I managed to load another one and shot her point blank in the chest while she was holding my leg in her teeth. I got one more in her at about 10 feet (in the butt though). She ran into the brush after that. So, while I still won't go into known brownie territory without my pump shotgun, I don't have any illusions that slugs will drop them in their tracks nor that I will have the presence of mind to point, aim for the skull, and fire one into the brain box. Incidentally, I found the sow just inside the brush line and did the obligatory skinning the next day while a trooper stood over my shoulder (never lifted a finger to the guy on crutches). Anyway, I don't think anyone should have illusions that when a bear charges at 40 yards that any weapon will stop them in their tracks unless the bullet finds its way into the brain/spine. I will be the first to admit that I was lucky enough to even hit the bear and not sure how many of us have the presence of mind when the time comes to really take their time to aim for and hit the head or spine of a charging grizzly.

TJ LANGLEY

In 2000 at a 40 year class reunion while discussing bear encounters a classmate informed me that her son was good friends with TJ Langley. I Googled TJ, made contact and received his story after a couple of revisions. Ten years later at another reunion I told my classmate that I'd acquired TJ's story and she said, "He's dead." Was I surprised. He died while solo hiking in Washington state's Glacier Peak Wilderness in October 2009. TJ'S bear attack story follows:

Ever since watching the film *Never Cry Wolf* many, many years ago, I've been fascinated by wolves. A quick glance at my bookshelf...*The New Wolves* and *The Ninemile Wolves* by Rick Bass, *Of Wolves and Men* by Barry Lopez, *Lives of the Monster Dogs* (not quite about wolves, but...) by Kirsten Bakis, *Never Cry Wolf* by Farley Mowat (the novel on which the movie was based) and *The Return of the Wolf* to Yellowstone by Thomas McNamee. This last book, an account of the reintroduction of wolves to Yellowstone National Park in the 1990's, set my life on a collision course with, of all things, a grizzly.

I'm not sure if my interest in wild places led to a curiosity about wildlife or if it was the other way around. Whatever the case, much of my adult life has involved spending big chunks of my free time in the outdoors. Aside from an "outdoor survival" class in junior high school, I've taught myself about wilderness travel, learned how to "leave no trace," and worked my way up from a first, nervous night at an alpine lake (no more than four miles from the highway) to extended backcountry trips (a seventy mile loop in the Canadian Rockies, hikes in Denali, the Brooks Range, the North Cascades, Glacier...). I would guess, if you add all the days up, I've spent at least a year, maybe two, in the wilderness. Often I have taken these trips alone. Yes, I've read the warnings. I know solo journeys are not generally recommended. Since my first trip or two, however, I have felt comfortable and at home in wild places. Besides, there aren't many people who think of sleeping on the ground and pooping in a hole as a fine way to spend their two week vacation! So, I go alone.

In September of 1999, not long after reading Mr. McNamee's book, I decided to spend my main vacation of the year hiking in Yellowstone. I hoped I'd catch a glimpse of one of the, by this time, fairly numerous wolves in the park. On other trips other places, I'd seen animals of all sorts—bears, deer, mountain goats, Dall sheep, elk, moose, caribou, coyotes. I'd even been on a trip where I'd seen more grizzlies (five) than people. Aside from tracks and scat, though, I had never seen a wolf. I was determined that this would be my year. If determination were the only requirement for a wolf sighting, I certainly should have seen one.

By the 22nd, after sixteen days and nights in Yellowstone, most of it in the backcountry, not a single wolf had crossed my path. I had tried a big multi-day loop hike, shorter day hikes, a cross-country mostly trail-free trip, and I drove much of the road system at dawn and dusk... nothing. Bear tracks, coyote packs howling in the distance, elk, bison, and a curiously friendly mule deer, but not a single heart stopping wolf encounter of any kind. I even sent a postcard home bemoaning the fact. I'm not sure, but I think my family got that card the same day the hospital finally got hold of them.

Only now, glancing through my trail guidebook from eight years ago, do I notice the following passage: My vacation very nearly over, I stopped in at the Old Faithful backcountry desk for one last permit. I would hike the Daly Creek/Skyrim/Black Butte trail system in the very northwest corner of Yellowstone. One last two-night trek and then the long drive home. By this time, I'd been in for permits enough that William McMillan, the ranger on duty, recognized me and knew me as at least competent enough to come back from my other trips. He checked to be sure the campsites I'd requested were free, printed up my permit, and mentioned that two other hikers had had a minor run-in with a sow grizzly and two cubs in the same area earlier in the summer. "Hang your food and keep a clean camp," he reminded me. Neither of us felt any need for concern—it was more just stating the obvious when traveling through bear country. Only now, glancing through my trail guidebook from eight years ago, do I notice the following passage: "The area is quite remote and problem grizzly bears caught in the park are usually airlifted by helicopter into adjacent Gallatin National Forest near this trail."

I can't remember exactly what time I hit the trail head, but it seems like it was late morning or early afternoon. Loaded a few last things into my pack, hefted it onto my shoulders and headed off toward my first night's campsite. I only saw two other hikers the entire afternoon and, before long, arrived at what I believed was my designated backcountry tent site. I found it odd that there was no bear wire. In the big national parks down here (Glacier, Yellowstone, etc.), most of the back-country camp sites have some sort of apparatus for hanging your food at night. Often, this is a heavy cable strung between two trees or poles with a series of lighter weight cables and pulleys attached to ease raising and lowering of food sacks, backpacks and anything else which might scent-attract a big fuzzy woodland beast. I set up camp, made dinner, slung my food bag over a tree branch with the small coil I always carry, and turned in for the night. *An uneventful day but beautiful—autumn in the wilderness...nothing better.*

I was up relatively early the next morning in the hope of covering a bit of ground and either making camp early or busting all the way out to the road, hitching the short gap between trailheads, jumping into my car and heading in to Bozeman where a shower and a beer awaited at my cousin's place. Not long after hitting the trail, I passed through the TRUE tent site, bear wire and all, that I thought I'd found the night before. It seems the park service had moved the camping area and my keen eye had spotted the now abandoned old site...well, in all honesty, I'd been a little tired and had convinced myself the old site was right instead of exploring further. Curious how these things happen sometimes.

A bull elk had been bugling much of the night and early morning, so, as the trail climbed up toward the "rim" portion of the Skyrim Trail, I kept my eyes peeled. Never saw the bull, but before too long, spotted a cow elk not far off the trail and enjoyed the small, powerful thrill I always feel sharing space with a big wild animal on its home turf. A nice start to my day's journey. I hiked ridgeline for the rest of the morning and, by early afternoon, found myself at my high point for the trip—Big Horn Peak (elev. 9930 ft). Must have been noon or a little after by this point, so I dropped my pack, pulled out my lunch, leaned back and tried to catch as much late September sun as I could. I reflected on how, in over two weeks in the heart of the "Serengeti of America," the closest I had come to any big predator was glassing a coyote from the Lamar Valley Road. I looked at the pepper spray (borrowed from Sean in Bozeman) clipped to my chest strap and thought about stowing it inside my pack as I certainly would not be needing it now. I resigned myself to yet another wilderness sojourn without a wolf sighting. In the end, I left the bear spray clipped to my pack within easy reach, but, fatefully, maybe dropped my guard half a notch.

After a leisurely lunch rest, I headed down the Black Butte Trail. This last leg was all downhill, so I moved at a pretty good clip. There seemed to be trail markers every quarter mile...annoying, I thought—nothing makes a short trail longer than knowing exactly how far you have come and being able to figure out precisely how much farther you must go. I had not gone very far before the trail left the wide open high-country meadows and headed back into more heavily forested terrain. At this point, several factors aligned against me just a bit: 1) I was moving quickly, intent on covering ground, keeping my options open for a possible run into Bozeman; 2) passing from open meadow back into trees, my eyes took a while to adjust; and 3) as mentioned earlier, I lowered my awareness the tiniest of degrees.

I had not been in the timber very long when I heard a branch snap off to my right, down- hill off the trail. I whipped my head around and saw two yearling grizzly cubs making an uphill run behind me. From the ranger's information I knew there were three bears in the area and knew, if encountered, I should back out of their territory and seek an alternate route; but now two of the little buggers had made that strategy impossible.

Still no sign of the sow, so I figured no choice but to continue the way I'd been going and hope she'd taken off with her cubs.

I did not run, but, as calmly and quickly as possible, I continued down the trail toward highway 191. Every few steps, I took a short look back to make sure the mother bear was not coming after me. One look—nothing. A second look—*it's a dog, it's a dog*!

I knew it wasn't a dog. I had my pepper spray clipped to the chest strap of my pack. That afternoon I stopped for lunch and actually thought, "I should just chuck the pepper spray in my pack... haven't seen a thing in two weeks." I had time to "un-holster" the canister, but fumbled with the safety and could not deploy in time. In retrospect, I'm sure it would have made a difference!

I grabbed my pepper spray, took one, maybe two tugs at the ring below the safety, looked at the can, realized I was tugging at the wrong thing... glanced up and saw it was not going to matter anyway...the sow was one bound away from my feet. I threw myself to the ground, pack toward the bear and hoped she would bluff...she jumped over me, turned, and I felt her jaws close over my forehead.

Pain, pain and the most frightening sound I have ever heard—the bones in my skull began to crack and white light exploded in my head... felt like my right eye was gone. Time slowed down or thought sped up—*I never thought I'd die this way... I'm seeing the lights, are the angel voices next?*

An image of my mother having to ID my torn, half-eaten body flashed through my mind...felt like my head was being peeled of all flesh...then a change; arms above my head for some reason and pain there, too...and the sound of bones grinding on bone or... teeth?...I opened my eyes, full of blood, red all I could see...gallows humor (I swear!) as I thought, "Uh-oh...I'm going the wrong way (to Hell).

And another shift as teeth sank into my back just above my waist... pain, pain now everywhere and I was lifted off the ground... *"Oh, God, this is bad...kidneys right there...why is this taking so long?... maybe... maybe... maybe I am not going to die... yet... but, how not?... I am so messed up... what must I (or am I going to?) look like? What is that sound?...* and I realized I was bellowing in pain, calling, hopelessly, for help; screaming, "Help me! I'm being mauled by a bear!" How strange.

And then, a sort of reprieve...nothing, no more teeth on me...but all I could think was, "pepper" and I clawed around in the dust...*found it! No! Binoculars*...and then it was like being tackled or... something... and I was off the trail and... flying...through... the...air. *WHAM.* Landed on a deadfall log, a short broken branch nub piercing my right butt cheek... nothing but blue sky above my one working eye...quiet...and the blue sky replaced by the muzzle of the sow, red with my blood... and I couldn't take those teeth on me again so I grabbed as hard as I could...my right hand at her throat...as if it would make a difference...and...she was gone... *really?... yes.*

I dragged myself back up to the trail and took stock of my situation... again, thoughts came at warp speed: *When did I drop my pack?* You're never supposed to drop your pack...*Can I carry it out?* No, your back is torn open...*Make a camp here and hope someone finds me?* It's Wednesday... no one will be here 'til Friday if you're lucky... and the bear might come back... *Hike out? Yep. Both legs work, one eye... how far?* Last trail marker... was it 4.25 or 4 even? Get moving."

So I started down the trail. Somehow figuring if I made it to the road I would be okay. I felt lightheaded and the breeze was cold as it dried the blood coating my face and head. Blood dripped from my back and plopped onto my right calf every few steps. There was something dangling in front of my left eye, maddeningly blocking my vision... I reached up to pull it away... gave a small tug and thought, "No, that might be something you need..." and stuck it to the drying blood beside my nose.

Every so often, I would stop and yell for help, loud as I could... just in case. Incredibly thirsty, so, when I crossed a small stream, I bent and scooped some water into my mouth... when I stood back up, nearly passed out. Decided there would be no more stops... just push on for the road. In spite of it all, still think I must have made pretty good time... as near as I can tell, two hours to cover four miles... and suddenly, there was the road.

I staggered out from the trailhead and waited for a car, waved my arms as it approached...watched, stunned, as it went right on by... watched another one do the same...This is crazy!...I moved to the middle of the road, waving arms, making the "slow down" sign and a third car went by...but stopped. I walked toward it, "It's okay, it's okay," one of the occupants called out, " We phoned 911! What happened to you?"

"I was mauled by a bear."

Before long, other cars stopped. "Here, lie down..." But I couldn't think how to do that... what part of me could I put to the ground? My back was flayed open, my front... well, I didn't want to tip my head forward...so I sat propped up on one arm someone offered a pristine white sweatshirt as a pillow...I felt bad knowing it would be ruined as soon as I touched it...And still, my brain seemed to be working all right—I did the math, figured it would be half an hour before an ambulance could make it out from West Yellowstone...a sheriff or state trooper showed up and then a ranger (who headed in on horseback, I think, to retrieve my pack and examine the scene) and I repeated my story, my name, age, vital stats, answered whatever was asked.

Sirens in the distance and the medics were there..."I'm gonna be okay, right?"

"We got you." That was all I needed to hear. But, into the ambulance and more questions and finally, "Can we get you anything?"

"Something for the pain might be nice..."

"Yeah, we're just waiting for the okay from a doctor and then we'll give you some morphine."

I overheard parts of a radio conversation and finally... well, the pain didn't go away, exactly, but I felt wrapped in cotton and I didn't much care anymore. Maybe I realized we weren't moving or maybe they told me why we were still parked... we were waiting for LifeFlight...I would have to be choppered to the nearest level one trauma center in Idaho Falls.

I stayed awake until the helicopter landed, or maybe passed out for a little while. They moved me from ambulance to chopper and the LifeFlight nurse introduced herself and the pilot.

Another short nap and I was at the hospital on a gurney clickety-clacking across a tile floor. And the waiting began. All I wanted now was the strange timeless sleep of anesthesia and to awaken feeling...better or at least sort of put back together. I would drift off and wake up, but never in a surgical theater. Always it was for something else...once for a CT scan or an MRI, once I came to shivering uncontrollably until someone wrapped me in a cocoon of heated blankets. Finally I was wheeled into surgery and put under and, at long last, felt that the worst was over.

And, for the most part, it was. When the anesthesia wore off in the ICU, I looked around for my family and was baffled that they were not nearby. I knew I had given out my folk's names and number in one of the many rounds of questioning. By some odd twist of timing, however, my adventure had fallen on a rare night out for my mom and dad— they did not get word of my mishap until about eighteen hours afterwards. It was disappointing knowing I would be alone for several more hours, but I killed some of the time pulling off my oxygen mask and, I'm told, singing "I Feel Pretty." (Good drugs?) I found the mask stifling; like it was keeping me from getting enough air...had to fight down mini panic attacks and simply breathe...relax and breathe.

When my family finally arrived, my greeting to them was, "What took you so long?" Still feel bad about that. (Sorry, Mom.) Once family was on the scene, many gaps in my perception of the attack got filled in. That I had dropped my pack during the frantic early moments of the encounter completely mystified me until my mother got word from one of the rangers...the waist and chest buckles on my pack were both still clipped when my pack was retrieved. The bear had peeled it off my back and bitten into both of my forearms in the process.

As for physical damage, I had an open skull fracture on my forehead—basically, a palm sized piece of my skull had been turned into a flap of bone (my nose was broken, the right orbit of my eye socket was crushed... the thing dangling in my field of vision as I hiked out? part of my left eyelid). There were three deep lacerations on my back and the tip of my iliac crest (part of the back side of my pelvis) had been cracked. A small chunk of my right forearm was gone (to this day I still have a "bear divot" there) and I was cut and scraped all over. Miraculously, my right eye was still there and functional (but, due to nerve damage, I could not raise the eyelid on that side. Even now, my peripheral vision is pretty bad to the right and the lid is still droopy. I learned the entire attack had probably taken less than a minute.

I spent six days in the hospital in Idaho Falls. I remember being pumped so full of fluids and antibiotics that my fingers looked like sausages... my chart listed my weight as twenty or thirty pounds heavier than my norm. My mom put me on the "prayer chain" at church and, though I would not call myself a religious person, I could definitely feel energy pouring into me from that corner of the world. *Powerful.*

It didn't take long before various media outlets got wind of my encounter. I have a vision of news crews lined up outside trying to sneak up to my room for film footage. I doubt it was that dramatic... I did give one interview...before long the news hit local Seattle papers and, for many friends, that's how word first reached them.

Upon my release, I opted to fly back to Seattle...a full day of driving more than I could face. My cousin, Willy, drove ninety miles from Bellingham to pick me up at the airport and take me to my apartment downtown. I did my best to take care of myself, but know I had a lot of help from friends. One of them, a surgical resident at Virginia Mason, lined up a great facial plastic surgeon to handle the round of follow up surgery necessary to complete repairs to my right eye socket, broken nose and damaged sinus passages. A week after arriving home, I was back in the hospital, but only overnight this time.

And that, for the most part, is my story. By November, I took my first hike...up to the lake where I'd spent my very first solo night in the backcountry years and years before. My journal entry from November 16th, 1999 reads: "Much has faded (pain, etc.), some still unchanged— slow healing, eye still frustratingly closed, but I think I'm learning patience and am appreciative of what I do have. Very good to be alive, very nice to have some of the little things back—being able to breathe through my nose, sleeping the whole night through, relatively pain free, less meds every day..."

Of course, I still had an insurance nightmare on my hands...the short version? The agent who sold me my policy misrepresented the level of coverage I had. I was looking at something like $114,000.00 in medical bills. Only after filing a claim with the state insurance commissioner AND hiring an attorney did I finally get the 80% coverage I'd paid for... and this was over a year later. I'm still paying attorney fees, but I can live with that.

I've been asked if I would do anything differently, given the chance... and, honestly? I don't think so. I don't see the pepper spray's making

109

much difference. That sow grizzly was coming hard and nothing was going to stop her and, damn, she was FAST!

This whole deal was a crapshoot...I'd bet five minutes either way and nothing happens—five minutes earlier and I see the sow crossing the trail and heading uphill...five minutes later and it is the cubs doing the same thing. From a worst-case scenario point of view, my timing was simply perfect. I hit that section of trail at the only time the sow and her cubs were an equal distance from me in opposite directions. Bad news.

Would I still go alone? Probably... there's still the hitch of finding someone else who wants to go! Besides, I've been on trips with buddies and, at the end of the day, we're probably moving the same way I was eight years ago—head down, fast and quiet. If there had been two of us? Well, maybe one would have been in better shape for the run to the road, but who knows? Maybe one of us would be dead. I don't see much point in playing "what if" or "if only..." This happened and it is part of who I am now. Life lies ahead of us, not back there over one shoulder. Would I carry a gun? Do I think the park service should allow firearms? No and no. Guns are heavy! I'd rather have a lighter pack or carry more food.

And I guess I feel there should be some places where you meet the wilderness, Mother Nature, whatever, on its own terms. We humans may not be four-hundred pounds of muscle, tooth and claw. We may lose in a heads up physical confrontation with a bear, but we do have big old brains and, most of the time, we seem to be able to think our way out of a jam. Besides, I barely had time to un-holster a can of pepper spray... nothing leads me to believe ANYONE would have had time to fire enough rounds to do more than make that bear even angrier!

One final note: A couple years after my attack, I was approached by "Wild Survival" to shoot a re-enactment. It was a fun couple of days (aside from being covered in red syrup during black fly season). As we finished up shooting the end of my hike out, the part where I'm trying to flag down a car for help, several cars actually stopped to see what was going on... the driver of one of those vehicles swears he saw a wolf run across the road not 200 yards from us. I was looking the other way.

KATHRYN DUNAGAN

Because I've lived in Alaska since 1987 and enjoy hiking, I've always had this fear of running into a bear. It was kind of like I didn't wonder IF but more a matter of WHEN it would happen. "What would I do?" I have read all kinds of articles on bear encounters and what a person is supposed to do or not do. Encountering a bear is something that I could not have predicted, exactly what would happen or how I would react.

The past few years my son Justin and I have hiked on several occasions. Two years ago, we hiked the Chilkoot Trail out of Skagway. Running into a bear on that trail, certainly got my adrenalin going. But after about 15 minutes of hollering and waving our arms, we convinced that bear to lumber off the trail, and we continued. That encounter went exactly like I had read about.

After camping in Cooper Landing with friends in August 2002, it being a beautiful day, Justin and I headed off toward Soldotna and Resurrection Trail. I had hiked this well traveled trail several times and I wanted to show my son Juneau Falls, thinking he'd really like to get some pictures of the spectacular falls. Judging from the parking lot at the trailhead, others had the same idea. The apparent number of hikers on the trail gave me a false sense of security that numbers would deter bear incidents. Still, I always hiked with bells on my pack, and a can of mace in case of close encounters.

With Justin taking his usual place in the lead, we headed up the trail toward the falls. I think Justin may have been slightly apprehensive, because twice he stopped dead in his tracks to ask me if I "heard this" or "saw that." His concern had me pretty nervous by this point. We continued talking and making lots of noise.

As we neared the falls, we heard the rushing of the water and met the first person on the trail. He was hiking alone. Justin, enthralled with taking pictures, busied himself and I visited the hiker for several minutes before he took off toward the trailhead. Justin climbed down into the canyon to get better views of the falls.

After about 45 minutes and four rolls of film, Justin was satisfied with the pictures he had taken. We began our return to the car with him in the lead. He even made the comment, "We'll probably see a bear, because I didn't reload any new film into the camera!"

Less than ten minutes later we rounded a tight corner of thick brush, and ran smack into a large brown bear. By the time we saw her, Justin was close enough to touch her. We took a step back, Justin yelling, "WHOA!"

Before I could respond, she jumped on Justin knocking him down into the bushes. I was unable to see what was going on and was so shocked that I couldn't remember what I was supposed to do! I backed up several more feet before my mind reacted, "What should I do?"

I simply froze. I couldn't make any sounds come out of my mouth. I felt so helpless, and worried for Justin. I really thought the bear was killing him. But luckily, within 30 seconds, the bear got off him (seemed longer) and turned to leave.

That's when I noticed a rather small cub on the trail with her. Justin jumped back onto his feet and came over by me. Because the bear was urging her cub off the trail, we thought it was over.

It was when Justin said, "I can't believe she bit me!" that I noticed his arm bleeding and some small tears out of it I was so relieved to see him alive that I hadn't even noticed the bite. In that split second, before we knew what was happening, the bear turned and bounded toward us. She brushed past Justin and knocked me flat onto my back in the brush.

Again my mind was racing. I really thought our lives were over. I just knew she was going to finish us off. By now, Justin was yelling at her and hitting her with his tripod. I really thought this would make her more angry. She wound up her right paw and swiped at my face. When I saw her huge paw coming at me, I shielded my face with my arms. I tasted blood immediately but felt very little pain. As quickly as she was on me, she jumped off and disappeared into the brush.

The fear that she would be back overcame me. I was hysterical and kept telling Justin, "We need help! We need help!"

He looked me straight in the eyes and said, "Mom, pull yourself together, there is no one out here to help us, we need to help ourselves!"

We looked for the can of bear spray—just in case she returned. Then we looked for my glasses that had been knocked off. We found only one lens. We decided to hurry back to the car. Justin wrapped his arm with his shirt, and handed me the camera. He armed himself with the mace in one hand and tripod in the other. He told me that we would run and make lots of noise all the way.

With the constant fear of the bear stalking us, I was in total shock!

Though it seemed we'd run for hours, it was only about 45 minutes later that we met a couple hiking up the trail. We told them about the bear and our encounter and suggested they turn around since their dog might also enrage the bear. Initially the man offered to walk back with us to the trailhead, but after hearing our story and seeing our wounds the woman proudly chambered a round in her rifle and said she wanted to go on

It wasn't until we neared the trailhead and heard voices from below us, that I felt we would be safe. Some people at the parking lot must have heard us talking, because they hollered up at us to say they had a first aid kit. I was so glad to hear other people that were willing to help us. Justin and I had decided, since he could not drive due to his right arm (we had a clutch) and I could not see, he would steer and I would shift to get us to the hospital!

One of the people in the parking lot was Dave Sabow. Kathryn provided me his e-mail and we wrote each other. I asked for Dave's input

which follows:

Ironically, Dave and I had spent an entire year in Juneau and had grown relatively accustomed to seeing bears on a regular basis. Black bears that is! When we got to the Resurrection Trail Head, we were a little distracted due to the car trouble we were experiencing. Dave Pavlik and myself were on a road trip from Juneau to Boston in a 1982 Toyota (with 200,000 miles on it!) We were actually tinkering with the engine when we heard some emphatic yells for help coming from the woods.

I yelled back, and I think it was Justin that shouted, asking if we had a first aid kit. I imagined that someone had twisted an ankle or skinned a knee, so I grabbed out first aid kit complete with alcohol swabs and few band aids. I was not quite expecting what I saw!

I had only just started up the trailhead to where I assumed the yells were coming from, when I encountered Kathryn and Justin coming out. Kathryn had taken a paw to the face and Justin had a nice chunk out of his forearm. I was immediately impressed by their calm. It was as though all of their adrenaline had been used.

Dave and I drove Kathryn's car for her to the Soldotna Hospital, and it was only when she was separated from Justin that Kathryn started to panic a little. Actually, it was during this time that I learned the most about Kathryn.! In an effort to avoid shock and keep her calm, I asked her many questions completely unrelated to the bear incident. I learned that Kathryn was at a major cross-road in her life, and saw immediately how proud she was of her son for his artistry and business ambitions.

After the incident, as I was absorbing the vastness of what had happened, I began to make some sense of the situation. I believe that everything happens for a reason, and I truly believe that the bear incident has given Kathryn the strength she needs to make a major transition in her life.

I had just finished a year of volunteer work at a homeless shelter in Juneau, and was going through a formative/reflective time as well. With that commonality, Kathryn and I just kept in touch. I cannot remember exactly how she tracked me down, but a month or so after the incident, I got an e-mail from her thanking me for my help, and we have continued writing sporadically.

Hope this helps! Let me know if you need additional clarification. Good luck with the book.

Dave Sabow.

EPILOGUE:

It wasn't until days later that I really realized what Justin had done to save my life. He was so brave at the time that he was fending the bear off me. But when he was being attacked, I couldn't think what to do, but stay out of the way, which may have been the best thing looking back, I felt terrible about it later thinking "how could a mother just let a bear attack her son and do nothing?"

I now realize how short life is, and how important it is to make the most of each day, as it may be our last. I also believe we were spared that day for a reason, I am not sure yet why but we were so very lucky.

GARY TITUS

I very much enjoyed meeting and visiting Gary Titus April12, 2007, in his Soldotna, Alaska, home.

Gary shared with me the highlights of a grizzly bear with a cub that he and Ellen Snoeyenbos encountered near his Twin Lake cabin 35 minutes by plane from Port Alsworth, Alaska. Gary's the real deal.

I live to hike. On my days off I'm out hiking some place. I like hiking the high country, above the trees, exploring new parts of Alaska. A lot of my hiking revolves around my love of history too. I like hiking old hunting trails, looking for remains of trapping cabins. It's all a passion of history and hiking actually combined. There's nothing like hiking. I moved to Alaska in 1977 to work as a wilderness ranger in Chugach National Forest, fortified by my Nebraska roots, hiking, hunting and outdoor living. Between work and recreation I walk a thousand miles a year.

In 1981 I became a Fish and Wildlife Protection officer (game warden) and in 1985 I bought land at Upper Twin Lake, 150 miles west and the past two years was Kenai National Wildlife Refuge wilderness park ranger and historian, which allowed me a great deal of time in the field, mostly on foot.

I met Ellen Snoeyenbos of Gardiner, Montana, in 2001. She's my age, 47, tall and athletic, loves the outdoors and hiking and works for the U.S. Forest Service. On her first trip to Alaska in June of 2001 I was eager to show her my cabin. To my great relief, she loved the place.

On the morning of June 13, 2001 my girlfriend Ellen and I climbed the mountain behind the cabin to see Dall sheep. The hike takes about two hours to reach the 2,800 foot view point. We walked a faint, old trail, making good time to the top. We ate lunch enjoying the spectacular view and sheep. After a while we began the return journey.

I commonly come across bears and I've been charged over a dozen times by blacks and browns—all bluff charges. It scares you. But they stopped. A couple of friends who have been mauled by bears say there's no time to react. It happens so fast.

Coming down the mountain and entering timber we transitioned from heavy outer clothing to compensate for the less windy conditions once we left the high country. We stopped next to a waterfall and changed out of our heavy clothing into short shirts, I threw my day pack on. Ellen did the same thing right behind me and I got ahead of her. It's steep right there and a waterfall to one side. The wind's coming down the lake like it does.

We started down trail again and I called out "hey, bear." That's what I say in the woods, whenever I get in a dense area where I can't see. "Hey, bear. Hey, bear." When I can see, I don't want to say anything because I want to see game but I don't want to be surprised by it in the brush.

I said, "Hey, bear," came around the corner and the bear was right there…maybe two, three feet away. If I had raised my foot, I would have kicked it in the head. There's nothing I could do.

I thought, "What a beautiful, blonde bear." It looked at its cub, then me.

I started to shout "Stop!" but the whole word didn't come out and she had me. That quick. I don't think she knew I was there. I did not see the cub until the sow grabbed me, just below the left knee at the top of the calf.

I had no time to turn and warn Ellen. No time for anything. I remember looking up at the lake saying, "That's it." It was so quick. You don't have time. I've been in law enforcement for most of my career. I'm trained in weapons. I qualify twice a year with weapons, shotguns and pistols. So I have to be quick, fast. There's just no way you're going to get a gun out, in my opinion, if it's a true charge. They're just too fast. I'm sure there's an exception out there. But it's fast, faster than most people realize.

I don't remember what happened.

Ellen said the bear grabbed me, picked me up and threw me on her back. Next thing, the bear's going down the mountain with me on her back. Ellen heard me screaming all the way down the mountain, about ten yards. Then she heard nothing. She thought I was dead.

But the bear had dropped me, turned and ran back after Ellen.

When the bear dropped me, I wasn't aware of anything up until that time. I was in shock. I watched the bear climb the mountain. I was mad then. I was trying to stand up. I did everything I could to get off the ground because I knew where the bear was going. I was mad. *Leave her alone.*

Ellen saw it coming and dropped to the ground to curl into a ball. The sow grabbed one of her feet in its jaws and headed down the mountain.

I was frantic to help Ellen, but there was nothing I could do. I tried to stand up, but couldn't. My left leg collapsed under me. I felt angry, frustrated. I forced my body into a sitting position. Right then, here comes the bear down the mountain, dragging Ellen by her foot. I threw a wild, impulsive punch at it. My fist connected. I don't know where. Then the sow dropped Ellen and came back to me. Its face was almost in mine. Its mouth was open. My hand was in front of my face, and it bit my hand. Although one tooth went completely through, I felt no pain. Then the bear was gone. We never saw it again. I was worried that it might come back, but I was even more worried about what had happened to Ellen. I said, "Ellen, are you OK? Are you OK?"

She asked, "Is the bear gone?"

I kept asking, "Are you hurt? Are you hurt?"

Ellen came up to me and looked at me. My foot was just flopping, I asked her to get my glasses. She kept saying, "No." Then she said, "I can't find them."

My left calf was torn, pants drenched with blood and I couldn't see well without my glasses. All I could see was blood. When Ellen looked at my leg, she didn't see any blood spurting. She feared leaving me in the event that the bear might return. We had no phone or means with which to communicate in order to initiate a rescue.

She helped me to a standing position. I don't remember much of the hike down. The pain must have erased the memory. I remember Ellen praying and looking at my foot, wondering what was wrong with it.

With my left arm around her neck we slowly headed down. I grabbed a stick for my right hand to support myself. Every time my left foot touched the ground, it turned down and to a right angle to my leg. Every step was sheer agony. I kept wanting to sit down but Ellen wouldn't let me—she was concerned that if I rested, I would lose the adrenaline rush. she worried that we'd run into the bear again.

She got off the trail and I re-directed her, "You need to go right." It's usually a fifteen minute hike downhill to the cabin but it took us a couple of hours.

I remember hitting the lake shore, looking at her and saying, "I can't go on. I can't go on." But she made me go on. I give her the credit for getting me down off that mountain. I kept wanting to sit down… "I've got to sit down just for a minute" because I was hopping on one leg. I had developed good hiking legs. But she wouldn't let me sit. Her determination to get me down off that mountain and the weight she had to bear of me leaning on her like that was incredible, she deserves most of the credit for remaining calm and helping me down the mountain.

We didn't really talk much about the injury or the trip out. It was spooky for both of us, especially for her, not knowing about the blood loss or how bad I was injured. Even though I was in shock, I was determined to get off the mountain. That's where your training comes in. When I'm hiking, I'm thinking okay, if I get hurt here I'm gonna do this…if I fall off this cliff, I'm gonna do this. You always play a scenario in your head because you've got time hiking. My hiking partner and I we've hiked close to 15 to 25 miles a day covering a lot of hard country. So you've got a lot of time to think. I'm playing those scenarios in my head. I think a lot of that is it's what you mentally train yourself to do because that's going to take over in stress situations.

I still had my day pack on. That's a long ways to go on one leg.

When we got to the cabin, I said, "You've got to get my glasses, my float coat, and you've got to take us across the lake. I know the ranger's there, I saw a kayak. She said, "I can't drive a boat." And so she put me in the boat and later on she kept asking me "is it safe, is it safe?" because the wind was coming down the lake hard, white capping. I kept saying, "It's fine. It's fine." I don't remember the boat ride at all.

Fortunately, park volunteer Kay Schubeck was there.

Lee Fink, the chief ranger at Port Alsworth, was just going to the hangar and just happened to hear the radio call from park volunteer Jana Walker from Twin Lakes and they all know me and my experience in the woods and they got the airplane headed for Twin Lakes with pilot Leon Alsworth, rangers Dennis Knuckles and Dan Young. A private airplane got going too.

About two hours later, Ellen and I were flown by floatplane to Port Alsworth, the nearest airstrip. They had a medevac coming down from Anchorage. From Port Alsworth a Life Flight air ambulance flew us to Anchorage. It was a long day. I don't remember most of it.

That night, a surgeon at Alaska Regional Hospital operated on my leg. My most serious injury was damage to the common peroneal nerve of my left leg. Without that nerve, I have no feeling in my leg from the knee down, but I haven't given up hope that it will heal. At least I can walk again, with the help of a brace.

Ellen's injuries amounted to a small scratch and puncture marks on her boot, her foot was black and blue as possible, clamped in that boot. Luckily she only had one small scratch, that was good.

I was in the hospital only a few days. They had me on so many drugs. I was on two different sets of antibiotics. I was taking Percocet almost every two hours and never felt it worked. It was hard just getting to the bathroom, most of my day was flat on my back wishing the pain would go away. Friends would stop by with meals and to visit. It was very hard time mentally…*will I ever hike again, work?*

But then in August I knew it was working. I threw the Percocet away because I don't like any type of pills, anything. The meds probably worked but I never thought it did.

My peroneal nerve was completely severed and the fibula crushed. I had four big holes in my leg.

Of course, my foot was locked in the down position. In July they got very concerned about that. Dr. Anderson said I had to go see Dr. McCord. He got very worried. He sent me to the hospital and they gave me spinal block. They were trying to get my foot back in the normal position, almost got it there but not quite. The general opinion was that I wasn't going to be doing much hiking anyway. I asked Dr. Anderson if I needed physical therapy, he laughed at me and said, "You'll push yourself harder by yourself, you would just drive them crazy."

I'm supposed to wear a brace. When I'm in the house I don't wear it. I won't ever be 100%. I've worked my way back into law enforcement, I've got this brace on. The leg atrophied. It took me a long time to get back in shape and learn how to walk with a brace. Last spring I went down to Arizona for training, we go every winter for refresher training in law enforcement, a week of very intense, hard training. We were doing ground fighting all afternoon and after this training I noticed my foot locked up, I can't move it down.

Dr. Anderson was coming almost every night because it wasn't healing right, he and Dr. McCord were responsible for pulling me through the healing process. The pain was incredible. In August I was put in a cast and began to build back my strength.

Last fall I went to Dr. Anderson. He's a hiker too, he knows how much I hate that brace. I started to notice movement in my foot so I asked Dr. Anderson if I could now not wear the brace, after I showed him the movement in my foot he said, "That's impossible." And I receive the best news of the day, I did not have to wear the brace anymore.

Since January I'm supposed to be back in it because they don't know what's going on. It's locked up. I'm back to hiking. I used to be a fast hiker but my friends tell me I now hike like a normal person. It doesn't stop me. I'm still doing the hard hikes, it just takes me longer.

I'm a federal game warden, US Fish and Wildlife. That's a collateral job now. I do about 40-45% law enforcement; my other job is cabin manager-historian-backcountry ranger. I also help restore historical log cabins for the Refuge and for the Kasilof Regional Historical Association.

The costs to repair my injuries ran over $95,000 dollars.

What caught me off guard was, the next spring after the mauling I had to fly back over to Twin Lakes to open the place up. I was still not moving much. A couple of friends flew over with me, just getting in and out of the floatplane was a challenge—it's tough when you're on crutches. My friend got the cabins all prepared for the summer. I just sat there watching for bears, saw several.

I had a shotgun with me everywhere, didn't feel safe in the woods. A place I've always considered safe. By the next fall, I'd had enough. I had what I call the demon to fight. *What am I doing I always felt safe in the wilderness and now I'm scared?* So I went over to Twin Lakes by myself. The first hike I was walking in a place where there were no trees or brush, I got down to a place where I couldn't see, and I backed off. But by the end of the two weeks I got over the fear. I'm back feeling safe in the wilderness, maybe just a little more cautious.

This past winter, I patrolled the refuge on a snowmachine.

This fall I had several black bears and a grizzly bear on the property again. I chased the black bears up the trail away, up the hill, screaming at them. I'm back to not being afraid. I now have a shotgun on my hikes, my hiking partner, his wife feels better when we carry it on our hikes.

Especially here on the Kenai population of people is booming. Bears avoid people moving from one area to another. Now it's harder for them to do it because houses are springing up as fast as can be. The Refuge is two million acres, but it's being encroached upon. Caribou Hills, a big brown bear area, is being encroached upon. There are more people in places like Tustumena. Previously you might see a handful of people all summer; now you see that many in one day. The bears are just being pushed. The Twin Lakes country…you never used to see people; now tourism is big there.

People need to rely upon what's given to you. Don't rely on weapons. Don't rely on pepper spray. You can take them, but use what you're given—your senses. Your sense of smell. If you smell something dead, back off. Your hearing. Listen for cracks in the brush. Bears make themselves known out there. If you hear something, pay attention, make some noise. Use your vision. Use common sense. If you walk into a thicker area, be aware there might be bears in there. When you're coming out of a thick area, if you want to see game, don't make noise…use your eyes now.

Rely on those things first. A weapon or pepper spray should be a back up. People blindly go into the woods with a shotgun thinking "I'm fine." They're not.

In an actual attack, it happens so fast you're not going to get a gun out. I keep thinking what I could have done differently to prevent the mauling...you do everything right in an automobile and you can still get in an accident.

The biggest thing is to be alert for bears in the area. You accept it, fine. If you don't, don't go out there. There are plenty of places without bears that you don't have to be there if you're afraid of bears.

Learn something about bears, their behavior. Who they are, what they do, why they do it. I don't consider bears dangerous, but part of the wilderness experience. I'm in their country.

I've done a lot of thinking since that bear attacked us. I never have blamed it for what it did. It was protecting its cub and we surprised it. We were way too close. Walking up that close to a bear is unusual. Maybe it had been asleep. With the noise from the nearby waterfall, it may not have heard us coming. A wind was blowing across the mountain covered the sound of our approach...probably carrying our scent away from the bear, too.

Our situation could have been worse. If Ellen and I hadn't been in excellent physical condition, we never would have made it down the hill. We didn't panic, but calmly thought out each step of what we had to do to get out of the fix we were in. I've always believed in letting bears know I was in the area. I stay in the open whenever possible, and I'm always saying, "Hey, bear. Hey, bear." From now on, when I'm not where I can see all around me, I'll be yelling louder and more often.

Another thing I plan to do differently now is carry a shotgun. Neither Ellen nor I were carrying a gun when we were attacked. In any event, a gun wouldn't have helped in that situation. Things happened so fast, I wouldn't have had time to pull the trigger, even if I'd been ready. The main reason I've decided to carry a gun is to protect other people. If a bear grabbed someone else first, I wouldn't want to be helpless. Our experience illustrates why it's more important to avoid close encounters than to put your faith in a firearm. Once you're in trouble, a gun may not get you out of it.

I don't put much faith in pepper spray. If a bear is approaching from a distance and the wind is right, and the bear isn't in a true charge, a shot of pepper spray might keep it from coming any closer. Pepper spray, like a gun, can give you a false sense of security.

I used to think I was pretty invincible in the woods. This attack taught me that I'm not. I had become too confident, maybe a little careless. There's nothing so humbling as being mauled by a bear. My run-in with a grizzly hasn't changed the way I feel about them. I still feel safer in the woods than I do anywhere else. My attitude—and Ellen's, too—is that the chances of another attack are slim to none. To me, being killed or maimed in an automobile accident is a far greater threat. With bears, I feel lucky when I see one. They're difficult to see, because it's their nature to avoid man.

Fear of bears is mainly fear of the unknown. Once you learn the bears' habits and which precautions you should take when you're in their home, the fear is replaced by a feeling of awe and respect.

PATRICIA VAN TIGHEM

In her book *The Bear's Embrace* the author expertly details the bear attack and subsequent terror which, ultimately culminated in her death. After reading the book, I hoped to gain a better understanding of a mauling victim's decision to end her life and I emailed Gordon Van Tighem, brother of the victim and mayor of Yellowknife, Northwest Territories. He was passing through Anchorage and we agreed to meet at Ted Stevens International Airport Thursday, March 9, 2006. He graciously commented on her bear mauling and filled in the blanks for numerous questions about his sister's tragic death.

Gordon told me Patricia and her husband "were on a camping trip in a national park, not allowed to carry firearms but they took appropriate precautions. They did all the right things. They checked at the information center of the park and were told no bears were known to be in the area. What nobody knew was that a sheep had died up there that brought in the bear. Rangers knew the bear. This was a recorded aggressive bear—it had taken the front end off a half ton with two wardens in it the year before.

"Patricia and Trevor were coming out and their paths intersected. It was just a complete fluke.

"The next day seven people went out in an effort to find the bear. The guy in the front and the guy in the back had rifles. The bear came at them and the guy in the front swung and shot from the hip. It was seven paces from them. The day before their accident, two teachers had taken forty-five school children up the trail.

"Even in adversity there was good fortune as so many things worked out right.

"They both assessed what was going on. Two guys helped get them to medical help. The other thing that saved them, they were both in excellent condition."

I asked Gordon how the family reacted to the news of the attack, how they were affected, what changes Patricia experienced, how the family responded to her needs, whether her decision to end her life was based solely on the bear mauling and attendant injuries and how her death affected the family.

He kindly stated about the attack, "If something would rivet you to your chair, when I got the news the first time, I had to call back twice. We went immediately to the hospital and there's nothing to describe what you see coming out of the operating room because the damage that's inflicted is unbelievable. I saw her when she came out of the surgery at three o'clock in the morning. You know it's your sister…the only thing you recognize is the lips. I don't know how many total stitches. The bear did most of the damage with its mouth. Bears go right for the face. They bite each other in the mouth, the disabling factor. The bear did its damage and took off.

"The family basically all came behind them. The family was at the hospital 24-7; even the hospital doesn't do that. The family got a constant underlying concern, more from some than others. Her mother was constantly going out to help and support. When everything was said and done when they were doing a wrap up for social workers and psychologists and stuff, it became very obvious that the family had come through it with a significant amount of strength. The caregivers, on the other hand, really needed some help. One thing the medical profession could learn is to actually listen to patients every once in a while.

"I've offered whatever support at any time if some want to get away for a while or if they need to do something. I've offered that but as far as knowing and intervening, I'm 2,000 miles away.

"The first few years after the encounter weren't too bad. There was a strong focus on remediation, basically physical. Then we started to run into some secondary effects. Some of the surgery became infected. Some of the medications were prescribed wrong. At one point one doctor took a look at the prescriptions and noted that you can't even have these two together. It's a matter of listening to the patient and also a matter of thoroughness I would think.

"A whole series of things continued for twenty-three years. It became a comedy of errors. Both of these people were medical professionals themselves and they had to tell their medical professionals certain procedures occurred to reverse certain situations. When you get into situations where you're constantly getting infected or other things are happening, you get into prescription medications which can also create a problem and then your mind changes chemically.

"After this happened the first thing that was done was to create a small textbook for nurses on how to deal with people with facial disfiguring accidents and starting new chapters of About Face which is a support group. Patricia was a very strong lady.

"If you do a Google search on her name some of the comments you get, that comes out again and again (her strength, determination).

"The initial accident was something that we keep going back to, one comment that stood out was, if you're in a car accident, it's an accident... you've gone through a windshield, it's all mechanical. In this case you're dealing with a rational mammal. It has to think to do what it's doing or it's instinct. That was something that built up over the years.

"The bear and pain were things that she never got over. If she hadn't been attacked, she wouldn't have taken her life.

"You had a vibrant, lively person that kept getting stopped on the street and asked for her autograph because they thought she was some visiting movie star in town from someone who looked in the mirror and didn't see herself. Out of that strength that we've all talked about, over the years things just built up.

"One of the things that she sent the psychiatrist at the end was a little card that had a mouse with its hands covering its face. It's lying in this bed of flowers and the mouse came to a hospital and was lying in a bed of chrysanthemums and felt great. The doctor came in and said, 'No, those should be geraniums. Get the chrysanthemums out of here.' And the mouse found that by covering his eyes and thinking that he was smelling chrysanthemums everything was fine. You've got to listen to the patient, who is experiencing the problems.

"You have to...if you can get into a regimen that works for you and see it through to the end...it's like somebody joining alcoholics anonymous, there are twelve steps. If you stop after eight, you're not finished. In her case she never went to the end of all of any of the treatments. Something always riled up or something. There were personal shortcomings as well. And the end that occurred...that wasn't the first attempt... going back several years.

"The accident and her death had a profound effect upon her children, as you can imagine."

MATE

There is a dearth of bear attack stories involving mating bears. Few people have observed such activity in the wild much less gotten close enough to be mauled by bear during the mating ritual. The only such case (which I covered in *Alaska Bear Tales*) I learned later was a fabrication. Even men who've spent their lives following bears admit viewing the reproductive act among bears is very rare. Ralph W. Young, storied veteran Alaska big game guide, said, "I studied brown-bear behavior and hunted them for 25 years before I ever saw a pair perform the breeding act. This must be a rare thing to witness, particularly in the heavy cover of southeastern Alaska. Even Allen Hasselborg, who lived alone on Admiralty Island for 50 years and was probably the greatest brown-bear hunter of the century, told me he had never seen brownies breed." (Ralph W. Young, Pg. 209, *Outdoor Life Bear Book*, edited by Chet Fish, New York, 1983)

KENNY HETRICK

In my quest for mating bear attack stories, I ran across Kenny Hetrick's experience which he had posted on the Internet. Kenny shared many of his and his wife's adventures including tiger and monkey bites, meat saw accidents and transporting Siberian tigers and jaguars. But the one that interested me the most was his bear mauling and his self-rescue. He told of being mauled by his pet boar and sow brown bears. I contacted him and he responded January 25, 2007, with permission to use his material. His story from personal emails and his website follows: (Source: Tigerridge@webtv.net Ohio Posted by: Kenny Hetrick at November 28, 2005 10:53 PM; and January 15, 16, 17, 29 and February 2 and 3, 2007)

My wife Roberta and I live in Stony Ridge, Ohio, on route 20 between Perrysburg and Woodville. I am a police officer in the 3500-resident village of Walbridge, Ohio, and an Ottawa County Deputy Sheriff. After returning from Viet Nam as a paratrooper, I worked for Chrysler Corp, became Golden Gloves and state boxing champion, coached boxing and collect vintage boxing gloves, books and mountain man paraphernalia. I have a Harley Davidson Repair shop, with tons of parts.

I've always loved animals and we began taking in unwanted animals thirty-five years ago—when the cuteness wears off, the owners don't want them. We started with a timber wolf and later a mountain lion. Our USDA license and other federal permits allow us to operate on five acres where visitors visit, school children love visiting.

We take care of all the animals which necessitates lots of butchering, every day clean up and whatever repairs that are needed. We never get enough butcher calls or road kills. I have to travel 450 miles with a trailer to buy food for these animals. I usually bring back 10,000 pounds of boneless fresh turkey meat. They love it, and it's good for them.

Very few people would want our job because the work never ends, and it's hard work every single day. Since the bears never hibernate, we feed them every day (they love road killed deer, horse meat, donuts, bread and whatever is sweet). We currently have 30 animals—8 Siberian tigers, 4 leopards, timber wolves, cougars, 6 grizzly bears, lynx, 3 lions, black and brown bears.

My wife is terrified of the bears, she goes in with the lions and tigers, but never the bears—she's smarter than I. Accidents will happen no matter how careful you are.

My bears all have big areas, and none is locked in a cage. Twelve-foot fences with an outside perimeter fence enclose my bears. About two feet from the fence are two strands of electric fence wire that keep the bears from digging, pushing, and climbing the fence. I'm always forgetting to shut it off and get shocked myself. The voltage isn't much, about like grabbing a spark plug. They are afraid of electrical current. Bears don't like to be shocked and after experiencing it once, they keep away from it. I go inside with these bears every day, to clean up and repair anything I find damaged.

On the day of the attack I was cleaning their area. I carried a 5-gallon bucket in my right hand. I reached down to pick up a deer hide lying outside the female grizzly's den box. She'd never been tame enough to handle safely and attacked me. She knocked me to the ground and bit completely through my arm, trying to pull me into her box. I heard my arm being ripped apart. With both feet I pushed against her box.

I screamed for my wife. Since she was in the barn, she didn't hear me. That's when the big 1000-pound male joined the party.

First, he hit me hard with his paw, gashing my head behind my right ear. The sow let go of my arm then the boar bit me right in the middle of my back, picking me off the ground in his mouth and shook me violently.

The power of these animals is beyond belief. I've seen my big male pick up the front end of a 2800 pound U-haul box like it was nothing. He's pulled fence posts from the ground, buried 3 feet in solid rock and cemented in place. He's turned semi-truck tires inside out. No human being on earth could do this.

My Carhartt jacket started to rip apart, and he dropped me. That split second was all the time I needed to crawl under the electric fence wire. The attack stopped as suddenly as it started. The fence was turned off but the bears didn't know this.

My wife finally heard me. When she got to the bear enclosure, I was still on the ground bleeding all over the place. She helped me up and rushed me to the emergency room. They X-rayed me. I spent 7 hours in the emergency room getting sewed up. Luckily nothing was broken. I healed up pretty good, have some impressive scars on my back and arm. And I'm alive.

I don't know why this happened. The bears have a huge enclosure and are over fed. Although she was never tame enough to handle safely the sow was due to birth any time and probably saw me as a threat.

Playing dead in my case would not have worked; they would have killed me for sure.

The electric fence is really great for bears. They come in different strengths, some are for five miles of wire, and the better ones are good for 75 miles of wire, of course, these are much stronger and cost more. I use one good for 10 miles of fence. Aluminum wire works the best with a brass ground rod for better travel of electricity. I've used the cheapest ones that cost $28.00—I think they have the worst shock.

Because I know the incredible power of these animals, I'm more careful now whenever I go in with them.

Bears give you no warning—they are cute cuddly teddy bears right up to the time they kill you. My bears were all young cubs when I got them. They came from out West and are Russian brown bears that were captive born. These type bears sometime outgrow the giant Kodiaks. Even as cubs, when they bite you, it leaves giant bruises. I've read most of the bear books and have studied bears for many years. When problems arise, I know experts who have helped me, like Dr Robbins from Washington State University.

Bears are not like the big cats…when they attack, they want you dead and won't stop until you are, in most cases.

I've adopted a sure fire bear stopper that stops a bear in its tracks. It doesn't hurt them and is not a spray or a weapon. A rubber snake, maybe three feet long works like magic. Hold it out in front of you where the bear can see it and shake it around like it is alive. They run every time. Now maybe you're thinking the bears in Alaska have never seen a snake, so therefore they won't fear it. They will not get close enough to find out, especially if you're shaking it. (APPENDIX 4)

FOOD SOURCE

Hunger is often given as a cause of bear attacks upon humans. During poor berry years (where frost, heavy rains or drought affected the growth) or decreased salmon returns in certain North American locales bear maulings have spiked. For the past decade or two those who study bears as professional biologists and managers have labeled such conditions food stressed. No doubt when bears are hungry, they are more agitated and less willing to sacrifice their food source or their territory to an interloper—be it four-legged or two-legged. Therefore, a hungry or food stressed bear could attack in defense of a food source or possible food source OR if its natural food source were not available, it may become predatory.

Unfortunately, a woman's compassion for an injured animal led to her demise from such a bear. Web Editor for the *Denver News* Wayne Harrison, reported such a tragedy August 11, 2009 ("Autopsy: Woman Attacked, Killed By Bear"). Apparently 74-year-old Donna Munson had fed wild animals from her wire-fenced porch for a number of years. In an effort to help a younger bear that had been injured by another bear, she set out hard-boiled eggs and milk. However, when the larger bear returned, she informed her brother that she was "going to chase it off with a broom." The meager mesh fence was not sufficient to deter the bear which killed her. Officials investigating the situation shot and killed two black bears on the premises, a necropsy revealing that a 400-pound boar had remnants of her shirt in its stomach.

Bears—especially big, old boars—don't want you messing with their food source and commonly protect it. In spite of some who claim a sow with cubs is the most dangerous, this boar IS the most dangerous! Gary Shelton refers to its protecting food as carcass defense. On page 132 of his *Bear Encounter Survival Guide* he says, "If you ever walk up on a large male grizzly defending a carcass, you will only have seconds to respond, and you'll have to do everything right to survive. Large males attack differently than sows or sub-adults; the intruder is usually dispatched quickly by a blow from the right front paw, then ripped to shreds for insurance."

SIG CASIANO

One of the most relevant stories illustrating Gary's point is that of Sig Casiano who was attacked by just such a bear in 2001 near Soldotna, Alaska. This boar was the baddest banana in the bunch. As Sig shared his story with me, I took note of several major points he made in man's defense from a determined or extreme bear, including the bear's size, its speed and power, being properly armed and practiced, having a back up weapon, a lanyard on his pistol and a shell in the chamber—great advice for man's safety against such an enraged animal, as well as other predators.

It was Sunday morning, late April 1998. Hunting season would start in about a week on May first. I had gotten a permit to hunt bear by bait in the Kenai National Moose Refuge and I decided to go out and set up my station.

I drove out to the parking area where I could see the lake. Because it was kind of heavy, I put my 55 gallon drum on a child's sled for transport. I had already cut a hole in the barrel and I had a chain inside it (in order to chain the barrel to a tree for storing bait). My two-burner Coleman stove was in my metal frame pack on my back.

I had my .300 on my right shoulder and my .454 Casul pistol holstered in a chest-shoulder holster. Because I've heard stories about bear's attacking people, I always wanted to be on the cautious side of things. Some of us try to prepare for things like this. Every time I go out, even for a hike, I carry a pistol or a rifle. I don't want to be surprised and not have the ability to protect myself.

I started walking down the trail across from the parking area and the trees were pretty dense. There was still about two feet of snow on the ground. The trail got narrower so I decided to come back down the road about a hundred yards to a trail I could use; it was maybe six feet wide.

I got about a tenth to a quarter of a mile down that trail when I heard this noise to my right. It sounded like I had startled a moose that was getting up out of its bed. I couldn't see anything because the foliage was really thick. I kind of bent down to see what was making the noise and I only saw a brown patch. As I stood back up, I could still hear it and it sounded like it was coming towards me.

The only thought going through my mind was why is this moose charging me? I reached up to grab my pistol and quickly realized that it was coming real fast. I've been around a lot of animals. I've scared moose up and never had one charge me. Bears too. They always run the other way.

I quickly unslung my rifle from my shoulder. I had a round in the chamber. When I'm by myself, I always have a round in the chamber. With someone else, I typically do not have a round chambered. In this case I did.

Right when I got it down, the moose was coming through to the right front of me. I released the safety, pointed the rifle and pulled the trigger. It landed about six-feet away from me, literally right at my feet. Because of the snow cover when the moose hit the ground, snow sprayed up.

That's the first time that I realized it was not a moose, but a bear. I immediately pulled back and put another round in…in fact I short stroked it and the case got stuck in there. I pulled it out and shot the bear in the shoulder. My third shot, I chambered another round and shot it in the shoulder again. He was still breathing so I pulled my pistol out and shot him in the chest one more time and he stopped breathing.

It happened so quickly. From the time I heard the noise till the time I shot him probably three seconds elapsed. I didn't have a lot of time to think about what to do. I had a half a second to realize I didn't want to use my pistol. And the other couple of seconds were taking my rifle off my shoulder, pushing the safety and pulling the trigger.

People asked me, "Why did you shoot so many times?"

I answer that I wasn't sure where I hit him the first time. I didn't know if I hit him in the head and knocked him out or if I hit him in the spine and crippled him. I kept shooting him until he stopped breathing.

I loaded my rifle back up with four more rounds. I heard noise in the brush and thought it might be a sow with cubs. I crouched to see what it might be. Then I realized that the noise was the brush settling from the bear's passing through in its charge.

I took my pack off and left it there and got in my truck and headed down Swanson River Road so I could get in cell phone range to call the Alaska State Troopers. I did not have a camera so I drove to a friend's at Longmere Lake to borrow a camera from him.

On my way I called my wife on my cell phone. I told her I'd be home late. She asked my why and I told her I'd just killed a bear.

She asked if it was hunting season yet.

I said, "No. I had a bear charge me."

She said, "What?"

I said, "I killed it and I'm okay. I didn't get hurt or anything."

She was all worried about my going back out. She didn't want me to go back out any more. I said, "I just can't do that. I love hunting. I won't get hurt."

I explained that it was an isolated incident that doesn't happen to every hunter going into the woods but that it's something that they should be prepared for because it could happen. Nine out of ten times a hunter is not going to be charged by a bear. I kept that thought in mind which kept me from being too worried about its happening again.

I went back out to set up my bait station a week later. And hunted. I didn't take a black bear that year but I had another brown bear in the area come into my station. Plus my wife kept requesting that I not go again. She mentioned at one point that I'd taken a bear and didn't need to go back again. She didn't want me to hunt bear again because I'd shot one. However, I reminded her that I'd taken a bear but I didn't get it—the state did.

When I got in my friend's house, I was able to contact the troopers and inform them of what happened. They were going to meet me out there.

My buddy and I got in my truck, had a camera and got out to Mosquito Lake. The troopers both had rifles. They were both standing there with M 16 style rifles, a shorter model. I thought that their sense of adequacy with the firepower wasn't very good. Their rifles would shoot more rounds, probably .223 caliber. More volume but not as far as fire power. I didn't feel comfortable leaving without my rifle.

They said, "Okay, why don't you show us where it's at."

I asked them, "Do you mind if I bring my rifle?"

They both said, "No. That's okay. You don't need your rifle."

I looked at their rifles and said, "Yeh, I think I'm going to take my rifle."

So we walked out there and got to my back pack. The one thing they wanted to do was ascertain whether I'd stalked this bear before killing it. And it was quickly noted that that wasn't the case. We hiked down the trail in two feet of snow. We could see my tracks walking in and his tracks coming through the woods, making a B-line right for me. So they quickly ruled out the possibility of my being out there hunting.

We followed his tracks for about a hundred yards and found a dead moose. You could see where the bear had bedded down on it. He'd been on it a couple of days but he hadn't eaten much of it. It so happens that that dead moose was on the trail that I'd started on the first time. I was pretty fortunate to be able to turn back and come back down the other trail because I'm not sure how it would have been otherwise.

As we walked through the woods following his tracks back, we noticed a number of broken trees. From the moose to the dead bear was a straight line. He was dialing in on me because of this noise that he kept hearing, this chain that was rattling inside of this barrel. He knew exactly where I was.

He'd knocked down spruce and birch trees that ranged in size from two-inches to four-inches thick, just knocked them clean off. The noise that I'd heard from the brush was all the trees breaking. The bear never went around any trees, he was running full speed. In fact right before I shot him, he hit a spruce tree that was probably five or six-inches in diameter and he didn't break that one—he bounced off of it when he hit it with his shoulder.

Initially they questioned me about my having so much fire power in the woods— both a rifle and a pistol. I thought it was a silly thought because I've read responses from people and results. The situation was exactly why one would carry a rifle and a pistol.

Neither of them knew how to skin a bear. Luckily I did. My buddy had actually brought a knife with him. I happened to have one with me.

I told them I would skin the bear I just needed their help moving the bear. There were four of us and we couldn't roll it over. I thought it was anywhere between the 1200 and 1300 pound range.

Federal guys came because it was on the refuge and he had to actually investigate too. It took five guys to roll the bear over onto its back so we could start working on it.

We got it rolled over and I started skinning it. I had them do some things for me like hold the legs and stuff like that. One of them almost cut one of the feet off. I started hearing this sawing noise and I looked up and he was sawing the foot off at the wrist, almost cutting into the hide (with my bow saw).

I told him not to do that. He asked me, "Well, what'd you bring the saw for?"

I said, "The saw is for cutting dead trees I would use for my bait station, not to cut a bear up."

You cut a bear up with a knife, through the joints.

We did a quick job on it. I cut it off at the wrists and the neck. I had brought another sled too. We stuffed the hide on the sled, and it probably weighed a couple of hundred pounds. We had a little trouble getting it out because it was so heavy. Even on the sled the rope kept breaking.

We finally got it to the road. Some tourists happened to be driving by at the same time. One of them asked if it was a moose. We told him it was a bear.

The authorities informed me that since it was killed in defense of life and property they would have to seize the bear. One of the things that I did that I kind of got scrutinized for was I took a claw off the bear.

They took the hide back to fish and game and the next day one of the biologists at fish and game called and asked me if I had the claw. I said, "Yes, I did."

He said, "You have to return it with the bear."

I said, "That's not a problem."

He was quite frank to me about it…"It is a big bear. There will be a lot of exposure. They need to really go by the rules on this one." So I respected that decision and got the claw back to them right away.

The Peninsula Clarion wrote a big story that I'd filched a claw which really got under the skin because I didn't steal…filching in my definition is deception and stealing. And I didn't know it was against the law to take a claw. And I gave it back when I was told about it.

Up to that point I didn't mind talking to the press about the incident but after that I wouldn't talk to anybody because I was wasting my time because they weren't telling the story. They reported other inaccuracies such as the size of the bear which was never weighed. I've killed enough bears to know that this one far exceeded their estimate of 500 pounds.

I was prepared to buy the bear at the Fur Rondy auction (usually each year at the Fur Rendezvous celebration in Anchorage furs are auctioned), to put a bid on it. But a couple of weeks after they actually got the bear, the Brigham Young University museum in Hawaii was doing an Alaskan exhibit and they requested a large brown bear, which I had shot. It squared 9' 6" and the skull measured 28 inches green.

Although the *Anchorage Daily News* reported the story most accurately, they quoted a state trooper implying that because this bear had pellets in its rear end from earlier run ins with humans, that it had lost its fear of people.

I disagreed with that. When I was skinning him, I found some birdshot BB's from a shotgun in his rear end. That doesn't necessarily mean he'd lost his fear of humans. This bear may have been around homes. It was fifteen years old. There's also the possibility that over time a bear hunter in a tree stand tired of the bear's presence, brought a shotgun and shot him in the rear end to get him out of there.

The reason that he charged wasn't because he'd lost his fear of humans. He charged because he was protecting his meal.

I've read lots of articles about bear attacks. A couple kind of startled me. In these articles the charging bear hit them and knocked the rifle from their grasp and they had nothing to protect themselves with. They had to either play dead or improvise. They were killed immediately.

Once you lose your pistol or your rifle, you don't have anything. You can punch a bear all day long and there are no definite results. If you punch him in the nose, you don't know if he'll run away or if he's going to continue attacking you. With a pistol or a rifle there's a definite outcome for the most part. You shoot him and it's going to have a pretty big impact on whether he decides to stay or whether you actually kill him.

That information caused me to buy a .454 Casul pistol, a very large caliber pistol designed for large animals like bears. I carry my pistol on my chest because the first thing you're going to do is jump on your belly and try to protect your head and your neck. If a bear ever got me on the ground, I would have a last line of defense with the pistol. If the bear went for my legs and tried to shake me to death, when he stopped shaking me, I would pull the pistol and shoot him.

If I had a rifle, I would use the pistol only as a last resort. I'm not going to pull the pistol out unless I have to.

Given the option of using a rifle or a pistol, always shoot your rifle before your pistol, even at six feet. Your rifle with the right round is lot more deadly, more powerful and has more impact on the animal that you're shooting than most pistols.

I recommend having a pistol on a lanyard so that it's always available. A lot of pistols don't have a place to put a lanyard but any gun dealer can weld one on.

For a defensive weapon I recommend a thirty caliber and up. My favorite rifle for protection is my .45-70. It's a lever action with an 18-inch barrel, easy to handle. When I'm fishing, I can put it on my back. It's a lot more effective than a shotgun. It is magna ported with hardly any recoil…anybody can shoot it, even a woman.

Another article pointed out that 90% of people that die from bear attacks where the bear was able to get their heads into their mouths. The people that lived typically were smaller bears that weren't able to do that. That's not in every case of course.

I would probably have died that day if I would have had pepper spray (instead of a firearm) because when I shot him, he was six-feet away and still running. Pepper spray would not have stopped him. I truly believe that pepper spray in my situation would have done me absolutely no good.

One of the benefits I had was I was wearing a metal frame. For me at the time I thought I had a lot of things in my favor. The two burner Coleman metal stove in my pack would have protected my entire back if he had gotten on top of me. He would have taken a bite out of everything he could take a bite of until he got some soft tissue.

The only soft tissue I had exposed is my legs. My thought afterwards if it happened was if he went for my legs and tried to shake me to death, after he was done shaking me, I would have pulled the pistol out and shot him.

A lot of people have said that my military training helped prepare me. That's quite possible. My military background enhanced my hunting abilities—anticipating noises around me and my environment, being aware of animals in the area and it prepared me for being comfortable with handling a weapon. I have no problem pulling the weapon down and popping a shot off when I need to. I've never been in combat but being in the military helped me be comfortable in handling a pistol and staying focused. Being comfortable with the weapon, pulling it down and shooting without asking any questions, without hesitating and without second guessing my judgment helped me. That's my nature too, I don't worry about a lot of things. I've been around a lot of animals.

It was a survival instinct as far as I was concerned. I was very, very lucky that I was not hurt. I've always recognized that. People told me that, especially fish and game people. I recognize that I was very fortunate.

I never thought this would happen to me and I'm sure that everybody who's ever been attacked by a bear never thought it would happen to them.

There are a lot of people out there who didn't understand why I did what I did, what I was doing out there or why I was hunting at all. I think they may understand it but I don't think they accept the reason that we have hunting and regulate the populations of predators and animals.

Several things impress me about Sig's story: 1) Noise did not deter the bear—rather, it helped locate the man; 2) large boars are very protective of their food source; 3) Sig's concern that spray would NOT have worked; 4) boar's determination and strength; 5) officials' suspicion/blame hunter—not innocent until proven guilty; 6) chambered round; 7) time elapsed; 8) pistol and lanyard—good advice; 9) being armed always; 10) in your face to anti's and huggers—a man's got to do what a man's got to do (kill a bear if necessary!)—11) shoot till they stop moving; 12) being prepared in the first place!

NO GOLDILOCKS

A fairly humorous story reached me via email June, 7, 2004, from my friend Tom Smith—he said he "Thought you'd find this story intriguing!" I summarized the forwarded tale from TN65X57@aol.com, "Canadian College Student Kills Bear with Frying Pan." (VICTORIA, BC PRWEB May 26, 2004)

As British Columbia college student Ryan, home on vacation, grilled salmon for his meal, a bear entered his home ala Goldilocks. Ryan had just sat down to eat when he heard the ruckus of what turned out to be a very uninvited guest. As he began to investigate, the door flew open and a large brown bear materialized in his living room.

The bear zeroed in on the salmon while Ryan contemplated his course of action. He shouted at the bear which disregarded the noise and sampled the salmon. Ryan threw kitchen utensils at the beast in an effort to get its attention. When a wooden spoon ricocheted off its head, it went for Ryan, rising on its hind legs to swat *homo sapien*.

The bear blocked his escape route to his room and a firearm so Ryan grabbed the cast iron skillet and shouted "bring it on, bring it on!"

Ryan jumped the counter. Standing 6-foot tall on all fours and weighing over 800-pounds the bear made for the college man. From a foot away Ryan swung his weapon, smacking the bear on the right side of its head. The animal was stunned and Ryan pummeled it with the pan. Fifteen thumps later the bear fell to the floor. Determining not to give the bear a fighting chance, Ryan continued pounding the brute for another five minutes before he called the police. When they arrived, they couldn't believe their eyes.

Officer F. Barnes of the Victoria crime scene investigation unit said, "It was the craziest thing I've ever seen…He actually killed a bear with a frying pan." Authorities estimated the bear came from a cave a mile distant.

Animal rights reactionaries felt that Ryan should have been prosecuted for his aggressiveness in killing a bear that did what was natural—breaking into his home for food! No doubt, they clamored, "Well, that silly student shouldn't have! The nerve."

PERSONAL SPACE

Bears have a home range and within that they have a personal space, just as people do. Depending upon their experience and temperament, these bears respond to others—be they bear, person or other animal. For instance, if a bear killed a salmon, fed upon it and a seagull landed nearby, the bear would be more tolerant of the seagull than it would be of another bear. When their personal space is violated, the bear reacts. Sometimes it retreats; sometimes it attacks.

SURPRISE

Usually surprise is connected with a bear's personal space or territory—when a person surprises a bear, it's within the bear's space; or the bear is protecting something and is surprised.

MIKE STASACK

Jaci Turner, a former student of mine who lives with her husband Mike Stasack in Sterling, Alaska, sent me the following story in December 1996. Mike calls his story "The Bear who Woke up my Life" and it demonstrates the danger of surprise.

Mike wrote that he and his 20-year hunting buddy and neighbor Bob Kuiper flew to hunt moose September 12, 1996. Mike dropped Bob at a lake and landed a mile away —they would hunt separately with moose moving back and forth between them—with plans to begin hunting the following day.

Mike hunted unsuccessfully the next morning, returned to camp for soup and a sandwich then taxied in his plane across the lake to access a ridge where he'd taken a bull the previous year. He secured his plane to the bank, donned his parka and rain gear for the light rain and wet brush ahead. He pulled on his backpack and grabbed his rifle and moved up the trail through thick stuff which he describes below.

I've always dreaded this section of woods because you really have to struggle to get through the next several hundred yards. Quietly slipping through the dense brush, my visibility was reduced to only a few feet. Then I got to open pockets where you could see 15 to 30 feet. I have never seen a bear in this area and wasn't even thinking of bear as I had visions of juicy moose burgers in my mind.

I had just reached an open pocket about 17 feet across when all of a sudden the brush started shaking violently in front of me. I heard an animal bellowing and my first thought was "My God, I'm gonna get charged by a moose."

Seconds later, an enormous brown bear head popped out of the brush and the bear rushed me on all fours, growling loudly. I was stunned as this nightmare unraveled. I kept telling myself *it's a bluff charge; it's a bluff charge.*

I didn't have time to release the safety on my .300 Weatherby Mag before he rose onto his hind legs six feet in front of me, his huge head over a foot above mine, my eyes fixed on his wide open mouth and those big white fangs. The last thing I saw was a huge right claw coming down across my terror filled face. As I fell backwards and yelled, I remember thinking *it's all over. I don't want to be looking up at him on my back when I hit the ground.*

Instinctively I rolled over onto my stomach and instantly he was on my back. I felt pain just below my shoulder and a few moments later he got off me. There was complete silence. I knew he was right there waiting. My face was in the mud and my hands were still clutching my Weatherby .300 Mag rifle underneath me. I had to play dead. I was too terrified to move anyway.

Seconds later I heard a rustling in the brush. I lay still some more. Is he just waiting in the brushy shadows for me to move before he attacks again? I couldn't stand it anymore. I turned my head to look back and didn't see him. I jumped to my feet and pointed the rifle and thought, "Now I'm ready to shoot you son of a b-----."

I shook badly and blood dripped from my muddy face onto my rain coat. I felt a slight pain in my back and felt blood against my shirt. The whole attack took no more than 30 seconds but I was O.K. I just wanted to get out of there and I talked out loud to myself, 'I just got clawed and mauled by an 8-foot, 800-pound brown bear and lived to tell the tale. I kept turning around guarding my back just in case. *Another half a mile and I'll be back to my plane*. Luckily, he didn't follow me.

Mike reached his plane and removed his backpack which had no bite marks on it. He washed his face with lake water and took off to the next lake to let his partner know what had happened, looking for the bear from the air. He saw neither the animal nor his partner so wrote a note to Bob then took off for medical help on a six minute flight to his home.

His neighbor Don Heininger drove him to Soldotna for medical help. Although the bear's claws missed his eyes, Mike received 40 stitches in his nose and upper lip and a few in his back for a deep tooth puncture wound.

A Fish and Wildlife biologist interviewed Mike and told him he'd probably surprised a sleeping bear, only 17-feet away.

AUDELIO LUIS CORTES

Since 1981 the privately owned company had been conducting seismic surveys for sub-surface mapping for oil at various times of the year, depending on terrain and environmental factors affecting accessibility to the areas. Their work consisted primarily of placing seismic lines (cables) with sensors (geophones) across the surface of the study area in a specific, tightly spaced grid pattern. These straight, parallel lines ran at 1/4-mile intervals through the area. A survey crew flagged trails to indicate the recording lines. A recording crew then followed the surveyors' marked trails and placed geophones. Holes were drilled and charges planted. Once the recording equipment was placed, an explosive charge was detonated, causing compression waves that the sensors received and recorded. Finally, the recording crew returned to collect the equipment.

Because marshes, ponds and small lakes polka-dotted the area and frozen ground provided better conditions for foot travel, they performed most of their work during winter months.

A couple of hours after noon on February 9, 1998, a six man seismic crew for Northern Geophysical of America worked a flagged trail in Kenai National Wildlife Refuge—in the Finger Lakes area of Swanson River Road a dozen miles northeast of Soldotna, Alaska. Hilly elevations varied from 20 to 30 feet upwards to 200-plus feet. Moderate brush, birch trees, saplings and two to three feet of snow covered the ground. The surface of most of the ponds had two to three inches of ice. The roadless area required helicopter transport—moving workers and their equipment to and from their base camp and their work site. Supplies had been left along the line at quarter mile intervals and crews carried or dragged the supplies and gear as they worked.

Training for wildlife encounters such as black and brown bears was provided. Workers also received topographic maps denoting surveyed and potentially occupied bear dens, giving them a 1/8-mile cushion around the den sites. The crew was not armed with pepper spray nor firearms.

Crew members carrying two-way radios were spaced 10 to 100 feet apart. As they set recording lines and sensors, they were unaware that they passed within forty feet of a brown bear den, uphill from their location. From the den opening, a man's head and shoulders would have been visible, allowing the bear to view workers as they passed below the den.

The first four men walked past the den before a bear emerged, a mere fourteen yards away, and attacked Audelio Luis Cortes, seizing his head and upper torso and carrying him ten feet down slope. A colleague ten feet behind Audelio climbed a nearby tree and yelled to warn the others, "Bear! Bear!"

The crew scattered, some climbing trees. The bear stayed with the victim for one to two minutes before walking to a tree occupied by one of the victim's co-workers. The bear stood and attempted to paw the co-worker's foot. When the bear left the site, the remaining crew radioed the base camp for medical assistance. At 2:05 PM the camp emergency medical technician arrived. The victim was pronounced dead from massive head trauma.

This was the second encounter of a denned bear during the project period and the first fatality for the company. (Source: Alaska Face (Fatality Assessment & Control Evaluation, Worker fatally mauled by brown bear, http://hss.state.ak.us/dph/chems/occupation injury/reports/docs/98ak006.htm)

Several hundred miles from Soldotna, other surveyors encountered a denned grizzly in 2007.

Two forestry surveyors—Moira McLaughlin and Daylon Johnson, British Columbians in their 20's—collected data on the mountain pine beetle south of Grande Prairie, Alberta while working for Alberta Sustainable Resource Development.

It was January. Hibernation time for bears. Yeah. But…this bear was not asleep.

One minute they're hiking down a steep slope; the next minute a grizzly comes from nowhere and knocks Daylon forward onto Moira.

The bear bit Daylon's leg and Moira's hand. Johnson hit the bear which lit out for other regions.

Moira and Daylon sat and regained their composure then radioed for a helicopter pick up. They learned later that they had accidentally walked over the bear's den, covered by 3 ½ feet of snow and a log. (2 forestry workers recovering after bear attack, Monday, January 22, 2007, cbc.ca *CBC News* www.cba.ca, Canada/Edmonton website)

WOUNDED

I copied and pasted this very interesting story from a website April 28, 2006 (www.sparksgenealogy.net/grizzly.html).

From The Webmaster: The following story was written by William (Timberline Bill) Sparks, who lived and hunted in Arizona in the late 1800's and early 1900's.   He was a well published author and poet. This story of his encounter with a Grizzly Bear and a fight to the death, (fortunately the bear lost) was published in one of his books.   The story was also published in the "Sparks Quarterly" and on the web site, http://SparksFamilyAssociation.net. I am also the Webmaster for this site.

FIGHT WITH A GRIZZLY BEAR
By William ["TIMBERLINE BILL"] Sparks, 1861-1928

In the spring of 1888 my partner, a man named Al Robertson, and I, were camped at the forks of Eagle Creek, near the foot of the Blue Range, and about fifteen miles above the Double Circle Ranch of Arizona.

"Al, if you'll wash the dishes, and bring in the horses, I'll go look at that trap we set down the creek," I said to my partner one morning, as he rose from the ground where we had been squatted beside the canvas manta, or pack cover, on which the tin dishes and plates that had contained our breakfast were spread.

"All right," said Al, "I'll have the horses here before you're back. What horse will I tie up for you? I want to start as soon as I can, for it will take me all day to ride to Slaughters and back, so I won't wait, for if there is anything in the trap it may take quite a while to trail it up and skin it."

After telling Al which horse I wanted tied up, I buckled on my cartridge belt, picked up my rifle and started down the creek toward the place where we had set a large bear trap the day before.

The camp was in a small open space on a point between the junction of two mountain streams, that tumbled noisily over their bed of boulders, between banks that were thickly wooded with black alder, ash, balsam, oak, cherry, walnut and pine trees, which in many places were festooned with wild grapes, Virginia creeper, and honey-suckle vines.

For several years there had been a considerable number of hunters in these mountains, who supplied the new mining camps of Coony, Carlisle, and Clifton, with fresh venison and turkey in winter; and winter or summer, hunted and killed the black-tailed and white-tailed deer, bucks and does alike, that abounded in the forests and hills north of the Gila River.

In summer they cut freshly killed venison into thin strips, which were salted and hung on a line until dry enough to be pulverized into powder when beaten with a hammer. When enough of this, "jerky" it was called, had been accumulated to load the pack horses, it was taken to one of the mining camps and sold to the Mexican workmen who, with their families, were very fond of it.

Bear of several varieties; cinnamon, black, brown and silvertip, as well as mountain lions, were plentiful, and until the advent of the cattlemen were only killed when the hunters were in need of bears' oil for cooking; or in the autumn, just before the hibernating animals holed up, when the fur and skins were at their best. I am aware that several great naturalists have decided that black and brown bear are one and the same species; and that the cinnamon and silvertip, or grizzly, is the same bear. But that these learned gentlemen, who have mostly gained their knowledge of wild animals from the writings of others, or from an occasional trip extending for a few weeks at most, to the wilds, are mistaken, I am sure.

The grizzly of California, and the silvertip of Arizona, are the same animal; and may be any color from almost black to a dirty gray. His hide is covered with thick fur, sometimes almost black, sometimes a purplish brown. Through this grows a mass of longer hair, usually somewhat darker than the fur, until it reaches through the fur, when it becomes silvery white, and I have often seen silvertips with a streak of white from the shoulders, where the long hair grew into a mane, to their rump. The genuine silvertip is broader between the ears than the cinnamon; shorter from a line drawn between the ears to the nose, and stands higher at the shoulders. In fact, a silvertip, that is not the product of a cross between the grizzly and one of the other species, has a sort of hump on his shoulders that no other bear has, as well as a character and habits that are different from those of bear of any other species.

The brown bear of Arizona is small, with a sort of curved head and long claws. He is covered with short, brown hair, often little longer than the winter coat of a cow, and if he has any fur at all, it is scanty and short.

The cinnamon is medium in size, between the black bear and the grizzly, and has long, reddish colored hair that covers a thick coat of fine fur, that is exactly the color of dried cinnamon bark. There is a difference in the shape of his head, and in his habits. He has no hump, but his claws are long like the grizzlies'. The full-blooded black bear is black; sometimes with a white spot on his breast; and has short front claws that are attached to fingers under the skin of his front feet, that are so muscled that he can climb a tree that he cannot reach around, if the bark is rough enough for him to insert his claws into its cracks.

No full-blooded bear of any of the other varieties can climb a large tree, though I have seen bears that were brown in color, but who plainly showed more of the characteristics of their black, than they did of their brown forebears, take to trees when pressed. As all these species cross, the cubs born of black or brown parents, that are mixed blood, may be of either color.

When setting a trap for bear, it was the custom to cut a heavy green pole, and drive it through the ring attached to the trap until only about eighteen inches of the larger end remained on the side of the ring from which the pole had been inserted. Then, if a bear got in the trap, in dragging the pole through the trees and rocks he would leave a plain trail, and could be easily followed.

But if no pole, or clog, as the hunters and trappers called it was fixed to the trap, and it was left loose, a large bear might travel for many miles before lying up. And if the trap was made fast, when it snapped on a bear's leg it might break the bones, as sometimes happened, and in such an extent that often a trapped bear would twist and gnaw off his leg above the trap and escape.

But this was in June; and the bear, as was their habit, had all gone to the higher mountains where there was food in plenty. Up in the mountain meadows, surrounded by forests of spruce, and quaking aspen, were many delicacies that appealed to the nose and stomach of a hungry bear. Yellow jackets were storing honey that only had to be dug for to be obtained. In many places the ground was matted with wild strawberry vines that bore countless crimson points of wonderful flavor. Wild oats were in the milk; and there were numberless dead trees covered with rotten bark, that a bear had only to tear off, with his claws, to secure great fat grub worms, that were far more grateful to the taste of an almost satiated bear, than the most tender venison.

On my last trip to town, a townsman had requested me to bring in a lion's skin, which he offered to pay well for. Lion were hard to find without dogs, and the trap had been purchased to trap lion at the time the

Territorial Legislature had made it mandatory on the supervisors of the different counties to pay a bounty on both bear and lion. But the counties of Arizona were very sparsely settled at that time, and were very poor; and the hunters brought in so many scalps of bear and lions that the different supervisors petitioned the next Legislature to repeal the bounty law, which was done.

As a lion caught in a trap would seldom travel farther than the first dense thicket, and the bear, as we supposed, were all higher in the mountains, we put no clog on the trap, but set it between two ash trees, and a few feet in front of another tree that was well covered with grape vines. A little basin, just large enough to secret the trap in, was scraped away with a stick, and when the trap had been placed in it and covered with twigs and leaves, the bait, a deer's head and liver, were hung on the tree on which the grape vines grew, and the other trees, so that an animal intent on investigating the bait would have to step in or over the trap to get to it.

Soon after I left camp I came to a place where the creek ran against a bluff. Pulling off my moccasins, and rolling up my trousers, I waded through the swiftly flowing water, slipping on the round boulders at times, but managing to keep my rifle and clothing dry. At several more crossings I repeated this; but at last came to the mouth of a small creek where the trap had been set. Stealthily approaching the place, I saw that the vines were torn, and the bark on several small trees broken and bruised by the teeth of some enraged animal.

When I stood over the spot where the trap had been set, I found that the ground had been almost ploughed up in places by a bear, whose footprints proved him to be a silvertip of enormous size. Different bear, when wounded, or caught in a trap, have no hard and fast rules in regard to their actions. One bear, suddenly finding himself griped in the torturing jaws of a clattering steel trap, may skulk noiselessly away, while another may frighten all the wood folk within hearing distance with his bawling.

But this bear had acted different from any that I had encountered before. The ground and trees showed plainly where he had swung and struck with the heavy trap, regardless of the pain he must have endured. In places the trap springs had dug holes in the soil that looked like a shovel had been thrust into it by some careless gardener, and saplings five or six inches in diameter were almost bare of bark in places, where he had snapped and torn with teeth and claws.

The "sign" or appearance of the torn vines and bark, and the tracks, proved that the bear had been caught not long before daylight, and as the sun was now not more than an hour high, I reasoned that the enraged animal would not travel after daylight, and might be in any brushy thicket, nursing his hurt, and the hatred that all bear must feel for a trap, and the men who set them.

So I slowly circled around among the trees until I found where the bear, evidently hopping along on three legs and holding the front paw on which the trap was fastened, above the ground, had left the narrow canyon valley, and started straight over a ridge that was covered only with scattered pine trees, and short grass, that made no covering in which a bear could hide.

Though there was no danger of coming suddenly upon the bear here, I climbed the ridge slowly, halting at times to recover my shortened breath. For a rifle is an arm of precision; and the man who has swiftly climbed a steep hill, whose breast is heaving, and nerves jumping from the exertion, cannot pull the trigger with any certainty, as the sights align on a moving or distant target.

And although the bear was encumbered with a heavy trap, I knew that when I came face to face with his bruinship there would be a reckoning on the part of the bear, if my bullets were not sent to the only immediately vital spot in a bear's anatomy--the brain.

The part of a bear's skull that contains the brain is long, and almost round, like a curved cylinder in profile, with a thick ridge of bone running from just in front of its junction with the spinal column to below a line drawn between the eyes. The frontal part is thickest beneath this ridge, and as the skull rounds, or curves, away from the ridge, it becomes thinner, but is still very thick, and in grizzlies often covered with several inches of hair, hide, and gristle. This was long before the day of high-powered guns, and even the heavy caliber black powder impelled bullets of those days would often glance and fail to penetrate the skull of a large bear, unless they struck it squarely.

But a bullet from the 45-90 that I carried would knock any bear down that it struck in the head; and neither I nor my companion hunters felt the least fear of any bear if we had a few yards of open ground to pump our rifles at him before he could reach us.

It was for this reason that, after reaching the top of the hill, I descended very slowly, always avoiding every clump of brush, and circling around through the openings until I had again picked up the trail, when it went into places where the bear might be hidden. I finally came to the bottom of the hill and a small stream of crystal clear water that gurgled between open groves of small timber. The bed of the creek was sandy, and from twenty-five to seventy-feet wide. The bear turned directly up the creek, and I followed, still carefully avoiding thickets and turns in the bank, where the bear might have laid up for the day. At last I found where the bear had left a thicket and crossed the creek, leaving a string of still wet tracks in the sand; which the sun had now heated so warm that it was evident the bear had heard me, and probably thinking the clump of brush he had laid down in was not so well situated for an ambush as he wished, had silently sneaked away while I was reconnoitering a short distance down the creek.

Presently the tracks led up a gently sloping hill, bare of underbrush, but covered with pine trees. As I slowly neared the top, I heard the rattle of a rattlesnake off to one side, and stepping a few feet toward the sound, I saw a small rattler coiled beside a hole near a large rock. Grasping a small boulder, I flung it at the snake, but missed my mark, and as the snake began to disappear beneath the rock, I hurled missile after missile, but without effect.

When the snake had disappeared, I slowly climbed to the top of the hill, and passing through the open pines, which grew so thickly here that it was slow trailing over the mat of pine needles, I picked up the trail where the bear had started down the farther hillside, which was pretty well covered with scrub oak and buck brush.

I did not follow the trail here, but traveled parallel with it, when I could see it in the soft volcanic ash which covered the hillside, or, when I could not see it, cut across where the course the bear was taking led me to believe it should be, still keeping in the open spaces until I could see the trail ahead of me.

At last I came to a belt of thick brush, and leaving the trail, I skirted this until I came to an opening, which I entered, and winding from opening to opening, came at last to a clear space about sixty feet in length, up and down the hill, which at that place sloped at an angle of almost 45 degrees. As I stepped out into this clear space near its upper end I could see the bear's track where he had hopped, and slid, down through the soft, ashy soil, and entered the brush at the lower end of the opening.

Thinking the bear was ahead of me, and holding my rifle in the hollow of my left arm, with my right hand holding its grip, my thumb on the hammer, and the trigger-guard, I stepped over into the bear's track just below the fringe of brush the bear had come through. Though I was gazing intently across the gulch, hoping I might see the bear ascending the opposite hillside, I had already chosen my route through another break in the brush just beyond the bear's tracks.

As I stepped in the trail I heard the rattle of a trap-chain above and behind me, and before I could turn, the bellow of the bear, not unlike the bawl of an enraged bull. I could not turn my feet on the steep hillside as swiftly as my body, and as I tried to face the bear, for I knew there was absolutely no chance for escape by flight, the bear came charging over the brush, snapping at my head, and striking with its unencumbered paw. Both myself and the bear were at a disadvantage on the steep hillside, and attempting to dodge a stroke from the bear's paw, I threw myself to one side and down the hill. As I did so, the rifle, which I had cocked as I tried to turn, was accidently discharged, leaving it with the chamber of the barrel empty.

I fell with such momentum that I turned over and over several times, like a boy turning back-somersaults, while the bear, his beady, bloodshot eyes flashing malignant rage and hatred, his ears laid back, and his grizzly gray mane standing erect, tried to check himself as he slid and rolled by me. Snapping like a monstrous dog, just as I stopped rolling, he sunk one tusk, all he had left--he had broken the others off biting the trap--in my thigh, and dragged me along as he slid down the hill.

When bear and man had stopped the bear was standing diagonally over me. The beast's tusk had penetrated my thigh and tore loose a whipcord looking muscle; and snapping again, the bear caught me by the same thigh. After some effort to balance himself, he rose up on his haunches and shook and swung me like a cat might shake a mouse. At last he slowly came down on his feet, and still holding me in the grip of his great jaws, flung or jerked me until my head lay down the the hill, while the bear's rump was up the hill, but his head, his jaws still grasping my leg, was turned almost at right angles toward his right, and my left.

I still grasped my rifle, for there was nothing else to hold onto. As the bear, still snuffling, clamped down again and again on my thigh, I slowly at first, and then with a quick sweep, brought the rifle around until it touched the side of the great brute's head. As I swung the gun, I worked the lever. The bear saw, or heard, and let go his hold on my leg. Just as his head turned and the muzzle of the rifle touched its side, a little below and back of the eye, the lever snapped, my finger gripped the trigger, and the crash and smoke that flamed out told me, even before the bear had fallen, that the scrap was over, for there were still several cartridges in the magazine, and even if the bullet did not reach the bear's brain, it would stun him into helplessness for several moments. But as my right hand jerked the lever and threw another cartridge into the barrel, I saw the bear collapse. His feet seemed to give way under him, and with a sort of convulsive shudder of the muscles, he sank to the ground and rolled over against the brush at the lower side of the open space, just as I, with a great effort, threw myself out of the way. When the bear stopped rolling, he lay on his back with his great paws sticking up, and the trap dangling from one of them; Man and bear were not far apart, and as bears have been known to play possum, I rose to a sitting position, and poked the bear with the muzzle of my rifle. But there was no doubt that he was dead. A look at the eyes, the great hole in the side of his head where the powder had burned the hair off, made that certain.

The bear had evidently heard me throwing rocks at the snake, and had circled around through the brush and waited beside his own tracks for his enemy. Had I followed the trail through the brush there can be little doubt I would have fallen an easy victim to the enraged animal. For, as it was, the steep hillside, and loose ashy soil that ran down the hill at every touch of bear or man, was the only thing that saved me.

I now thought of my leg. It felt numb and dead; but I soon found there were no bones broken; but the blood was flowing freely from the wound made by the bear's gnashing tusk. Pulling out my pocket knife, I cut and tore from my cotton flannel undershirt--all I had on except trousers, moccasins and hat, enough strips to tie a bandage around my leg tightly above the wound. Then, picking up my rifle, I looked again at the magnificent animal that luck alone had enabled me to conquer; and limped down the hill to the bottom of the gulch, and then on down to where I knew there was an almost ice-cold spring.

When I arrived at the spring, which bubbled up from a small fern-covered cienaga, or marsh, I lay face down and drank my fill. Then, slowly limping, I went down the gulch until I came to a place beneath a giant mountain cypress where the bear had dug out a wallowing hole. In spring, when the bears begin to shed their winter coats, they greatly enjoy a mud and water bath, and into one of these wallows I scrambled, not without considerable difficulty. I had observed that although I had tied the bandage tightly above the principal wound-- for the broken tusks had done little damage, and the grinding teeth had bruised and not cut-- with every limping step the blood spurted out afresh. So, after sitting in the cold water for perhaps twenty minutes, I re-bandaged the leg tightly, and finding a dead sapling with a fork about the right size for a crutch, I broke it to the right length. Then, leaving my rifle and cartridge belt, I started for the camp.

It was now about an hour before sun-down; and I was about five miles from where the trap had been set, and about six and a half miles from the camp. Leaning on the improvised crutch, I limped down the canyon to the creek, and on down the creek as I had come. Dark came on, and the rough and narrow fork of the sapling rubbed and chafed my armpit until I stopped and tore the most of what remained of my shirt into strips, and wound it around the fork of the crutch. Then I hobbled on, hour after hour, through the darkened woods.

Limbs, and vines, and thorns reached out and tore and scratched my exposed skin, but I did not care. I did not think my wound was serious; and while other men of my acquaintance had killed bear in hand-to-hand conflict, none had ever met such a monster as I had, --except for the slight handicap of the trap for the bear, --fought and killed in a fair fight.

Bear, like hogs, are very heavy for their size. But this bear was larger bodied than a fair-sized cow pony; and although it was June, the season of the year when bear in the foothills are usually poor, he was fat and sleek; a meat-eater that had not gone to the high mountains, but had remained in the lower country to prey on the cowmen's cattle.

Finally, I came to the main creek, and stumbling along to the accompaniment of the cries of night animals and birds, wet, weary, and sore, came around the point only a hundred yards or so from the camp. Through the trees I could see Al standing by the campfire. At last I crossed the smaller stream and climbed up the bank to the welcoming fire, and the well-meaning but clumsy ministrations of my partner, who finding on his return after dark that the horse he had tied up for me was still unsaddled, knew something had happened, but could do nothing until daylight made it possible to follow a trail

Next morning, long before daylight, Al saddled up and went after the gun, rifle, trap and hide. At that altitude the nights were cold, and he found the skin still in good condition. After skinning the bear, he returned to the camp, and, loading me on an easy gaited horse, started for the nearest town, about sixty miles away. That night we stopped at the Double Circle Ranch; the next at McCarthy's Mine, and on the following day we arrived in Clifton, where we sold the bear's hide; and I remained until the wound in my thigh had healed.

****

To give credence to his story of the grizzly bear, Sparks obtained two affidavits which he included in his book. Each was written on the letterhead stationery of the Office of Sheriff of Gila County, Globe, Arizona. These two statements appear as follows:

****

October 5, 1925.
TO WHOM IT MAY CONCERN:

My name is J. H. Lacy. During the year 1888, I was Company Physician for the Arizona Copper Company at Clifton, Arizona. In June of that year William Sparks was brought into Clifton suffering from wounds on the left leg and thigh inflicted by a bear. It seems that he caught a big Silver Tip bear in a trap and following him up came upon the bear suddenly and was attacked before he had opportunity to defend himself. The wound was a severe one and was several weeks in healing. I was the physician who attended Mr. Sparks. The hide of the bear, which had been killed by Mr. Sparks, was on exhibition for several weeks in Clifton. It was a very large Silver Tip hide.

[Signed] John H. Lacy, M.D.

Sworn to before me this fifth day of October 1925.

C. E. Burleen,

Notary Public, Gila County, Arizona.

****

TO WHOM IT MAY CONCERN:

My name is J. A. Lord. I have known William Sparks for the past 38 years. During the year 1888 I was a practicing dentist in Clifton, Arizona. Sometime in the spring of that year, Mr. Sparks was brought into Clifton suffering from wounds inflicted by a bear. I saw Mr. Sparks shortly after he was brought to town. His thigh was very badly chewed.

[Signed] Dr. J. A. Lord

Sworn to before me this fifth day of October 1925.

C. E. Burleen,

Notary Public, Gila County, Arizona.

Wounded bears are nothing to trifle with as the following story indicates—the nearly indestructible grizzly was well armed, took the heat and had amazing stamina. The hunter made a couple of faulty assumptions and fired a couple of very long shots. The story also raises doubt about the family canine.

The hunter dropped a caribou then watched a grizzly for an hour before deciding to shoot it. Firing twice from 200 yards, he knocked flesh and bone from the animal but it escaped into the alders. The hunter and his wife followed the blood until it ran out. Deciding to look for the bear the next day, they returned to camp 8 miles away near mile 40 of Alaska's Denali Highway.

Next morning the couple returned to the blood trail accompanied by their Russian bear dog. They spotted a flock of ravens and concluded that the bear was dead. After an hour's fruitless search the couple returned to the site of the shooting. That's when their dog rumbled from the alder jungle hotly pursued by one wounded and very angry grizzly, snapping her jaws and singing a tune.

Before the hunter had time to react, the sow knocked him down where he kicked at her while she tried to bite his face and neck. As he struggled to bring his .458 rifle into play, the bear bit his calf.

He shouted for his 100-pound wife to shoot from 5-feet away. Amid the chaotic noise of the bear's roaring and the man's shouts, she held the rifle over her husband's head and touched off a round from her .338 into the bear. Every time she shot, the bear dropped him. Two more rounds finished the bear. The hunter and his wife were amazed that the bear was still functioning and continuing the attack, picking him up in its jaws and shaking him.

The hunter suffered teeth puncture wounds on his right calf. When they skinned it, the couple found that the bear's heart was missing. (Source: "Injured grizzly attacks hunter," HARROWING: Woman kills bear at close range as it attacked her husband, By Peter Porco, *Anchorage Daily News*, September 14, 2002)

PREDATORY

The family fed feline is amazing to behold in its pursuit of birds or squirrels in the yard. However, when it comes to stalking prey, it is an amateur compared to the wild bear which rustles its own grub. Just like the cat's stalking maneuvers, the bear's stealth takes it within striking distance before it attacks, which ends in devastating results unless one is prepared to stop such action.

Tragically many people fall prey to predatory bears and it appears, more will likely become victims…as Gary Shelton states, "During the next 20 years, there will be a continuous increase in predatory attacks on people by both grizzlies and black bears…Bear populations are increasing all over North America…protected bears lose their fear of people and do not try to avoid them. Bears that do not fear people are more likely to be predatory…human death rates and property damage by bears will have to reach epidemic proportions before present-day policies are influenced." (*Bear Attacks II Myth and Reality*, Pp. 41-42)

In his *Bear Encounter Survival Guide* Gary Shelton wrote "Predatory attacks by grizzly bears…will become more common as we inflict less mortality on bold bears…" (Pg. 85) which I paraphrase: we do our fellow humans a disservice by allowing predatory bears to prey on them. Or another way, we need to kill all bears that prey on people.

All bears can be dangerous. Too often people think of a black bear as "harmless as a dog." Not so. Blacks do attack and do kill.

On March 27, 1999 Gerald Eugene Smith posted "How Dangerous Are Black Bears?" on the Suite University website (www.101.com). He details the dangers of black bears stating that "Canada is the place where black bears are at their most dangerous." British Columbia and the area along the Alaska Highway—especially Ft. St. John and Ft. Nelson—are by far the most problematic.

He says that "British Columbia has roughly five times as many serious attacks and fatalities from black bears as from grizzlies…from1978 to 1994, there were 27 attacks by grizzlies and 2 fatalities. The black bears caused 78 attacks with 9 fatalities…there may be as many as 3 predatory black bear incidents in a single week."

People spending inordinate amounts of time in these areas are at higher risk. They must take every precaution, travel with a partner (keeping him in sight in areas of high bear activity) and carry a large canister of bear spray and a big ("Crocodile Dundee type") hunting knife—easily accessible for quick use. Shelton recommends they carry a stout walking stick and at least one person in the party carry a rifle in .30-plus caliber. They must convey that they are prepared to fight.

He comments on the predatory black bear's sudden attacks from cover, often coming from the rear and says that, "A lone human has little chance even if armed. One very lucky man who did survive such an attack did so because he accidentally left the safety off and a round chambered. He only saw a black streak out of the corner of his eye before he was knocked down. He kicked at the bear, which grabbed his boot and started dragging him into the woods. He put the rifle under the bear's chin and fired twice, killing it instantly."

Gary Shelton shares a story that a reader sent him describing a child-stalking black bear (*Bear Attacks: The Deadly Truth*, Pg. 61).

In 1994 Dave Keddington and his wife of Fairbanks, Alaska, were visiting a favorite and very popular salmon fishing stream. It is twenty yards wide and extremely swift. During a salmon run, easily one hundred people line the shore. On the opposite stream bank was a family of five. A small child, unobserved by its mother, played about 100 yards downstream from the family members. Dave observed a large black bear emerge from the woods on a direct course for the child.

Halfway to the child the bear sighted the mother walking toward the child. The bear immediately stopped, stared at the woman 10-15 seconds and quickly retreated into the woods. No one in the family was aware of the bear's presence. Dave states that the child was 25 yards from death when the mother's presence changed the bear's mind.

Dave's assessment was that the bear figured the mother was a greater threat than the tiny child and thus it retreated.

A man and female companion were not so fortunate when they visited Algonquin Provincial Park in Ontario. A number of scattered islands polka dot Opeongo Lake, the largest, in the park. These islands are easily accessible from the park highway. It was the thought of canoeing and camping at the lake in October 1991 that attracted Raymond Jakubauskas, 32, and Carola Frehe, 48. When others realized that they were late in their return from their outing, a search party was organized. Before long their bodies were discovered, guarded by a black bear. The Ontario Provincial Police determined that soon after reaching Bates Island the couple began setting up camp and preparing a meal. A boar black bear appeared and struck Carola as Raymond attempted to fight off the attack with a paddle, evidenced by welts and bruises discovered later on the bear's body. The bear then killed Raymond and spent the following five days dragging their bodies to a hide and feeding on them.

IAN DUNBAR

One of saddest and most horrific attacks I've ever heard of regarding bear-man encounters, primarily because the bear came right into the yard in daylight, is the story of Ian Dunbar. I've summarized it from Gary Shelton's *Bear Attacks: The Deadly Truth.*

In their British Columbia subdivision, a dozen miles from Mile70 House and 85 miles south of Williams Lake Lisa Dunbar kicked a soccer ball with her 4 and a half-year-old kindergarten son Ian. When they heard the phone ring September 16, 1994, mother and son went onto the ground level deck. Lisa entered the house via the sliding glass door to answer the phone while Ian removed a rubber ball from his pocket and began bouncing it on the deck. It caromed over the 3-foot high railing and into the yard half a dozen steps away.

Ian retrieved the ball while Lisa spoke on the phone. She looked out the front window at what she thought was a black dog trotting from the front toward the back yard. When she heard Ian yell "Mum," she dropped the phone and ran to the back deck. She knelt on the railing bench and reached over, grabbing Ian by the shoulders when she discovered that what she thought was a dog was, in fact, a 220-pound black bear. As she lifted Ian, the bear grabbed him by his side with its jaws and jerked him from her grasp.

Screaming, Lisa jumped over the railing onto the bear's back then kicked frantically at the animal in an effort to get the bear to release its grip on her son. She smacked it with a flower pot, broke a shovel and a broom over its back and hit it with a fish tank full of dirt but the bear continued violently swinging her son in its jaws from side to side, hitting his head against the floor joists of the deck.

She jumped onto the bear, reached for its eyes and pulled back on its eyes which infuriated it. The animal dislodged her and roared for the first time, chasing her and knocking her down. She fled through the sliding glass door and closed it on the bear's hind foot as it stood up reaching through the opening for her. She kicked at its foot. Ian whimpered and the bear returned to the boy with Lisa in hot pursuit.

Two neighbor men had heard the melee and jumped into a pickup, drove up the driveway as close as possible to the bear and honked and yelled. The bear swatted the truck and bit at the front tire. It swatted the ground before attacking the truck again and running around the satellite dish, growling and blowing.

John Davidson lurched from the truck and ran to Ian and Lisa, who scooped up the lad and ran for the truck. She climbed into the cab and began mouth-to-mouth resuscitation, feeling the air escaping his lung through his side. As they sped toward the hospital, John told her to grab some blankets and that an ambulance was on the way. However, within twenty-five minutes Ian took his last breath.

Many aspects of this story are troubling. The first neighbor on the scene had run to retrieve his rifle but could not find his trigger lock key. He underwent emotional trauma because he couldn't help. Although no one had mentioned it to the Duncan's, they later learned that the bear had been in the neighborhood for three weeks (some people had fed it).

This was a habituated bear, having been fed and familiarized to people by people.

At least two people had an opportunity to kill that bear before it attacked Ian but chose not to for fear of being charged with destroying it for preventative reasons. "Up until about ten years ago, nobody in B.C. tolerated a bear hanging around, no matter how remote the risk of attack was. Now, however, we must not touch them, no matter how many there are. Think about how those two people must feel who didn't kill the bear when they had the chance." (Pg. 76, *Bear Attacks: The Deadly Truth*)

Another factor about this incident is extremely troubling. Besides the loss of their son Lisa and Dave Dunbar were subjected to spineless phone callers who blamed them.

Shelton does an excellent job in this section of his book addressing the failed policy of a government which does not allow its citizens access to firearms for their personal protection (and he also covers in this book the need for counseling bear attack victims, grizzlies as tree climbers, aggressive bear behavior, preservationists, pepper spray and playing dead and dangerous beliefs). Did I say that this book is a MUST read!

I concur with Gary Shelton's following assessments in *Bear Attacks: The Deadly Truth*:

"If they're (anti-hunters) successful in getting bear hunting banned, more people will be killed."(Pg. 65)

"Preservationists always try to blame people for bear attacks…No matter how well you keep your yard, there are those people who will try to blame you for what happened." (Pg. 71)

"It's also extremely unfortunate that Canadian firearms and ammunition storage laws make it virtually impossible for rural citizens to quickly defend themselves against dangerous animals." (Pg. 76)

The source for the following two interesting incidents is www. mainguides.org. On April 17, 2003 a forestry logging foreman surveyed cut sites alone in northern Quebec. Tracks in the snow indicated that a 400-pound male paralleled him for about 55 yards, moved ahead of him in order to ambush him, attacked him from 16 yards, mauled and killed him before dragging him into its den. His body was recovered the next day after a search and rescue team shot the animal. ("Fatal Bear Attack Shows Need for Vigilance," April 17, 2003, Ontario Forestry Safe Workplace Association [OFSWA]).

An 18-year-old, 5-foot-3, 105-pound female hiked a trail in Wawayanda State Park in Sussex County. She'd just crossed a bridge when she looked back to see a black bear standing on the bridge. She began backing away while watching it 30 yards distant. She tried to run when it attacked her. The bear knocked her to the ground and she threw a hard elbow to its snout. The blow allowed her time to escape as the bear stood on its hind legs and sniffed the air. Officials refuse to identify the woman who received a set of 4-inch welts on her midsection.

State Department of Environmental Protection spokesman Jack Kaskey stated, "This bear was in predatory mode…This was classic predatory behavior. The bear was out to eat her. She had to fight for her life." ("Predatory Black Bear Attack," Jim Lockwood, Newark Star Ledger, August 12, 2003 [New Jersey] Staff writers Kristen Alloway and Brian Murray contributed to this report. http://www.nj.com/news/ledger/jersey/index.ssf?/base /news-3/105539953559010.xml The previous news item is also available from the Daily Record News website)

MARY BETH MILLER

Yellowknife outdoor enthusiast and athletic marvel Mary Beth Miller was apt to be found jogging, canoeing or mountain biking. Miller moved with her family to Yellowknife when she was 6-years-old and competed in cross-country skiing and speed skating as a teenager. When she turned 18, she switched to biathlon, which combines cross-country skiing and shooting.

In 1999 the sport rewarded her efforts with a bronze medal at the North American biathlon championship in Canmore, B.C., which helped pave the way for her being named Female Athlete of 1999 for the Northwest Territories.

Miller attended Augustana University College in Camrose, Alberta, where she graduated in 1999 with a B.S. in biology and physical education.

She had worked on the Barren Lands as a wildlife technician involving the surveys of numerous species that included both bears and caribou.

With hopes of making the women's national team Miller arrived in Valcartier, one of two national biathlon training sites. When the 24-year-old competitive biathlete arrived at the centre near Quebec City, she was familiar with the dangers of the outdoors. Nevertheless when she learned of the sighting of a black bear the previous week, she was not overly concerned. She knew and respected nature.

Because of the difficulty of finding a running partner on short notice, Mary Beth jogged alone on a popular running trail that day in July 2000. A black bear assaulted her from the side. She momentarily broke free but was dragged down by the bear and fatally mauled.

Though she took her dog along for bear protection on her training runs at home, she was alone that day, on a trail where others had seen bear tracks but never had much reason to fear for their safety.

Mary Beth was a charismatic, fun loving and generous woman. She wanted all to be on the same footing and shared her athletic success secrets in hopes that all could compete fairly.

Four days after Mary Beth's death wildlife officials destroyed the bear they think responsible for her attack. (Source: "Biathlete Killed by Bear," *Maclean's Magazine*, July 17, 2000, Brenda Branswell, Cheryl Hawkes, www.canadianencyclopedia.ca)

MARCHUK BOYS

May 1995 Daniel Marchuk and cousin Brenton Marchuk drove to a tree planting operation in British Columbia. They set up their tent in the trees, surrounded by 70 other campers. After breakfast the next morning Daniel returned to his tent to grab his camera and was surprised by a charging black bear that knocked him down from behind.

Remembering advice about playing dead if attacked by a bear, Daniel rolled into a ball, clasping his hands behind his neck. The bear bit his head and lapped the blood, repeatedly stopping and starting anew.

Even though the young man yelled as loudly as possible, the noises of a nearby stream and running generator blocked out his repeated shouts for help; and he decided to take action before things got worse. Dan grabbed the bear by the nose and lips and twisted, causing the animal to retreat long enough for Dan to rise and run. The bear dropped him again.

In the meantime Brenton was approaching the tent when he saw the wrestling match and intervened. He ran up and kicked the bear in the backside with no results so he grabbed a chunk of wood and beat the bear on the back with it. The bear stopped long enough for Dan to rise and run again, but he'd gained only ten yards before the bear ran past Brenton and pulled Dan down again. Brenton ran to it and continued beating it with the wood until the bear released Dan, then the cousins ran toward the cook tent yelling "Bear!"

They ran past some employees and reached the tent but before they could escape inside, the bear sank its teeth into Dan's leg and pulled him down again. By now campers had emerged from around the area and tossed rocks and sticks at the bear which retreated to the rear of the tent where it remained until the camp foreman and another man who had heard the commotion arrived with their rifles and killed it.

Here is an example of a predacious black attack in which 70 campers in various stages of activity prepared for a day of work. (Gary Shelton's *Bear Attacks: The Deadly Truth*, Pp. 52+)

A troubling question: Would this bear have done that thirty years ago?

DENISE SATRE

Another predacious black attack in *Bear Attacks: The Deadly Truth* is one of the most disturbing stories that I have ever read. It portrays a government's firearm policy as a serious threat to its citizens. And it illustrates, once again, the danger of habituated or people conditioned bears. A summary follows.

Sven grew up on a ranch and possessed outdoor skills that served him well—he was expert with firearms and horses. In his teenage years he was forced to kill charging bears twice: once to save a friend and once to save himself.

At the age of 20 he moved to Australia, later to New Zealand and finally to New Guinea where he met, married and had two sons before his love brought him back to the valley where he grew up.

He and Denise Satre returned to British Columbia's Tatlayoko Valley in 1995 to discover that things had changed. Ranchers were no longer permitted to kill predators unless they were caught in the act of killing livestock or human safety was in imminent danger. And bears had changed.

Their numbers had increased alarmingly, and their attitude was different. "It used to be that when people saw a bear, which was seldom, it was just a blur as it ran away. Now many of them are not afraid of people..." (Pg. 199)

One day while driving down the lane near their ranch in the valley, Denise pointed out a black bear to her two small sons Alexis, 5 and Zachary, 4. She honked her car's horn in an effort to scare it off. It appeared unafraid as it moseyed toward the brush, stopping to stare back before departing. Denise told her boys about the dangers of a bear with no fear of man.

When she saw her husband Sven and told him about the peculiar behavior of the bear, he seemed unconcerned that a black bear could present much danger, especially from the safety afforded him horseback.

Little did she know when she watched the bear that it was the one to attack her husband within days.

Friday June 14, 1996, 53-year-old Sven and his 16-year-old ranch hand James Rempel rounded up cattle from the brush. James was afoot, armed with Sven's rifle and driving cattle to the road while Sven rode one of his horse. They had agreed to rendezvous around 7:30 PM but Sven never made it. Alarmed, James searched for two hours.

When his search failed to turn up his boss and Sven didn't appear, James called for help from the nearest phone around 9:45 PM.

Unaware that James had phoned for help, Denise left home with her two sons around 10 PM to search for Sven and James.

In the meantime, four men arrived to help James—Edward Gano, Troy Harris, Matt McIntyre and Henry Lampert.

Later Denise met the searchers on the road and supplied them with two additional flashlights before returning to a neighbor to call for reinforcements. She acquired a shotgun, flashlights and a flare gun from her friend, left her boys there and returned to the search.

Five men sharing three flashlights and a rifle spread out in the dark, calling and looking while Denise drove the roadway calling for her truly beloved but there was no answer.

Around midnight they found Sven's horse, the halter hooked to the saddle by a broken cinch. They led the horse to the road where Denise dispensed her gear when a second group of seven searchers arrived. Using a dog they back tracked the horse but failed to find anything except the saddle blanket. The group decided to await daylight to provide better visibility and to avoid disturbing any tracks. At 3 AM Dave Hall phoned the RCMP for Search and Rescue assistance.

An hour later phone calls resulted in more area volunteers along with more firearms, equipment, blankets and food.

At daylight Alex Bracewell and Edward Gano led a party of eight into the woods. The concerned searchers were committed to find one of their own. Alex carried a .30-30 carbine and loaned his scoped .308 rifle to Edward. Within fifteen minutes they sighted a black bear. When they yelled, the animal remained motionless, but a second shout got it moving.

With Denise following closely Alex, Edward and James cautiously approached the area, guns at the ready. That's when they found Sven's body. It was just after 5 AM; Denise rushed to her husband and cradled his body.

Les and Colleen Harris led Denise away while the three others hid and waited for the bear to return, planning to dispatch it. Chomping its jaws, snarling and blustering, the bear appeared in a short time. Edward ended the bear's destructive activities with a single shot, much to the delight to the waiting group around the campfire below.

Evidence indicated that Sven had used an axe to cut alders from the trail for at least a mile. A bear track then intercepted Sven's saddle horse tracks, its tracks plainly visible on top of the horse's. The bear stalked Sven for a half mile. The walking gait of both animals increased to a trot until the last hundred yards where both animals were in full gallop. Churned up earth and divots turned marked a sharp left turn where the saddle rolled. Sven flew from the saddle, ending up on the ground armed with his axe. The black furred death machine awaited him. What were Sven's chances?

Momentarily the horse stood nearby before panicking and exploding away into the brush, returning within 200 yards to the trail—during which time she lost the saddle blanket and the saddle cinch broke.

At least three times the bear moved the body, indicating that the searchers had disturbed the animal, an average to large sized male in prime condition.

Gary Shelton received a letter from Denise in which she explained that she was upset that a biologist blamed people for being in the bear's turf and that she no longer feels safe on the ranch.

KRISTY ABBOTT

When she hit the trail, her intent was to enjoy her outing. Her plan was to jog on Kupreanof Island's Petersburg Mountain Trail near Petersburg, Alaska. She was not expecting an encounter with a bear. It was around 5 PM on a July 2002, evening when Kristy Abbott of Harrisburg, Oregon, spotted a thin, gaunt black bear up ahead. Her fondness for hiking and kayaking did not include boxing with bears. The 27-year-old adventuresome and athletic woman stopped and triggered a hand-held air horn. The bear responded by charging her.

Kristy, a former U.S. Marine looked for a weapon. She faced the animal, determined not to turn her back to it. At first, she poked it with a stick, trying to keep it away from her. Then she got behind a tree and attempted to keep the tree between her and the bear. For fifteen minutes she went one way and the bear tried to cut her off. Constantly watching the bear and exploiting her chances, she backed away from it and toward the Kupreanof State Dock trail head. The brief encounter dragged on and on. For an hour and a half she stood toe to toe with the bear, trading blows. In the end she smacked the bear on the head with a large stick (possibly hitting it in an eye) and the bear vamoosed.

Kristy sustained claw and bite (puncture) wounds on the backs of her legs and was treated at Petersburg Medical Center. She has since returned to her job with American Safari Cruises. (Sources: 1) "Oregon Woman fights off Alaska bear," Associated Press, July 12, 2002, www.igorilla. com; 2) "Woman vs. bear woman wins," Katie Pesznecker, *Anchorage Daily News*, July 12, 2002)

BRENT HUGHES

Brent called me a few years ago with an interesting story about black bear behavior and Brent's decision regarding his personal safety. He sent me his story in an email April 27, 2008.

Brent spent three summers at a friend's Matanuska River Glacier cabin east of Anchorage some 100 miles. He loved the solitude and the freedom where he enjoyed nature, baking bread in a Dutch oven in his woodstove (the scent was heavenly and a principal delight) and working on various projects, which included some serious hiking. He was pretty much on his own with no one else around.

He spooked a black bear from his deck in mid-June 2002, by calmly stating to it that "you're not supposed to be here." And he had a couple of other encounters with bears that summer which ended with the bear's hightailing it. He did have a closer encounter with one during an extended 4-day hike up the glacier when he discovered that approach did not work and he called upon his .44 Magnum before the bear left on its own. But when he reached his home cabin, Brent had a most traumatic experience involving a bear which he relates.

Over the next couple of days I re-acclimated to "normal" life again by immersing myself deeply into a many-years-long math project which I was very nearly finished pursuing. It was a brilliantly glorious sunny morning, bread was baking in my Dutch oven nestled in the wood stove, and as I sat hunched over my notebook, driving in the final triumphant connections to deriving Abel's famous theorem of the impossibility of formulaic solvability of the quantic equation, the deeply cognitively intoxicating trance of the moment was interrupted by the impossibly unfathomable footsteps of what seemed to be yet another "large dog," not five feet from me somewhere now outside on the front porch, approaching somewhere near the closed door.

No telling how long it would have taken me to refocus from my contemplative stupor of the last stages of Abel's celebrated finale, were it not for the astounding appearance of a large black head in the corner of the large, low-lying window just feet from me now. I was shocked, but now no stranger to the thrill of close encounters with black bears—I again, calmly called out, "Hey, what are you doing here?" nonchalantly anticipating returning to my math.

But this black bear did not leave. It was staying. And stared at me. Interesting.

"Hey, beat it!" Oh, no, he had no intentions of leaving. He had but one plan, as it turned out. This clearly brought matters to a whole new level— and fast! Absolutely intent in driving matters to their proper textbook response, I stood up and, with the stern voice which had served me so successfully on my adventure only days before, I yelled confidently, gesturing with my arms, "Go on, beat it!!"

This is where the drama begins. Almost as if mocking me, as if to say "Is that the best you can do?," the bear slowly raised up on its hind legs and with its forepaws extended up "spread eagle" on the window pane, began bouncing its nose against the window as if perplexed that there was some impediment to its coming on in for what it appeared to have every intention of "getting."

Keenly aware that the morning's activities had been permanently reconfigured, I began to sense a slip into a primal state of "fight or flight." I had absolutely no intention of flight, but fighting with a bear was not really what I wanted to be doing this morning. I again yelled, and the bear dropped to all four feet. But then it raised up on its back feet again, and apparently more intent on getting through the window as it intensified batting its snout against the window.

Having had enough of this game, I immediately turned to go up to the loft where I kept my .44 Magnum pistol. Ascending the ladder to the loft, I was shocked to see the bear race past the side window to my left. As I reached my gun, kept by the loft window, I felt a calm settle over me, presuming—still in an emotionally primal state—that the bear had taken off, down the bluff in the same way the black bear had done on that rainy morning back in June.

I became noticeably unnerved when instead of relief at its disappearance, it was instead directly below the loft window, again standing on its hind legs with forearms outstretched upwards toward the loft window—staring straight at me! Alright, I get it. It wants ME!

I have but one last textbook act to employ, and by ripping the mosquito netting I had taken such pains to meticulously erect, I fired a single warning shot into the ground only a few feet from the bear. At that instant the bear raced off two steps, stopped, then loped back to its previous position under the window, and again raised up on its hind feet. That was really quite enough for me.

It is at this point that I reflexively move into a primal mind-set to make the decision to fight this thing with potentially lethal force—I abruptly moved to "autopilot," the first time in my life I have ever actually been in a potential "life and death" duel with another living entity. With gun in hand, and clearly "rattled," with rubber legs—simultaneously deeply confused and keenly focused—I climbed down the ladder to meet whatever "fate" was imminently to unfold.

As I stepped off the ladder, out of the corner of my right eye I caught the black streak of the bear racing back around to the front window to meet me. Up on its hind legs it went, front paws spread high on the window pane, now determinedly banging its head against the window, staring straight at me—only feet separating us as I now was screaming at it in a primal tone of voice that I had never heard before, and unnerves me to this day. I reflexively grabbed a pan and banged it on top of the wood stove in a last-ditch effort to exhaust the standard textbook methods of attempting to scare away a bear.

This bear had not read the book. This bear had but one game plan—clearly! As I realized in that escalating cauldron of directed yelling and conviction of potential impending doom for one of us—I silently passed into the ultimate reflex: feeling I had exhausted every option to halt imminent doom, I instinctively and defiantly raised my gun to just under its lower jaw, and now actually angry that it had forced my hand to this point, and with a loud blast, I executed this "murderer"!

(From a natural primal emotional flow I cognitively concluded it intended to "kill" me – but everything was pretty much "autopilot": I just wanted this "kiddo" to go play somewhere else. When it finally sunk in that it intended to press the issue of "getting" me, I felt it wanted to KILL me—again, at a fairly primal level. That is just a really, really surreal moment of raw reality. Not something I ever even contemplated in my imaginative meanderings throughout 59 years of life. So, yeah, the primal emotion during the instants that were flickering by were "this animal, given a chance, is going to do everything it can to KILL and EAT me!" Once that registered in a primal "mental space" I have never experienced before, I saw the bear for what was to me obvious: the "lad" intended to "murder" me in a macabre sort of way, I suppose that is a bit of a comical slant to characterize the starving guy was willing to settle for a weird looking 2-legged moose. But from my side of the window, the scenario pressing upon my mind was that the guy was going to "murder" me.)

The deadly tension that could have filled the cosmos at once vaporized—all was still!

The bear looked completely bewildered as it harmlessly, abruptly sat back on its haunches and just stared at me for what seemed like a perplexingly long period of time. Then very slowly, it leaned slowly to my left and simply toppled over across the door way. I instantly stepped to the window and looked down on the porch.

My indomitable rage and resolve to execute this "murderer" in the fleeting moments prior to the gun shot abruptly turned to profound sadness as I took the two steps over to open the door, only to witness the bear's claws slowly close while a final film of blood expanded from one nostril. I was so devastated with such profound sadness that I dragged a chair over to the doorway and just slumped in it, staring at the bear, lying in a massive pool of its own blood. [*It was to be several days before I emerged from the "slump" of having terminated the life of another living being. Odd that we kill a mosquito without giving it a thought,*

161

yet here I was having participated in the second saddest event of my life having killed a fellow mammal roughly my size. Sad stuff. Really sad. I am largely still not over the sadness. Yet I am sure I would not hesitate to respond to a similar threat in the future. A truly, profoundly contemplative life event, to be sure.]

After about an hour, I gathered my wits together, stepped over the bear and packrafted across the river to report the event to my friend who instructed me to eviscerate the bear and he would fly over to skin it and fly the hide back over for preparation to submit to the Park Rangers. I was amazed at finding that all of the bear's organs were practically like cellophane—there was very little mass to any of the organs. The intestines were completely devoid of any food with the exception of a few pathetic small green berries.

Upon delivering the hide to the chief ranger he said that the bear was starving, that teeth were worn down to the gum line and that it would never have made it through another winter. He said I probably did it a favor and a favor for the local population of cabins along the highway, inasmuch as bears in such a desperate condition due to starvation show no fear of humans and will invade domestic areas in desperation.

In retrospect, as badly as I felt about killing this bear, it was some consolation that had I not had a gun I might well shudder to contemplate an alternative outcome. I am deeply intrigued with whether or not bear spray would have been a successful deterrent. I now am an ardent supporter of bear spray based solely upon studies and accounts provided by others. But I think a firearm in a remote camp or domicile certainly is prudent in relatively remote bear country. For me, this will forever be more than a philosophical musing.

Was the visitor on that rainy June morning also visiting the environs of the nervous moose that beautiful evening prior to my four-day glacier adventure? And if so, was that visitor the same old boar that made its fateful calling during my early morning math studies—while baking bread?

Lest anyone be curious, the bread ended up over baked. I really should pay more attention next time. (APPENDIX 5)

PAUL and CHRISTINE COURTNEY

What may have started out as a "punk" adolescent bear trying to prove himself or a just plain curious animal, turned into a predacious attack.

Paul and Christine Courtney married in 1995 and immediately began a series of outdoor activities in order to satisfy their longing for the outdoor life which included hiking and canoeing. Although their knowledge of and experience with bears was limited, they chose to visit and enjoy the Yukon in June 1996. They flew to Whitehorse and rented a car to use in their sightseeing. Then they went to Kluane Provisional Park to spend a couple of days hiking and a night in the forest.

They viewed a park video on bear encounters that advised visitors on proper bear protocol and what to do if encountering one. They rented a metal container for food storage, hiked five and a half hours from the trailhead and set up camp for the night. Probably the only two people in the area.

Knowing that they were not permitted a firearm by park rules, Paul spent a restless night on the sloping ground compounded by the possibility of a bear problem. He felt vulnerable even though they did not discuss the threat as a couple. He was more than eager to leave the next morning for the second half of their hike.

They continued, taking pictures and enjoying their time together, anticipatory to their arrival at their vehicle later in the afternoon—glad that they had NOT seen a bear.

Two hours into their return they rounded a bend in the trail and spotted a bear a hundred yards ahead, approaching them. After traveling a couple of dozen yards they noted that the bear was following them. Hoping the bear would be distracted long enough to allow them to escape, they shed their backpacks. Unfortunately the bear ignored their packs and approached them, head down and soundless—a definite predatory posture.

Terrified, they acted upon misinformation and made a bad mistake— they chose to play dead. When the bear momentarily disappeared from their view, Paul assumed the play dead posture on the ground—fetal position with hands clasped behind his neck. Questions persisted in his mind: *Where is the bear? What is it doing?*

Then Paul heard Christine's call for help. He jumped to his feet and ran to his wife who lay on her side in the fetal position. The grizzly bit at the back of her neck.

Grabbing a 4-foot branch, Paul beat on the bear. For twenty seconds the bear endured the branch before it lunged at Paul and bit him in the lower leg. Paul stumbled downhill and behind a tree and the bear returned to Christine.

Paul immediately rushed to his wife's aid, again beating the bear with the branch.

Christine felt Paul's actions increased the bear's aggression and told Paul to stop. When he asked her if he should go for help, she concurred.

Picture this. They had hiked five and a half hours to reach their locale. Consider the length of most bear attacks—20-30 seconds. If a bear can break bones, remove ribs, scalp and inflict multiple injuries in 30 seconds, what can one do in 45 minutes? What is the likelihood that Christine would be alive when Paul or "rescuers" returned?

Paul bolted for the trail. He thought the trailhead was about three miles away. He reached the valley and crossed the river numerous times in his downstream travel. His trot, favoring his injured leg, became a limp. He continued while yelling for help in hopes of alerting someone.

When he spotted a person, Paul assumed he was nearing the trail and blurted out his situation. Because of the man's heavy German accent, it took a while for Paul to communicate his need. The man helped Paul down the trail to the parking lot. Then others engaged. One drove him to the park visitor's center where Paul hastened inside and expressed his emergency.

After the officials heard his emergency and the locale of the attack, Paul saw two men leave with firearms. However, it was an hour before two helicopters arrived and departed to locate Christine. Meanwhile other employees tried to console Paul.

Twenty minutes after the choppers had left, one returned for Paul's help in locating the attack scene. Although he could not find the bear or his wife, Paul succeeded in finding the general location. Shock began to affect him and he was returned to the center and given sedatives.

Two more agony filled hours elapsed before authorities returned and Paul learned about their efforts. They'd found and killed the grizzly which was in the process of burying Christine's body.

Paul was flown to the Whitehorse Hospital. (Source: *Bear Attacks II Myth & Reality*)

Even though Paul Courtney and his wife knew the risks about grizzlies, it didn't help. Paul later told his story "I Saw My Wife Get Killed by a Bear." From *Stuff Magazine*.com on line, 2/24/2003, as told to John Parrish.

We turned a corner on the track, and there it was. The brown coloring and the hump between its shoulders confirmed our worst fears—we were standing right in front of a large grizzly bear.

We'd both seen bears before, but this was different. For starters, the bear was only 100 yards away. There was no one else around, we had no weapons and there was nowhere to take shelter. In hushed voices, we debated what to do. I wanted to get off the road and into the bush so the bear couldn't see us, but my wife, Christine, thought it would be better if we walked backward slowly and allowed it to see us, in the hope it would slip away at the sight of humans.

It was the last day of our vacation in the Yukon, a wild and beautiful territory bordering Alaska and British Columbia. Our plan was to hike into the outback for a day, camp overnight in our tent and then walk back out the next day. We had left the Kluane National Park visitor center at about 11 AM to hike into the woods. Like most people from British Columbia, we knew a bit about bears, so we knew the risks. But we also knew the statistics, which show the risks are small and that bears usually avoid people. No one had been killed by a bear in Kluane.

After camping overnight—taking all the usual precautions, such as making sure we didn't cook next to the tent and keeping our food in an airtight canister—we'd packed up and moved out at first light. We wanted an early start because we were supposed to catch a flight to Vancouver later that day. To make good time, we headed back toward the visitor center on an old logging track. Two hours later we spotted the bear.

As we stood there stupefied, I noticed that the bear didn't seem to be aware of our presence. Quickly, I put an end to our indecision and persuaded Christine to follow my suggestion and make for the trees. Things might have turned out differently if we'd done what she'd wanted, but I'll never know. We went about 20 yards into the bush and came to a clearing. That's when I looked back and saw that the bear was coming after us.

One moment we'd been walking along happily, and within seconds we were in deep trouble. "Let's put our packs down," I said. I thought the bear would stop to investigate them. But he didn't. He just kept coming. You can't outrun a bear, and there were no big trees we could climb. It seemed our only option was to follow the advice on the information board at the visitor center: play dead.

We both dropped to the ground and got into fetal position, with our hands across the back of our necks for protection. A bear can break your neck with a single bite. In no time at all, the bear was standing over me. I was curled up tight and couldn't see him, but I knew he was there. I could hear him sniffing, and I could feel his hot breath on my face. He nuzzled me for what seemed like five, maybe ten minutes, then lost interest. That's when he padded over to Christine. I could hear him sniffing her and then heard something that filled me with dread. She began crying for help—the bear was biting her.

I felt fear like I've never felt before. I didn't know what to do, but I jumped up and scrambled around for a piece of wood, anything to hit the bear with. The bear was clawing at my wife and biting through her hands, trying to get at her neck. I picked up a branch, the strongest I could find, and attacked him.

I beat him around the head with all my strength. Blood was splattering the ground, and the bear seemed oblivious to what I was doing until, suddenly, he turned toward me. I tried to run, but only got a short distance before he knocked me down by taking a chunk out of my leg.

There was no pain. Shocked, I fell and managed to drag myself behind a tree, thinking, I'm going to die now. But then the bear headed back to Christine. It was like one of those nightmares you can't wake up from. I half hobbled, half ran back, picked up the branch and began hitting the bear again as it bit and clawed at her. I was screaming in fear, but Christine was so brave. She shouted for me to stop and said I was aggravating the bear more with what I was doing. "What should I do?" I asked desperately. "Go for help," she yelled. "Go for help!"

It was decision time. I could stay and continue attacking the bear or leave, try to find help and pray he'd lose interest in her. You can't make a decision like that without doubts and regrets, and I've gone over mine many times since. I'd tried fighting the bear and that hadn't worked. Should I have fought the bear harder? I don't know. I'd tried as hard as I could and still had no success; going for help seemed like the only option.

It was only about three miles to the visitor center, but in my panic I somehow got lost. I didn't know where I was, and as each minute passed I knew Christine's chances were getting worse. I ran along a riverbank yelling, not knowing where I was going. At some point, I don't know after how long, a hiker came out of the woods. I must have looked deranged. I told him what had happened and asked him to help me find my way back.

When I burst into the visitor center, it didn't take them long to figure out what had happened. A couple of guys armed with guns left immediately, and two helicopters were to follow. I felt ill now—it was the shock. And I was going out of my mind. The helicopters seemed to take so long to arrive, and nothing was happening.

A couple of hours passed. They gave me a tranquilizer and made me lie down on a stretcher. Someone strapped me to it, and then they told me: They had found Christine's body. Nothing in my life has ever been as awful as that moment. The bear had savaged her to death by the time they reached the clearing. He was digging a hole to hide his kill when the park rangers got there. They shot him and recovered Christine's body.

The bear was an adolescent male, about three years old and under seven feet in height. When its stomach was cut open, they only found bits of Christine's clothing; he hadn't begun eating her. I've never felt angry toward the bear—it was just doing what bears sometimes do.

Grizzlies are dangerous and unpredictable, and we were just in the wrong place at the wrong time. On another day, the same bear might have walked right by us, but on this day something about us alerted the predatory instincts in that grizzly.

Last year I went back to the clearing in the woods. It was a bit like a pilgrimage for me, I suppose, and I thought about whether Christine would still be alive if we'd followed her plan instead of mine. I've asked myself a thousand "what ifs" since then. What if I'd been carrying a weapon? What if I'd been stronger? I'll never know the answers. And nothing's going to change the fact that Christine died that day.

GLENDA ANN BRADLEY

Having read about the Smoky Mountain tragedy shortly after it occurred in May 2000, I contacted some people via the Internet and received little information, kind of a run around from agency to agency. I then Googled "Glenda Ann Bradley."

I became very angry when reading about the senseless death of a woman whom everybody loved. She'd gone to college and returned to Cosby, Tennessee, to teach at Jones Cove Elementary School.

When Glenda Ann Bradley and her former husband Ralph Hill left to enjoy a beautiful Sunday outing in the most visited national park in America, who could have guessed what they would experience? Around 2:00 PM Ralph left Glenda resting on the trail so that he could try one more fishing spot.

When Ralph returned and found Glenda Ann's pack near the confluence of Goshen Prong and Little River trails, he called for her but received no response. He looked into the woods and spotted two bears forty yards away. They guarded Glenda Ann's remains.

Ralph shouted and threw rocks at the bears, but they refused to budge. A dozen hikers, drawn to Ralph's cries for help, joined him trying to chase the bears from Glenda Ann's body. The animals showed no fear of the people and weren't about to give up their prey.

Hearing the ruckus, another fisherman saw what had happened and left for Elkmont Campground to find a park ranger, arriving about 5 PM; and a ranger was immediately dispatched to the scene.

For nearly three hours, Ralph and the group of hikers and campers watched in horror as the bears fed upon the 50-year-old school teacher.

Park rangers arrived just after 6 PM, saw the animals and shot them with their service weapons. The bears were sent to the University of

Tennessee of Veterinary Medicine Department for a necropsy.

Wildlife biologists had tagged the sow for research in 1998. To their knowledge she had not shown aggressive tendencies toward people up to the time of Glenda Ann's attack.

I am not alone when I state that Glenda Ann would be alive today had she carried a lethal weapon such as a handgun—I believe a .22 pistol would have saved her. But a larger caliber would have been better, like a .38, a 10 mm or a magnum in caliber .357, .41 or a .44. (Sources: 1) www.WorldNetDaily.com, "Where's the outrage for Glenda?," Henry Lamb, Posted: May 27, 2000, 1:00 AM Eastern, (Tuesday, January 30, 2007), 2) "Bear Attack in Great Smoky Mountains National Park," www. imagesbuilder.com/gsmnp/bear-attack-in-smokies.)

You can die alone as did Glenda Ann Bradley or surrounded by people...on a world class fishing stream or at a world renowned hot springs.

PATTI REED MC CONNELL

How could people be attacked by a bear in a public park? How could there be no means of self-protection...or even park officials prepared to protect campers.

Even though this was a predatory attack, I've chosen to place it in Chapter 10 Controversy under the heading Sensationalism...which will become evident to the reader.

GEORGE PETER DOERKSEN

George Peter Doerksen had earned his Ph. D. in Entomology and specialized in dragonflies. He was totally consumed by his study of the little "helicopters" and his photography and documentation of the insects. Although a sawmill employee in Tahsis, B.C., he had taken leave to visit Liard Hot Springs Provincial Park to further his studies for the University of Victoria.

The 41-year-old man had been in the area several weeks and was well known to the park staff. He worked out of his tent where he camped alone within 400 yards of the Liard Hot Springs grounds. His tent was near his vehicle about 200 yards from the Alaska Highway in an area not frequented by the general public. George kept a clean camp site and stored his food in the recommended manner.

Through countless days and nights in the field he had developed the idea that bears would not bother you if you didn't bother them. In spite of his sentiments about bears, however, one night George expressed concern about a bear that had visited his camp. Although park policy did not permit him to carry a firearm, he probably wouldn't have anyway. Nevertheless, he determined that if the bear returned, he would shout to scare the animal from his camp.

The night of July 30 was the last night anyone remembered seeing him at the Lower Liard Lodge. A couple of days later two young women, concerned about his absence, decided to check on him at his camp. They hiked to his tent on August 2, 1981, and discovered his tent smashed. Next to his car they saw a pool of dried blood. Further concerned, they returned to the park. The Park Ranger contacted the local Royal Canadian Mounted Police at the Fort Nelson detachment who in turn contacted the Conservation Office in Fort Nelson.

Two local trappers were asked to search the area of George's tent and vehicle.

Even though no problem bears had been reported in the area, reconstruction of the scene confirmed that a bear had visited George. His pants, shorts, socks and boots were at his tent. A large quantity of human blood not far from the shelter indicated that George had tried to escape the bear. His bed clothes were undisturbed in his tent, indicating that he was not dragged away but rather that he may have been carried or he may have run from the tent only to be overcome by the bear at that point.

Four-foot tall grass and dense brush compounded the search effort. However, during the initial search, ground searchers spotted a large bear and tracks measuring 10-inches across, made by a grizzly. Unfortunately, the dense brush prevented anyone from shooting it. Officials conducted an extensive three day search that included a professional hunter, ground searchers and a helicopter crew. From the air a second tent was discovered but it was unconfirmed as to whose it was and how it got there. On the morning of August 5 a grizzly was spotted from the air about 80-feet southwest of that tent. However, it disappeared into the thick brush.

The indications of the search revealed that after the bear had fought George near his tent, it dragged him through the tall grass to a ground cache about 100 yards, depositing him in heavy brush before raking four inches of soil and leaves over him. Evidence revealed that the bear fed on him for two to three days.

Officials never caught the guilty bear though they tried unsuccessfully to lure it to a bear trap with a foul moose carcass.

The coroner confirmed the bite marks on George's skull were made by a larger grizzly.

There is grave danger in assuming that you are safe from bear injury in bear country. Although George felt that his safety was assured, he was wrong. (Sources: I am indebted to Mike Cramond and Lori Jeffrey—for his authentic research-books and for her kind consideration and efforts in sending me the highlights of the incident. 1) *Of Bears and Man* and 2) email from Lori Jeffrey, Administration Clerk, Ministry of Environment, Ph: (250)787-3496 Fx: (250)787-3490, Lori.Jeffrey@gov.bc.ca.)

ESTHER SCHWIMMER—New York infant

August 2002. Woodridge in the Catskills. Family vacation. Infant asleep in a stroller in the front yard. "Bear! Bear! Bear!"

That was the scene at the Schwimmer family's summer bungalow in New York when Rachel Schwimmer heard a neighbor screaming. When Rachel saw the 150-pound black bear burst from the woods, she marshaled her two and four-year-old children to safety. However, before she could return for her five month old Esther, the bear had grabbed the baby in its jaws and headed for the woods.

Joined by her husband Pincus, Rachel and friends and neighbors yelled, waved their arms, chased the animal and threw rocks until it dropped Esther and fled into the forest. Pincus, sustained injury when he tried to tackle the bear.

Esther was rushed to Ellenville Hospital.

Officer David Decker of the Fallsburg police shot and killed the bear with his .40-caliber pistol. Unfortunately, the severe injuries to her head and neck resulted in Esther's death. (Sources: 1] "Woodridge Focus Of Tragedy," Matt Youngfrau, Sullivan County Democrat, www.sc-democrat.com; 2] "Parents look on helpless as bear snatches baby girl and kills her," John Innes, The Scotsman, Wed., 21 Aug 2002, http://thescotsman.scotsman.com)

ELORA PETRASEK

In April 2006 a mother from Clyde, Ohio, southwest of Sandusky, and her children visited Chilhowee Recreation Area in the Cherokee National Forest some 22 miles east of Cleveland, Tennessee. Susan Cenkus, 45-years-old, her daughter Elora Petrasek and her two-year-old son, Luke recreated at a pool below Benton Falls on Chilhowee Mountain in the Appalachians. That is the good news.

The bad news is that a black bear aggressively scaled a fence, bit Luke in the head and picked him up. Susan and others pelted the bear with rocks and sticks in an effort to deter it. Then the animal mauled her.

During the ensuing melee 6-year-old Elora ran from the area.

Rescuers arrived and provided medical support to Susan and Luke before flying them to Erlanger Medical Center in Chattanooga. Susan sustained eight puncture wounds in her neck and dozens to her body and was in critical condition. Even though Luke suffered punctures to his skull, he fared better as his condition was listed as stable. Doctors expect mother and son to make a full recovery.

In order to provide safety for campers and to allow rescuers to search for Elora the campground was evacuated. The Forest Service temporarily closed the campground and several roads and trails in the attack area. Forest rangers and local hunters searched for Elora.

When one of the searchers was a hundred yards down the trail from the falls, he discovered the bear guarding Elora's body.

Supposedly one of the men shot at the bear with a small caliber pistol but no blood or sign of an injury was noted. Finding the animal took precedence. In hopes of catching the bear, officials baited traps with pastries. Dogs were brought in. Wildlife officers planned to put out more traps.

Three days later one of eight traps baited for him caught the bear. It was euthanized and sent to the University of Tennessee's College of Veterinary Medicine in Knoxville. (Sources: 1] "Six-year-old killed in bear attack; mother, son expected to recover," Created: 4/14/2006 4:49:34 PM, Updated:4/14/2006 7:26:31 PM, 2006 Associated Press; 2] "Rangers catch bear after deadly attack," Animal suspected in Ohio family's mauling euthanized, Sunday, April 16, 2006; Posted: 6:08 PM EDT (22:08 GMT), www.cnn.com; 3] "Rare black bear attack kills girl in US campsite," *The Guardian*, Oliver Burkeman , Saturday April 15, 2006.rce)

RICHARD and KATHY HUFFMAN

What if you do everything right and you still have a bear in your lap?

That question was raised with the deaths of Anchorage attorney Richard Huffman and his teacher wife Kathy when they were discovered at their camp site. Some said that they did everything right, like Al and Joyce Thompson three decades earlier (*Alaska Bear Tales*). However, the facts may prove otherwise. In the case of the Thompsons, they set up their camp and seem to have done everything right. They slept beneath a visqueen lean-to when awakened by a brown bear which reared up and dropped onto the shelter. They escaped with injuries and scars. However, the Huffman's may not have known of grizzly activity in the area where they camped.

Rafting guide Robert Thompson and two clients spotted the camp and a blonde grizzly on Alaska's Hulahula River. The site was a shamble—gear strewn about, tent collapsed and both inflatable kayaks shredded.

Thompson wanted a closer look and paddled toward shore where a bear stood among the debris.

That's when the grizzly lunged toward them.

Hastily retreating, they dug their paddles into the water. The bear pursued them downriver—alternately plunging into the water to swim after them and taking to the shore and running parallel to the river. Fifteen minutes and a half mile later the bear was in the river only forty feet away and gaining.

Thompson rifled through his dry bag for his handgun and contemplated firing a warning shot. While anticipating his next move, he watched as the current slammed the bear into a boulder. The grizzly climbed onto the rock and watched the people as they drifted downstream.

Using his satellite phone the guide called authorities in the Inuit village of Kaktovik, twelve miles downriver on Barter Island just off the northern tip of Alaska in the Beaufort Sea near the Canadian border.

What began as a celebratory sixteenth wedding anniversary float in the Arctic National Wildlife Refuge ended tragically for Anchorage couple Richard and Kathy Huffman. They were experienced in the outdoors and camped safely and wisely. They always kept a clean campsite with their food in bear proof containers; they made a habit of cooking meals miles upstream before floating to their camping area. And the couple meticulously cached their edibles and toothpaste in bear proof containers away from their tent.

While loading his Cessna 206 preparatory to flying them to their drop off point, Tom Johnston of Kaktovik's Alaska Flyers, noticed the couple's gear—an emergency position indicating radio beacon, dry bags, bear proof food containers, canisters of pepper spray and a long gun in a soft case. Ever cautious, Kathy thoroughly grilled him before takeoff: what was his flying experience? What about his airplane's emergency equipment—where was it? What were his dispatcher's and state trooper's phone numbers?

Eight days after their June 23 departure onto the river, Richard and Kathy beached their kayaks and made camp for the night. Sometime that night a healthy grizzly showed up. He was six-feet long and weighed 300-pounds.

Responding to Robert Johnson's phone call, pilot Bob Mercier of the North Slope Borough Search and Rescue roared onto the scene in his Bell 412 helicopter. He hovered above the Huffman's camp and spotted the grizzly lingering near the deceased couple. Although the bear ran off a quarter mile, it did not leave. Because there were human fatalities, the pilot flew straight to Kaktovik and picked up Officer Richard Holschen of the North Slope Borough Police Department. On their return, the helicopter again scared the bear away from the bodies. Mercier touched down so Holschen could investigate.

Holschen, armed with a shotgun, waited for the bear to come closer. Although Holschen had successfully driven polar bears from town and whale carcasses, he was unnerved to see the grizzly lumbering back toward the campsite.

Meanwhile Mercier lifted off and his co-captain, Randy Crosby, chambered a round in his rifle. He then dropped the grizzly with four shots.

Initial examination of the scene revealed that Rich Huffman had tried to fend off the bear. His .45-70 CoPilot rifle was located near his leg with three rounds in the magazine, none in the chamber, the lever was extended. The couple was likely startled awake and trapped inside their tent with mere seconds to defend themselves. A personal locator beacon (PLB), still in its case, was located approximately ten feet from Kathy's body. The grizzly had fed on both Richard and Kathy.

Dick Shideler, biologist for the Alaska Department of Fish and Game, inspected the scene and discovered that almost every piece of gear was chewed and/or ripped apart. Although the campsite beneath the bluff along the river was protected from the wind, the bench above the camp where the tents and couple had been dragged bore signs of recent bear diggings.

The deceased were taken to Barrow and transported from there to Anchorage for funeral arrangements.

Some locals question a developing trend. The summer before the fatal attack Arctic Wild guide Jennifer van den Berg shouted at a bear that showed no signs of fear. Just prior to the Huffmans arrival, backpackers were bluff-charged by a grizzly.

The day before the Huffmans were discovered, a bush pilot dropped off recently retired USFW wildlife biologist Fran Mauer in the refuge. Concerned about the increasing bravado of the local bears the pilot asked Fran if he was packing a gun.

Having a bear about your camp is nerve tingling. Robert Thompson, the river guide who found the Huffmans' campsite, believes that a floorless tent, an electric fence, and a loaded pistol (that doesn't need to be cocked) might help future campers. He never uses bear proof canisters as he would rather have them eat the food than generate interest in him. He recommends stacking cook ware on food containers so that a snoopy bear will make noise while going for the food and thus alert the campers. An environmentalist and lifelong trapper and guide, admitted that his encounter with the grizzly was a determining factor in his decision to shoot to kill if another grizzly chases him.

My personal observation is that this was either a rogue bear with a chip on his shoulder or one that had previously encountered humans and successfully frightened them to its camp raiding advantage. I further theorize that they may have survived, maybe not even been mauled, if they'd had a dog in camp to warn them, a portable electric fence, a possible audible (to bears) electric buzzer, a Tom Hron PackAlarm or a motion detector audio instrument—something attachable to tents, packs, clothes. (SOURCES: 1] *Anchorage Daily News*, 7/7/05, "NECROPSY: Report offers no reason why bruin attacked couple," JEANNETTE J. LEE, The Associated Press, July 6, 2005; 2] U.S. Geological Survey: www.absc.usgs.gov, "ANWR Grizzly Attacks: They Did Everything Right," Jonathan Waterman, National Geographic; 3] personal email from Don Grimes, February 21, 2008)

And here's further nitwittery from the don't-eat-or-bother-animal-types:

An Associate Press piece, "BERLIN POLAR BEAR CUB AT CENTER OF ANIMAL RIGHTS BROUHAHA," on the Internet March 21, 2007 presents polar bear cub, cute, cuddly Knut. After he and his twin were born last December, their mother ignored them. The brother died. Zoo officials chose to raise the cub. However, one righteous individual proclaimed that it was inhumane to feed wild animals by hand—it breaks animal protection laws. He wants the cub killed. What? Would a living animal choose to live—whether in a cage or in the wilds—or be dead?

Methinks this protestor had too much fruitcake at Christmas and it hasn't worn off!

GREG FLAATEN

Two men pedaled their bikes through the timber. They regaled in the ride. That's when they spotted the bike and the bike helmet. Robert Earl and cycling buddy Robin Borstmayer rode the popular, densely wooded trail east of Tunnel Mountain Road on the outskirts of Banff. Earl immediately recognized the bike as that of Greg Flaaten, a fellow riding enthusiast. All three worked for the city of Banff.

Then they heard a shout from the woods off to one side, "Help, help me!"

Another shout warned them of a black bear's presence in the area. Realizing that the bear was between them and the victim, they formulated a plan—Banff town manager Earl remained while Borstmayer rode to the nearest campground for help.

When Borstmayer reached the campground, a park warden and a Royal Canadian Mounted Police officer returned with him to the attack site. Once on scene they observed drag marks and signs of a struggle. The young bear guarded its "catch," pacing and refusing to depart. But as people became more numerous, it reluctantly slipped away, periodically reappearing beyond a knoll some 50 yards distant. After 5 or 10 minutes the officials finally dispatched it and discovered that it was a male weighing about 120 pounds and appearing undernourished.

Flaaten, a 41-year-old experienced mountain biker and avid outdoorsman, wore headphones as he cycled alone. He had spotted the bear stalking him before it gave chase and separated him from his bike. The bear bit and clawed him while dragging him 75 yards from his bike, ten or fifteen minutes before his rescuers discovered his bike and broken helmet.

Flatten suffered chest and arm injuries and was rushed to Banff Mineral Springs Hospital thence medevaced by STARS to a Calgary hospital. He will need months of rehabilitation after reconstructive surgery to repair damage to his chest and right arm.

The bear did not damage the arm's artery or blood loss could have seriously compounded Flaaten's situation, causing loss of limb or life. (Author's comment: And this was a measly 120-pound bear) (Sources: 1) May 14, 2006, *Canadian Press* © 2006, Sunday; 2) "Bear attack victim 'lucky'", Sherri Zickefoose, szickefoose@*theherald*.canwest.com and Craig Douce, reporter/photographer for the *Rocky Mountain Outlook*, Sunday, May 14, 2006, Calgary Herald © The Calgary Herald 2006; 3) "Bear mauling victim faces months of rehab," Emma Poole, epoole@ *theherald.canwest*.com, Monday, May 15, 2006, *Calgary Herald* © The *Calgary Herald* 2006)

ISABELLE DUBE

Three friends jogged along a hiking trail near Silver Tip Golf Course west of Canmore, British Columbia when they encountered a grizzly around 2 PM June 5, 2005. Although her two friends ran toward the golf course, 35-year old mother and wife Isabelle Dube, Canmore resident, climbed a tree. The two hundred pound grizzly followed her up, pulled her from it and killed her.

Within minutes three mountain bikers—Cameron Baty, Brent Rosvold and Ari Carriere—hove onto the scene where the bear acted as if it were guarding a kill and approached them from behind a downed tree. The bikers retreated to the ninth fairway at Silver Tip, where the victim's jogging companions had fled to safety.

Isabelle's companions and the mountain bikers directed RCMP and fish and wildlife officers to the scene where they shot and killed the bear. It was the same one which had been wandering the area for weeks and had been live trapped, fitted with a radio collar and moved to an area inside the east boundary of Banff National Park. (I've wondered about the possibility that journalist Mike Cramond, author of numerous bear books, was correct. He theorized there might be a connection between mauling victims and man handled bears—those tranquilized, collared, tagged and tooth removal. He also questioned the relationship of numerous bear mauled victims in areas where man handled bears were transplanted.)

(Sources: 1] "Skiing Community Feels Loss of Isabelle Dube," Fri Jun 17, 2005 12:00 AM MDT, Canmore says goodbye to mom killed by grizzly: www.canmoreleader.com; 2] "Grizzly kills Isabelle Dube of Canmore," Bob Remington (rremington@*theherald.canwest*.com) www.trailpeak.com, Mon Jun 06 09:49:24 PDT 2005, *Calgary Herald* Copyright ©2001 - 2006 TrailPeak.com, Vancouver, BC)

DR. JACQUELINE PERRY

Vitas Abrutis and his son Rytis scared off a nuisance black bear that had bothered them about 50 miles north of Chapleau,Ontario, in Missinaibi Lake Provincial Park. Within thirty minutes they heard a man screaming, "Help, help!" as he frantically paddled his canoe toward them. Vitas noticed blood on Marc Jordan when he approached and heard him say that his wife was dead in his canoe. Deep wounds were noticeable on her body. Both Vitas and Rytis helped Jordan from his canoe and with the removal of his wife's body.

It appears that the same bear the Abrutises chased away earlier attacked Dr. Jacqueline Perry, 31, and her husband Marc Jordan, 30, at their remote campsite. Jordan stabbed it with a knife as the bear attacked his wife. The area is home to a large population of black bears, with increasing sightings since 2005.

The area's remoteness caused an hour delay before rescuers arrived. Jordan was flown to a Sudbury, Ontario, hospital suffering from severe lacerations. He was expected to require surgery and was listed in serious but stable condition Wednesday.

Police and wildlife officials hunted for the wounded black bear.

The attack is just the latest in a rash of bear attacks across Canada. A Manitoba man fended off a black bear in early September, just one week after a black bear killed another man in the province.

There have also been four grizzly attacks in Alberta since June, including the fatal one on a female jogger near Canmore (Isabelle Dube, above). A woman in British Columbia was also mauled in May.

"The black bear population in Ontario has exploded. It's just ballooned out of control," said Jim Lawrence of the Canadian Outdoor Heritage Alliance. The Northwestern Ontario Sportsmen's Alliance and the Canadian Outdoor Heritage Alliance say the spring hunt would help manage the number of black bears. They say without the hunt, bears no longer fear humans and consider people part of their "wilderness buffet."

Wildlife officials are predicting more encounters with bears as people continue to encroach on their habitats. (Source: "Fatal bear attack renews calls for bear hunt," Thu. Sept. 8, 2005 9:57 AM ET CTV.ca website, CTV.ca News Staff)

TOM TILLEY

After reading about the tragedy of Dr. Jaqueline Perry and her husband's efforts to fend off a bear with a Swiss army knife, Tom Tilley, 55-year-old outdoorsman from Waterloo, Ontario, Canada purchased a hunting knife. He had reason to express his gratitude for the information when he faced a black bear and used his knife to protect his dog in July 2006.

Tilley was four days into a twelve day canoe trip. While portaging his canoe near Wawa, some 136 miles north of Sault Ste. Marie, Tom heard his dog Sam, an American Staffordshire, growl at an approaching bear.

Tom spotted the bear stalking him and waved his arms while backing slowly away from it. That's when the animal cut off Tom's escape route.

That's also when Sam stepped between the bear and his master, distracting the 200-pound bruin which grabbed Sam by the back in its jaws.

Tilley jumped onto the bruin's back and stabbed it with his 6-inch blade.

After verifying the bear was dead Tilley noticed that he had a hand wound and that Sam had a couple of puncture wounds. Tilley paddled nearly an hour before encountering two Americans with a satellite phone.

Tilley praises his dog's warning and his love for his dog in the relative non-injurious outcome. (Source: July 23, 2006, 55 Year Old Ontario Man Kills Bear With Knife, The Right Stuff, Black Bear, Human Predation, *Natural History*, http//nevermelted.com)

Two hours after they called for help a cargo plane arrived, taking Tilley and his faithful pooch to Wawa where they received medical treatment. (Sources: 1] Ontario man and his dog survive black bear attack, Saturday, Jul. 22, 2006, CTV.ca News Staff, www.torontoctva. com, 2] Canoeist stabs bear to death in Ontario, www.cbc.ca)

DRILLER

In September 2002, a British Columbia oil driller boarded a helicopter in an effort to reach a mountain area where he hoped to make radio contact with home. On the return to his remote mining exploration camp he asked the pilot to drop him at a drilling platform. He planned to run a water line to another drill site preparatory for the night shift. The pilot dropped him off and departed.

Having been in the area for several weeks, the crew maintained a clean camp which negated visits from animals foraging for garbage. Neither the driller nor his crew had observed any bears in the immediate vicinity.

Nevertheless, sometime in the ensuing couple of hours as the man worked alone, a black bear attacked him.

When two workers arrived at the site two hours later for the night shift, they found the driller's backpack and a roll of hose in the trail. Cautiously approaching the drilling platform, they climbed onto the rig and found blood.

Next they were confronted by an aggressive black bear. They started a chainsaw and burned a torch to scare it.

Then they looked for their colleague and found his body thirty feet from the platform. The next morning the healthy animal was found and shot. Human remains were found in the animal's digestive system. Officials speculated that the bear may have never seen man previously. (Source: "Black Bear Kills Driller," [A Bongarde Media Company] Safety Smart! http://safety1st.gsfc.nasa.gov/safetynet/fatality)

ADELIA MAESTAS TRUJILLO

She lived in Cleveland, New Mexico, where she reared her children in traditional ways, using her wood stove to prepare beans and tamales. She demonstrated her love for family and friends by teaching and working with them. Adelia Maestas Trujillo, 93-year-old mother and grandmother, devoutly began each day with prayer. Although spunky and strong-willed, walking became harder with age; nevertheless she got around just fine and she insisted on living in her tin roofed adobe house.

After becoming a widow in 1989, Adelia worked with nearby elementary schools in the foster grandparent program where the children called her "grandma." Pleasant and deeply religious, she often visited the Mora Senior Citizens Center where her sister-in-law Ermelina Romero often joined her. One of Adelia's trademarks was blessing others, "May God bless you. May God take care of you."

Even though it was common during summers for Adelia and others to see bears leaving the foothills in the Sangre de Cristo Mountains to help themselves to the abundant chokecherries, plums and apples in surrounding meadows and roadsides, the summer of 2001 was different. The previous winter's frost had killed off much of the grasses, berries and young plants that bears rely on. Dry conditions didn't help. Neither did the orchards around Mora and Cleveland.

Bears dominated discussion in the valley 7,000 feet above sea level. A hot spot for community conversation was David Rael's El Nicho en Mora café which was a favorite hangout for Adelia. She frequently visited with friends at a booth near the front of the café after Sunday Mass.

Although hungry New Mexico bears harassed farm animals, dragged one camper from his sleeping bag and ransacked numerous kitchens, who would have thought that one would kill Adelia?

Saturday August 18, 2001, her son, who lived next door, went to his mother's and found her body in the kitchen next to her bedroom. He had heard nothing unusual.

Investigation by officials revealed that a bear had entered the house through the kitchen door where they found a broken pane of glass. They discovered that Adelia had cooked no foods, none was sitting out nor was there refuse that might attract a bear during the daytime attack.

The medical examiner listed the cause of death as multiple bite wounds inflicted by an American black bear.

News of Adelia's death shocked and sickened friends and neighbors. Some expressed fear. One lady told of being afraid at night and asking God to help her. Another lady admitted that she feared for her children's safety during the day and that she no longer trusted bears.

Using tracking dogs, authorities followed the guilty bear, a 4-year-old boar weighing 250-pounds, found it and shot it a half mile away.

In 2001 the Department of Game and Fish in Raton, 80 miles northwest of Mora received four times as many bear sighting phone calls as in the previous worst year—about 100 bear complaints a day. Because of potential danger to people, numerous bears were destroyed in the Moreno Valley and outlying areas.

During the same time frame another New Mexico resident had problems with a black bear in his house. (*The Taos News*, August 23-30, 2001, Taos, New Mexico, "Taos man shoots bear twice in his kitchen," by Cornelia de Bruin)

Tuesday morning August 21 Charles Dean was awakened by loud noises. He interrupted a 300 pound black bear which was snooping for food in his kitchen sink. Charles fired a couple of rounds at the bear which promptly fled the house. His microwave oven and a couple of cabinets were not so fortunate as the bear.

Trackers followed the bear with tracking dogs, and ended the 10-year-old burglar's bent for breaking and entering. According to the bruin's rap sheet, he had previously been in trouble with homeowners. (Sources: 1] *Sangre de Cristo Chronicle*, Thurs., Aug. 23, 2001, Jessica Johnson, staff writer, Vol. 27, Number 34 Angel Fire, NM; 2] 93-year-old woman becomes first victim in the past century, www.bitterroot.com/grizzly, September 4, 2001, Bear attack hits home in New Mexico, by DEBORAH BAKER Associated Press)

CLAUDIA HUBER

In October 2014 my daughter Jill sent me a link to a mauling fatality near Teslin Lake, Yukon Territory. Internet articles revealed that on Saturday the 18th Claudia Huber and Matthias Liniger's dog Kona was barking. Matthias went outside to calm the Alaska malamute and discovered a grizzly in the yard. Matthias entered the house to retrieve his rifle during which time the bear entered the domicile through a window. Both Claudia and Matthias exited the house, the bear attacked Claudia, Matt shot and killed the bear and hastened his seriously injured wife into his Toyota pickup and to medical treatment twenty minutes away at the Teslin Medical Center. Although CPR was performed for half hour, Claudia's injuries proved fatal.

Officials discovered the boar was 25-years-old and 100-pounds-underweight (375 pounds). The animal was not starving and there were no food attractants found at their Four Mile Creek home.

(Author's update: While surfing the internet December 30, 2015, I came across a piece from CNN, "Coroner: Woman mauled by grizzly died from gunshot wound" Dec. 25, 2015. After the autopsy Chief Coroner Kirsten Macdonald reported a tree branch deflected Matthias' bullet, striking Claudia in the chest.)

Predatory attacks chart from above incidents:

Date	Victim(s)	Type bear	Fatal
7/1980	Stephen Routh	black	
7/1981	George Doerksen	grizzly	X
1981	Marty Miller	black	

11/30/93	Don Chaffin	polar	
9/1994	Ian Dunbar	black	X
5/95	Daniel Marchuk	black	
5/96	Sven Satre	black	X
5/96	Christine Courtney	grizzly	X
8/97	Patti Reed McConnell	black	X
8/97	Ray Kitchen	black	X
5/2000	Glenda Ann Bradley	black	X
7/2000	Mary Beth Miller	black	X
8/2001	Adelia Maestas Trujillo	black	X
7/02	Kristy Abbott	black	
8/02	Ester Schwimmer	black	X
9/02	B.C. oil worker	black	X
10/02	aunt	black	
6/05	Isabelle Dube	grizzly	X
7/05	Richard, Kathy Huffman	grizzly	XX
9/05	Jaqueline Perry	black	X
4/06	Elora Petsarek	black	X
5/06	Greg Flaaten	black	
7/06	Tom Tilley	black	
10/14	Claudia Huber	grizzly	X

Gary Shelton states in *Bear Attacks II Myth and Reality*, (Pg. 34), "Most tourists who come to B.C. aren't afraid of black bears and have no clue that a black bear could stalk, kill, and eat them."

As Jim Leslie hiked solo on the popular McHugh Trail southeast of Anchorage, armed with a .44 Magnum pistol, he encountered a 250-pound mother black bear with two cubs. Instead of exhibiting typical behavior and fleeing, these bears closed in on him. As they closed the distance, Leslie fired a warning shot, scaring one cub up a tree. However, when it descended, the bears advanced toward him. They made solid eye contact, never taking their eyes off him as they advanced, making no sounds.

When the bears got inside one hundred feet, Leslie fired another warning shot with his handgun. One bear jumped off the trail and, to his joy, the others followed and left.

He later admitted to being afraid for his life.

One official stated that he felt the bears were somewhat habituated to humans. (Source: McHugh Creek hiker tells of being stalked by 3 bears, ENCOUNTER: Jim Leslie says behavior of sow and cubs was out of character, CRAIG MEDRED, *Anchorage Daily News*, June 1, 2003)

My friend Cas Gadonski suggested the preceding story demonstrates textbook behavior of a mother bear teaching her cubs how to hunt—surrounding people with their cubs, advancing noiselessly, zeroing in on the victim… "In yesterday's *Anchorage Daily News* there's an article about a hiker at McHugh Creek on the south outskirts of Anchorage. He has a .44 Magnum handgun and a cell phone. He was approached and surrounded by 3 Black Bears...momma and 2 young ones and they were stalking him. He was in a panic, called 911 for help, fired 2 warning shots...and finally the bears left. Go check the story out...it is poorly written with the typical Left-wing newspaper attitude of 'oh, bears frequently do this, they cause no harm' type of color. Fact is Larry, this guy was in deep do-do and he knew it. I've heard of grizzlies doing the same thing...momma teaching her young ones how to hunt as they surround the victim and slowly move in for the kill." (Source: email from Cas June 2, 2003)

While hiking the Campbell Tract in east Anchorage in August 2002, Gene Trumbo ran into two black bears—a big one and a small one. He immediately turned around to retrace his steps with the larger one following him, not 50-feet away. Every 50-feet Trumbo turned and yelled at the bear which pursued unfazed, actually closing the gap between them.

At that point Gene rushed the bear, frightening it into leaving. ("If you bully back, they think people are more dangerous than they look," said Alaska Department of Fish and Game bear man Rick Sinnott.) (Source: Hungry-looking black bear gives hikers a scare, Stubborn pair of Campbell Tract bruins worry Fish and Game biologists, Zaz Hollander, Craig Medred, *Anchorage Daily News*, August 16, 2002)

I surfed the Internet July 29, 2006, and listed the following dealing with bear attacks, causing me to wonder if we're witnessing more bear attacks and increasing attacks by blacks?

Fatal bear attacks by decades:

Total	black	grizzly	polar	unknown species
2000's	17	12	5	0
1990's	11	2	6	3
1980's	9	0	7	2
1970's	4	2	2	0

1960's	3	1	2	0
1940's	1	0	0	1
1916	1	0	1	0

MYSTERIOUS-UNUSUAL ATTACKS

Some bear attacks may not fall under a defensive or a predatory attack. Perhaps they are of such a nature as to be described as mysterious. One such attack took place in a national park. Maybe the animal had been conditioned by its association with people and chose to impose its will in this case. I emailed John Conard as follows:

Sent: Monday, February 23, 2004 3:13 PM
Subject: your query
John,
Thanks for your kind query. My son-in-law forwarded your message. I just returned from ID and mother's funeral.

I'd be delighted to see your story. Suggest you paste to your email because I can't open attachments. Looking forward to seeing it. Am constantly looking for good stories (hopefully to be presented in the words of the "victim"--since it's their story and best told in their words).

thanks again.
Best wishes,
Larry

Dear Larry: I'm sorry to hear about your loss. These times are always tough for families.

I appreciate your willingness to read my letter.

This is a letter that my Great Aunt Florence Shanstrom wrote to her mother (my Great Grandmother) on Sept. 8th, 1930. I have the original in my possession. The original is pretty powerful because by the end of the letter you realize that Florence typed the letter one-handed on a manual typewriter because her left arm had been terribly mauled by a bear. I spent about 4 hours typing this on a PC with a good word processor and I was worn out! If you are interested I would be happy to send you a copy of the original. It has a totally different feel than this "sanitized" e-mail version. Still, it is a good read.

Here is the letter. I have corrected a few of the more obvious typographical errors.

Dear Mother, Sept. 8, 1930

We arrived home today, or this morning, at two o'clock. We thought we would rather keep on coming than to stop because we could rest all day after we got here; it was a lovely night to drive and we are glad we did come on as today is rainy and we would have to be so careful. I am very much better and stood the trip very nicely and was stronger when I got here than when I left the hospital. Riding in the fresh air was good for me, but part of the time I thought I could not ride any farther or sit up any longer. My arm is healing up nicely. I cannot use it at all yet nor even move my fingers. But as soon as the new tissue is strong enough and is built up enough I can take the left hand and make the fingers work and they will soon be all right again. But I cannot yet because it would tear the arm apart. The whole thing seems so unreal. We had such a nice time until then.

We arrived at the park Sunday evening just in time to camp for the night, got up early next morning and started out to see the sights. Our route took us first to the geysers for which I am now thankful because otherwise I could not have seen them. They are very beautiful and wonderful. But I could not keep back the thought that someday the whole thing will blow up and I am sure it will do so. As you walk around looking at the geysers your feet almost burn. And as you watch the geysers bubbling and boiling and then see them spouting way up in the air you realize that underneath is an immense cauldron of boiling water and fire. All around are openings of various sizes with steam escaping constantly so that from a distance it looks like the whole place is on fire. There are several pools of boiling mud that looks so wicked the mud boils constantly day and night; then there are many pools of hot water, deep, quiet, beautiful; to me each pool seemed so menacing and I said to the boys it is beautiful but terrible, almost horrifying. On some of the pools it looks like flames leaping up from the water and one pool called Fire Hole looks like a roaring furnace of many colored flames. It is steam instead of flames though and is colored by varicolored living organisms of a very low form of life which live in the hot water and are reflected in the steam. There are lovely terraces containing every color of the rainbow. We spent all morning looking at these things then got something to eat and started on the next part of our trip through the park and had gone about two miles when we saw a black bear near the road side and decided to take a picture of it.

So we stopped and took the picture. We saw so many people taking pictures of bears that we did not think there was any danger especially as we did not go near but kept our distance. While we watched we leaned against the car; we could not get in until the boys did and suddenly the bear started over towards us and first thing we knew he was right by us and before we could think he rose up on his hind legs and made a grab for me. I dodged but he got my arm in his mouth and bit out a big piece between the elbow and wrist and scratched the rest of it badly. We all yelled and I ran around the car. Then the bear started to get in the car via the front door which was closed. But he squeezed in through the glass part which was open. Esther (Florence's young daughter) was in there on the back seat and oh it was so terrible to see him climbing in and we could not stop him. We had things packed on the other side of the car and could not open those doors. But he couldn't get his hind legs in so he picked up a package from the front seat and made off with it. It turned out to be a sack of canned goods that we had bought for our supper.

Until after he left I did not know that I was hurt so badly. My arm just had a stinging, burning sensation and when I had time to look at it after the bear had gone I was shocked. There was a hole five inches long and three inches wide with the bone exposed. We were two miles from a ranger station. So we hurried there and asked where we could get a doctor. The ranger said "One hundred miles from here." I asked him to tell us just how to get there so we would not have to lose any time getting there. He asked are you sure you need a doctor? We have a trained nurse here. Will she do? I said I must have a doctor quick and removed the bandage I had put on my arm. he said you need more than a doctor, you need a hospital and I will open up a shorter road for you so you will only have to go fifty miles. It is a one way road and you will have to go the wrong way over it. But just keep right on going as I will open it up and keep it open and cleared for you until you get there. No one will stop you and I will telephone the doctor to be ready for you.

The road was like all roads in Yellowstone Park, a dangerous one full of sharp curves and steep grades so it took us two hours to get to the hospital. The doctor took me in the operating room and after looking at the wound said is the damnedest worst arm I ever saw and I can't give you anything to ease the pain while I am working on it. If it was just a cut to be sewed up I could use a local anesthetic. But I have to pull the remaining flesh together to cover that big gap in your arm and we will have to fight like hell to make the flesh live after all that strain is placed on it. It can't live if it is numbed from anesthetic in addition. I can give you ether if you insist but that will lessen your chances of recovery. That arm is worse than dynamite and you need all your resistance to counteract the bear bite.

I said go ahead I can stand the pain all right. He told me I could lay down if I wished. But I said I would rather sit up. Then he tied up an artery and two veins and took eighteen stitches. Each one an inch back from the edge of the wound and even then, three of them broke because the strain was too great. He cussed like a trooper. When he had finished and I had not made any sound or groaned or anything he said "you are a brick" and the nurse who was helping said "Oh I'll say she is a brick." Then he said "I can't turn you loose with an arm like that. You will have to stay here and fight like hell." And I said, "I have fought like that before so I can again." Then he had a nurse put me to bed and I laid there fifteen days and did fight like hell to get well. The first two days he had the violet ray turned constant on my arm. He had made the arm look so much better than I had thought possible. It had just one long seam five inches long and it seemed to be healing up so nicely. I was quite pleased.

But on the sixth day it all blew up. Every stitch had become infected and the doctor had to take them out, then the seam began to spread. So he took some more stitches. And two days later they were too full of pus and had to be taken out. Some of flesh decayed and had to be cut out. The doctor said "that blankety, blank arm has not done one thing I wanted it to do, blankety blank, blank. You have been a wonderful patient though and we will win out. It is just a case of beating the game and you are doing your part. It is the poison from the blankety, blank beast's teeth that is doing the damn work now; it is what I expected. I had a really hard time with it. but oh I was so thankful that it was me instead of one of the children. And thankfully, it was no worse.

Last Monday the doctor said that if I really felt that I must go home he thought I could go the next day, but he advised me to stay longer and would graft some skin on the raw part. But I felt that if it would heal up at all I was lucky and better leave well enough alone and school had begun too. So at three o'clock Tuesday PM, he said I could go and sent a nurse to dress me. The boys had the car all packed and waiting so as soon as I was dressed we started.

The hospital is up in the northwest corner of the park so we had to come seventy-five miles through the park and it was an awful ride. Of course, I noticed it more than the others because my nerves none too good by that time. The road is very narrow and full of sharp turns and steep grades. We crossed the continental divide there too. when we were about half way we saw a a large sign which read "look out for rolling stones and blasting." We could not turn and go back. There was no room to run in so we went on and nothing happened except that we were all tired out from the strain. As we went through the east gate we all said,

"Thank goodness we are out of the park". All that road was on the side of the mount, a shelf road. We camped that night a few miles from the park. I couldn't walk alone nor dress or undress. So the children had to help me with everything. I did not think it safe for me to sleep in a tent so we slept in cabins each night and ate at restaurants. Each day I gained in strength and today I can go alone if I don't go too far. We started early each day and drove as late as we could and yesterday we decided we would try to keep on until we got here.

Vernon (Florence's husband) was very much surprised and glad to see us. He had wired me to come on the train, but I could not let the children come alone over those mountains. I asked the boys to write to you every day while I was in the hospital and thought they had done so until I got here. I am sorry they did not. I was too sick to ask them or to a talk much. I found your letters and Jessie's (Florence's sister) this morning and am so very glad to get them. I sent you a card every day along the way and mailed the last one jut about ten minutes before the accident. I don't see where they went.

Everyone was so very, very good to me while I was laid up. It is a government hospital, but we had to pay of course. It is only open during the park season and is filled with people who come there for a vacation and wind up in bed there instead. When I went there they only had one bed left and it was in a room with two other women. I was thankful to get it but I asked them to give me the first room they had vacant. Soon a man was able to leave and I expected to get that room next morning. About midnight two nurses came in and moved me. I asked what the grand rush was about and they said we have another patient and want you to have the single room.

It was a beautiful room. People who live there send flowers to the hospital and the nurses kept some in my room all the time. One day two of my friends from here came in. They had gone to the telegraph office to send a message home and the operator told them I was there so they came right over. I guess this is enough about the accident.

We slept this morning until ten o'clock and just as we were ready to sit down to breakfast here came Ben Romig and a friend of his. He did not know I had been gone and did not stay long. He said he will come back soon. He wanted to find out the road to your home and plans to go and see you this fall. This is a very crude letter. I am using my left hand on Elmer's typewriter and hit the wrong keys half the time. I don't seem to be able to get any punctuation marks at all.

They had some rain while we were gone so our yard looks nice now. I will try to get someone over to come in and clean up the house. It is very dusty all over. Miss Reis has quit going out to work and does baking for a store. It won't be long now until I can do some work myself and oh won't I be glad when I can. I am absolutely out of danger now and my arm is healing fast. The seam is nearly grown together and although the place where he had to cut out the dead flesh is raw and bleeding some it will soon heal over. It was just the top part that he had cut out and the bone is all covered. There will be a bad scar but just now it doesn't seem to make me feel at all sorry. I can only feel a great thankfulness because I did not have to lose my arm and because it was not one of the children. I use cuticura on the wound and you know that it is so soothing.

No the Government cannot be held responsible. Although I think it should be. When you enter the park you have to pay three dollars for a permit to drive your car in the park. And on this permit it states the government is not in any way responsible for accidents of any kind. It also says that anyone who teases or molests the bears or other animals will be prosecuted and fined from one hundred to five hundred dollars. So if I had bitten the bear I would have been arrested and taken to the park officials and fined. but as it is I stand the pain and expense and all. I have since read a govt. pamphlet in which it states that there is no such thing as a tame bear. All bears are treacherous and some are vicious it all states that the ground around the geysers is composed of travetine and is very thing and dangerous to walk on. But the only way you can get one of these booklets is to send to the government and ask for it, and the average person does not know there is such a book. There should be signs up where people can read them. They soft-pedal all the dangers and advertise the tame bears, etc., and people are invited to come each evening to see the bears eat their supper. Big logs are placed around for people to sit on and they don't know that two rangers with loaded guns in hand are watching every move the bears make. When I told the ranger I needed a doctor he described the place where that bear was and asked it that was where it happened. I said yes then he asked if it was a big black bear. And said I know him he has become mean and we have been trying for several days to shoot him. We will get him now. If people knew what we do they would not come to the park. He said a bear will be nice to three people and then without any warning bite the fourth one. While I was in the hospital ten people died from heart attacks. The doctor said it was the high altitude that caused it and that no one should go there unless they are sure they have a good heart. I think the dangerous roads helps to cause the attack.

People should be told the true conditions there. This government booklet says that the park is of volcanic origin and no geologist would dare to say that it will not at some time erupt again. Electric Mountain is so charged with electricity that if you stand anywhere on it and touch anybody or anything you will receive a terrible shock and you simply can't stay on it in a storm. We walked all over that dangerous travetine in blissful ignorance as all the others we saw. There are many beautiful things in the park worth seeing but I think people should know the dangers so they can avoid them. The boys saw people whose cars had been ruined by bears. The glass broken and tops caved in and upholstering torn off the seats.

When we left you we went to Denver as we had planned we just missed a terrible storm and part of the way water was running over the road but not enough to be dangerous at that time. Next morning we read that the road was washed out so we had crossed none too soon.

Next morning we went to the automobile club to find out about the roads. They told us that all the routes to the park were closed and would be for ten days because of washouts. We could stay in Denver or go over the mountains to Salt Lake City and west gate of Yellowstone Park. We thought we might as well be driving as waiting so we went on after a night and morning at Idaho Springs. I wanted so much to go to Central city but it was raining and did not seem best to go. But it would have been nothing compared to what we went through later.

The only road open was the one through Idaho Springs and on over Berthoud Pass. When we got to Salt Lake City we learned that the road we came over was closed just about half an hour after we started. We drove one whole day in second gear and only went fifty miles. The mud was terrible, and it was a shelf road very narrow with a deep canyon below. We met a few cars and the folks looked as scared as we felt. Each time we met a car both had to stop and someone from each car got out and helped push the cars past each other. Otherwise one car would have gone over the cliff. This was near Rabbit Ear Pass, we got a cabin that night with a stove and fire. Next morning the mud had dried off so it was safe to go. I was going to stay at that cabin until it was safe. All day on that awful road with not chance to stop. No chance to turn back, no place to stop. No cabin or house or filling station. Nothing but mud and upgrade all the way. It took twenty gallons of gasoline to get us that fifty miles and we pulled in that filling station with our gas tank almost empty. Maybe I wasn't glad to see that cabin too.

It was getting dusk and so cold. The rest of the trip was not so bad and when we to Salt Lake City we went to the auto club to ask about the route to the park and the girl at the desk asked how we got there. We told here and she said you could not have come that way because that road is closed and has been since Monday noon. We said we have been over it ever since Monday noon too. We had a nice time at Salt Lake City and all went in bathing in the lake and had a grand time. We drove around and saw the city then headed north for Yellowstone. This road was just opened up while we were at the auto club. The state engineer came in while we were waiting and said we have just this minute opened the road to Y.P. It is bad but cars can get through with care. The road was fairly good but oh the wreckage along the mountainside was terrible Cloudbursts and landslides had destroyed many homes and we saw families with shovels and picks trying to dig their way into their homes which were buried two thirds deep in mud and rocks. Many houses were destroyed and only the front wall and porch left standing. When we entered the park the ranger told us that all the other roads were closed and people waiting for a chance to go on. At Cody were two thousand more than the town could take care of and they were sleeping in the school houses, picture shows, and churches. They reached the park two days after we did. This brings us up to where I began my letter and I had better stop. It will take a week to figure this out. This is Monday now. I started yesterday but have written most of it today. I can't work so I might as well write even if I have been too long winded.

Will you please let Jessie read this too and I will write to you both soon. I too felt that I should not go to Y.P. that is why I did not mention it sooner. I hoped some real reason would develop for not going and when it didn't I tried to talk the boys out of going. They wanted to go and I decided it was silly no to accept Vernon's gift of that trip. I wasn't real sure that it was the park that held the danger for me although it seemed to be. I would very much rather have stayed longer with you.

Sending ever and ever so much love I will stop.

Florence

KEN CATES

If it could happen to Ken Cates, couldn't it happen to anyone? A genuine outdoors-Alaskan, given to the pursuits therein—hunting, fishing, hiking—Ken had knocked around Alaska forty-five years. The outdoors was his second home.

Who's to say what really happened that Tuesday in May 1999. Reminding his wife Sharon of 35 years that he'd be home around 4 o'clock, Ken left his Soldotna, Alaska, home at noon for a standard hike up Funny River trail half dozen miles from town in the Kenai Wildlife Refuge, home to moose, wolves, black and brown bear.

A glorious spring day beckoned him, cloudy with mid-fifty-degree temperature. Shouldering his camouflaged backpack and his Winchester .280 bolt action rifle, Cates set off from the trailhead.

However when he hadn't arrived at his appointed time, Sharon's concern mounted. Something serious had happened or he would be out by now. Two hours later she and a friend drove to the Funny River area where they spotted his truck at the trailhead. He wasn't there. Sharon called the Alaskan State Troopers at 10:00 PM and they tried to reassure her that people often work their way from the maze of trails, arriving late no worse for wear.

Sharon knew her husband. This guy was an expert marksman who reloaded his ammo in his basement. He was experienced in the woods. He'd made many safe, solo trips. He was in excellent physical condition, a plus for the slender, 5' 10" 53-year old. Where was he? Was he okay?

They'd have to search for Ken. Sharon called Ken's hunting buddies and friends. They knew he was in trouble.

Early the next morning forty people showed up to begin their mission. A Civil Air Patrol plane searched from the air while the ground party followed a foot and a half wide sliver of muddy trail through the leafless spring timber. The searchers noted Ken's boot prints. Before long, to their surprise and consternation, they discovered a set of brown bear tracks over Ken's, traveling the same direction.

Two miles from the trailhead and just beyond a 90 degree bend in the trail the searchers came upon Ken Cates' body. Ken bore tooth marks on his head, which proved to be a single bite that crushed his skull and killed him instantly.

Ken's rifle lay several yards away, a spent cartridge on the ground and a spent round in the chamber with his third cartridge in the magazine. Brown bear hair and blood were found on a nearby tree, indicating that Ken had hit the bear somewhere at least once.

Atop his MSR stove on the ground was a pan of water. Evidence indicated that he'd prepared to heat water for his Top Ramen soup when a bear surprised him.

Some speculate that the bear stalked Ken and attacked as he prepared his meal, perhaps taking advantage of the distance Ken may have been from his rifle. Or perhaps the bear and Ken met by coincidence. Maybe the bear surprised Ken's cooking efforts.

In spite of an exhaustive search, the bear was never found. Some wonder if it died or may yet be lurking in the forest.

Adding to the mystery was the discovery of a dig next to the trail. Why would a bear scrape away ground cover and dig a hole if not to prepare a food cache or to dig a wallow to escape the heat? Some say that brown bear boars do not cotton to human urine…and that they tend to make a dig in such spots where it is encountered. Is it possible that Cates relieved himself near his cooking area and the bear took exception to his action? (Source: www.ultimatesportsmen.com, Tales of the Ultimate Sportsmen, "Bear Attack" by Jim Oltersdorf, Writer/Photographer, Soldotna, Alaska)

TARA EDWARDS, JENNIFER SCHRAGE and STEPHANY THOMAS

I was amazed to hear about three ladies who had an encounter with a bear in Anchorage's Kincaid Park in July 2008. They told me they were jogging when they saw the bear, I said, "Yeah, it probably thought 'there are three hot chicks. I think I'll jog with them.'"

I met them at the Edwards' home January 19, 2008, and they were ebullient in their portrayal of their experience…so much so that when I attempted to transcribe their comments, different voices interrupted each other and I had trouble discerning which voice belonged to which lady. I decided to summarize the beginning of the interview then to conclude by using their names for identification followed by their comments. Their comments rivaled three excited teenagers at an Elvis, Beatles or Jonas Brothers concert.

Prior to their experience six months earlier Tara Edwards, Jennifer Schrage and Stephanie Thomas had stretched, warmed up and started on their morning run on the dew covered dirt trail that wound through birch trees among the low birch covered hills. Jennifer suggested they depart from usual and start from Jodphur. Temperatures registered in the high 50's when they left the parking lot between 7 and 8 AM.

Before long they jogged onto Lyderberg trail, crossed the bridge and started up the long gravel hill that parallels the road, toward the chalet. They ran abreast with Stephanie in the middle.

They were ten minutes into their run and part way up the hill when Jennifer said," Oh, there's a bear." They agreed it was cute, adorable and huge. Jennifer added, "Man, I've lived here for such a long time but I've never seen a bear." At that point the black bear was 200 yards in front of them.

They thought they could make noise and the bear would be long gone by the time they reached its location.

That was okay with Stephanie who was not thrilled with the possibility of a race with the bear—she knew she was the slowest in the group and admitted, "All you have to do is not be the slowest one…and that would be me. If we get in a race with a bear, I'm pretty sure I would lose."

They considered their safest means of avoiding the bear and getting away from it.

After they passed the bear's location, Tara was looking over her shoulder and said, "You know what, guys, it's just following us. We may need to get off the trail." They turned back to the Lakewood bridge and began talking a little louder and made more noise. *Yoohoo!*

Jennifer stated, "We were in the worst place we could have been at Kincaid because there were no trails to get us anywhere other than the Lake Loop.

Stephanie admitted, "What was normal for us, we would not see anyone. So I thought 'if anyone comes along, it would a flat out miracle because we never saw anybody while we were...there never were bikers or anything.'"

Jennifer said, "Run faster; you have to run faster."

Stephanie thought, "I'm like, 'I'm running as fast as I can.' I was trying my hardest but I have no kick." Then she turned her head to look back and all she saw was black fuzz. She announced to the others, "I felt something on the back of my leg."

Jennifer said, "Oh, you did?" And thinking they needed to get to another trail, she bolted into the underbrush. Then she realized *there are no other trails out here.*

At that point the women realized that they needed to regroup, that they weren't supposed to run and shouldn't.

Watching Jennifer leave them, Tara and Stephanie were thinking that Jennifer did not make a good running buddy.

When Jennifer left the trail, the bear skirted around Stephanie, pursuing Jennifer who was ten yards off the trail in the alders, devil's club and tall grass. Tara and Stephanie yelled, "Jen, the bear's right behind you!"

The bear had no trouble but Jen picked her way through the foliage.

Jennifer: That's when I tripped. It was slick. I fell and did a full face plant spread out.

Tara: You had to roll over just to get up. And you had dirt and moss all over your back.

Jennifer: That's right. And some on the front too.

Stephanie: I remember the bear standing over you. I think it was over

	you but not like over the top of you but over the back and you were kicking it. You weren't actually making contact but you were kicking and saying, "Go away, bear! Go away, bear!'"
Jennifer:	I don't remember any of that. I'm sure it happened. I felt like he kind of like jumped over me. Then he got up. We were probably a few feet apart and we both basically crawled back onto the trail. So now he was on the north side of us. I remember I got back onto the trail and was trying to get up and that.
Tara:	I think that we were frightened enough that Stefanie and I had sticks and we…
Stephanie:	We were screaming, "Go away, bear!"
Jennifer:	We all basically would scream, "Go! Go away." We were clapping our hands. I was hoarse for days.
Tara:	The bear was back behind us here and Stefanie and I with sticks in our hands and trying…
Jennifer:	Are we supposed to play dead right now? Because I thought with a black bear you were suppose to be big and wide. I knew all this stuff.
Stephanie:	We were having an ongoing conversation about what are we supposed to be doing? What are we doing wrong? And it would not go away. We tried everything.
Jennifer:	He stood by a tree and looked at us. Maybe 6-feet-tall. He wasn't a baby. When I tell the story, maybe he was a couple of years old. Like it just left his mom, maybe. Is that right?
Stephanie:	We were trying to find sticks. Usually when we're running, we're kicking sticks out of the way and jumping over them. And we were like "where are the sticks?" We could not find sticks.
Tara:	Stephanie was stuffing sticks into my hand.
Jennifer:	We all…there was a period of time I was in front. There was a period of time you were in front. And there was a period like the stick time she was in front. But we basically walked back down Niagra and half way down that I didn't realize it was the same bear that we had seen. I thought it was the

mother, I was wondering *how many bears are out here?*

Stephanie: *Aahhhh.* I always thought it was the same bear.

Jennifer: In my mind was, *Okay is there a mom that we're going to be seeing some time soon. Are we going to be seeing more bears?* We kept walking down…

Tara: If we stopped or took a step toward it with our sticks and waved them around, it would stop and…

Stephanie: It would go up into the devil's clubs and then it would circle us.

Tara: We had to move faster to keep it from cutting us off. We'd step toward him and he'd back off and he'd come back behind us again.

Stephanie: As soon as it was out of our sight, we would try to…

Jennifer: Take about fifteen steps

Stephanie: It would just…boom, be on the trail in front of us again.

Jennifer: It would get into the grass and we thought, *oh, he's gonna leave, he's gonna leave…* and he'd come right back out of the grass and just as close as he was before. When it started following us…

Tara: I remember looking at my watch and it was 37 minutes and…

Stephanie: Our families are all pretty much home asleep.

Jennifer: We might not be home for hours.

Tara: I wondered how much longer it would be that others will know that we're not coming home…

Stephanie: We were walking backwards and it kept up with us. If we walked backwards, if we stopped, it would ease towards us. If we ran, it would run after us. We couldn't get away from it

Jennifer: Once we thought the bear was leaving, we sprinted to get distance between us. It was like thirty seconds and the bear came back onto the trail. I kept thinking, "*My kids are in bed! They don't even know I'm here.*"

Tara: Why is this bear so persistent?

Stephanie:	We're thinking, *"What can we do? What are we doing wrong?"*
Tara:	But we thought the three of us together had more safety. I didn't think that we would die regardless of how bad it would get.
Jennifer:	Halfway through I was fearful that we may not make it out of this because we had a long ways to go. I remember thinking this, *When people are in a bad situation about to die, they have a sense of calm. But we were talking...and I remember having a sense of is this happening? Am I calm or am I just trying to get out of the situation?*
Stephanie:	We all had the sense that it was very probable that we would get injured. I thought if the bear charged, one of us would get hurt badly. But with three of us, I figured that two of us wouldn't let the other one die. So one of us might get hurt badly.
Tara:	Over and over I just kept thinking *how is this going to end?* I knew it couldn't go on forever but it seemed like forever.
Jennifer:	I didn't think I could run far enough back to get to anything and if I run, then all of a sudden he's gonna really get upset.
Stephanie:	We were only an arm's length away from the bear a lot of the time. If I would have leaned over slightly, I could have hit it on the nose any time I wanted to because that's how close it was to us. It never growled. It just kind of moved its head from side to side.
Tara:	It was so close...it wasn't working any more...stepping toward it and it just kept coming...I remember thinking *How close should I let it come? What will happen if he gets any closer?* Then I panicked since it was within 15 inches of my leg.
Jennifer:	What are you going to do? Tara had her arm up, I'll never forget. I go, "Tara, I don't think that's such a good idea." And it goes crack! And I go *UUUUUU!* And that was the first time he was further away from us. She hit him on the nose. The bear shook his head as if startled and then backed off. I found a kind of club and I was, "We're not...NO!" Then we got to the next trail and the road was next to it.

Stephanie:	The bear followed us onto the road.
Jennifer:	I thought for sure when we got to the road, it would be gone. There's no way it will stay.
Tara:	They had done some construction…so that the rocks on the side…I threw like a girl but we were all throwing rocks at the bear.
Stephanie:	We never hit it. It was just across the road from us.
Jennifer:	He was much farther from us than he had been. Then a construction worker came around the corner in a pickup truck.
Tara:	Two trucks, a big one and a pickup truck. And we were waving at them and they stopped.
Stephanie:	The bear was still hanging around on the side of the road.
Tara:	When the smaller truck came close enough to be between us and the bear, we jumped on the truck, we could see the foliage moving.
Jennifer:	The driver said, "It's only a black bear." And we yelled, "Just drive!"
Stephanie:	We were clinging to the side. He said he'd get in trouble if we weren't in the back. We climbed to the back of the truck and at that point I looked at my watch and it was 54 minutes. He took us to the park entrance by the "Welcome to Kincaid Park" sign… he wouldn't take us further because he had to get back to work.
Jennifer:	Had we gone on the trail we were 4 minutes from the car. But we were NOT going back into the woods. The bear was on that side of the road.
Stephanie:	We were willing to go way out of our way to get to our cars as opposed to the shortcut on the trail.
Jennifer:	We hopped off at the bridge.
Tara:	We were trying to run but our legs were so heavy…they hurt.
Jennifer:	There was a police car coming down…
Stephanie:	Which I had never seen before. Of all the mornings we've

been out there I've never seen a cop. Year around. Never seen a cop.

They kind of freaked.

Jennifer: "You know what?" I go, "We just had to deal with a bear. For a long time. He goes, 'You girls get in and I'll give you a ride.' "

Stephanie: I've never been in the back of a police car before.

From the time the bear brushed Stefanie's leg until the group reached safety at their vehicles was less than a mile and a half but it seemed like it took forever. Jennifer stated, "It felt like it was probably five miles. But at the end of the day we never ran a full three miles from the car to where we were." The bear stayed with the ladies fifty-four minutes.

The Alaska Department of Fish and Game was notified and Rick Sinnott didn't take long to find and dispatch the bear.

Jennifer stated, "The rest of the day I was talking fast...I was talking to a friend of mine on the phone...she said you weren't making sense... you could just tell from all of the adrenaline I was out of it. *If my mother hears about this from anybody else.* I finally had to call her and tell her the story which she handled well. And the next day I started getting really sore in my stomach and my calves. I think because we had all that lactic acid, all that adrenaline was stored in our bodies and we never finished.

"I remember I slept. It was 6 o'clock. And Tim basically got the kids' dinner, got them baths and got them to bed and I never even woke up till the next day."

The women acknowledged that they were totally unprepared for an encounter with a bear. They wore shorts, T-shirts and running shoes. They had no protection. They agreed that they wouldn't know how they'd react if the bear had bitten one of them.

Stephanie said that, "At times I was panicky, *this is bad*. At other times I felt I could handle it. It was such a long time. I asked myself *what are you doing!?* "

The day after the event the women awoke exhausted and sore. All three were paranoid for some time. Tara concluded, "It's ironic that I so often act as though 'it could never happen to me, and then when it does happen, it's hard to feel safe again.'"

DON WELTY

A few years ago I heard that one of Sam Fejes' guides had a run in with a bear. I was able to track down Don Welty who moved to Alaska from Ohio in 1981 and began guiding in1985. He is married to Lynn and has two children. Don is 5' 11" and weighs 185 pounds. His job experience includes guiding, commercial fishing and 12,000 hours as a commercial pilot.

When I contacted Don, he kindly agreed to share two stories with me in which he credits God for saving and blessing him. In the first account the bear reached Don; in the second one, it almost did. His stories "Two Close Calls" follow.

Our mode of moose hunting entails dropping hunters into camps via aircraft in which the "airstrip" is a swatch of ground thirty feet wide and 200-400 feet in length. Only the slow-flying speed and maneuverability of a Super Cub makes it possible to operate on any of these makeshift landing sites. Once the hunter and guide begin their hunt, we fly over their camp every other day to check on their success or to re-supply them with food or other necessities. Moose season in southeast Alaska coincides with the relentless fall and winter storm cycles. The almost continual rain and wind makes for some difficult flying and hunting conditions. On September 23, 2004, the weather was improving with small breaks of sunshine between the scattered rain showers.

Steve, a packer, and I left the lodge in the late afternoon after a 2 day wait on whether to check on camps. If any of the hunters had been successful, I would drop Steve off to help pack out the 700 pounds of meat, cape and antlers that would have to be carried to the nearest landing spot. Steve, fresh from Arizona and having packed out a half-dozen moose already, was relishing the adventure and feeling strong. His strength was certainly needed as landing sites are infrequent where the moose hang out. We took off from the lodge heading west. After flying through sporadic rain showers, we passed over a camp and saw from the air that they had been successful and really needed Steve's help. As I circled the strip, it was apparent that the heavy rain from the day before had flooded the area. An estimated foot of water lay on the strip making a safe landing and take-off impossible. We talked to the guide using a VHF radio and told them we would have to try again in the morning. The guide was not too happy about that, but since we had no option, we headed back to the lodge.

As we passed down the shoreline praising the Creator of all this beauty, I thought of a pair of winter-shed moose antlers I had seen the previous season. They would make a unique decoration at the lodge and provide a chance to stretch our legs.

The shining sun along the beach line to the south beckoned us to take a more southern route back to the base camp. We enjoyed the occasional rainbow and a beautifully lit up surf line, still wild from the last storm.

Since we didn't have enough daylight to check any other camps until morning, we decided to land on a small but flat sandbar about a mile from the shed moose antlers. We were both eager for a break from the unending chores at the lodge. Steve was enthusiastic as always. If all went well, we would be back in the air in thirty minutes with plenty of daylight to make it back to the lodge. Steve had borrowed a .45-70 lever action gun for his packing trip, so because this was prime bear country as well as moose, we instinctively took it along.

We crossed a wide, sandy area, traveling into or across the light north wind. As we approached the low brush ahead, we began to talk out loud and shouted an occasional "hey bear" to allow any bears in the vicinity to leave ahead of us. As the brush got higher, we were pleased to see a moose trail leading in the direction we wanted to go. This made for easy walking.

Moose prints were abundant with an occasional old bear scat, but no fresh bear tracks. Expecting to see or hear a moose, I stopped when Steve said, "What's that?"

I then heard the woofing alarm of a bear. I hollered, "Bear! Give me the rifle." Steve handed me the rifle and I levered a round into the chamber and let the hammer down slowly, shouting, "Hey, bear, get out of here!"

Forty to fifty yards ahead a bear stood up. As we continued to talk, we waved our arms so it could see that we were people — not small bears! It was, I estimated, about an 8-foot boar. It was square-headed and dark brown over its entire body — a medium-size boar and larger than most sows in this area. No teats were visible or sign of cubs.

Since no sign of a kill was apparent, such as carrion birds, I expected the bear to turn and run off. Instead, after standing up for maybe five seconds, the bear charged. No sound, no angry, irritated look, just a full-speed charge. As Steve continued to yell, "Get out of here!" I leveled the quick-handling .45-70 lever gun and cocked the hammer. I was still hoping this was just a bluff charge, but at less than ten yards, I had to shoot.

It was coming straight on, its head a bit lower than mine. The rifle's sights were steady between the bear's eyes, which were locked onto mine. For a split second I thought of the trouble killing this bear in self-defense would cause. No matter, the boundary was crossed and I pulled the trigger.

The hammer fell, but all I heard was a *click*!

Thinking I had a dud shell, I quickly worked the action and at two feet tried again, only to hear another click. What a sick feeling. I knew that only God could save me now. Some confusion after the contact left me lying in the brush pulling myself into a fetal position still trying to work the gun. How I held onto the gun at the impact or received no injuries from the bear's running into me at 25 MPH, I still don't know, but I was now lying fifteen feet behind where I had been standing seconds before.

The ground trembled and I felt the jaws of the bear slip over my head. As he bit down, I heard a sickening, crunching sound and was amazed that I was still alive! This often called "kill bite"—because few life forms ever survive it—could have been fatal had the bear shaken me as they often do.

Panic struck as I heard Steve's voice, thinking he should be playing dead. I got up, knowing I had no way to defend him except to distract the bear back to me. As I looked through a cascade of blood coming down my face running into my eyes and blurring my vision, I realized that Steve was okay. Then his words broke through my mental fog — "Help us, Jesus." He was ten feet away and had thought the bear had killed me. Instead, after the one bite and hearing Steve, the bear looked up at him and ran off into the bush. Thank you, Lord!

Both of us were pretty shook up. We endeavored to stop the bleeding by tightly wrapping my head with a rain jacket. Upon examination of the gun, we found that a safety, unlike any lever gun I had ever used, was blocking the hammer just short of the firing pin and needed to be pushed sideways to fire. Ironically it was a safety feature new that year. We reloaded with the only two shells we could find and made a plan on how to get back to the plane safely.

The bear had run away the same direction we had to go, so we waited and watched for fifteen minutes or more before heading back to the plane.

We walked downwind now, alert for any sign of movement. When we arrived at the beach, we knelt down and praised God for bringing us out of the attack alive and asked that I would be able to safely fly us back to the lodge before nightfall.

As we neared the plane, I gave Steve a quick rundown on how to operate the radio and what to do if I passed out. I felt alert and had no serious pain yet although I realized I probably had a serious head injury.

In spite of a heavy rain and hail squall in the vicinity of the lodge, the Lord answered our prayer and we made a safe landing just before dark.

We told the crew at the lodge what had happened and began cleaning the wounds to prevent infection. One canine had penetrated my skull near the temple, the others stopping at the skull. It was decided that a rescue helicopter should be called since it was impossible to get to help in an airplane until morning.

Pain started to set in, followed by shock. Along with it came severe headache, nausea, chills and shivering to the point I didn't think I would make it through the night. I asked my daughter Rene, who was there in camp, to call a friend and start a prayer chain, which she did. I held on the few hours awaiting the Coast Guard helicopter's arrival.

I had developed a swelling in my neck, with increasing pressure and pain, which the doctors later said they couldn't understand. However, prayer was working on me already. By the time I made it to Anchorage on a Medevac flight from Cordova, the neck swelling was gone and the pain stabilized.

Doctors did a Cat scan and determined I had one skull fracture but no damage to the brain. Now the concern would be to make sure meningitis would not set in, so they started me on a strong antibiotic. I was able to leave the hospital on September 26.

Along with many friends' and neighbors' prayers, visits and calls, a quick recovery followed.

I thank God for His gracious protection and for the loving gracious people He has placed in my life. I want to thank the brave, selfless Coast Guard crew that came to get me in the dark, stormy weather, and I thank all my friends and family for their faithful prayers.

I am reminded of these scriptures: 1) "The prayer of a righteous person is powerful and effective." James 5:16; 2) "What is man that You are mindful of him, and the son of man that You care for him?" Psalms 8:4

Story two

The following fall my wife Lynn and I had gone out to Prince William Sound with some friends on a late November deer hunt. Snow covered muskeg, clear sky, and cold temps graced our hunt. This late in the year most all bears would be hibernating setting me up for a "letting my guard down moment." We both had been successful in harvesting a deer and were enjoying a beautiful evening as we drug the deer down to the beach.

I had a deer attached to a harness that went around both shoulders that let you pull hands free. The system works great except for one small detail—the harness was under my pack, requiring the removal of the pack before being able to remove the harness.

After a mile or so we neared our destination a few hundred yards from the beach and passed through a small patch of timber where a small stream began to flow. I had my rifle strapped on the side of my pack and it began hanging up on branches. We stopped for a rest as we broke out of the trees and I removed my pack and unstrapped my rifle to avoid the same problem. I then got back in the harness, put the pack back on, then strapped the waist belt and sternum strap, a move I would soon regret.

With the pack securely on over the drag harness one cannot get free from this "anchor" quickly. We were just starting to move away from the edge of the trees into the meadow ahead. Looking back into the trees after hearing approaching footsteps, Lynn asked, "What's that?" As I turned to look back at her, she said, "Bear!" Being the last thing I expected to hear this late in the season, it seemed as if I moved like molasses. Since I was attached to the deer on the end of the harness, I was unable to get very far away from the trees in order to give myself some room.

Now I know how a dog feels being chained to a tree with a bear in the yard! I did manage a few steps back as I chambered a round, popped the scope covers and safety off, and shouted, "Get out of here!" (I've got to stop saying that!)

Knowing the bear now heard us, smelled us and probably saw Lynn move, I thought he would hold up in the timber. I was wrong. As he got to the edge of the trees at about fifteen yards, he looked at me and with no hesitation came straight for me. He had that same "locked in look" and made the same low growl as the last bear I had an unfavorable encounter with in September the year before. I thought to myself "here we go again."

I pulled the trigger at fifteen feet. Fortunately, I had turned the scope magnification down to the lowest setting earlier, but even at that, his head filled the whole scope and was too close to be in focus. This time, unlike the last time, the gun roared. Oh, how sweet the sound.

The whole event from Lynn's warning of "bear" to when I shot, was maybe three seconds. Why the bear, an eight-foot lone boar, didn't hold up in the trees and made such an aggressive move, remains unanswered. After confirming that the bear was dead, we headed down to the beach with the deer and met up with the rest of the party. After giving a short explanation, I was able to recruit a friend to help me go back and take care of the bear. After some "in the dark" pictures and two hours of skinning we loaded the pack and headed for the boat. Since everyone had to return that night to town, I never did get to go back in the daylight to see how long the bear had been trailing us. Bear season was still open and I had a tag so I was able to keep the hide, unlike a normal "defense of life and property" bear.

I am so thankful to my favorite hunting partner, my wife, for her warning and quick response to get out of the way. And I am most thankful to my Lord Jesus for delivering me out yet another predicament.

For those unfamiliar with Alaska, Don guided a remote, roadless area—reached only by air, water or foot.

JOE HUSTON

It was my good fortune to meet Joe Huston in July 2007. While I sat with my friend Andy Flack at a picnic table eating sandwiches from Sara's in Anchorage, Joe taxied up to the Trail Ridge Air dock in a De Havilland Beaver on floats. He walked to our table and Andy introduced me to his friend and colleague. Then Joe chatted about his bear scrape— he said he'd allow me to use it, stating, "I never gave it to anyone because I was waiting for the right time." We considered a number of titles before settling on "Death was a Whisper Away."

I think you'll be as amazed as I was when you read Joe's story.

I grew up on the west side of Washington state's Cascade Mountains near the small logging town of Eatonville. I spent most of my days fishing and hunting until I entered the military in 1987. After the military, at age 24, I finished my pilot's and mechanic's licenses with Pierce College and a local flight school, General Aviation. When work started to slow down in Washington, I considered Alaska. I already had many contacts in Alaska as part of my family was in Ketchikan and Anchorage and a few of my Washington relatives worked seasonally in the Great Land. I headed to Alaska in 1995 looking for adventure. I found it. Many times over.

The day that I arrived in Anchorage I had three solid job offers. I worked a mechanic job at Merrill field for a year and a half while rebuilding an Aeronca Sedan airplane my Dad and I had partnered in. Then I finally picked up a flying job.

In the spring of 1997 I started flying for Tikchik Narrows Lodge, a lodge located fifty miles north of the western fishing village of Dillingham. The lodge is in Wood-Tikchik State Park which includes the famed Tickchik Lakes—a half dozen lakes that drain into Nushagak Bay in Bristol Bay. Considered by myself and many others to be the best freshwater fishing in the world, the Tikchiks and Bristol Bay are indeed a piece of heaven on earth to the outdoorsman. Accompanying the largest salmon runs in the world this area is also home to an equally abundant population of bears, moose, caribou, wolves and other Alaskan critters.

This location is truly in the middle of nowhere, the bush of Alaska. The lodge is located on a peninsula that juts south from the mainland between two lakes, each approximately ten miles long. The peninsula essentially cuts the lakes in half and actually forms a very short river, maybe two to three football fields in length. Nuyakuk Lake lies to the west and Tickchik Lake is on the east. It is a beautiful spot.

Normally my day started with some exercises and a morning jog out on the runway. The 1,800-foot-long gravel runway connects the lodge to the mainland. Along its course the runway has water on each side and the strip stretches forty to fifty feet at its narrowest width. The best way to get a decent workout is by running back and forth from one end to the other. This day was no different. It was July first 1997. In my cabin I warmed up with some stretches, sit ups, pushups and floor exercises. I headed out the door and started down the runway. My jog usually consisted of three or four times up and down the runway, I would jog at a fast pace for a harder cardio work out.

I reached the end of the runway on the first leg and turned around, not knowing that I had just passed by a brown bear that state park investigation would later determine was lying in the bushes a short distance off to the east side of the runway. The bushes were so thick that they concealed him from me as I passed by him again. Moments later I heard something coming up behind me.

I turned my head to see this bear somewhat off to my right side, perhaps thirty feet away and gaining on me. My initial instinct was to run faster. I increased my stride a few steps and realized I can't outrun the bear. Better stop and bluff. When I stopped, the bear was maybe ten feet away and looked a little surprised. I began waving my arms and, ironically enough, said to him a few times, "Go home."

At this point his back faced the mainland. I felt that because there was more cover toward the mainland, it provided him a sense of security. My back faced the lodge side of the peninsula to the south, which was approximately 1100 feet from where I stood. That section of runway and water was open area.

When he started to circle me and move towards the lodge side of the peninsula, I knew I was in trouble. After a few seconds he jumped at me and hit me in the back with his left paw. The blow opened up my chest and punctured my right lung with a quick jab of his front paw. The right paw simultaneously hit my right thigh and this effectively flipped me over and mashed my head into the gravel. I tried to dodge his attack but he was too fast.

When I lifted my head up I was on my belly, he grabbed a hold of my right thigh, I watched with horror as his teeth sank into my flesh as if it were butter. He tore right into me with what seemed to be very little effort. He took a couple of bites out of my thigh and then grabbed my shoulder with his mouth. At this point he shook me like a rag doll. I think he actually had my whole body off the ground a couple of times and was just tearing at my shoulder. We were eye to eye and I could hear all of the bones in my shoulder coming apart, the sounds resembling those of a dog chewing on chicken bones.

For the first time in the twenty seconds or so of the attack, I thought he was going to kill me. I honestly thought *This is it*.

In the weeks preceding the attack I had read Larry Kaniut's first book, *Alaska Bear Tales*. I remembered that quite a few people had escaped death by playing dead. That's when I immediately began the performance of a lifetime! I held my breath, went limp and played it for all I could.

Seconds after I did this the bear stopped the attack. Still holding my shoulder in his mouth for a moment, he suddenly dropped me. He circled around me and stuck his face in mine, I presume to see if I was still alive. I continued playing dead the best I could. Next I heard him run off into the brush alongside the runway. I remained still and held my breath as long as I could. Finally unable to hold my breath any longer, I gasped for air. I immediately heard the hole in my back blowing air through the wound with every breath. I knew from my military training that this was very life threatening and that I needed to get help fast.

Putting pressure on my limbs to see what I had to work with, I tried to get up. My right leg and buttock were torn up badly and bleeding a lot, but the bones and joints were intact and functional. My shoulder was bleeding heavily and was just a mash of clothes, blood and flesh.

I got myself up and began hobbling toward the lodge as fast as I could go. I had approximately four hundred yards of runway to go and then I needed to go another five hundred feet into the lodge courtyard. I lurched along, somewhat running and hobbling. I was amazed to hear the gushing sounds of my wounds and blood sloshing and could literally see blood shaking and splattering off of me as I went along.

Mentally I was racked with the fear that the bear would come back and attack again before I could make it to the lodge. I was barely able to keep myself going, I could not withstand another attack. I was focused on surviving this event.

After what seemed an eternity I finally hobbled up to one of the cabins at the lodge and knocked at the door. One of our staff members answered and I mumbled, "There's been a little trouble on the runway." I must have been a sight because the poor gal couldn't move for a few seconds. I kept telling her to go get the owner because I knew I needed to be flown out to get medical help ASAP.

She ran up to the main lodge and I staggered into the courtyard. After noticing me, four or five employees came to assist me as I collapsed on the grass in the courtyard wracked with pain. They packed towels around my wounds to stop the bleeding. We had all sorts of help by then. One of our guides was diligently loading his shotgun and another employee that must not have had much first aid training kept saying, "Oh, this looks bad." The morning had turned quickly from a picturesque fishing lodge environment to a survival scene.

The quickest and easiest way to Dillingham was going to be the lodge airplane, a Cessna 206 on wheels which was down at the runway, 500 feet away. We began moving that way and by the time we got there, the rear doors were open for me and I was helped into the back seat. Within seconds the owner of the lodge showed up with a "Stat" kit—a briefcase full of first aid items meant for larger scale accidents, including sutures and morphine.

One of our guests was an anesthesiologist, who jumped in the back with me while the owner jumped into the pilot's seat and fired up the engine. As the plane warmed up, I realized that I had flown the airplane in from Anchorage the night before, leaving an hour or less of fuel in the tanks. At this point I could not talk much, my breathing was shallow, my right lung was collapsing and the left would soon follow if I did not get a chest tube put in.

We lifted off the runway and I immediately could see what I had not realized all morning, the fog was down to the ground. Visibility was absolutely terrible. We flew low along the lakeshore towards the outlet, a tactic used only in extreme weather conditions.

My in-flight doctor was trying to find a vein in my arm. I had lost so much blood she couldn't get an IV started in my arm. I begged for the morphine. I was in so much pain and stress it was unbelievable. At that point she put down all of the equipment, looked me in the eyes and asked, "Are you saved? Do you know Jesus Christ?"

I thought, "Well, surely now I am going to die. The doctor has given up on helping me and is giving last rights."

I remembered when I was a child, we had gone to church for a short period in our lives and went on a field trip with the church youth. I had given my heart to the Lord on that trip. I told her "yes" and she began praying over me. Mostly I remember her saying the Lord's prayer, "Our father Who art in heaven, hallowed be Thy name, Thy kingdom come, Thy will be done." After she started praying over me, the stress left completely. All of a sudden it didn't matter whether I lived or died. I had a peace about me that I have never felt since then or before.

We were flying low over the Nushagak River now and could follow it down to Dillingham if necessary. However it is the long way and we didn't have much fuel onboard.

We turned around a couple of times because the fog descended to the trees. I began to think that we'd be forced to land on a sand bar, out of fuel and I would bleed out. I felt that this was looking really grim.

A few minutes later I passed out and when I awoke, we were on final approach to the Dillingham airport. We had made it! I had never seen a sight so beautiful. We touched down and the ambulance was waiting. Some friends from Dillingham were there also and the back doors of the Cessna opened up. The medics and my friends reached in to grab me. My body had stiffened from intense pain and I didn't want to move because I knew it would be even more painful. I eventually let the medics and our friends get me out.

I was rushed to Kanakanak Hospital where I was stabilized and a chest tube was inserted to re-inflate my lungs at the hospital. I am eternally grateful to them for the work that they did. A life flight aircraft was dispatched from somewhere way up north and later that day I was flown into Anchorage and admitted to Providence Hospital. Another facility I am eternally grateful for.

Dr. Tower and his staff left my wounds open and cleaned them for a couple of days. The surgeries to clean them went well and I never did develop any infections. It took three consecutive surgeries to put my shoulder back together—Dr. Tower is a genius in his profession and did some out of the box thinking that worked really well on me.

The lodge owner and park service never did find the bear. The attack was investigated by the park service, it was a young bear. Maybe 400 pounds. The experts say that the sub-adolescent bears sometimes do not know how to deal with humans. In the fall of that year our caretaker shot a bear that was trying to break into a freezer at the lodge. It fit the description of the bear that got me but we will never know for sure.

I still spend a lot of time in the woods fishing and hunting. I do a lot of bear hunting, occasionally guiding a hunter or two on bear hunts. Even though I could hold a grudge, I don't hate bears. I respect them, they are magnificent animals.

I am careful about where and how I jog. Running kicks off the predatory instinct in predatory animals. Period. Watch it around mountain lions, wolves, bears. There are many documented attacks on joggers from all three of these animals. And that list is not all inclusive.

When I awoke from the first surgeries, I asked the doctor how close I came. He said that he could see the artery in my neck exposed in the wound, another fraction of an inch and he said I wouldn't even have been able to get up after the mauling. I would have bled out right away. The silver lining of this cloud is that it set me on a course to find out who God is and who I am. This is a lifelong pursuit and I am glad that this incident pushed me into this search. One that I feel every man should be on.

RC HARROP

It is very unusual for a bear to attack a group of more than a few people, so when RC Harrop told me about his story while I signed books at Alaska Wildberry Products during the summer of 2001, I asked him if he'd share the experience, which follows.

Most of the time I have been able to work around, avoid, or chase off any problem or curious bears. Prior to this the worse actions I have ever had to take was pop a couple caps off into the air to chase off some very curious ones.

I'm the director of the Youth Enrichment and Outdoor Adventure Program for Youth Services at Fort Richardson located in Anchorage. We use the Alaskan wilderness as our hook and conduct a year round program teaching kids how to deal with life. Subjects include drug abuse, gangs, conflict resolution and leadership, the emphasis upon helping them build up their confidence and self-esteem. We accomplish our goals by running trips that include rafting, kayaking, fish camps, backpacking, rock climbing, glacier traversing, ice climbing, ski camps, winter camping and a low ROPES course.

My military experience (a retired Army officer with airborne ranger background) has enabled me to guide trips into the Alaskan bush for over ten years. During that time I've had 20 to 25 close encounters with brown and blacks bears, but none were ever like this. However, this encounter scared the hell out of me.

We'd just finished serving supper, three hours after beaching. We'd had time to play an awesome game of ultimate Frisbee. Our group included thirty-five adults and students and we were nearing the end of the two week Forty Mile-Yukon River float trip in August 1999. Suddenly the kids yelled there were a moose and a calf crossing the island's small stream. Then they yelled that a bear was chasing the moose.

We were about 10 miles inside of the Canadian border on the Yukon River, camped on the high sandbar of a large island. A small stream dissected our island. I turned around and saw a dark colored bear run the moose and its calf into the brush about 437 to 547 yards away. Moments later the moose—minus the calf—emerged at high speed with the bear right behind it. She plunged into a deep side stream that cut through the island. As the moose hit the deeper water, the bear initially chased it but finally stopped when it got to the point where it had to swim. This was about 273 to 328 yards away from our camp.

The bear emerged from the water, shook, stopped and looked at us. It paused for a moment, then started running towards our camp. It covered 109 yards before it ducked into the brush. We heard branches breaking and the bear approaching at a high rate of speed. I ran to grab my weapon, which was still on the raft.

Because of our group size and the fact that we had several high risk students, we had chosen as part of our risk assessment for this trip to leave our weapons unloaded with trigger locks during the day (on other trips I carry the weapon on my hip).

The weapons consisted of one .44-Magnum Blackhawk and a 12 gauge shot gun, and they only came out at night after the kids had gone to bed and things were quiet, and in anticipation of a bear's walking into the camp.

I grabbed my pistol and ammo and ran to get in front of the group where I figured the bear might come out. Once in front of the group I dropped to my knees on the sand and had time only to load three rounds before I heard the kids yelling more. The bear exploded from the brush, crossed the stream and a sand bar at a dead run and headed toward the group that had formed a circle with their backs against the Yukon.

The bear went straight for two of my staff who'd moved between the bear and the group. I was hoping that this was going to be just a bluff charge but the bear was not acting like any of the other ones I had encountered before.

Because he charged straight at my staff, I didn't finish loading my weapon. I dropped all but one cartridge onto the ground and spun the cylinder. I immediately fired one round into the air.

The grizzly swung and charged straight at me. I pulled the trigger to fire another warning shot but the hammer fell on an empty chamber. At this moment my two staff members charged the bear that was less than ten feet from me.

The bruin backed off about 10 to 15 feet and stood up. Since I wasn't sure how many rounds I had loaded, I dropped to my knees and put the last round I had in my hand into the pistol. I lined up the cylinder just in time. The grizzly charged.

I did not want to shoot a bear because I had a bunch of kids watching and I was in Canada with a revolver on a US Army sponsored trip.

However, this bear was not acting normal, refused to back off and was more aggressive than any that I had encountered in the past.

Brent Morgan had placed himself between the bear and several of the kids who were separated from the main group. Intent on reaching him, the grizzly did not slow down.

I finally fired when the bear was about 8 feet from me. As the 300 grain hot load hit him in his left shoulder, I watched the top part of his shoulder explode in fur and meat. Immediately after I fired, my partner Joe Nash, who had retrieved his 12 gauge shotgun and had taken a position behind me, fired and hit the bear in the center of his chest with a 600 grain sabot round.

I immediately fired again hitting bruin in the neck and jaw area. Simultaneously Joe hit him in the right shoulder. I fired a third round that hit him center mass in the chest, and about the same time Joe hit him in the gut. When he took the hit in the gut, he finally turned away from Brent (he was less than five feet from him). The bear ran about 30 to 40 feet away, stopped and turned around and started to charge again.

I fired but was out of ammo. Joe then fired, hitting him center of mass of his chest. At this point the bear ran off into the brush. We could hear him moving in the brush so I yelled at the group to pack up the rafts and get the hell off of the island. Joe and I set up a perimeter, reloaded and our group retreated from the island in less than 15 minutes. I could not take the chance of the bear charging the kids again so I did not take the time to let him bleed out and track him down. We moved down river, found a new campsite and went to bed.

Although it seemed longer to me, the group agreed that from the time he broke from the brush running at us to the time he finally ran off into the brush, was about 50 to 90 seconds. Joe and I fired so close together that the group heard three shots during the main part of the charge.

Prior to starting the trip we spent a lot of time teaching the kids what to do in case of a bear attack (I am the bear expert on Fort Richardson and give all the wilderness safety briefs for the installation). Most of the kids had done exactly what they had been taught—they had formed a tight circle and were yelling at the top of their lungs or blowing whistles that they had around their necks. Only a few of them were by themselves off to the side of the group (afterwards they stated that they didn't know what was happening till they heard the gun shots).

None of the kids or adults had run to attract attention after the bear had broken out of the brush. We were downwind from the bear. The adults thought the bear was trying to work towards a small group of kids off to one side. They could be seen in a couple pictures taken by a news reporter that was along with us. The reporter had grabbed her camera and was able to take several pictures of the bear running off. She took a picture right when the last shotgun blast hit the bear (I have copies of these pictures).

Most of the adults commented later that the bear looked skinny. Joe and I figured that the bear was somewhere between 7 to 8 feet tall. His tracks were about two-thirds the size of most of the bigger brown tracks that I had seen before. Joe and I figured that he was probably 3-4 years old and was not good at his hunting skills yet. The adults that were in the back with the kids said he was acting as if we were a herd of caribou.

I am a hunter and have read your stories and know that browns can take some heavy hits, but it didn't strike home till I saw this one take three .44 mag rounds and four 12 gauge sabot rounds and never even slow down.

Upon our arrival at Eagle I reported the shooting to the Immigration and Customs authority, (he was the only person of any authority in town). He said that he would let the Royal Canadian Mounted Police know about the shooting. I then reported it to my higher headquarters. I did not tell him that I had used a pistol in the shooting. For validation I have a copy from the Fort Richardson paper where they ran a small article on the incident.

(APPENDIX 7)

JOE MONASTRA

Afognak Elk Hunt Cut Short By Brown Bear or Does a Bear S**t in the Woods? Yes, but He Doesn't Like it When You Do.

As told by Joe Monastra

1 Oct 2006

My buddies, Rodger and Darrin, and I flew from Kodiak to Afognak Island on the afternoon of 1 October 2006 with Seahawk Air. Afognak is the second largest island in the Kodiak Archipelago and is on the northeast end of the chain. I had drawn an elk tag and Rodger and Darrin were going for black tail deer and to help haul elk if I harvested one. Our destination was the southern end of Laura Lake, so we could easily access the old logging roads that etched the landscape on the east side of the island. Rolan, the pilot, had dropped off hunters before in this area and said camping spaces were few and far between because of the uneven terrain around the lake, but he thought that one or two of the bights on the southeast side of the lake would do. The extreme south end of the lake was unworkable, as it's a swamp, so we ended up about a third of a mile north from the southeast tip of the lake in a bight with a small stream. The area around Laura Lake has two hard and fast rules: first, if the area is flat and clear of any major vegetation, it will "squish" under foot; second, if God can put devil's club in a spot, he did.

Our camp site was only about fifteen yards laterally from the shore but near twenty feet above the water line, in a flat mossy area we had to clear out. It took about 3 hours of work, but we finally cleared the area, set up our tents and our portable bear electric fence (we had to dig a shallow trench around the campsite to ensure clearance for the wires, so the fence wouldn't short). To this day I have no idea if the bear fence actually works or not, but I've never had my camp damaged by a bear while using one. At just under four pounds, the fence is a light enough item to bring with you anywhere for peace of mind.

The day had turned to early evening, so we decided to scout while it was still light and try to figure out how to get to the logging roads. We were less than a half mile to the edge of the nearest logging road and we could see the clear cut hills from our camp. But the Afognak forest canopy is thick and dark—so thick we could only get signals on our GPS or satellite phone if we stood in a clearing. We quickly surmised that following the game trails was a better option than straight line bushwacking.

Everything on that island uses the same well worn trails. We found elk tracks, deer tracks and bear tracks (very big) laid right on top of each other and as well as the their scat. We didn't make it to the logging road that night; we ran out of light and decided that clamoring over deadfalls by flashlight was a bad idea. We returned to camp and got a good night's sleep.

Monday, 2 Oct 2006

We set out after sunrise and found the logging road after much chagrin. We had wanted the most direct path (like I said we were staring at the clear cut hills a half mile out) but deadfalls and debris from the storms and logging make it near impossible, or at least very dangerous, to clamor over. This is where we learned that the game trails were about the only answer, and once we mapped which ones went where, we got around relatively easy.

The logging roads themselves were an easy walk, but were getting overgrown with alders which slowed us down in places and increased our "pucker factor"; when in the alders we couldn't see more than a few feet in front of us, and it was obvious from all the tracks and scats that the area had lots of bears. Later that afternoon, Darrin shot a deer near the top of one of the clear cuts. We decided to drag the forked buck down to the bottom of the clear cut and then to the logging road that headed back to camp rather than back up to the top of the clear cut and logging road from which Darrin shot the deer. It was a poor decision. We should have just butchered it on the spot but we were concerned about visibility. The clear cuts were not "clear"; logging ended over twenty years ago on this part of the island, so the clear cuts were full of old logging debris, alders and vegetation that was chest high.

It was brutal going dragging that deer through that stuff; it took us an hour to get it down to the road. Now with a clear field of view around us, we butchered the buck, and packed the meat back to camp. We hung the game bags in a tree about eleven feet or so off the ground. We ate dinner and then hit the sack. Life was good.

Tues, 3 Oct 2006

We spent most of the day hiking and glassing in the Seal Bay area. We saw lots of elk sign but it was weeks old. Overall it was an uneventful day, with one exception. When we left that morning, we noticed that the remains of the deer carcass we left off the side of the logging road had been picked on by the foxes (we even caught one in the act). However, when returning that evening, the carcass had been totally obliterated – leg bones, skull, everything had been crushed and broken into tiny bits. On the game trail back to camp, we found very fresh, steaming bear scat. Our camp was unmolested, either through luck or due to the bear fence, but we built a big fire that night and made lots of noise just to be sure that a bear wouldn't enter camp.

Wed, 4 Oct 2006

Despite our best intentions, we got up after sunup, still tired from all the hiking the day prior. We were set about the morning routine of eating breakfast and prepping our packs to leave. I had to heed the call of nature, so I grabbed a roll of toilet paper, my wet wipes and rifle and headed out of camp and over the small saddle to the northeast to find a good sitting log. I almost left my rifle in my tent, save the nagging voice in my head that told me to bring it – you should always listen to that voice. I stopped less than a hundred yards from camp and about eighty yards downwind from where we had the deer hanging. The saddle was formed where two bights in the lake met; so our meat and camp were on one side of saddle and we had agreed to do our more formal nature calls on the other. I surveyed the area twice, found a good sitting log, dug a cat hole, laid out my wet wipes and set my rifle up against the log. I decided I would sit with my back to the lake, which was about fifteen yards behind me so I could keep a look out into the forest. I snapped a branch off the log to give myself a little more leg room, then dropped my pants and just as I was sitting down, I thought to myself "I stink! I really need a shower!" (only later did I realize I had not smelled myself), and then I heard what sounded like a stampede…a deep rumbling through the forest. I've hunted long enough to know which animals sound like what in the woods, and this did not sound like anything I'd heard before. I instantly knew that I was in trouble. I grabbed my rifle and lunged forward; it is generally agreed that this decision saved my life.

I'm no great bear man, but from what I've studied, bears are primarily left "handed" and usually swing for the head of any threat or prey. This bear was already swinging, and that lunge forward moved my head out of the strike zone. Instead the bear struck me at a downward angle with a single claw on the flat of my back midway up my right lat. While actually just a glancing blow, it felt like I had been hit with a baseball bat with a nail at the end of it.

I sprawled forward and ended up on my back but before I could do anything, the bear loomed over me. All that I saw was the triangle outline of his huge head, and I watched with detached terror as the white of his claws whizzed by my face. And then as quickly as it happened, and for whatever reason, he popped his jaws, and backed off, running about 10 yards or so away from me. He turned around and stared at me. I screamed "Bear! Bear!" while really meaning, "Help! Help!" With a shaky hand, I flipped the safety off on my rifle and quickly pointed it from my hip at the bear. I could not aim: my scope covers were still on the rifle, I was still on my back with my pants around my ankles and my brain was not processing quickly enough. I pulled the trigger. The bullet whizzed over the bear's head and killed a trophy class spruce tree. The bear broke into a sprint back up the saddle but parallel to me. I chambered another shell, and shot again to ensure the bear continued to run from me. Again, I hit another spruce tree. The bear disappeared over the saddle, in a dead run on the trail back towards our camp. The next thing I heard was six shots in rapid succession.

When I finally made it back over the saddle (my pants still around my ankles no less), I saw Rodger was standing in the trail with an empty .44 Magnum revolver in his hand. There was no sign of the bear. Apparently, when he heard my screams and shots, he dropped his morning oatmeal and came to my aid, only to encounter the bear at a full sprint coming at him from the opposite direction. Their encounter occurred at less than 20 feet. He instinctively emptied his gun, hitting nothing but trees in the thick woods. The bear tore through woods, disappearing quickly into the heavy brush and shadows.

I told Rodger the bear "pushed" me, at the time I did not know how else to describe it. My brown polypro shirt was not torn, but when I pulled it off, I was bleeding from a gouge in my back. The shirt must have stretched over the bear's claw. Rodger and Darrin cleaned out my wound, and dressed it. I wanted to stay and finish the hunt, but both of them thought I needed stitches and were worried about possible infection. I put on my pack, and the weight of it against the wound made me realize they were right. I was high on adrenaline, and I felt no pain. That would eventually change. We decided to end the hunt. I was not seriously injured and did not consider the situation an emergency, so we opted just to fit into Seahawk Air's schedule for our pickup, rather than request an emergency trip.

While we waited for the plane, we looked for the bear just to be sure it wasn't wounded and left out there for another hunter to encounter. After three hours we found no blood, hair, or any other sign of a hit. We then packed up camp and waited. The pickup was uneventful, and Rolan told me I had the distinction of being his first client "touched" by a bear.

That night in the Kodiak emergency room, I received treatment for a 3 inch by 1/4 inch wide by 1/4 inch deep gash in my back. I did not get stitches because it had been 12 hours since the attack, and stitches would have increased the chance for infection. I just ended up with a wider scar. That night, we caught the last flight out of Kodiak back to Anchorage, and then drove home. I spent the next few days hugging my wife and kids more than usual.

By all accounts, we had done nothing wrong. Our meat and food were up in trees and out of camp. We had been clean. The best I can figure that bear had come in the middle of the night to try and get that deer out of the tree. After the attack, we found tear marks in the bottom of the game bags. He was tall enough to paw at it, just not tall enough to get it out of the tree. It appeared he bedded down behind a huge deadfall that was on top of the saddle near the meat pole; on one side of the fallen tree the earth had been scooped out and large shallow depression was clearly visible. When I walked past that area the next morning, he slipped in behind me, walking along the lake shore out of my field of view. He must have either viewed me as a threat or a deer – I was just wearing my thermals and brown polypro shirt at the time. When he realized I was neither, he broke off his attack. He was a big bear; his paw prints were as long as my boot (size 9) and those game bags, which he could touch, were eleven feet off the ground at least. According to Rodger, the bear's back was noticeably higher than waist high, as best he could determine as the bear ran by him. We estimated it was close to a nine foot bear and about 800-1000 pounds. We did not report the attack or shooting as a DLP, or Defense of Life and Property. Seahawk Air coordinated with Fish and Game at our request, but since there was not conclusive evidence we had hit anything (other than spruce trees!), there was not duty to report.

The whole incident reminded me of the opening scene from *Pulp Fiction*, where the two hit men played by John Travolta and Samuel Jackson, survive a point blank shootout without getting a scratch.

I can honestly say that bear probably spent his day in the bear coffee shop with his buddies having the "miracle versus freak occurrence" debate. I know for my part, it was a miracle, to escape from such a predicament with just a bragging scar and a great bar story. I believe in God, and I believe we all have a guardian angel. Both were looking out for me that day. In fact, besides the scar, the only other damage was the loss of my cross. I had worn it around my neck every day for over a decade, including every mission I had flown over Iraq and Afghanistan. Not sure the exact moment it came off, but after the attack, I just had a broken chain, with no cross, hanging around my neck. A replacement cross was the first thing I bought when I got back home.

One final thought -- he was a beautiful bear, colored like a milk chocolate bar, and moved with power and speed you had to witness to believe. Rodger and I have talked many times about that day and both of us remember the same thing about that bear; he shuddered with every step, as his powerful muscles sent ripples through his fall fat layer and coat. It is amazing how the mind can allow for such detached fascination while the body is engaged in the pressing matter of survival. I was glad that both bear and man walked away relatively unscarred from the experience.

Another unusual means of dealing with bears occurred in September 2010 when a British Columbia man walked along. He saw a black bear which was no surprise; he thought his shout would send it on its way. Wrong. Jesse Mengler looked for a weapon when the critter charged him. The man spotted a hand-sized rock on the ground and picked it up. As the bear reached him from his elevated position, Mengler tossed the rock hitting the animal between the eyes and knocking it out. He hit the bear on the head several times with the rock and it wandered off into the woods where Mengler assumed it died. (You Tube, TMTV.net, Kootenays).

POLAR BEAR ATTACKS

Because a small number of people inhabit polar bear country where villages and agencies have prepared extensive avoidance information for the locals, I've listed polar bear attacks separately.

About the late spring of 1999 I received a call from London and the British Broadcasting Service inquiring whether or not I could provide them a list of polar mauling victims they might be able to interview. I told them that Polar bears do not maul—they eat. A polar bear investigates anything that moves as its next meal, and it's not likely that a person mauled by one would be around for an interview. Polar bears rarely bluff charge.

Having received email pictures of some particularly ghastly injuries on a man and a dead polar bear, I wanted to discover their derivation. On August 7, 2006, I entered "polar bear tent" on the Internet and reviewed www.snopes.com. I condensed the following account from their site. Last updated 2 August 2006. The Northern News Services covering Canada's territories described the attack:

Inuit guide Kootoo Shaw, guided three U.S. hunters 45 minutes outside of Kimmirut on September 2, 2003. The men were not aware that a bear was in the area which just showed up in camp. It first approached the Americans' tent and tore through it before heading for Shaw's tent. "He started ripping through and we managed to get out through the door," Shaw said. Shaw ran from the bear but tripped on a rock as the bear pounced on him. As the bear bit and ripped at the man with its teeth and claws one of the hunters shot and killed it.

The seven foot bear inflicted lacerations to Shaw's scalp requiring 300 staples to close. It also broke two of his ribs.

Another predatory polar account appeared on line. Source: "four Quebecois campers survived a brutal polar bear attack," Terror in paradise, AARON SPITZER, Nunatsiaq News, PO Box 8, Iqaluit, NU X0A 0H0 August 3, 2001 http://www.nunatsiaq.com/archives/nunavut . I emailed the editor 7/21/06 with no response as of 4/24/08.

Four medical professionals from the Gatineau region of Quebec slept in two tents the final night of a week-long canoe trip down the Soper River which flows through Katannilik Territorial Park into Soper Lake. On the morning of July 27, 2006, they planned to canoe the final nine miles to Kimmirut.

Ed Fortier 32, Patricia Doyon 25-years-old, Alain Parenteau 31-year-old and Anne Dumouchel, 33 anticipated no problems as all but Patricia had extensive outdoor experience.

A huge polar bear, its head five feet off the ground, shuffled silently toward the tent of Fortier and Dumouchel, rousing them from their sleep. Fortier felt something pushing against his feet through the tent wall before the animal scratched the roof. When he and Anne screamed, the bear walked toward their partner tent. Doyon and Parenteau awoke as the animal approached their tent.

Moments later the bear ripped open the end of the tent as Doyon and Parenteau fled from the side door. But they did not escape. Nanook grabbed Alain and began slashing at him with its claws as he lay on his back trying to protect himself with his feet while scooting backward. One claw gashed his neck within an inch of his jugular vein. Before long his T-shirt was bloody and shredded. His campmates stood nearby yelling at the bear and throwing rocks at it.

Then the beast lunged for Doyon, tossed her to the ground and slashed her head, back and thigh. Fortier pulled out his knife and stabbed the bear in the throat with its 3-inch blade. Although the knife seemed inadequate, the animal ceased the attack and lumbered down the beach.

Fearful of the bear's return, they hastily tossed their gear into their two canoes and pushed off toward Kimmirut. In no time it was obvious that Doyon and Parenteau were too weak to paddle, causing the group to lash the canoes together with Fortier and Dumouchel paddling.

The others encouraged Parenteau, who lay on the bottom of the canoe shivering, his wounds not bleeding arterially. They scanned the shore in the event of the bear's return and finally reached Kimmirut by 7:30 AM where they awaited a medevac flight to Iqaluit. That afternoon Parenteau was safe in the Baffin Hospital. Doctors expected Parenteau and Doyon to recover.

Although officials sought the bear, it was never found.

ITAY HELED emailed me from Canada requesting phenomenal survival story contacts and followed up his search on April 16, 2007, with the following story which I condensed.

Lydia Angiou was in her yard with her two younger children in February 2006, when she noticed a polar bear observing her 7-year-old son and two friends playing hockey a short distance away at the Ivujivik youth center. Thinking only of protecting her son, the tiny 41-year-old mother ran toward the animal initiating a chain of events.

A youth center worker saw Angyiou kicking the bear and screamed "polar bear!"And a child ran to tell 33-year-old Siqualuk Ainalik about the bear. Siqualuk ran to his brother's house, grabbed a .303-caliber rifle and headed for the youth center.

When he arrived, he saw someone fighting a polar bear. Siqualuk fired three shots into the air with no effect upon the animal. He then looked the bear in the eye and it moved toward him. Ainalik shot it four times then checked to see that Angyiou was alright…and that the bear was NOT!

Tiny Lydia Angyiou, in shock and covered in blood, was taken for medical treatment to the nursing station. In spite of her adventure, she was alright. (Sources: Polar bear no match for fearsome mother in Ivujivik, Jane George, February 17, 2006, http://www.nunatsiaq.com/archives/60217/news/nunavut/60217_03.html; 2006: Nunavik's top story, A woman tackled a hungry polar bear and lived to tell the story... http://www.sikunews.com/art.html?artid=2562&catid=4, Publiser: 30.12.06 00:55)

DON CHAFFIN

When I first contacted Don, he told me he couldn't talk because his bear attack was being litigated. Later I actually researched for his attorney and Don shared information with me. Don does not tell his entire story here but I included this material because of its timing and research-note taking value.

Don Chaffin visit, kidney dialysis center off Tudor, Wed. Nov. 10, 1999 Include his mauling/predatory. Get from him/find his biz card.

On the way from the Suburban into the center I unzipped my cammo coveralls and tied the arms across my chest. I walked into the building and saw a man in a baseball hat and a red western style shirt sitting on a couch to my left. I walked to him, actually looking beyond to the other end of the room forward and off to the left before asking, "Are you Don?"

He stood and said "yes," and I extended my right hand and said, "I'm Larry."

Don appeared to be around 6'1 or 2" tall and pretty solid. He wore a pair of beige-tan suspenders a couple inches wide that matched the beige in his shirt collar. He said, "Sit down." I did and I began the conversation by asking what had ever become of his court case. We spent quite a bit of time with his detailing his attorneys and the background of the case, five years in the waiting, Don's original request for a settlement and his disappointment in the time delay. Toward the end of our visit Don told me a little about his attack but stated that "I've never told my story to anyone, not a living soul." I told him that when his story was told "first, it needs to be in your own words and second, it needs to be acceptable to you in print."

I visited with him from 2:00 to 3:40 PM then went to see Tom Smith. It was interesting because Tom introduced me to a lady (and later her husband who alluded to "our pastor Fred Voss knows you") and Don Chaffin's name came up. I told them I had talked with him less than an hour earlier.

Don commended "Alex, my friend who saved my life. He should have been recognized and given an award but he received criticism and a reprimand. Anyone who would stay in a room where another was being mauled and eaten by a bear deserves recognition, not reprimand." He said that he'd been to Houston a number of times to have reconstructive surgery, that "they took bone from here and here (indicating his left hip area) and put it in here and here (indicating his right temple and right cheek areas) and rebuilt my eye socket so my eye would stay in. My right eye used to be my best eye, but now I have blurred vision out of it. They told me my right eye would never allow vision but I have some."

December 8, 1999

Went to center, referred by worker to nurses' station, went in, saw Don, held up *Outdoor Life* magazine and he motioned me back, shook hands, introduced me to his wife Betty, spoke few minutes, he invited me downstairs for turkey dinner.

We went and visited an hour (2:10-3:00 or so). A pilot, owner of 180, sat down and talked. Previously owned a PA12 and then Super Cub people suggested he buy, but preferred the 12 for room. Owned an 11 before that and said it was too small and wouldn't hold enough of a load to be practical. He said he hauled out 2 caribou and friend with 12.

Don told me a little about his mauling. He'd been working a crossword puzzle and rose to leave room. Folded paper up and put it in pocket or may not have. Saw polar bear at window and started by when it broke window with paws. He grabbed a magazine, rolled it up and swatted it in the face until if fell back to the ground. He ran around table and tripped on stool at end, fell. Meanwhile bear came back through window and lunged across table and onto him as he rose to leave.

He said that the docs in Houston removed about an 8-inch piece of bone from his pelvis which they used to replace the cheekbone which bear had removed, that he had to hold up his eye lid with his hand in order to get it to work, but that the docs repaired that.

Much of the material I've researched outlines plans for towns or villages and work related areas for protection against polar bears. Many villages have polar bear watch or warning programs. Authors of *White Bear* state, the "greatest incidence of human injury by (polar) bears was mining and oil exploration camps during winter operations." Pg. 149.

One internet web site provides the following warning (www.thepoles. com), "The best protection against polar bears is a gun. Shotgun is the standard of Canada and a Magnum handheld the choice of Russia. The shotgun should be 15 calibers and not greased. Keep it outside the tent at all times or it will ice up. Tie a string to it leading into the tent for fast reach. Protect it in a durable plastic bag and carry it in a padded gun cover with a shoulder strap. Carry it with you at all times, don't leave it on one sled when returning for the other. Mantle and test fire occasionally. The gun provided at Resolute Bay with names carved in its handle has a history of malfunction, especially in very cold temperatures. We advise to stay away from it.

"There are flares available to scare off the bear. The accounts for their use have however been somewhat disappointing. The bears have ducked and then kept on with their business of mugging sleds.

"The weak part of the bear spray can is the aerosol pump that can freeze in cold temperatures. Keep the spray inside your clothing while traveling and inside your sleeping bag at night. We carried it on us, then pulledl it out and tested it in below -40C. It worked fine every time."

Other advice regarding polar bears: "…the Innuit that we interviewed said they would never travel in polar bear country without a firearm." (Pg. 70, *Polar Bear Conflicts with Humans* #3, Susan Fleck, Steve Herrero, Department of Renewable Resources, Yellow Knife, NWT, 1988).

"Eleven of the 15 wildlife biologists and officers interviewed felt that Parks Canada should change its firearms policy to allow visitors to northern parks inhabited by polar bears to carry firearms…" (Pg. 73, *Polar Bear Conflicts with Humans* #3, Susan Fleck, Steve Herrero, Department of Renewable Resources, Yellow Knife, NWT, 1988).

CHAPTER 6
PUBLIC SAFETY

THE NEW BEAR

In general bears-of-old wanted little to do with people. Fifty-plus years ago both blacks and grizzlies fled man's presence. Supporting this concept are three telling quotations from 1961, 1998 and 2004:

1) In 1961 famed outdoor writer Jack O'Connor wrote in *The Big Game Animals of North America*, "The chances of a hunter being mauled by a black bear are about the same as being struck by a meteor."

2) Denise Satre, whose husband was killed by a black bear, wrote Gary Shelton, "There was something else important we were unaware of—the change in black bear behavior. It used to be that when people saw a bear, which was seldom, it was just a blur as it ran away. Now many of them are not afraid of people, and we see bears all the time." (*Bear Attacks: The Deadly Truth*, Pg. 199, see Satre story in predatory section herein)

3) Kevin Frey with Montana Department of Fish, Wildlife & Parks states, "We assume bears think gunshots are dangerous, but they have no way of knowing this. Maybe it used to be that way, but that's not passed on through the generations anymore. This is a different bear here now." [Underlining is Kaniut emphasis] (*Where the Grizzly Walks*, Pg. 233)

Times have changed. And so have the bears.

From the mid-Twentieth Century, the heyday for *Outdoor Life Magazine* colleagues Jack O'Connor and Ben East, until 2017 bear behavior has undergone change nationwide. Ben East shed some light on this initial change… "it's close to unheard of for a bear…that attacks and kills a human…then carries the victim to feed on. There have been at least three substantiated cases…in the United States. Strangest of all, each time the man-eater was a black bear, not a polar, grizzly or big *brown.*" (Page 68, *Narrow Escapes and Wilderness Adventures*, Outdoor Life, E.P. Dutton & Co. New York, 1960)

Because of this drastic change from what was "normal" bear behavior, your friendly neighborhood North American bear became more brazen and less fearful of man… therefore more likely to stir up trouble.

We are witnessing the unprecedented habituation of these predators to humans. The key concept here is habituation. Man has allowed bears to become more and more familiar with mankind.

The formerly bashful bear evolved into a different animal, receiving numerous names depending upon its behavior or the lexicon of those referring to him. The bear hanging around campgrounds became *panhandler*. The bear that interrupted man's activities in an ongoing fashion became known as *nuisance*. Later that bear was labeled food *conditioned* or, arguably, *habituated*. The city-dwelling bear became *urbanized*. The bottom line is that these bears have become accustomed to man's proximity and a dangerous familiarity has developed. This bear is now common in back yards seeking dog food, bird seed or garbage. In many ways the food conditioned, habituated and urban bear are one and the same. I agree with bear author Gary Shelton who addresses this animal as the *new bear*.

It's the same panhandler we've always known but it now has a batch of attitude thrown in. And man has taken on a different attitude toward this habituated critter. Consequently we have taught it that we will co-exist with it, which has emboldened it. For a generation or two it has taught its cubs that man is a pansy.

This new bear knows humans are harmless. It does not fear man because we protect it. It is more aggressive because we tolerate it more; we hunt it less—some states have outlawed hunting bears with hounds. We don't hurt this bear nor aversively condition it…which will result in more human interactions within a generation or so. We currently manage it in a manner that places its safety before the safety of humans.

Numerous bear "experts" tell us we can co-exist with bruin if we just give it a chance. There are others with equal bear expertise who agree with the theme of this book and the fact that bears are and should be considered dangerous. A number one voice for the people is Gary Shelton. He alludes to a paper presented in 1987 by Erik S. Nyholm in which he attributes increased bear behavioral change to protection of bears. Shelton further states,

> "…we are slowly entering into a new era in our relationship with bears. There will be more bears in B.C., and much less negative-conditioning-influence by people on bear behavior. This will result in more human/bear conflict, and more bear encounters that are hard to survive. Some bear biologists would disagree with me on this subject–not because of clear evidence to the contrary, but because they fear that such a concept could be used to justify the hunting and control killing of bears in order to reduce bear danger to people." (*Bear Encounter Survival Guide*, Pg. 7 Introduction)

Let's take a look at the situation from the bear's point of view. *Hmmmm. There's a two-legged up ahead. No reason to fear him. I don't see a smoke pole. On second thought, I've never seen a firearm. I only know about them from hearing Grandpa Teddy talk about two-leggeds in the old days. They shot their smoke poles and injured or killed some of my kin. But they've changed. They don't seem to want to hurt us anymore. So there's no reason to fear them. It also makes it easier to get closer to them and their homes where we can have our way with them. I guess we of the bear clan can thank their leaders for convincing them that we are to be admired and saved for a new generation. And our numbers are growing by leaps and bounds.*

Since about 1995 this new bear has grown more assertive, almost disdainful of man. Aggressively hanging out in broad daylight. And it seldom flinches in man's presence. Gary Shelton shares a story of one such black bear attacking a young man amidst dozens of campers (*Bear Attacks: The Deadly Truth*, Pp. 52-plus—see Marchuk Boys in this book). Here is an example of a predacious black attack in which 70 campers in various stages of activity prepared for the day.

Would this bear have behaved in this manner thirty years ago?

And what about the next bear?

Bears in the 'Hood

During the first thirty years we lived in the same south Anchorage house (1970 to 2000), we saw three bears between our house and the New Seward Highway a mile and a half away—one every ten years. From 2000-2005 we saw 2 to 5 each summer **in our yard** and 7 visited us in 2006. In 2008 we had a juvenile delinquent black bear in our chicken

225

run which I effectively pepper sprayed—that's the year my wife began carrying pepper spray when working in the yard or garden. The year 2009 was a slow year as we saw only one black bear by our mailbox. In 2011 we saw 9 blacks. What's wrong with this picture?

ADF&G roundly scrambles to educate city dwellers, to assure us we can co-exist with their bears. We Anchorageites are criticized for putting garbage out too early for garbage pickup—it's bad policy because it tempts bears. Our local fish wrapper spawns criticism of bad people, such as those who have bird feeders.

And, no, we don't have bird feeders. Not a chance. Am I supposed to plow under my raspberry patch, dispose of the garden, deep six our chickens, disallow grandchildren in the yard, keep my wife in the house, sell her horse, stop putting out trash?

Although there are way too many instances of people's carelessness with food sources, the number one attractant for bears in Anchorage is moose calves, of which we have an abundance. Media does not mention ADF&G's allowing a growing number of moose to propagate in town, attracting more and more bears to one of their favorite meals, moose "veal"! Every year the bears show up when the calves are born.

Because they are omnivorous, bears eat anything that tickles their fancy. They are especially fond of tender victuals, like elk calves. "The grizzly follow the elk, and after they come out of hibernation and get their fill of green grass, they naturally take to elk calves. Occasionally they include the mother on the menu." (Pg. 173, *The Only Good Bear is a Dead Bear*) You might say the moose is Anchorage's version of elk; these bear magnets endanger people. A couple of years ago my friend Frank Kufel told me that he heard about a woman in Anchorage who exited her home to find a moose carcass leaning against her house with a grizzly chowing down on it.

We have so enabled bears to habituate to man, either directly or indirectly, it is common to see them regularly, even in our cities where stories of urban bears are legion. Before Alaskan statehood in 1959 those bears would have been on the dinner table. However, it's now politically incorrect to harm a bear so the citizens of Anchorage are blamed—it's bad people behavior...it seems we're supposed to invite them into our homes for coffee and donuts. Brace yourself, some of these bears and stories may be coming to a neighborhood near you.

Whereas Alaska Department of Fish and Game biologists are addressing the predator problem in the field, it seems the biologists' counterparts in the city have a different view of bear numbers.

Nationwide city bear stories seem to be on the increase.

When a black bear broke into her Agawa Road home, Lisa Spirko and her children took refuge in their bedroom, called for help and exited a window to safety when police and a biologist from Fish and Wildlife responded to her. The bear fled through another window and was shot and killed. ("Bear Invades Home –Ordeal for Terrified Mom & Her 2 Children," Vernon, New Jersey Web News, June 12, 2003, www.vernonweb.com/vwnews.htm)

Entering her attached garage to fetch an item from her car near Grand Marais, Minnesota, Heil-Smith, 37, ran into a black bear sow and its cub. She opened the door while chatting on her cordless phone and was surprised to see the bear between her car and the side of the garage. With nowhere else to go, the critter rushed Heil-Smith who attempted to shut the door, only to discover the animal was too strong. The sow wrapped its forelegs around the woman who fell backward. That's when Heil-Smith overcame her fear with anger because the bear was in her house. She stuck her knee up so the bear couldn't bite her and grabbed its nose, simultaneously yelling, "Get out of my house!" After the bear left Heil-Smith, the lady's punctures and scratches necessitated numerous stitches at Cook County North Shore Hospital. ("Woman Fends Off Bear Attack in Her Own Garage," Clint Austin, *The Atlanta Journal-Constitution*, Knight Rider Newspapers, September 24, 2003)

Canadian Margaret Montgomery, 81, let her dog out one evening only to have the dog chased into the lady's garage by an apple eating bear. In an effort to protect her dog, Margaret held onto the bear and punched it. She grabbed a garden hoe and pummeled the bear with it, driving it off. The lady suffered claw marks to her face and chest and a puncture wound in her thigh and was taken by ambulance to Mindemoya Hospital. (Ontario Federation of Anglers & Hunters, "Manitoulin Senior Fends Off Bear Attack," Margo Little, *The Sudbury Star*, September 26, 2003, Ontario, Canada)

June 8, 2006 Stan Walchuk, Jr. filed an internet piece "Riding In Bear Country" on *Equine Trader*. Until the early 1990's he'd had relatively few bear encounters. He alluded to half dozen grizzly scenarios — one pinned his family at their blazing campfire; one rushed his six pack horses; another mauled a nearby camp neighbor; one attacked a hunter on an elk kill and another pummeled an elderly gentleman. However in the past few years he has experienced "more serious bear confrontations" than during his previous twenty years.

Returning from a charter fishing trip with my daughter Jill on May 18, 2008, we heard the news about another bear caper. A bear broke into a couple's house in south Anchorage above Potter Marsh and inspected their refrigerator and freezer…spawning this little satire from my pen.

Honey, time to sell the house. Yep. First it was the dog food that Fish and Game wanted secured. Next came bird feeders. Can't enjoy the birds anymore because the bears might want their food. Upped the fine from a hundred bucks in 2007 to 300-plus in 2008. Then it was garbage.

If dog food, bird feeders and garbage cans attract bears what does that say about backyard barbeques, fruit trees, berry patches, gardens, chickens, ducks, pigs, cows, goats, pets, fish smokers, small children and slow moving senior citizens! Not to mention (again) moose calves.

And what about the recent infusion of salmon into Anchorage's creeks? How many bears do those streams attract? How long has the Alaska Department of Fish and Game been stocking these bear attracting streams? How is it that they can fine a person for "feeding" bears when Fish and Feathers stock Anchorage streams with salmon and allow the rampant propagation of moose?

To top it off, we now have the ultimate perpetrating bear attractant— food storage appliances in the form of freezers and refrigerators… INSIDE the house!

Looks like we have four options, Dear: 1) stop eating refrigerated and frozen food, 2) put some neighborhood bears on the dinner table, 3) erect a croc-filled moat or 4) move to a safer area free from four-legged predators, say Detroit, LA or Chicago.

How does the garbage outside-the-house problem solve the bear-inside-the-house problem?

It doesn't.

While surfing the Net in 2009, I read and summarized some bear-man events—all from Colorado and the *Denver News*. On July 8… "Boulder man watching TV didn't know bear was inside house" related that a bear entered the home of Bruce Rice who watched the Colorado Rockies while talking on the phone. Bruce's neighbor Peter Schinkler alerted him. The two men chased the bear from the house before Bruce's dog Buzz treed it. Wildlife officials shot the bear with beanbags and it left. Because the Division of Wildlife acknowledges that bears can smell food from three to five miles away, they encourage people to remove pet foods and bird feeders from their homes. Division of Wildlife manager Chris Mettenbrink stated, 'We wanted to put the fear of men back into them.'

"Bear Shot Inside Colorado Springs Home" (July 13) relates a Colorado Springs homeowner reported that a bear forced open the back door of his home. The man's roommate yelled. After the bear roared from a staircase, the homeowner shot it with a .45-caliber long Colt pistol.

"Bear burglar keeps coming back" (July 26), homeowners Hillary Grady and her husband were surprised and shaken up when a bear tore a screen from an open window and accessed their kitchen. This was the Grady's second bear burglar surprise to which officials responded by bean-bagging the nearby bear."

And on July 27 "Bear Breaks Into Home, Terrorizes Family" reports a Boulder family, having spent ten to fifteen years watching bears roam their neighborhood, received an uninvited guest on a recent Monday morning. Awakened by their Russell Terrier-Shepherd mix, the Fischer family discovered a bear ransacking their pantry. Shotgun wielding husband Paul gave the bear an opportunity to exit but it rushed him. He shot it three times, wounding it before the family escaped to their car. The bear lunged toward arriving deputies who dispatched it inside the dwelling. The family indicated they'd seen the 120 pound male bear on the property several times—it attempted to enter the home Tuesday before returning on Thursday to break into one of their vehicles.

After I emailed Tom Remington in 2010 requesting permission to use his bear blog, he granted permission to include the following:

Black Bear Blog by Tom Remington Colorado Woman Eaten By Bear, August 8, 2009.

Officials in Ouray, Colorado are thinking a bear is the cause of a 73-year old woman's death because a bear was found over her body eating it. The same officials point the finger at the woman, faulting her with her own death because she continually fed bears, the report says.

An autopsy will be performed on the unidentified woman and a necropsy on the bear in efforts to determine if the bear found eating on the woman was the same bear that might have killed her.

In the meantime, reports are coming out about increased human/bear encounters in Ouray County, Colorado, the same area where this woman was apparently the target of a hungry bear(s).

Officials point a finger at a lack of natural food and people not taking care of their personal garbage as the two major reasons encounters are on the rise. While there's little that can be done about the lack of natural food, brought on by natural climate conditions, it appears officials are bent on focusing on only one very small aspect of bear management

– increasing fines to those who refuse to take care of their trash. They actually think this is the remedy.

Granted, if you don't want bears rummaging through your garbage and posing a potential risk to you and your family, then people should do what they can to minimize the problem. On the same token, not once in the two articles I have referenced in this piece, did any wildlife official or anyone else mention the idea of control of bear populations.

Why is it that all the blame is put on resident's lack of effort to reduce bear encounters and none on the fish and game department and other wildlife officials to better manage bears? When you decide to buy a home, camp or cabin in bear country, you assume a certain amount of responsibility to learn to deal with bears and other creatures. But by the same token, you would expect fish and game to take responsibility, other than levying stiffer fines, to control bear numbers. Since the beginning of time, we have had to deal with seasons when there is a shortage of natural food.

So, are we to assume now that buying a home in Vail, Colorado is living in bear country and if a bear gets hungry enough and opts to munch on one of the family members, we need stiffer fines for that same family? Will a $10,000 fine deter a hungry bear?

And here's another question I've been chewing on for a while. If officials keep raising fines on people who won't take care of their garbage, who won't stop leaving food out on their dining room tables, who refuse to stop baking cakes and pies, who go outside and garden, who mow their lawns, who entertain guests on their back yard patios, who allow their children to play in the yard, and suppose in theory every ounce of man's property was "bear proof", then what? None of this will stop bears from getting hungry. None of this will create natural food when Mother Nature dictates the bounty. None of this will control the populations of bears.

In theory, once the state creates their perfect little restricted world, complete with multi-thousand dollar fines and there are still bear/human encounters, are we then to expect humans will be expected to stay inside 24/7 and lock their doors, bar their windows and live in fear?

Tom Remington - it's Tom's story

In 2010 three Anchorage stories captured the headlines which I wrote editorialized:

1) Jeff Johnson of Eagle River, Alaska, a few miles northeast of Anchorage, intervened when a black bear managed breaking and entering into his chicken coop. He approached the coop, thinking the bruin may have left, when he looked into the hen house and saw the bear eating a

chicken. He held a hunk of plywood against the window entry and kicked open the lower chicken door so the cluckers could escape. Meanwhile his 20-year-old son Seth called police and returned to his father with a .30-06. Jeff shot the animal and arriving police polished it off with their shotguns. ("Bear helping himself to chickens gets shot in coop," JAMES HALPIN, May 29th, www.ADN.com.)

2) Michael Weiman, 64, shot and killed a brown bear on his property in Eagle River after it chased his wife Memorial Day evening—a great and heroic story on Memorial Day! Give him a medal. He saved his wife and perhaps others. While his wife Marianne walked the family Boxer Mojabe, a punk brown bear charged and Marianne shouted. Michael responded to her screams with his .44 pistol, shooting 3 shots into the ground near the bear. It fled; they escaped into the house; it returned. At that point Michael did the right thing and dusted it with his .30-30 rifle— one shot. Dead bear. Thin the herd. ("Dog intervenes in grizzly attack, but bear is eventually shot," LISA DEMER, June 1, 2010, www.ADN. com)

3) Property owners John and Barbara Lopetrone were surprised by a black bear IN THEIR HOUSE on Upper Huffman Road, fled to the bedroom and called police while it ravaged their kitchen. Police told them to stay in their bedroom and not to make noise while they chased it from the house with hot water. It had entered via an open 1-foot wide window. Police indicated that the bear might have to be eradicated if it returned. Duh! ("Black bear chased off by police returns to Hillside home," JAMES HALPIN, July 14, 2010 11:07 PM.)

The following year police shot and killed a black bear attempting to break into an eastside Anchorage residence Friday. Anchorage Police Department spokesperson Lt. Dave Parker said the incident happened at about 5:14 in the evening, when a black bear tried to get into a house on the 2400 block of Glenkerry Drive, near the Anchorage Baptist Temple. (*Anchorage Daily News* on line, Michelle Theriault Boots, 6:14 PM AKDT, July 1, 2011)

Today's news caught my attention: "Soldotna officer kills bear in residential area," *Anchorage Daily News*/adn.com (September 9, 2011). A large brown bear roamed the Soldotna, Alaska, neighborhood for nearly a week when police officials brought its roaming to a stop. It had rummaged through multiple yards, including ripping the lid from a chest freezer. After numerous calls to the police regarding the foraging animal, officer Victor Dillon dispatched it with a shotgun as it attacked him from twenty-five yards. As you might imagine, some folks were upset while others were supportive of Dillon.

I selected one well written response from the site—lilylee wrote:

"The old-timers on the Kenai Peninsula kept a gun handy and shot bears in their areas, no questions asked, they understood how dangerous it was to have a bear nosing around in the neighborhood. Most of the Kenai Peninsula is a wilderness plenty of room for bears to be in and some bears who get use to humans are dangerous.

"It appears that the homesteaders way to deal with the bruins have had no effect on the bear population 50 yrs later.

"One has to be realistic. One man in Kenai told me he had several acres and today he had 4 brown bear on his property. All animals need a certain amount of space to forage, when any animal population exceeds that capacity they will compete for space and it is stressful on the animals.

"I love the animals of Alaska but for a decade or more there are many stories of encounters with the bear population in the Soldotna and the area bear population is too high."

While emailing a friend in Pelican, Alaska, Christmas wishes in 2011, he related significant bears in the 'hood information. He titled it "Bears and Such" and allowed me to include it here, anonymously of course:

Enjoyed your articles on thinning the herd; we share similar sentiments. I first resided at Pelican some 45+ years ago, the summer of 1966 to be more precise. I never saw an Alaska Brown Bear until the fall of 1970 when I was up on the tidal flats of the Lisianski River. After that they were still somewhat a novelty until about the 1980's. Recently they have been seen on the boardwalk in Pelican, one chased a man into a house last fall.

In 2010 about 15 homes were broken into (unoccupied) on the west side of town. In 2011 the bear(s) continued to break in on the west end and then moved east and out to our cove 3 miles SE of Pelican, we had 6 homes broken into. It has not been uncommon to see a bear or bear(s) on the beach in front of our home and this past June a boar and sow came walking up our boardwalk 20 feet from our back door.

In talking with "old-timers" I was set straight on why there are so many more bears. In the 40's thru the 70's it was common for one or more local salmon trollers fishing in Lisianski Inlet to shoot any bear seen on the beach. Bill Mork, a lifelong resident of Pelican, told me he had shot 35 bears in his past. These old trollers have long since died off and they have not been replaced.

Bears were not tolerated within the Pelican City Limits. Pelican had no garbage dump other than the inlet, (not a good thing), but it did deprive them of an easy food source. In the late fifties or early 60's, "Pelican Bear Control" is reflected in a photo of a sow and cub lying dead on the boardwalk in the center of town. The recidivism rate amongst bears in Pelican was zero.

After the events of last fall I have decided to practice a zero tolerance on a bear close to the house. If they appear to be a present threat or a potential future threat to our property or family then they may have a heart problem. We have entirely too many in our immediate circumstances. I accidentally walked up on one last summer and found myself twenty feet from a full grown Brown Bear, luckily it was not a sow & cubs or just one in bad humor that day. The bear was in the front yard of my neighbor's home not 25 feet from a house that was later broken into that fall.

It is now common to see bears in Pelican and 10-15 or more on a cruise to the head of the inlet. Sooner or later a child or a person not very ambulatory will have a tragic encounter with a bear either in Pelican or on the property of one of the outlying residences. I have heard of one solution to the overpopulation problem; "see'em, shoot'em, and shut up".

Lisianki Skiffer   12/26/11

As 2011 drew to a close, it was appropriate to summarize bear activity in my neighborhood. While returning from helping family friend Chester Meeks in Montana in mid-October, another family friend and neighbor Tamie Hollingsworth, a few blocks south of us, attempted to exit her home, only to be confronted by three grizzly cubs of the year. About the same time another friend Dave Goggins sent me a YouTube clip of the orphans, filmed by neighbors the Lindstrands. Within the next month these cubs were at a neighbor's around the corner and a large sow grizzly, cub her size and cub of the year were eighty yards behind us at another neighbor's. I kept expecting to see these bears until I learned that ADF&G captured the orphans ("Catching orphaned bear cubs proves to be no easy task," by Mary Pemberton, AP, *Anchorage Daily News* on line, Nov. 14, 2011). ADF&G cited a man for dispatching their mother outside his house.

After some serious sleuthing (ADF&G referred me to Alaska State Troopers who refused to provide the man's contact information) and with the help of my friend Leonard Hackett, I was able to locate and interview the shooter and his wife. They were harassed for their venture with the sow grizzly that was making herself a nuisance with the family chickens. He shot and killed the bear and was surprised to discover in the darkness four sets of bear eyes watching him. Shortly thereafter the long arm of the law invited him to pay a fine of $5,000 and to spend two years in their gray bar hotel. He pled guilty and was fined $2000 with no jail time.

Here's a man defending personal property, killing a nuisance bear IN THE CITY. Officials had been called a dozen times in the past with not one single response to his concerns. After he dispatched the bear, he was threatened and criticized. Here's a man doing what any self-respecting, responsible citizen would have done. Yet he was harassed, belittled and demeaned by the local constabulary. He should have been feted with a medal for doing what officialdom refuses to do—protect the neighborhood from wandering bears. (After speaking with the shooter, I discovered that he attempted to keep the hide, thus the fine. Had he turned in the hide, I'm guessing he may NOT have been fined. Nevertheless he was defending his property whereas the ADF&G did not.)

In mid-November our family friend Brian Hosken showed me a picture of a large brown bear track in his parent's driveway off Clark's Road. And on November 25, while reading the newspaper on line, I noticed bears are still about, primarily around Service High School and Hilltop ski area. ("Brown bear seems to have put off winter nap, roaming Hillside," HILLSIDE: Ski club groomer reports multiple sightings. By ROSEMARY SHINOHARA, *Anchorage Daily News*, November 25, 2011.)

More than likely this same bear bulldozed his way from Abbott Road, through a roadside berm, across our friends Melinda and Dave Skeins' yard and onto their driveway, leaving 15-plus-inch tracks in late November or early December. Bears hibernate, right?

In 2012 the opening round of Anchorage man vs. bear began Saturday evening around 6:00 PM May 12. A brown bear bushwhacked 57-year-old Howard Meyer on a hiking trail near his home up Eagle River valley. Some of the looney fringe related they saw no reason to go after the bear which posed no threat to man (*Anchorage Daily News* internet site, "Brown bear attacks hiker on Eagle River Valley trail," by Michelle Theriault Boots, May 14, 2012).

A distant neighbor Carol K. shared an intense bear story that occurred very near her Anchorage home. She titled the story "Forty Steps."

Our neighbors' moving sale in late May of 2012 included a "rocking moose" that just didn't look right. Closer inspection revealed fresh slash marks on its formerly-stuffed head and body, and the ground littered with its fluffy contents. One neighbor then reported he'd seen a large grizzly bear lumbering through the yards the night before. Taste-testing the 'fake' moose, speckled with leftover oatmeal, surmised the mom. Fortunately, the only sign of bear that day.

The next morning brought light fog, but an otherwise nice start for a short 5K from home, enough to get the heart pounding. While my dog usually joined me for companionship, and for extra ears, eyes and nose, this time he stayed home to rest his aging, achy knees. Heading up, around and down to a rushing creek was scenic and peaceful, and I soon made the turnaround back up the hill. As I approached the 4-way stop where I would turn left, a moose cow and calf suddenly bounded across the road ahead of me. I stopped, held my breath and checked all around for anything that may have startled them. No sign of dogs, cars, or…bear. Within seconds, a small, softly buzzing motorbike drove down from their direction and then putt-putted the other way.

I resumed jogging, barely rounding the stop sign, when a woman in an SUV opposite me made a careful turn to her right and waved. As I thought she must be referring to the animals down the road, I nodded to acknowledge I was aware of the moose and continued a few more steps. The SUV lady also drove a few more feet, ever so slowly. Puzzled, certain all was clear, with an alternate route planned if the skittish moose were near, I suddenly realized the SUV lady was now pointing behind me—frantically. I noticed a large, silvery German shepherd in her back seat, sitting still, without barking.

My instant 180 degree turn brought me face-to-face with a massive brown furry head on a humped back, complete with golden brown eyes, a wide mouth making whuff-whuff sounds, as thick curved claws clicked on the pavement reminded me…I was IN THE WAY!

Diving right into a gnarly brush-filled ditch did not seem effective enough to avoid a slashing—or worse—BEQUICK. BEQUIET. Dashing to my left seemed a little more hopeful where an old Mustang was abandoned—OUTTA SIGHT. OUTTA MIND—in a driveway straight across the road. SUV lady remained in place as I all but flew in front of her and—PLEASEBEUNLOCKED—flung open the Mustang passenger door. Ducked into the car, lurched across the seat to blare the horn—OUTTA SCENT. OUTTA REACH—I caught sight of Great Big Grizzly coming around the front of the SUV, slowly only to sniff the air, then veering toward the Mustang. I had to completely rely on SUV lady to honk rev her engine, screech tires, if the door did not open and there was no other cover—and now to find the car horn did not work!

As I hunkered down, still stretched for the horn, the SUV lady pulled closer as one other red vehicle slowly passed the driveway. SUV lady and

I signaled to each other that Great Big Grizzly was gone. For whatever reason, he had quickly turned back to the road and soon disappeared.

I, too, went back out to the road to thank the SUV lady. As we recapped the ordeal, it was clear that it wasn't clear. Neither of us knew if the bear had initially chased the moose down from the upper road, if the motorbike startled the moose which triggered the bear, unbeknownst to me-the-jogger-who-got-in-the-way, or was Great Big Grizzly chasing me then noticed the moose. SUV lady didn't see the bear until the stop sign. I don't believe the bear was behind me before I'd turned at the stop sign, but was already heading downhill or waiting in the ditch for the moose. I felt I'd been extra vigilant along the whole route, and would have heard rustling in the ditch, or claws clicking on the pavement much sooner and would definitely have been overtaken on the uphill.

While we talked, the red vehicle stopped ahead and an older woman got out. She came toward us, actually wagging her finger and shouting: "Didn't we know not to ever, ever run from a bear?! Didn't we know that would be considered harassment?"! He was probably a 2 to 3-year-old which would now be shot because of us! Not, "are you OK—what happened?..." rather an outright attack and assumption we were intimidating a grizzly! I hardly think it looked like SUV lady and I were out to take close up photos. Now, that's what really got my heart pounding.

Her unbelievable accusations were much more disturbing than the actual bear encounter. I tried to explain she obviously did not see or know what happened. I wondered who was harassing whom? I also wondered if, as she walked back to her car, the bear reappeared and chased her, whether she would even appreciate being forewarned as I had been. I fully accept that I was inadvertently part of Nature's chase, and could easily have experienced a seriously different outcome that day. I respect responsibilities of outdoor life, wherever that may be. I do not feel that I was interfering or otherwise doing the wrong thing in that situation.

At any rate, SUV lady offered a welcome ride home, so we shared a few other bear encounters over our many years in Alaska, though none quite like this one. Her old German shepherd, mostly blind and deaf, even seemed to agree. I remain extremely grateful my creaky four-legged buddy was not with me that morning.

Later on, I returned to the stop sign to double check the distance to the Mustang. Forty steps—40 up, 40 down, each time. Roughly 120 feet from…a Great Big Grizzly barreling its enormous, rippling body downhill. Milliseconds, really, to decide the next step. Had SUV lady not appeared when and where she did, I may not have had those few seconds for those forty steps.

Ironically, the very next day's news reported a large 2-3-year-old grizzly male was indeed shot and killed within five miles from my "run-in," during its attack in a llama pen later that night. Other reports rolled in that summer of grizzlies breaking down chicken coops, dog houses, GARAGE DOORS, not to mention maulings. Even my ol' dog warned us more than once of the new, glossy, brown cub in our woods with mama watching. Sadly, our other male grizzlies were also shot and killed by October of that year in our area. While black bears have regularly scurried about our neighborhood, these recent encounters are very different, and very dangerous. Be quick. Be quite. Until time to be loud. And never assume.

While surfing Drudge Report April 7, 2013, I was drawn to a story about a man who was cited by the police for killing a charging bear in his yard. Having seen a bear in his yard recently, the man carried a shotgun.

The coppers said the animal created no danger to people.

The eco-nuts said the shooter should have called officials.

The bear—which is supposed to live free in the wilds—is in man's yard. That's reason enough to dispatch it. Again, we have a prime example of the value of the human as juxtaposed to that of the animal kingdom. Had the man—or other human been killed or maimed, would the bear be charged for a crime? ("Auburn Man Facing Charges After Killing Bear In His Backyard," http://boston.cbslocal.com/2013)

We're being brainwashed by government agencies like the NPS and the animal rights BULL-oney. Some of the animal rights armada feel that animals supersede humans. We are in a pitched battle with the earth worshippers who seem to think that the environment is of greater value than *homo sapien*. It becomes even more incumbent upon us with common sense to stand tall and provide information that will allow safe passage in bear country—not safe passage for the bear but for man!

Increasing predator numbers—(and other nuisances)

Mounting predator numbers will probably increase predator-human interface which will likely result in injury or death to both. On March 8, 2010, local news media reported the discovery of a female body near the roadway a mile outside Chignik Lake, an Alaska village of 150 people.

Four people returning from Portage Bay on snow machines had noticed gloves and blood on the road and stopped to investigate around

6:30 PM. They read the signs in the snow—a set of person tracks interspersed with wolf tracks and accompanied by a trail of blood and drag marks leading downhill. The riders proceeded a short distance and found Candice Berner's remains.

Hastening to town they alerted others and later that night several people spotted wolves in the area, apparently completely unafraid of the humans. Alaska's State Medical Examiner concluded the cause of death was "multiple injuries due to animal mauling." Wolf tracks indicated as many as four wolves participated in the attack.

After the death of local 32-year-old teacher Ms. Berner, a spunky, 4-foot, 11-inch tall lady who hailed from Slippery Rock, Pennsylvania, and whose interests included boxing, weight lifting and running, townspeople feared for their safety and patrolled against further area wolf activity. (Sources include The *Anchorage Daily News*, Villagers unnerved by fearless wolves, by JAMES HALPIN, jhalpin@adn.com, March 11, 2010 and FoxNews.com, TEACHER MAULED TO DEATH BY WOLVES IN ALASKA, Friday, March 12, 2010.)

In the fall of 2010 wolves terrorized citizens of Port Heiden, Alaska, a village within 50 miles of Chignik Lake. The continued disappearance of family pets caused the State of Alaska "open the season" so to speak on Old Yellow Eyes—time to thin the herd.

It is interesting that so many people defend the predators, often with emotion instead of knowledge—interesting that so many of them defend the indefensible. While reviewing my research on wolf attacks just before Christmas 2015 I decided to visit the internet and input "North American wolf attacks." Wikipedia listed 36 North American human fatalities up to 2010.

During the fall of 2010 and winter 2011 wolves gained the attention of officials at Elmendorf-Fort Richardson base in Anchorage. Administrators decided it was time to reduce wolf numbers because of reported encounters between people and their pets. On Wednesday February 9, the *Anchorage Daily News* carried a piece alluding to joggers encountering and escaping wolves and along with the piece came the attendant pros and cons of saving Mr. Wolf and Company.

Follow up that scenario with the following. The *Anchorage Daily News* reported the extermination of wolves on the Anchorage army-air base. Mike Campbell wrote March 25, 2011, "State kills 9 wolves on base," (PREDATORS: Risk of attacks reduced, Fish and Game officials say). During a 6-month predator-control program at Joint Base Elmendorf-Richardson Alaska Department of Fish and Game took action against a pack of 14 wolves known to visit the base and munch on pooches and kitty-cats. Some laud the action in the interests of public safety, but the eco-nuts went ballistic over man's regarding public safety over that of the beasts among us.

Ol' Lar says, "Why can't we learn to live with the gentle creatures living in our driveways and eating our pets? They're not hurting us…and besides, we invaded their land! We're just selfish. I'm ashamed to be a human. Blah, blah, blah. Poor babies. Sometimes it's hard to differentiate the tree huggers from the tree sap they're hugging!"

If you're so inclined, you can visit the World Wide Web and read endless accounts of animal attacks upon humans. For starters Fox News. com reported "Nanny Rips Baby Girl From Jaws of Coyote in California Sandbox," Saturday, May 03, 2008.

And from articles.latimes.com "Concerns Grow Over Coyotes," May 10, 2008 by David Kelly, Times Staff Writer: Since the 1970's experts have recorded 111 coyote attacks on people in California, a 3-year-old Glendale girl killed in 1981. These opportunistic predators will attack small children the same size as their prey. The yotes living next to people lose their natural fear of man.

Other animals affecting financial interests as well as personal safety include feral hogs (our Swedish friends the Kalls tell us they are also out of control in Sweden, and extremely aggressive). While surfing the Internet July 11, 2010, I ran across a piece detailing the threat to our North American populace and pigs. Reported on http://quazen.com/recreation/ outdoors/the-pig-boom Knewf in Outdoors June 7, 2010 wild boars exist in forty of our fifty states, their numbers having doubled in the past twenty years. Their physical size has also doubled from an average 150 pounds to over 300 pounds, some as heavy as 500 pounds. Their numbers (guesstimated at over 4 million) are increasing faster than they can be eliminated by hunting or trapping.

As the hog population increases, so does the potential for human encounters, people becoming targeted more and more for attacks. As you might expect, animal rights groups are incensed with the killing of feral hogs.

I read more about hogs February 7th on Fox News on line ("No Oink About it, Feral Pig Problem Spreading," by Ruth Ravve, February 7, 2011, FoxNews.com). The piece explained numbers of feral hogs (at least 4 million but actual numbers unknown) and "more than $8 million worth of damage every year," which does not include damage to the natural environment, native species and diseases they carry that can affect humans. Within six months of their birth the hogs can birth litters of 13 and do so every 1.5 to 2 litters a years. They are attacking pets, people, yards and other landscape—their damage resembles a bulldozer's plowing. At least one state is authorizing hunting license holders to shoot swine on sight. No closed season. No limit. But some animal rights folks disapprove.

"Don Anthony, of the Animal Rights Foundation of Florida, said he doesn't believe the swine are causing all the problems that are claimed." He feels that the state should neuter the hogs to keep the population under control because these wonderful beasts have been in the U.S. for 500 years—regardless of the fact that the brutes are hog-handling America. Ol' Don says, "We should be used to them by now. Killing them is barbaric and unnecessary."

Says Ol' Lar, more nitwittery on parade... looney bin homo sapiens with total disregard for common sense, on a mission to save the hogs. Don is a prime example of someone with no clue as to the safety and economic welfare of his fellow citizens. But he would probably instantly jump on the band wagon to declare an elderly lady who allowed animals to die in her care as unfit. I refer to a piece I read while surfing the internet February 23, 2011, about "An elderly disabled woman lived inside the home with all the animals, authorities said. She could face animal cruelty charges."

The piece talks about the deplorable conditions within the dwelling and the 70-plus animals therein with NO mention as to the lady's welfare. In my backwoods way of thinking, this screams volumes about where our society has come. We're more interested in the animals than the "elderly DISABLED woman." Where are her neighbors? How many of them took the time to look in on her? After the fact, the finger pointing remains...a "bad" woman who allowed animals to die. She is elderly AND disabled. Perhaps has dementia. Let's hear it for the U.S. Humane Society but not for the lady! ("Dozens of sick and dead animals in Long Island Home," MYFOXNY.COM, Tuesday, 22 Feb. 2011).

Other examples of animals' increasing and causing problems worldwide follow:

In Bavaria at the end of November 2006, www.igorilla.com reported hunters chased 15 wild pigs from the cemetery that subsequently invaded the town, terrorizing people and doing up to $10K damage in a shop.

June 25, 2008, FOXNews.com noted a predatory cougar in New Mexico. Robert Nawojski, 55, was reported missing. While state game and fish employees searched for him, they encountered a mountain lion which they shot and wounded before finding the remains of Nawojski, partially buried.

The third week in July 2008 Fox News carried a piece alluding to brown bears causing havoc in Russia, primarily at Kamchatka where two mining guards were mauled and eaten. The article alluded to numerous other accounts of bears entering towns and creating problems.

At the end of October 2009, I learned that a woman had been attacked by coyotes and Googled "coyotes kill lady" and found numerous related articles. The following comes from Newshound by J.R. Absher, the Outdoor Life web Pg. (October 29, 2009, "Killed by Coyotes," by Gerry Bethge): A couple of coyotes attacked and killed a solo hiker in Cape Breton Highlands Park, Nova Scotia. Even though others responded to her screams and alerted park officials, 19-year-old folk singer Taylor Mitchell succumbed to her injuries the next day in the hospital.

With the introduction of gray wolves into Yellowstone, encounters between them and people have skyrocketed:

Houndsman Shane Richards lost three hounds to wolves near Headquarters, Idaho, in September, 2011. Within the past few years other hound hunters have lost their dogs to wolves.

In October 2011 archer Rene Anderson hunted elk about ten miles from Headquarters, Idaho. She carried a .44 Magnum at her husband Denny's suggestion and dropped a wolf which was stalking her at ten feet.

Countless other stories abound, like the couple camping near Cedars on the North Fork of the Clearwater, kept up all night by wolves howling outside their wall tent before the family escaped to their car.

Readers Digest addressed the increased numbers of predators and their aggressiveness in November 2003. In the article "Man Eater" David H. Baron discussed both the increase in mountain lion population and parallel attacks upon humans and their pets. David delineated the fact that increased deer numbers have returned the big cats to their former hunting grounds which are now changed by increased human habitation and dwellings as well as roadways and expanded city boundaries, complicating the coexistence of man and beast... "And humans themselves were different. Unlike the Native Americans who once hunted the cougar for its skin and meat, and unlike the miners and ranchers who killed the cougar out of hatred, these people craved the presence of wildlife. Many had moved to the area just to be closer to nature." (Pg. 166)

Once cats and bears habituate to man, both pose a threat to him. Chris Thompson, who killed a bear in the line of duty as a police officer in Soldotna, Alaska, said, "Once bears lose their fear of man, they can become really dangerous. When this happens, I don't think people and bears can coexist." (*More Alaska Bear Tales,* Pg. 249)

Carel P. Brest van Kempen shares increasing population and the blame game on his Internet blog

"As changing human attitudes replaced predator bounties with protective legislation, the large carnivore population in the lower 48 has become larger than in any time in the past century. Of course, the human population is also at an unprecedented high, so it's tempting to chalk the recent spate of attacks up to a redistribution of probability. Of the 12 recorded Black Bear fatalities in the lower 48, and the 45 fatalities in Canada and Alaska, the vast majority occurred where bears have little contact with Man, so habituation to humans can't be blamed—but that's exactly what's being blamed for the Mountain Lion attacks out west.

"For several years, a number of experts warned of precisely the kind of incident that happened to Shir Feldman last week. David Baron's 2003 book, *The Beast in the Garden* was a response to the 1991 mauling death of 18-year old Scott Lancaster in Idaho Springs, Colorado. Barron agreed with biologists Michael Sanders and Jim Halfpenny, who believe that the behavior of Mountain Lions in Colorado's eastern Rockies is changing. The advancing urban/wildland interface and a growing population of Mountain Lions that are rarely threatened by humans add up to a dangerous mix, according to these men. The urban interface creates excellent deer habitat, which attracts the cats, who are losing their fear of man."

I emailed Carel January 5, 2007 and he responded the same day with the following email:

Hi Larry:

Thanks for your message. I'd be happy to permit you to use my quote. Please attribute it to me. My surname is "Brest van Kempen" (three words, only 2 of them capitalized). My first name is Carel.

I'd also appreciate it if you could send me the chapter when the time comes.

Best Wishes,

Carel P. Brest van Kempen

http://www.cpbrestvankempen.com

In Defense of more Critters

What place should predators—especially bears—occupy in our cities? Two groups have strong feelings on this subject—those who protect bears and those who protect people.

At least four groups of people are interested in protecting bears: the fish and game managers, other state and federal agencies, animal rights groups and individuals.

If, according to some estimates, bear numbers in North America have increased 40% in the past 20 years, what have the departments of fish and game to say about it? Through my efforts with the Alaska Department of Fish and Game to reduce bear numbers the last several years, I've come to the conclusion that the biology boys would rather manage us than their precious animals.

Their most recently retired bear man, Rick Sinnott, apparently sought to incorporate bears into city living. From the International Association of Wildlife Filmmakers 2007, site comes the following (note: European spelling):

"But perhaps the single most important factor in maintaining the rich biodiversity in Anchorage is one man, Rick Sinnott; area biologist for the Alaska Department of Fish & Game. It is his brave and ground-breaking approach to conservation over the last 15 years that has created the current remarkable situation. Rick passionately believes that humans and wild animals can live side by side, and that conservation in a modern, rapidly urbanising, world is not just about preserving areas of untouched wilderness like large scale museum exhibits, but about maintaining and appreciating the essence of wilderness wherever we live. In Anchorage that appreciation and acceptance of wilderness has meant some very large, and potentially dangerous, animals living cheek by jowl with some quarter of a million people.

"This approach to conservation is not some ill-considered new age idea that Rick has just come up with, far from it. It is an idea that has been with Rick since he was at collage; a line from Henry David Theroux 'In wilderness is preservation of the world' has struck with him and guided his approach to managing the wildlife in the city. Nor is Rick just an ideas man, he has an exceptional blend of qualities that has allowed him to put his philosophy into action; an outstanding level of understanding of wildlife and a real passion for his work, coupled with the toughness and resourcefulness developed from a childhood spent in the great outdoors and several tours of duty in Vietnam as a marine sergeant." (www.iawf.org/uk)

In order to eliminate predators in town my family theorized that it would take an extreme event—such as the death of a child— to get the attention of the game managers and those with other official capacities.

As of November 10, 2017 the Alaska Department of Fish and Game website "A Summary of Anchorage's Wildlife" indicates an estimated 250 black bears and roughly 60 brown bears live in the Glenn Highway corridor between the Knik River and Portage, roughly 75 miles, fronting the Chugach Mountains…"one-third of these bears spend at least part of the summer in or adjacent to residential areas in the Anchorage Bowl, Eagle River/Chugiak, or Girdwood. Judging by the number of cubs, the black bear population is probably increasing; this is further supported by the number of calls to ADF&G from residents, which have sharply increased in recent years…(brown bears) are also occasionally attracted to the Anchorage Bowl by winter-killed moose, abundant moose calves in spring, and spawning salmon in streams. Because of their size and potential aggressiveness, brown bear use of residential areas presents a definite human safety risk.

"The number of both black and brown bears in the Anchorage area has increased in the last three decades, due to hunting restrictions and availability of human food sources."

"In the Anchorage Bowl, moose are also abundant, with approximately 200-300 in the area year-round, and about 700-1,000 moose in the winter… population is controlled primarily through starvation, vehicle collisions, some calf predation from bears and wolves, and limited hunts on the two military reservations..an average of about 156 moose were killed in vehicle collisions in the entire Anchorage area each year… Moose…(pose) a hazard to drivers during the winter, and individual moose can become aggressive when under stress or protecting their young or territory. People have been stomped to death by moose in Anchorage (in 1993 and 1995), as many as 50 to 100 dogs are injured (some killed) annually, and cross country skiers and dog mushing teams using city trails have been charged on numerous occasions…moose are becoming more aggressive toward humans in the past decade. ADF&G has to destroy some individual aggressive moose each year."

I've told my wife if there are 100 sows in the bowl and they have twins every year and 25% of them live, that 100 becomes 125…extrapolate it from there. In 2017 there were 34 reported bears killed in Anchorage by citizens and officials…what, exactly, is the value of having bears determine our lives for us?

My wife and I heard on the news today that a biker had been seriously injured in town. This is one year after the IAWF praised Rick Sinnott's hope to have bears rubbing shoulders with people, but probably not in the way Sinnott had hoped. I wonder how Alaska's game managers feel about the summer of discontent experienced by several people, including those three attacked by grizzlies in Anchorage. Karl Vick wrote "Bear attacks hit record high in Alaska," August 17, 2008, *The Washington Post* (from AZCentral.com). The piece is very telling about the cavalier attitude of these game managers - clearly indicating they perceive no danger from bears.

EAGLE RIVER, Alaska - Most times, in Alaska, the bear eats you.

But this summer, in a record year for maulings, Devon Rees managed a draw with the grizzly that leapt onto him as he sauntered home between a stream brimming with salmon and the busiest highway in the state.

"Bear comes flying out, gets its fight on," said Rees, 18, nursing his wounds on the couch of his grandmother's trailer perhaps 60 yards from the scene of the Aug. 4 battle. Bandages covered puncture wounds on the inside of both his thighs, and blood seeped through the gauze around one elbow. His jeans lay in shreds on the floor. His left eye was puffy from the swat of a massive paw.

"She was moving around like a dog will when it's fighting," said the 5-foot-11-inch, 215-pound Rees, who had been at a friend's house until 2 AM watching a movie called "Never Back Down." "It was fist to claw."

In a typical year, Rees would stand out as the Anchorage area's one and only mauling victim. These days, he's just a face in a crowd of them, notable chiefly for defying expert advice that playing dead is the best way to survive after spooking a grizzly.

At least eight Alaskans have been battered by bears this year, with three maulings in five days in early August. And though no human fatalities have been recorded, the summer of the bear is testing Alaskans' carefully calibrated relationship with wildlife, an evolving attitude that differs from views in the Lower 48, where grizzlies run half as large.

"Most places in Alaska don't have a persistent problem with bear or moose, because if it's anywhere near the village, they shoot it, no questions asked," said Rick Sinnott, the Alaska Fish and Game Department biologist charged with reconciling the 350,000 humans who reside around Alaska's biggest city with the wildlife who live there, too. "It's the Last Frontier mentality: You don't tolerate any risk from wild animals."

But at least until this summer, Anchorage residents were more inclined to live and let live, many residents being from "outside" and intrigued by the sight of moose wandering through the city as well as by the predators that stalk them.

The joke used to be, Anchorage isn't too bad because it's only two hours from Alaska," said Sean Farley, a bear biologist with the Fish and Game Department. "The truth is, Alaska is right here. We've got bears.

We got moose. We got wolves. You name it."

And this summer, a poor season for salmon has made the bears loiter longer at Anchorage streams and be less tolerant of interruption.

"If you don't get enough to eat, you get cranky," Farley said.

The first attack, on June 29, was one of the worst. Petra Davis, 15, was cycling in a marathon bike race at 1 AM on a trail beside a salmon stream in the city's Far North Bicentennial Park. In the darkness, with the wind whipping the cottonwood trees, she may have careened broadside into a mama grizzly. It chewed through her bike helmet, crushed her trachea and cut into her shoulder, torso, buttocks and thigh.

"She was on the ground, sitting up, bloody, her cellphone out," said Sinnott, who heard a recording of the call Davis managed to place to 911. "She was apologizing because she had a hard time talking."

She got out the word "bear." Another rider directed paramedics.

Suspicion centered on a grizzly sow with two cubs that had been the subject of a half-dozen reports in the area over a six-week period. One jogger said he discovered the sow running behind him and pulled himself forward as its jaws snapped shut an inch from his rear end.

The next attack came July 23, a few yards from the front door of the Kenai Princess Wilderness Lodge, 100 miles south of Anchorage. Abi Sisk, 21, had just stepped onto a trail in the 11 PM twilight. She was bending to look at flowers when a grizzly lunged.

"She heard growling, and all of a sudden it was on her," said Dan Michels, the lodge manager. A guest heard "what he thought was laughing," from the parking lot and saw the bear with Sisk's head in its mouth.

The beast ran off after the man ran toward it, waving his arms and shouting. Sisk, a housekeeper, survived, partially scalped and with a broken jaw. Since May, a dozen bears have been shot on the Kenai Peninsula after threatening humans.

"The idea of bears is so predominant and so much bigger than the animals themselves," said Sherry Simpson, a University of Alaska professor and author of a book on bears and humans.

Farley, the biologist, has worked with grizzlies weighing 1,000 pounds, and he laughed aloud at Rees' vainglory. For appreciating the overpowering strength of Ursus arctos horribilis, Farley recommended a video shot five days before Rees's encounter, in the same town, by a woman who at first mistook for her baby's cries the sounds of a moose being killed by a grizzly.

"They got to do something about these bears," said Scott Simpson, a shipping executive, pausing at the scene of the Rees attack and voicing an opinion heard more and more often around Anchorage. "I've been all over the backwoods here and never seen it like this. The prevalence this summer is just staggering."

The sense of crisis took hold on Aug. 8, four days after Rees's encounter, when at 5 PM Clivia Feliz jogged onto Rover's Run, the city park trail where Davis was attacked. She had run 800 feet when the ears of her border collie, Sky, went straight up. Two grizzly cubs were 30 feet ahead on the trail, sniffing the ground.

"I'm thinking, Where's the sow?'" Feliz said from her Anchorage hospital bed. Not seeing one, she turned and ran back down the trail. The cubs gave chase. Feliz veered into the woods, figuring that "if I disappear from sight, maybe the cubs will just forget, like kids."

"But they were still coming."

Before she saw the mother bear, she heard it, first on the trail, then crashing through the brush. Feliz, 51, lay down behind some dead trees. The cubs "blew right by me," but the sow veered her way.

"I could see her nose go up. She scented me."

The bear was on her in seconds. There was no growling or clicking of teeth. It just stared at Feliz, huffing, then lunged at her head and "chomped right down" on the arm Feliz brought up reflexively.

For a few seconds, the bear simply held her captive, pushing Feliz's head and shoulders with its paws and mouth but not biting.

"She was just staring at me," said Feliz, a massage therapist. "And I was thinking I should protect my vital organs, because if she bites me in the stomach, you know, a lot of blood there. I drew my legs up. There was another huff. She bit down, but she bit down very deliberately this time.

"I could feel the ribs cracking. I knew she had bit into something, like an organ." Four ribs snapped, partially collapsing a lung.

Her screams of pain did not faze the bear, which held her down a few more moments, then left the way the cubs had gone. Feliz waited a few minutes before staggering back to the trail, her right arm hanging useless, with a crushed brachial artery, her left arm held against her bleeding torso. Sky reappeared, and when they reached a road Feliz flagged down a passing car.

"I know about bears. I've lived here 12 years," she said. "I'm not blaming anybody else. The bear was the bear and did what bears do."

That sensibility remains common across a state where fishermen routinely carry guns.

"I don't see it any different than New York in rush hour: You just have to pay attention. Our cars just have hair and teeth," said Don Smith, a telephone technician packing a .45 along with his fly rods as he prepared to float the Russian River, not far from the Kenai Princess Lodge.

Grizzlies routinely fish the bright teal waters alongside humans in what "feels like joint custody," said Sherry Simpson, the professor.

In Anchorage, trails placed beside streams are used both by bears and by people who often forget that a city can also be part of the wild. Analyzing the DNA from fur collected from thistles and wires, Farley found that 20 different bears passed near the stream where Davis and Feliz were mauled. Radio-collar tracking indicated that when salmon are running, bears are almost always within 100 yards of the stream and, therefore, the trail.

"There's the problem of enhancing salmon streams that run through cities," said Simpson: "Ring the dinner bell."

I wonder how our game managers justify three grizzly maulings in town juxtaposed to creating an asphalt wilderness for the state's animals? One has to wonder if Sinnott's theory of wilderness motivates him to turn the city into wilderness in order to save the world! But, wait. Others share his passion.

With regards to public safety and city officials allowing dangerous animals to run rampant, are we talking common sense or comical sense? Jonathan Serrie wrote a piece for Fox News on line November 16, 2011, regarding the increasing numbers of bears and the official attitude toward them: "Suburban Bears? Oh, My!" According to Adam Hammond, wildlife biologist with the Georgia Department of Natural Resources, bears in yesteryears were considered varmints and killed wherever and whenever encountered. The increasing numbers of bear hunters has not reduced suburban bear numbers—as bear numbers increase, so does their range, expanding from wilderness into the suburbs.

Whereas past activities controlled city bears, Hamond reflects what I consider the "new" view of game management when he stated:

"It's a great thing that the bear population is doing well. The only struggle we have as managers is just to try to minimize problems so that basically bears behave. And usually bear behavior is directly tied to human behavior…bears pose little threat to humans if they're just passing through.

"But residents near a bear sighting should take trash and pet food indoors to prevent the wild animals from lingering…If people will help the situation by just making these non-natural human provided foods unavailable to bears, we'll really have very few problems."

In a nutshell it appears fish and game managers want people to manage bears for them. If people do not provide food for the bears, everything will be hunky dory. And I'll have to remember that bears pose little threat to humans...IF they're just passing through! *Hmmmmm.*

To make matters worse, the game managers are changing. When Gary Shelton discusses the new bear, he also addresses new management. "Mr. Shelton observes that B.C's preservationist-driven bear-management policies, strengthened in 1994 and 1996, have discouraged hunting and thereby decreased bears' fear of humans. B.C., he says, has too few hunters and too many bears." (from the emailed Liard Hot Springs mauling story forwarded from Loussac Library Feb. 2, 2006: Record: 1, Thank goodness the Americans had a gun, Authors: De Cloet, Derek, Source: Alberta Report/Newsmagazine; 09/01/97, Vol. 24 Issue 38, p25, Persistent link to this record: http://search.epnet.com/login. aspx?direct=true&db=f5h&an= 9709300029)

And Shelton acknowledges that "They are young, radically left-wing, and ordained to the brotherhood of cause-science. These medicine men had the mission of interpreting nature for us laymen who are incapable of getting it right." (Pg. 241, *Bear Attacks: The Deadly Truth*)

While finalizing this book and "googling" "Algonquin bear fatalities," I came across the following piece which sheds further light on Gary Shelton's comments about changing game managers and their philosophy. From *The True Free Press*, *Mountain Laurel Review*, June 15, 2K1, Killer bears in Bradford? (mountainlaurelreview.com)

"Two days ago we commented on the local Game Commission officer and her stupid remarks about black bears invading the city. She told us that residents of the City of Bradford had better get used to them. They, in so many words, were a fact of life and people like Mark should arm themselves with slingshots and marbles and just would have to live with them...Many of you laughed when I said that the bears had more rights than people. Many of you thought that it was another of my exaggerations to make my point. Believe me, I wasn't. They do and it becomes very obvious when the local enforcement and safety officer does absolutely nothing to protect property owners from this nuisance and potential threat...we should all be outraged at the complacent attitude of Rose Luciane of the Pennsylvania Game Commission... We are talking about the City of Bradford and the backyards of a residential neighborhood. We are talking about the safety of children...Let's hope the people of Bradford don't follow the instructions of this silly woman... All it will take is for one child to be carried off or one person attacked and injured. Then what will happen? How can they explain that?"

I wonder what number of other states' agencies share this bears-in-town philosophy. If the new bear and the new biologists aren't enough to concern us, I refer you to the animal lover enclave—the tree and bunny huggers and environmental nut jobs, whom I call econuts. I have no axe to grind with animal right advocates nor official agency personnel; however though they may mean well, they fail to realize the inherent dangers— more territorial-range conflicts (food competition) and more young bears' being killed and/or pushed-dispersed from dominant animals' ranges and into people space (i.e., during the last several years the bear population has exploded in the upper hillside east of Anchorage as well as the Russian River and other areas on the Kenai Peninsula of Alaska).

Allowing the increasing numbers of bears in America is nothing new. Way before *More Alaska Bear Tales* was published in 1989, Alaska game managers were in "action":

"The (police) chief kept calling the Fish and Game asking them to come over: 'Hey, the bears are tearin' up my garbage cans. They're tryin' to get in the house...the Fish and Game would come over and shoot Roman candles at the bears, run them off, but the bears would come back...one big boar...chased the kids...(who) barely made it to the house...'These other bears are bad enough, but I'm not putting up with one chasin' my kids.'

"The Fish and Game didn't do anything about it." (Page. 148)

Is Fish and Game sworn to protect and serve the public or to promote and save the predators...or prosecute and savage the public?

We have allowed officials and the animal rights crowd to shove these animals down our throats. Paradoxically those wanting to save the bears are actually doing more harm to them as well as creating more man-bear conflicts. There is a bitter pill connected with their lobbying and authorities' acceptance of their agenda...a pill called over-protection that has bears less fearful of man and more aggressive. We don't need to swallow it.

On October 9, 2003, Debbye posted a telling comment on http://fim. ondragonswing.com/archives/004367.html: "It wasn't so long ago that predators tried to avoid humans because they knew we (or our weapons) were deadly. Now, thanks to the nature lobby, they've learned we are an easy meal."

What management practices address this issue?

On another level we endure different wildlife messages, such as the misleading concept that animals have rights…assigning them equal, if not more, value than humans.

In the first place pets and animals should be given necessary respect and care. However, animals do NOT have rights.

Another misleading concept is that proposed by so many well-meaning officials—the idea that people and animals can co-exist in a wonderful earthly Nirvana. I believe it is this attitude that motivates wildlife officialdom to place animal safety above public safety.

While perusing *Anchorage Daily News* on line May 29, 2012, I read "Moose injures girl in Eagle River stomping," by Michelle Theriault Boots. The piece detailed how two young girls attempted to escape a moose which ultimately stomped one of them. Noting some of the comments following the piece, one stood out—a powerful reflection of "What's Wrong with This Picture?" Author flyfish sarcastically captures the prevailing attitude by Anchorage officials when it comes to big, wildlife and public safety.

Flyfish posts: "Shame on those parents for letting those kids outside to play. Don't they know it's spring and our wild animals run the show here in Anchorage. Wake up, people. Keep your kids and bird feeders inside where they belong. And for goodness sakes, stay off all the trails that we've spent millions of dollars on: they are now animal trails. Enjoy your video games, kids."

And another example I discovered on msnbc.msn on line Feb. 22, 2012: an animal rights advocate wanted to dust a fellow human for wearing fur. "Feds: Ohio animal-rights activist offered $850 for random fur-wearer to be killed." Meredith Lowell, 27, has been charged with soliciting murder in what federal authorities say was a plot to kill someone wearing fur as part of an animal rights crusade. This came to light in November when the FBI was notified about a Facebook Pg. created by Lowell who assumed the alias Anne Lowery.

And how about those animal lovers/hunter haters who vent their rage over the killing of an African lion named Cecil in July 2015, but say nothing about the millions of aborted human babies and Planned Parenthood's (euphemistic name) butchering babies and selling their body parts?

In separate incidents Friday June 23 and Saturday June 24, 2006, fishermen shot black and brown bears that charged them on Alaska's Russian River. Both shooters carried .44 caliber pistols which deterred the charging bears. Though the animals were still on the loose Monday the 26th, the black was later shot a few miles west of the river and the brown was dispatched downstream from the ferry.

The ever popular Russian River salmon stream has become overrun with grizzlies. In July 2006 one fisherman claimed to have seen as many as six brownies one day. Aggressive bears hijacked fishermen's catches. Over the past dozen years, fishermen on the world famous river complied with the bears' demands. What will become of this fishery and other bear infested streams? The bears are either being forced out from areas upstream by fiercer bears or finding it easier to hassle fishermen. Either way, both man and bear are in jeopardy.

Why am I the bad guy in the bear's kitchen? Why am I the villain when he's in my back yard? If he's armed, can't I be armed? Am I any less entitled to safety in the woods than the bear? Why should he be allowed to inflict injury or death upon me with no risk to him? If I go for a walk in town, shouldn't I have the expectation of being safe? If a mugger confronts me, shouldn't I have recourse? Why, then, shouldn't I have recourse from injury in bear country, which might also be in town?

After Wes Perkins was severely mauled near Nome, Alaska, in 2011, and lay at death's door, people's beastly nature appeared, touting animal's value. One site proclaimed the bear was executed by rednecks and the human victim "unfortunately survived." Yes, the looney bin fringe showed its head again.

Maybe the animal rights gang will reconsider their stance on saving bears when they learn about the bear's interest in their wine grapes. *The Capital Press*, December 30, 2005, reported "Grape-munching bears have caused bunches of trouble in Northern California wine country. Some winery owners have summoned authorities to trap and shoot black bears…that plundered their vineyards. The killings have sparked debate over the future of wildlife in the nation's most famous wine-growing region…" one winery owner "Paul Maroon said he had tried scaring off the bears, but resorted to getting rid of them for good because he feared they might hurt his field workers."

Tsk, tsk. Maybe the wine drinkers would rather have their wine than the bears. Could it be that a grape will accomplish what people with common sense could not?

Thin the Herd

Let's focus momentarily on Alaska's largest city and the recent adoption of its theme Big, Wild Life. What exactly does that mean? I get the big part. I think the wild refers to wilderness. The part I'd like to focus on is life. Whose? People's or animals?

When it comes to common sense, the following two statements from Gary Shelton's book *Bear Attacks II Myth & Reality* are very revealing,

> "During the next 20 years, politicians and biologists will have great difficulty devising workable solutions for managing bears…because the ever-increasing bear population will cause serious havoc." (Pg. 213)

> …"there will be a continuous increase in predatory attacks on people by both grizzlies and black bears…Bear populations are increasing all over North America…What goes with more bears is not just more encounters because of numbers alone, but more encounters because protected bears lose their fear of people and do not try to avoid them. Bears that do not fear people are more likely to be predatory.

> "Unfortunately, human death rates and property damage by bears will have to reach epidemic proportions before present-day policies are influenced. We should be asking ourselves this question: Is it really necessary to allow bears to reclaim all of their former range and their status as dominant species in order to guarantee their future survival?" (Pp. 41-42) (APPENDIX 10)

Our neighbor, Guy Sines, who grew up with our children, addressed his concern for this growing issue in the *Anchorage Daily News* way back in 2006. Guy agreed to allow his piece in this book and Frank Gerjevic of the *Anchorage Daily News* emailed me the newspaper's permission—

RE: Guy Sines' piece:

Larry,

The date was July 25, 2006, and I don't think there's any problem excerpting the piece in your book as long as you credit Daily News and the publisher of piece.

Hope this helps.
Take care,
Frank
Frank Gerjevic
Editorial Writer | *Anchorage Daily News*

Here's Guy's input: "Wild animals don't belong in urban setting" COMPASS: POINTS OF VIEW FROM THE COMMUNITY by GUY

SINES

For four decades, my parents have left their trash in garbage cans at the base of the driveway of their lower Hillside home. It keeps the garage from becoming smelly, and bears were never a concern until recently. Sure, our trash cans got rolled by stray dogs once a week or so, but enforcement of existing leash laws eventually put an end to that problem.

Now we have state wildlife biologist Rick Sinnott penalizing folks for doing what they've always done with their garbage, rather than actually dealing with the issue.

And if that weren't enough, he's now telling people that it's not a good idea to raise chickens and rabbits on the outskirts of the city. Again, this penalizes people for normally acceptable behavior, while ignoring the problem, which is that there are wild animals living comfortably within city boundaries.

When I was a kid growing up on the lower Hillside, a moose sighting was an occasional thing, and the moose were typically skittish and would run when spotted. You never, but never, saw a bear in town. As time went on, the Hillside fall hunt was canceled to appease the politically correct and naive Lower 48 oil transplants. The moose population in town exploded, the moose became comfortable then belligerent, and lo and behold, the wild animals that use moose for food, i.e. bears, eventually moved in as well.

Now we have a problem that is on the verge of becoming a serious public safety issue.

Humankind has historically built settlements for, among other reasons, protection from wild animals. Moose and bears do not belong in a city. Nowhere else in the world is this asinine view tolerated, and for very good reason. Wild animals are a safety hazard to humans.

The approach of the Anchorage Assembly in dealing with this issue is to find some type of compromise between the people on both sides of the issue. Well, trying to find a compromise with people who are out of touch with reality is irresponsible at best. A command decision needs to be made for the good of public safety, regardless of how unpopular it is to the bunny-hugging lobby.

I have no patience for the the-animals-were-here-first crowd, nor for the people who claim that wild animals living within the city are one of the factors that contribute to our quality of life.

When I head out to the cabin, just this side of Denali Park, nary a moose do I see. However, I'll drive past half a dozen in the seven miles it takes to get from my home to work. The moose population within the Municipality of Anchorage is staggeringly disproportionate to the population in adjacent wilderness areas. The moose have figured out that they're safe here, give birth here, and enjoy the ease of walking on roads and trails kept clear of snow.

I have been charged by moose nine times in the past decade, while running, skiing or mountain biking on the municipal trail system and while walking in my suburban neighborhood. And don't tell me I need to be more aware. When you round a corner on a trail and find a huge bull standing in your path, "awareness" is next to meaningless.

The manner in which I exercise awareness is that I no longer go for walks unarmed, as I will not become a link in the urban food chain.

Bottom line: Wild animals do not belong in an urban/suburban environment. Mr. Sinnott needs to stop trying to appease the bunny huggers and take a common sense approach to this dangerous public safety issue.

I'm not a litigious man by nature, but I encourage anyone who has the misfortune of being charged, trampled or mauled by wild animals within the city to file a lawsuit against the municipality, as litigation seems to be the only language they understand.

(A little over three years after Guy's compass piece, I sent a similar one to the *Anchorage Daily News* in response to a question for a bear manager. (APPENDIX 11)

On Sunday November 28, 2010, our daughter Ginger Risch walked a few miles from her Huffman home to our house on DeArmoun Road and stated that she'd met a lady on her walk who had brown bear on her deck within the past few weeks. It was at this time that I heard about our neighbor John Kaiser and his episode with Mr. Brown Bear. I contacted John and he provided his following story "Neighborhood Encounters of the Furry Kind":

On a Tuesday night around 1:00 AM just as I'm ready to retire, my Chesapeake retriever, Shelekov started growling. Only two weeks earlier we experienced an intense encounter with a love-starved bull moose rattling my neighbor's house and his nerves. I figured the moose might be back.

I opened the door, blocked the dog's exit and slipped outside onto our second story porch, listening for any sign of what may have alarmed her.

I heard what sounded like breaking branches and leaves or garbage bag material being shredded. As I proceeded to the edge of the deck to see what was going on, I thought a moose was trying to scrape velvet from his horns by the deck. Sure enough this big brown body with his head down is trashing it back and forth on what looks like a white kitchen garbage bag on the ground. I yelled, "Hey, what are you doing?"

With a pose of annoyance as if to ask, "Who dares bother me?" this big, brown, wide head lifted up slowly. I was looking at the biggest brown bear I have ever seen, outside of the zoo in the Lower Forty-eight. I was a good seven feet above the ground and what seemed like just a few above his head while he stood on all four legs. He could have stood up and swatted me right off the porch if he had wanted too. So I quickly moved away from the edge of the deck, almost in shock at what I was seeing, and yelled again. With that, all he did was turn and take two big hops away and then start walking casually toward the back of the yard and the wooded easement.

He had gotten into a kitchen garbage bag I had missed due to a fresh 2-inch snowfall that day. He didn't even go near the garbage cans as he came into the yard. Next morning I measured his tracks at several spots in the snow and they consistently measured 9 x 12 inches. According to fish and game estimates that makes this about a 10-foot Alaska brown bear, the kind of giant usually relegated to Kodiak Island or the Alaska Peninsula. I almost felt like I was dreaming, since I had never expected to see such an enormous carnivorous monster invade our four children's backyard where they played every day with each other and friends.

My moral to my moose and bear encounters: more firepower is better, and I won't go outside anymore with a .44 Mag to confront a disturbance in the middle of the night. I put the .44 away—instead my first line of defense for going outside will be an assault 12 gauge shotgun loaded with 00 buckshot and slugs instead. I'll be armed adequately to fend off an attack at the level that unveiled itself the night of the crazed bull moose.

At the end of June 2014, our daughter Jill related an event of our mutual family friends Steve and Lana Weurth and I called them for the details. Steve summarized their combined story:

I was jogging near my Anchorage hillside home when I encountered a large black bear. It was the width of the road away from me and I gingerly passed while keeping an eye on it. A passing car stopped and asked me if I'd seen two grizzlies. The next day while jogging the same route, I looked for the black bear but did not see it. However when I rounded a bend in the road, I came face to face with two grizzlies. The bears loped toward me. I backpedaled, running as fast as I could in reverse.

I launched myself onto a deck at a nearby home and banged on windows. Although cars were in the driveway, no one responded.

I spotted a passing car and waved to it. About then the rear bear bumped into the hind leg of the first bear which turned to swat the second bear. That's when I made my getaway, running to the car while the bears settled their differences.

I grew up here and I've never seen so many bears on a regular basis. I've seen more bears in Anchorage than ever before. (As of August 13, Steve had encountered 8 bears while running near his home)

About the same time frame to the credit of Alaska Department of Fish and Game, they announced "because of public safety concerns" that they "decided to euthanize the bears" that have wandered Anchorage's Government Hill neighborhood for the second year in a row—a sow with four cubs. (*Alaska Dispatch News*, Tegan Hanlon, April 16, 2015) Unfortunately after a hue and cry from neighborhood residents to raise money to save the bears, recently elected Governor Walker directed the animals' relocation. The family was captured within days and relocated into the wild; they will either return or be an impediment to bears where they're moved. But wait a minute. As of June 22 the bears are no longer with us. Seems the hubbub they've created near Hope, has led to their removal from the planet—mom and three cubs, one remaining at large. (I read something once about "survival of the fittest.")

August 2015 Larry Yepez of Midpines, California, was startled by a black bear on his porch the morning of the 13th when he stepped outside. *The Washington Post* story stated that black bears had become a problem lately. So, why weren't they dispatched so that he wouldn't have to fight one for his life on his porch?

Civic Duty

I define civic duty as an activity that requires action on behalf of the best interests of a community. All too often officials don't or won't act on behalf of their citizenry therefore a citizen steps up for them. Sometimes civic duty requires a citizen to do right even if it is wrong. By that I mean, the citizen acts in the best interests of his community even though officials (and others) might deem it wrong. For instance, if a beautiful stream overtime becomes overgrown with trees or brush that deny the public from enjoying the stream, a man who removes the offending limbs, brush or trees does his civic duty.

Our children grew up enjoying playing in a stream near our home. Over the years that ten to fifteen-foot wide, foot-deep, clear stream became choked with tag alders whose branches obscured the view of the stream. Because the eco-nuts seem to value all things natural and oppose our liberties, the approach to the stream was labeled taboo—can't play in the water any more. It's a salmon stream. I guess that applies to shoreline brush also. After a couple of years' missing the view, someone decided to do his civic duty. The shoreline brush is long gone. Imagine that. Civic duty.

Another example involves the overgrown brush on street corners that obscures the driver's view of oncoming traffic. Removing that vegetation and allowing total visibility provides greater public safety and amounts to civic duty. Same as moving a log from the roadway or filling in a nasty pothole before the officials have time to respond. That might even include engaging a bad guy instead of waiting for officials to show up. *Hmmmmm.*

Then there's the illustration of the wild animals roaming about town oblivious to the safety of citizens, mirroring the somewhat similar attitude of officials who are oblivious to the safety of citizens while allowing wild animals to roam about town. Were some citizens to dispatch such a "wandering" bear from his yard to protect his children, that man has done his civic duty...and performed parental responsibility. After hearing numerous shotgun and rifle reports during the summers of 2012 and 2013, I'm pretty sure neighbors were doing their civic duty. For which I thank them.

One such man, a friend and former student, told me about doing his civic duty. During the summer of 2013 he shared his concerns about marauding bears in Anchorage and felt it was his duty to keep an eye on his neighborhood. He had a 10-foot and a 7-foot brown patrolling the neighborhood. Because the big boar came through every three days on a regular basis, he chose to eliminate it. He did the same with the sow. It also became necessary to eliminate black bears that were too close to his children. Perhaps they were DLP kills; but those bears will be a threat to no one in Anchorage.

An *Anchorage Daily News* Opinion piece written by Jim Lieb, wildlife biologist living near Palmer, Alaska, appeared in the *Anchorage Daily News* August 7, 2016. It addresses this issue therefore I'm including it: For safety's sake, consider a brown bear hunt in the Anchorage area

After reading Rick Sinnott's July 31 *We Alaskans* article on bear attacks in Alaska, and the prior piece by Laurel Andrews titled "Bear Scare," I would like to expand the discussion to brown/grizzly bear management. Every summer for years now, various state and federal sources and the media have been telling folks about bear encounters and how to deal with them.

While I do agree with some of the advice presented to the public, including do not run, fight if it's a black bear, and play dead if it's a brown bear, I balk at suggestions we must live in fear…that we need to avoid going into the woods alone or to always be talking and making noise, wearing 'bear' bells, and we should avoid any area where a bear has been seen (for at least a week or two).

This approach has been described as 'learning to coexist with bears when we venture into their home.' An alternative view, possibly politically incorrect, is Alaska's wildlands are also our home, to be utilized in a reasonable fashion, and should not require we go forth with extreme trepidation.

While spending time in most of Alaskan wildlands probably should include, among other things, a comprehensive knowledge of bear ecology and behavior, appropriate firearms and the skill to use them, and possibly bear spray, should such preparedness be considered necessary everywhere in Alaska? Might there be a few areas exceptions could be made?

One such area has the highest human use (number of miles of foot traffic per square mile per year) in the state, plus one of the highest percent of brown bear attacks in the state…namely game management Unit 14C, which includes Chugach State Park and Anchorage. If there ever was a place in Alaska that might warrant special bear management, it is here.

One component of such management seldom mentioned in the bear encounter discussions is hunting. The Alaska Department of Fish and Game has a limited hunting program for brown bears in Unit 14C, entailing two small drawing permit hunts in a small portion of the west half and a conservative season in the more remote east half. Harvest data for 14C over the past 10 years shows an annual harvest averaging 1.5 brown bears, approximately 1.5 percent of the unit's estimated population.

Compare this to Unit 13 to the north. The hunting regime throughout this area is much less conservative (1 bear per year with no tag requirement). Harvest over the past 10 years has averaged 145 brown bears, representing approximately 10 percent of the unit's estimated population.

I have lived in Unit 13, and have had close encounters with brown bears there on various occasions. While my sample size of 12 is small, every such bear I've bumped into on foot ran away, moved away, or stood there while I moved away. Of course, none of these bears were sows with cubs of the year, so there is indeed a luck component here.

But I've talked with various long-term residents of Unit 13 who also feel hunting makes a difference in how these bears behave. And while nothing here suggests adverse bear encounters can be reduced to zero, increasing the harvest of brown bears could help.

Note hunting regulations in Unit 13 are part of an intensive management program to reduce predators of moose and caribou. What I'm suggesting for consideration is an intensive management program in Unit 14C to reduce adverse encounters with brown bears.

Others have suggested a similar approach. The late Charles Jonkel, who ran the Ursid Research Center in Missoula, Montana, in a 1994 article on brown bears, stated "hunting pressure automatically teaches bears to avoid humans." He also cited an aversive conditioning research program that captured problem brown bears and brought them into holding facilities where they were repeatedly confronted by humans and repelled with chemical sprays.

Treatment was complete when the bear fled instantly to the "sanctuary" portion of the enclosure. The bear was then returned to the wild. This captive process, called "bear school," lasted 4 to 6 days. While nothing like that is being suggested for Alaska, this program does affirm bears can readily learn to avoid humans.

There is a more extreme management option I've heard suggested for the Anchorage area: make Chugach State Park a brown bear-free zone. The park encompasses 774 square miles, representing approximately 1/10th of 1 percent of Alaska's approximately 600,000 square miles of brown bear habitat. So we're not talking about adversely affecting the species as a whole to any appreciable degree. Of course, this would require at least legislative action, which is unlikely to happen given the almost guaranteed outcry from the Lower 48 wildlife preservationists.

A "Star Trek" "phaser" set on bear-stun and tucked in the belt of everyone living in, or venturing into, bear habitat would no doubt successfully resolve most close encounters of the bear variety, and probably stimulate the development of re-enforcement of bear behaviors beneficial to humans. But unfortunately we'll probably have to wait a while for such technology to arrive. On the other hand, who knows, maybe a modified "Taser" will prove to be the 'Model T' of the eventual "phaser."

In the meantime a Unit 14C brown bear hunting program focused on generating a minimum harvest of 10 percent of the population per year could be considered. If nothing else, we should have a trial program to see if the number of bear encounters and attacks decline.

A very interesting parallel between cats and bears exists and authors Jo Deurbrouck and Dean Miller raise a compelling point in their *Cat Attacks* (Introduction, Pg. xiii):

"Can we share habitat with big, wild creatures, and ignore the rules those creatures live by? Can we continue to pretend, living side by side with such an effective predator, that we are never prey?"

While perusing Fox News online September 11, 2009, I ran across the following disturbing confirmation that it is time to reduce city bear numbers. I summarized the Associated Press piece "Bear Attacks Colorado Man Inside His Home." While his three dogs barked, the Aspen home owner went to the first floor to investigate. He was rewarded for his efforts by a blow to the head from a large black bear. He was taken to the hospital and treated for non-life-threatening injuries. Wildlife officials have killed at least nine bears this summer and police have responded to 200 bear sightings in August alone (the previous August they responded to 16).

I used to tell people to be careful in bear country. However, nowadays bear country could be your living room. We need to address the new bear that greets us at the door…or the refrigerator. Do we welcome it and its probable problems or do we remove it? Andre Champollion wrote of his 1903 bear hunt on Alaska's Admiralty Island for *Forest and Stream* ("Hunting the Alaskan Grizzly," May 2, 1908). Some authorities stated that grizzlies will not attack without provocation to which he replied, "This is true probably of localities where these animals have been extensively hunted and the fear of man and guns has been so thoroughly inculcated in them that their only idea is to beat a hasty retreat…" (Pg. 46, *The Only Good Bear is a Dead Bear* by Jeannette Prodgers).

Resulting from 2017 bear fatalities in Alaska, KTUU ran a piece. In 2014 Suzanne Knudsen was mauled by a brown bear very near the Bird Ridge fatal mauling site. She is getting back into the hiking scene, carrying pepper spray and a pistol. She is concerned for her grandchildren whose parents grew up in the area.

Three things stand out from the on line article: 1) more bears, 2) stocking steams with salmon and 3) habituation. Knudsen "believes more bears have populated the area since the state began stocking Bird Creek with salmon." Another lady, Desiree Petcoff said, "It kind of begs the question, are these bears becoming desensitized to human beings?" ("Alaskans on edge" after two deadly bear attacks in one week KTUU news, June 25, 2017)

Fish and Game fines a man for feeding bears 90 miles from Anchorage...yet they are more guilty than he because they "feed" bears all over Anchorage by allowing moose calves by the dozens. Those mobile "garbage cans" are the primary reason bears are here. Another contributing factor is the salmon stocked in our streams the past 20 years. Another, people who want wildlife in town. Have you researched the amount of financial, emotional, physical pain produced by moose injuries in Anchorage? Have you children or grandchildren? Our kids grew up on Rabbit Creek where salmon were NOT stocked, in the 1970's before ADF&G became Sinnottized with the nonsense of coexistence. Have you a neighbor who loves Alaska but drives from her garage to the hose in order to water her lawn due to her fear of bears? Do you have a wife who loves to be in the yard...without pepper spray or a guarding husband? If your neighborhood has thugs, which odds do you prefer being concerned about, 100 or 1? I address all this public safety in my new book SAFE with Bears. I've lived here since 1966 and know no better place to live...but the bears can be seen outside of town.

While wrapping up this tome in 2017, I compiled some Alaska bear sightings and/or situations from May 2017. The summer of 2017 witnessed bears everywhere in Anchorage. There were an unprecedented number of human-bear encounters. Granddaughter Sarah facebooked me the end of June, noting two dozen bear sighting posts of Anchorage bears within twenty-four hours.

Aprox. day

MAY 25 homeowner shoots brown in yard, Douglas Island, AK

JUNE

17   fellow volleyball players Robin Robbins and Bill Morrow shared bear info—Robin's phone pix of brown sow and three yearling cubs in his yard above Potter Marsh; Bill Morrow said 8 blacks roamed Moose Run golf course;

19   black kills Patrick Cooper;

       black kills Erin Johnson;

       three attacked by brown in Eagle River;

(June 19 marked a tragic and highly unusual day when 16-year-old Patrick Cooper was struck down while competing in a mountain race less than twenty miles from Anchorage. And within a day another black bear mauled two women, killing one of them.

Erin Johnson, 27, and co-worker biologist Ellen Trainor, 38, were ambushed near Pogo Mine in the vicinity of Fairbanks. Both women had undergone bear safety training and carried pepper spray, which may have saved Ellen. Another senseless bear fatality, similar to that of Cynthia Dusel-Bacon forty years previous.)

24 Rodney Meeks and son see black and cubs at Kincaid;

26 black breaks through Anchorage Zach Landis' bedroom window;

brown attacks two Joint Base Elmendorf-Richardson bikers;

brown attacks man and dog (near Hope);

27 ADF&G removes brown-killed moose near Anchorage's Service High;

black bear in Juneau liquor store;

Eagle River brown shot in defense of life or property;

Eagle River black shot in defense of life or property;

28 cub in Dave Parnow's neighbor's house;

30 Elliott Clark, 11-year-old kills-saves family from Brown w. 12 gauge shotgun; neighbors 2 houses away have bear in yard

JULY

3 Goldenview family 2 miles south have grizzly moose kill in yard— ADF&G tell them they can't shoot unless the bear attacks them

4 Centennial Park tent mobbed by black; woman inside sleeping bag playing dead

5 neighbor across street has bear in yard; Granddaughter dad viewed brown sow's 2 cubs above Upper Huffman

7 Anchorage Muldoon residents feeding as many as 5 bears

10 Granddaughter and dad observe 2 griz cubs Upper Huffman;

12 Granddaughter grazing horse in front yard, 2 guys tell her they saw black block away; family friends took picture of black sow and cubs at Kincaid park; neighbor had black looking through her window and a brown in her neighbor's yard; Girdwood homeowner Robin Renae Thatcher has black killed in her kitchen

14 (?) ADF&G whacks Service area sow as possible threat to public Brown-grizzly in Sitka kills and begins devouring Karelian Bear Dog at owner's home…commenter Beth Lang said:

I have 2 kids and live in this neighborhood. The dog in question was loved by just about every kid down this way. When these kids aren't by my house they are up where the dog lived. It just so happened to be a big day for baseball so most of the kids were either at the field or getting ready. I can guarantee if it were any other day most of the kids would have been up in that part of the neighborhood. Is it going to take a kid getting attacked for people to realize this bear is a problem? The people that live down here have gotten a lot better about taking care of their garbage. The garbage issue is what started the problem. That bear was taught to look for food around the houses here. At this point the only way to stop it was to kill it. It breaks my heart that the dog had to pay the price. It so easily could have been one of the kids. I'm not sure why they mentioned that the dog was not tied up. The dog is always tied up or on a leash when outside. Were they supposed to leave him tied and not give him a chance to either do his job and chase the bear away or get away from the bear?? There is no point in placing blame. It's a problem regardless and it needs to be dealt with before momma bear teaches more of her cubs the same nasty habits.

15   Bear was shot-killed while eating homeowner's dog

17   I saw sow black and 2 cubs, Crestview-De Armoun (about a mile from home); grizzly charge, man picks up dog, bear veers off into woods after moose calf

18   Sitka homeowner shoots brown chasing his dog, officials finish it off next day.

SEPTEMBER as of the end of the first two weeks we've had blacks and grizzly throughout our neighborhood—in the road in front of our home, up the neighbors' driveway and on the power line behind our home.

OCTOBER: black bear walks into Ted Stevens Airport area post office and is dispatched.

Ken Marsh, spokesman for the ADF&G in Anchorage, kept his word and sent me the municipality statistics on bear kills for the past six years. About the same time with November running out the clock on 2017 the *Anchorage Dispatch News* ran a piece about bears in town, more than likely using Ken's numbers. The Sunday edition front-paged "Nearly 4 times more bears were killed this year in Anchorage than in 2016" by Tega Hanion, November 12, 2017. From 2012 to 2017 the numbers looked this way:

Year	Total	Black bear	Grizzly	Killed by
2012	18	5	3	agencies
		6	4	citizens
2013	7	1		agencies
		4	2	citizens
2014	10	2	1	agencies
		6	1	citizens
2015	22	7	1	agencies
		12	2	citizens
2016	9	2	2	agencies
		3	2	citizens
2017	34	16	1	agencies
		15	2	citizens

Hanion quoted Anchorage's bear biologist, "I would bet good money that trash was a factor in almost anything that happened in the neighborhood." (Page A 14) The article suggested back to back human fatalities in June may have created a less tolerant public, online posts aroused public awareness, perhaps there are more bears in town. The biologist admitted…'we're kind of speculating on some of this stuff." And numerous theories included:

maybe bears knew they could find trash;

maybe more bears chased moose calves into town and found trash;

maybe it had something to do with salmon in streams;

maybe it was some other issue with a food source;

maybe new residents in the neighborhood weren't accustomed to seeing bears.

Instead of considering the attractants and theories for the increased number of dead bears, might a biologist be more concerned about the explosion of bears in the municipality? Nothing in the article addresses game management. Is it reasonable to think that bear removal from cities would reduce costs for monitoring and removing them periodically?

Because "coexistence"—man and bear—seems to be on the minds of so many, I've listed some recent Anchorage area bear attacks—close calls, maulings or deaths: dog walking Gary Boyd; Gabriel Wintters rushed three times; three grizzlies and four blacks killed in defense of life and property (2004); mauled by grizzlies: Devon Reese; Petra Davis; Clivia Feliz (2008); Jeff Johnson, Weiman, Lopotrone, John Kaiser (2010); Soldotna officer; fall-winter grizzly, Hosken; Skeins, (2011); Eagle River Howard Meyer; Hillside jogger (2012); Steve Weurth; in house (2014); government hill black and cubs (2015); three attacked by grizzly; one fatality; 1 brown and 1 black shot in Eagle River in defense of life or property; black bear in Zach Landis' bedroom; brown attacks two Joint Base Elmendorf-Richardson bikers; black bear and cub in Anchorage hillside home. (2017)

In lieu of all the bear activity, especially in Anchorage, how is that coexistence with bears working? Coexistence implies living in the same environment peacefully, making the same space possible for both, in this case bears and people. How do you explain a woman's fear of going outside her home as peaceful coexistence? If coexistence works, why is it necessary for a man to guard his wife in the yard all day as she works in her flowers?

When will this bear reigning end? With predator and other nuisance animal numbers increasing nationwide, when will Americans take the hint and reclaim their safety by eliminating numerous predatory animals from the neighborhood? What are your game officials doing to provide public safety?

During the summer and fall of 2018 I sent emails and letters requesting suggestions of reducing bear numbers in Alaska neighborhoods, addressed to the Commissioner of Alaska Department of Fish and Game, public relations personnel, the bear guy and each ADFG board member. The silence I received from them was deafening therefore I'm hoping with the election of a new governor, he will appoint a commissioner of fish and game who will NOT depend upon citizen polls and that the commish will drop the hammer on the ADFG board and demand they establish a realistic bear policy that protects the public instead of bears.

(Author's note: my wife told me she heard on yesterday's news [June 5, 2019] that 47 bears were reported killed to ADFG in 2018)

My question regarding the increasing numbers of bears in neighborhoods: in the interest of public safety isn't it about time to reduce bear numbers? Shouldn't there be some kind of moral imperative to place the safety of humans above that of animals? Or will the managers continue to promote personal satisfaction over public safety?

The ball is in your court...or, more accurately, the bear is in your yard...or your house!

CHAPTER 7
OBSERVATIONS

GENERAL

Ideally, no one should be injured by a bear. However as long as people think that "it will never happen to me" or because they refuse to learn of the bear's ways or because they agitate bears by pushing the envelope, there will be bear attacks. Bears attack when or if they want to—provoked or unprovoked. Maybe their only reason is that they're having a bad hair day. Or that you disturbed them for some reason unknown to you or them.

If contact results in a mauling, what is its cost—to you, your family, your companions, the bear?

Responsibilities

When you enter bear country, you inherit responsibilities—to you, your party, those awaiting you and your party's return, the animals you encounter and the environment. We have a responsibility for our welfare in passing through the outdoors as much as we do in our regular environment. How can we best prepare ourselves for an outing? What dangers must be assessed and prepared for? How can we assure ourselves and our loved ones that we will return safely? We need to take whatever precautions necessary to assure the safe, uninjured return of our companions.

But the responsibility for our safety does not end there. We are also responsible for the safety of the forest and its inhabitants. How can we best keep those animals alive? What kind of activity will enable a wild bear to continue living even though our paths cross? Man must move throughout bear country in such a way as to minimize man-bear confrontations.

My concern for human safety revolves around the most effective means of self defense. I am eager to present what works best and/or should be allowed for your personal safety.

Because any bear—black, grizzly or polar—is capable of seriously injuring or killing you, it is important that you have a plan for your self-defense. If you enter bear country, you're at the mercy of the bear. Would you rather be at his mercy or have him be at your mercy?

It is your responsibility to research the safest methods for avoiding human injury as well as bruin injury—pepper spray, noise, flare gun, dog, pistol, shotgun, rifle.

Before entering bear country it would be a good idea to run down the following check list to ascertain your preparedness. If you cannot answer them positively, you may wish to forgo the outing.

1. Do you have a means of communicating with civilization?

    a. A PLB (personal locator beacon)?

    b. An ELT (emergency locator transmitter)?

    c. Cell or satellite phone or radio?

    d. Does this device have proper energy or back up supply?

2. Are you taking a bear dog—one that will deter a bear and not "retrieve" one to you?

3. Do you have a dependable partner?

    a. Will he stay with you?

    b. Can he administer first aid?

    c. Is an injured victim safe from further encounters or injury (in your absence)?

4. Are you prepared to stop a charging bear?

    a. Is your weapon of choice capable of doing so?

    b. Are you properly trained in its use?

    c. Can you bring the weapon into play within a split second's notice?

Education

Your best chance of seeing a bear is at a zoo, bear viewing place, salmon stream or garbage dump and probably while you are above timberline, flying or driving.

What percent of people learn about bears before entering the woods? Maybe 10%? What is the best source of information? How much is enough/too much information? What is the appropriate action during a bear encounter?

It's likely both man and bear could avoid injury or death if man knows more about bear behavior. Arm yourself with information. What causes bear attacks? How can you avoid a bear? How can you survive a bear mauling? How hard it is to hit a charging bear? To stop one?

If your bear experience is limited, gather whatever it takes in the way of knowledge and assimilate that into your repertoire of understanding, then sally forth determined to be confident, fearless and cautious. Be willing to learn and to back off a dangerous situation. Leave your arrogance behind.

Gain understanding about your new environment. Just as people venture into the desert with little knowledge about its dangers, so people enter bear country. While driving the friendly roads of Alaska I frequently see people walking the shoulders as if there were no bears in the state... just wandering along miles from a dwelling or a vehicle in which they could take refuge. They must not know that Alaska is wilderness from border to border with towns and villages sprinkled here and there! I would be the last person on earth to paddle a canoe into hippo country. So why do people insist upon walking wilderness asphalt without adequate bear protection?

A truly tragic fatality could have been prevented had the victim been aware of the dangers. *Crocodile Attacks* relates the story of Ginger Meadows who was attacked and killed by a crocodile in Australia. Had Ginger known about crocodiles, do you think she would have gone swimming? Likely not.

It is important to tell people of the dangers of bear country and possible encounters with bruin, as you would inform visitors about snakes, etc.

When visiting a new place such as a park, ask officials about bear activity and the proper etiquette while you are there.

Myth

Numerous myths, misinformation, misstatement and misguided ideology pervade bear information and related topics. Unfortunately, some people accept these as fact. Such include the idea that bears don't run as well downhill; grizzlies can't climb trees; bears are sluggish and bumbling; sows defend their cubs to the death; a sow with cubs represents the most dangerous bear to encounter. A major misconception is that bears won't bother you if you don't bother them (see *Night of the Grizzlies*).

1. Many people proclaim or accept the concept that man intrudes or invades bear country. They argue that urban expansion is detrimental to bears and other animals.

   People have been expanding into the wilderness for centuries. So what? Is man supposed to stop procreating? Is he supposed to be confined to some narrow strip of land where animals do not reside?

2. People have fewer rights than animals or, put another way, animals

have rights! AND animals have more rights than mankind.

Say, what?! Animals have rights? Domestic animals deserve consideration and safe treatment, unless, of course, they're destined for the dinner table. And since when do people have fewer rights than animals?

3. People cause injuries from bears.

    In most bear-people encounters involving human injury, people got too close to a bear's space. The bear's nature may well cause it to retaliate against the human. Sane people do not enter bear country with the idea of having a bear inflict injury upon them.

4. People deserve injury from bears.

    Why would any person "deserve" to be injured because he got too close to a bear? Too many ignoramuses assign injury to people as if the person deserves the injury.

5. Being tolerant—not hunting/reducing bear harvest—decreases human injury.

    On the contrary, less hunting and averse conditioning results in more bears, bears that are less fearful of humans and an increase of human injuries from bear (or predator) attacks.

6. If you don't bother them, they won't bother you.

    Tell that to Tim Dexter (Treadwell) and others who were injured or killed by bears. Bears can bother you about any time they take a notion to do so.

7. Bears only attack when provoked—you're safe if you don't agitate or encroach on a bear or its space.

    Bears don't even know what they're going to do in given situations. Provocation includes predatory habits. Is it possible there's no such thing as an unprovoked bear attack—something provoked the bear into the action? So if a bear's hungry, he is provoked to procure food.

8. Sows protect their cubs.

    Not 100% of the time.

9. It's possible to bond with bears, to become friends and compatriots. Even though they're wild animals, a person can become pals with them.

    James Cap'n Adams did for a while, however he died from a head wound inflicted by one of his pet grizzlies. Timothy Dexter died in his mistaken belief that he could bond with bruin. A pet grizzly nearly took off the thumb of my friend.

272

10. If you try real hard, you can reason with bears.

Stephen Routh looked into a black bear's eyes and "tried to reason with him" before realizing it WAS unquestionably a WILD animal. Forget reasoning with it.

11. No record exists of a bear attacking a group of more than four people.

APPENDIX 7

RC Harrop, where a bear attacked his group of 35 people

Patty Reed McConnell /Liard Hot Springs story (100-200 bathers/ recreators)

Marchuk cousins (70 in camp)

Norway early August 2011, 80 campers most between 16 and 23 years old when 4 mauled, one killed by polar bear.

Forest Wagner's group had 14 individuals

Michael Justa and Anna Powers' group had 22 guests

12. "…if you elicit an aggressive response from a bear it is because you scared it and the bear is simply protecting itself, its cubs or its food." (Source: 2015 Chamber of Commerce and Visitor Center booklet from Alaskan city.)

Bears may act aggressively as a result of being scared; however this statement does not go far enough. Predatory bears are naturally aggressive, whether scared by man or not. In this book I addressed numerous situations with aggressive bears that were not "scared." Those bears which invaded homes were not scared--Brian Knowlton, Claudia Huber, Adelia Maestas Trujillo. What about RC Harrop's bear? Numerous predatory attacks such as Isabelle Dube, Ian Dunbar, the Courtney's, Kristy Abbot, Patti Reed Mc Connell and Elora Petrasek were not caused by scared bears.

Athleticism

Another concept to consider is that of athleticism. It is my experience that more athletic persons evade and avoid certain accidents—their reactions are quicker and their response better than non-athletes. I believe this applies to bear encounters also…where an athletic person probably has a better chance of escaping.

Children

Never leave young children unattended. I'm amazed at people who allow their children to play in the yard where parents have actually seen bears wandering through. In *Bear Attacks: The Deadly Truth*, Gary Shelton describes an incident Dave Keddington of Fairbanks, Alaska, sent him. (see beginning of Predatory section in Attack chapter)

Personal Traits/Abilities/Characteristics

You must be in control. Call the shots. Rather than letting the bear dictate the situation, you determine the outcome. Decide and prepare ahead of time to be the one in control, rather than allowing bruin to make that decision for you. I'll be at the mercy of my weapon and my experience...not at the mercy of any bear and his arsenal. Thank you very much.

Preparation

Preparation involves mental, emotional and physical conditioning that will guarantee safe passage in bear country. If you can avoid a mauling, by all means avoid it...garner the necessary information and skills to detour around the bear or to stop it. Take precautions; take proper action. A major requisite to safety is to gain outdoor experience. In the book *Danger Stalks the Land* I delineate specific survival preparedness.

The outdoorsman owes it to himself, his family, his companions and to the bear to know himself and to prepare himself.

Practice

Plan your work then work your plan. Whatever you plan to incorporate in the woods or in town for safety against bears, you need to practice. Many people have told me they can outrun or out-climb a bear...or "take one with my pistol." When was the last time you practiced running, climbing or shooting?

If you plan to escape a bear attack by climbing a tree, how many times have you practiced climbing a tree within the last year, what type trees are at your disposal and can the charging bear climb trees...and, do you have time to reach the tree ahead of the bear?

If you plan to stop one with pepper spray or a high powered rifle, when was the last time you used either? When was the last time you practiced being three feet from a bear that stood up in your face?

The best precautions are useless if not practiced and learned in a reactionary mode. If you plan to escape a bear by spraying it with pepper spray, how many times have you practiced un-holstering, aiming and discharging the propellant and at what ranges and in what type weather conditions?

Practice numerous activities: using a flashlight and acquiring a weapon in the dark of a tent. Practice caution, bear awareness and the use of whatever weapon you choose for self-defense. My friend Eddie Feigner, founder and pitcher of the 4-man softball team The King and His Court, told me some years back that "practice makes permanent." It develops muscle memory.

Marti Miller was stalked by a black bear weighing 175 pounds. She did not want to shoot it. It is interesting to follow her logic and to note the benefit of practice in *Some Bears Kill* she states (Pp. 64 and 65):

"...it looks like he's tracing my steps...I took it as a red flag...It was as if I were trying to draw lines in the sand. I figured I'd leave my thirty-pound pack and climb farther up the ridge; that way if the bear was following me, he'd be distracted by my pack and I'd have some space... My plan was to climb another two hundred feet up the ridge and watch what happens...the bear came out exactly where I had...It did not touch the pack. The bear looked right at me...*This bear was trying to circle behind me...I'm here. I'm alone. I have to deal with this...nobody else is going to come to your rescue...*

"We looked at one another one hundred feet apart. I have dogs and horses and am used to speaking in commanding tones. I yelled in my deepest, gruffest voice, 'Get outta here!'

"The bear looked at me and shook its head laterally. It didn't clack its teeth together. It didn't slather. After shaking its head, it continued its purposeful walk toward me.

"I aimed at the bear's nose. At the moment before pulling the trigger— perhaps what made me shoot—I thought of my daughter Caitlin, and I thought of my friend Cynthia who had been attacked by a black bear. I knew that the bear could be on me at any moment. I had control of the situation and I didn't want to lose control by letting the bear charge. I pulled the trigger, but I did not hear the shot. As soon as I pulled the trigger, the bear went down, 'fwump.' And then I heard the echo. It took me by surprise that the bear dropped. I remember pausing, taking the gun away from my shoulder, and thinking in a surprised way, This thing worked."

Only when you can react automatically—and, often, quickly, can you hope for safety in bear country. You need to be so practiced that your action is as automatic as the subconscious insertion of your vehicle key into the ignition, brushing hair away from your face, shifting gears in your automobile, tying your shoes, taking a 3-step approach for hitting a volleyball or compensating for wake turbulence from a heavy jet in the cockpit of your private aircraft.

If you have prepared yourself and practiced the necessary steps for survival, you will be able to perform in the most critical aspects of a bear encounter.

IT DOESN'T MATTER WHAT YOU KNOW IF YOU DON'T PRACTICE IT!

Confidence/being cool

In his very interesting book *Notorious Grizzly Bears* W.P. Hubbard alludes to human scent and fear, "I believe another factor many hunters do not realize when they are faced with a charging grizzly is: sub-consciously the hunter, under such circumstances, has a touch of fear in his system which creates a scent given off by his body. The grizzly detects this fear-scent, which, along with his rage, increases his boldness and temper beyond the point of reason or caution." (Pg. 73)

Mike Cramond comments about confidence and fear as significant in the bear-man encounter scenario in *Of Bears and Man:*

"Fear may have something to do with triggering attacks. It is quite commonly known that people who are afraid of dogs are often the ones who get bitten by them. All my life I have been accepted or avoided by dogs, even vicious ones, because I don't fear them. I am wary of them. I approach the snarling or barking dog straight on, talking to them both reassuringly and demandingly if necessary. My body language may also tell them that I'd kick them under the jaw too, if necessary. Or I carry a stick, or make the grimace of picking up a stone from the ground. Dogs know all those movements from experience with other men. You don't even need to pick up the stick or stone. They know the maneuver, and they expect the stick or stone to come up in the hand. The gesture usually cows them, makes them circle—often they leave at a dead run. Too, as I do not really fear them, they detect none of the adrenaline that is released into the bloodstream and immediately transmitted through the skin of a fearful human.

"The grizzly bear, even the famed and ferocious man-eater of Alaska's Admiralty Island, backs down before an adversary of unquestioned courage. Stan's (Price) life with bears had shown him that they recognized dominant authority, and where there was nothing for them to prove or lose by attack, the best route for them was to retreat...

"Fear may have something to do with triggering attacks...the smell of fear...is a very real thing...I have had to handle people in great terror, and their odor is best described as skunk-like. I have smelled the same odor in frightened dogs and cats, so I am inclined to believe that this smell may also trigger an attack from an animal." (Pg. 84)

Being attentive to things and aware of your surroundings and relevant activity and assessing the situation are very important. Keep your head. Do not panic. Have a pre-determined mind set. Express confidence (even if you don't feel confident) and a powerful body language posture to bluff the bear. Bears understand body language—that's how they react to other bears. Out-bear the bear!

Cramond further comments, "A gun actually does something for the psyche of the man who carries it. It allows him to feel more confident and convey confidence in 'body language' to the bear. Thus a man standing firm, believing in the infallibility of his gun, has a greater edge for bluffing a bear off… I believe it's the man's confident bearing rather than his gun, that makes the animal flee." (*Killer Bears*, Pp. 295-296)

CHAPTER 8
STRATEGIES
Many considerations could affect your strategy for safety in bear country.

Visibility

Visibility is paramount.

Many bear mauling victims have stated that the bear was too fast, giving them little or no time to react. Greater visibility would have given them more time. You must have at least twenty yards of visibility in 360 degrees if you hope to minimize a surprise or other attack. The visibility provides better assessment of a bear's presence and that space should give you a one second cushion to bring a weapon into play. It also gives you a better view and ability to ascertain the bear's movements and behavior.

Apprise yourself of your surroundings and constantly assess what is going on in the environment—preferably 50 yards minimum visibility allows you to determine any dangers. Is the bear alone? How close is it to you? Can you readily reach safety?

On July 27, 2003 family members and I hiked the Chugach Mountains bordering Anchorage. The two-foot wide trail wound through thick alders with a couple of stretches of 200-yard alders providing zero visibility.

We encountered 21 people and their dogs—2 ladies hiking, 2 ladies jogging, a man and a woman with 2 dogs, a young tenting couple with a 12 gauge shotgun fastened to his backpack, 2 more couples with 2 dogs each, 3 adults with 3 children and 2 dogs, 1 guy jogger with 2 Siberian huskies, 1 guy jogging with a Heinz 57 dog and 1 guy hiking briskly. With the exception of the couple with the shotgun, I observed no pepper spray or firearm. With the wind blowing a steady 30-40 miles an hour, I wondered about the effectiveness of pepper spray, and I wondered about the two wounded brown bears I know of which dug holes in ambush of their pursuers who saw nothing of the bears until they were very close and observed the bears' ears above the holes.

And a couple of years later my daughter Jill and I saw two brown bear 3-year-olds in that same valley.

The summer before our group hiked Flattop Mountain. My son-in-law Brad Risch jumped from hiding ten feet away behind some mountain hemlock. I had time for nothing but surprise.

Travel in open areas—the better you can see, the better your chances of avoiding a chance or surprise encounter. The best way to avoid surprise—at close quarters…steer clear of brushy areas.

Reaction time

A former Los Angeles police officer learned in his training and told me that it takes the average person eight tenths of a second to recognize a threat before he reacts. If a bear charges from 30 yards, a person has 2-3 seconds at best. If nearly one second has elapsed in recognition of the crisis, the person has 1-2 seconds before melt down. If you're armed and able to engage a weapon, how many times can you pull the trigger on a can of pepper spray, pistol, shotgun?

Improvise

Use whatever's available—poke the bear's eyes or nose, thump it with a stick, club, a knife, bang stick or spear. The skull between the eye and ear (temple) is the thinnest place on a bear's skull. It might be that you could penetrate this area with a knife, rock or stick. The nose is also tender and some people have hit the bear on the nose, tweaked it or stuck their fingers up the nostrils to deter the bear's actions. Other areas of vulnerability on a bear's head are its eyes, its ears and its tongue.

Never give up…keep fighting…and trying everything. Michigander Art Legault thought of his pocket knife, brought it into play and saved himself from a sow black bear. In 1980 Stephen Routh deterred the bear temporarily by switching it in the face with a small branch then swam into the lake and pushed water toward the attacking bear. Ann Quarterman and Christine Bialkowski went toe to toe with a grizzly and Christine kicked it in the nose, sending it on its way. Greg Brown kicked a brownie off of him. Helmuth Port screamed into a grizzly's ear and it left his tent. Guy George reacted instinctively and swung an ice axe into a grizzly sow's head and throat.

In 2010 I read about a man who was awakened in his tent by a polar bear: (www.ca.news.yahoo.com, "Man punches polar bear, escapes attack," Friday August 13, The Canadian Press). Wes Werbowy heard a large male approaching his tent, inhaling with the snuffling sound they make while pursuing quarry. Wes immediately wondered about his shotgun which was at the front of the tent, and he started to unzip his sleeping bag. Before he knew it, Wes was facing the bear which stood on his shotgun, only two feet in front of the man. He then remembered an old Inuit trick…the most sensitive part of a bear is its nose, a great target in an emergency. Wes punched the bear as hard as he could and the animal instantly swapped ends and left.

What are the chances of surviving a bear attack by turning the tables on the animal and attacking it? Would it be so surprised that it would bolt?

A 76-year-old Japanese man, Noboru Toyoshima, ran into a mother bear with a cub, he remembered a friend's input, "Bears can't move easily when grabbed face-on. That's when the man from Kyowa, Akita Prefecture, turned his mountain hike into a charge-the-bear action. He rushed the animal and hugged it. They struggled a couple of minutes before the man kicked its legs and tripped it. Both bear and man tumbled a dozen yards down the slope. The bear rose and fled, leaving the man with claw marks on his head and shoulders. (Source: CreekBed.com/ venture news, World Wide Web, 76-year-old survives bear attack by hugging, Friday 19th July 2002)

Make eye contact

Although bear experts espouse the idea of not making eye contact with a bear because it's an act of aggressiveness. I say, "Balogna." If a bear confronts you, you need to think and say, "Yo, Mr. Bear, behave yourself or there's going to be bloodshed—yours, not mine."

While surfing the internet in August 2003 I ran across some comments that I thought very apropos for this section about attitude, eye contact and body language. I emailed the man who posted the information for permission to use his comments. He informed me that he chooses to remain anonymous. However he is an Alaskan who has spent years in the outdoors and has encountered a variety of big game animals. He wishes them no harm but in an endeavor to understand and get along with them better, he has experimented with a variety of body language and eye contact. His user name on the predator website is huntersnorth and he permitted me to include his name as Mark G.

He posted the first of the two posts March 13, 2003. Here he responds to another poster about fear, eye contact and facial language:

"Holdengr, I doubt Canadian bears are any friendlier than American bears, even though it appears certain that Canadian people are friendlier than American people. Maybe your generally friendly attitude has affected your bears!

"I have had a few uncomfortable encounters with bears, but the vast majority of my encounters have been very benign. I see bears (and other wildlife) often because I have had an outdoors job here in Alaska all my life, in addition to a couple of hunting trips and several fishing trips every year. It's certainly true that the more time you spend in the bush, the more wildlife you will see.

"I also firmly believe that your body/facial language is understood by animals just like you understand the words in this message. If you show fear, they know it instantly. If you show benign curiosity, they will tolerate you. If you give them the 'evil eye', they will likely flee...or fight. I've experimented with this with bears, wolves, moose, and crows. I've found that, of those four, the moose is (by far) the most unpredictable."

In the second post huntersnorth provides extremely helpful information about facing down a brown bear (posted March 14, 2003):

"Several years ago I was fishing alone in a large hole in the Talachulitna River that was just full of silver salmon. A 3 or 4 year old brown bear showed up on the opposite side of the river, perhaps 70 yards away. He was very un-happy that I was at 'his' favorite fishing hole. He started popping his teeth. Then he started pouncing with his front legs and whoofing. Then he walked over to a nearby tree and reached as high as he could (literally on his rear toes) and clawed up the tree, all the while looking over at me to see if I was impressed.

"While all this was going on I simply continued casting & retrieving, and giving him an occasional direct glance. After his tree performance I decided that I should either send him on his way or leave myself. So I simply set my rod down, took the rifle off my back, crouched a bit, and cocked the rifle while bringing it up to my shoulder, all the while giving him a direct stare (and probably squinting my eyes a bit). The effect of these actions were pronounced and immediate. His performance stopped, his eyes bugged out a bit, he turned around, and quickly set out to look for a safer fishing hole. I didn't say a word of English to him, and if I did he wouldn't understand anyway. But I 'told' him everything he needed to know, he understood perfectly, and reacted appropriately."

Look the bear down (look it IN THE EYE). Put on your best and most violent appearance of confidence and kick-butt mentality (or what some call "threat display"), because animals are aware of your attitude and demeanor. Show this 4-legged beast that you mean business.

Tell old fuzzy ears that you are man—"Whoa, bear! I'm man. I'll kick your fanny."

Although I have no empirical evidence, some suggest making yourself bigger than the bear (bears posture, bluffing other bears by standing sideways, etc.). Hold arms over head, hold up a coat, bag or pack to emphasize your size. If you're in a group, get your partners to do the same, in a confident modulated voice telling the bear to buzz off.

Move away from the bear, always maintaining visual contact with where it is and what it is doing.

On the subject of backing away from a bear, I had one young woman exhaust herself in April 2000 telling me that "you never back up from a bear in a close encounter because it is a sign of cowardice that bears recognize…and they only become more aggressive." She explained, "I was taught by the biologists and the US Forest Service people I worked for while guiding on Anan Creek in Southeast Alaska." After listening to her, I wondered how much of that theory was based on the fact that they are not allowed to carry a firearm in that situation…but rely upon pepper spray as their sole deterrent.

Therefore it is a bit misleading to let the listener think a can of pepper spray and holding your ground will suffice…not to mention that her bears were sated on salmon on the stream she guided, not necessarily interested in testing anyone's defensive weapon whether pepper spray or other.

She persisted in her theory and I told her that as a pragmatist I applauded her, "If it works, practice it." At length she asked me what I would do in a confrontation with a bear to which I commented, "I'd look it in the eye as I do menacing dogs, talk to it in a commanding (not yelling) voice, 'Yo, bear, I'm man. I'm not here to hurt you. In fact I'm moving away. Have a nice day.' And if the bear took my moving away as a sign of cowardice and attacked, I'd blow his butt off." End of story!

Raise your weapon and prepare to use it. Decide ahead of time whether you're going to fire a warning shot or save every bullet for the bear.

Talking down and eye contact

Although Allen Hasselborg lived alone for decades and was mauled by a brown bear, "The 'Bear Man' of Admiralty Island advocated talking bears down. He believed that it didn't do any good to bluff a bear because the bear was too intelligent. Hasselborg advocated getting firm with the animal and telling it to back off; and others witnessed him telling bears to go away, which they did." (Pg. 269, *Alaska Bear Tales*)

Hassleborg talked down more than one bear over his career. (see *Bear Man of Admiralty Island*) He displayed a confident persona and walked the talk. He bluffed the bears but was able to back up his bluff with a high powered rifle—even though he was mauled twice. (1912 and either 1938 or '39)

John M. Holzworth shared Hassleborg's theory in *The Wild Grizzlies of Alaska*, Pg.. 19, "…they're (brown bears) afraid of you if you face them."

Another account of a brown bear encounter portrays Allen Hassleborg using his voice and eye contact. The bear charged two men and Hassleborg from fifty yards when he "brought his gun to his shoulder for action. He barked a sharp command. 'Stop that, boy! Stop it! Stop it quick!' If his words had been bullets, they could not have been more effective. Slithering and sliding on the beach, the huge animal brought up short, shaking his head in surprise…Across ninety feet of mud and mussels in the gathering dusk, the three humans and one thousand pounds of disconcerted grizzly stared at each other.

"Suddenly, the spurt of courage that had inspired his charge deserted the bear. He turned tail and ran a few yards, then stopped to gaze sulkily back at the trio, as if debating his course. Then he slowly walked toward the shore, punctuating his retreat with glowering looks at his conquerors." (*Bear Man of Admiralty Island*, Pg. 142). Hassleborg's philosophy was, "If a bear starts for you, be firm with him and tell him to go back…" (Pg. 145)

And Hal Waugh, one of Alaska's most well known master guides believed that bears recognized changes in the human voice and that a person remaining calm and speaking softly to the big bruins of Alaska one could often talk them out of a charge or other aggressive action by standing one's ground.

Dalton Carr tells of talking down a grizzly in his *Tales of a Bear Hunter*. I've included part of his Pp. 46 to 47: "Since I was not really hunting, I was carrying the lightest rifle I own, a sporterized .303 Enfield (Jungle Carbine) with iron sights. As I approached the second meadow, heavy woods hugged the trail's left side. The sun had melted most of the snow on this part of the trail, so I walked along very quietly.

"Ten yards ahead the trail made a sharp left turn. I stopped, and for some unaccountable reason I felt a reluctance to make the turn. I put the rifle in the high ready position, flipped off the safety, and took up the slack on the military-style trigger. At that moment I heard a soft woof, and a large shape materialized out of the dark forest at the turn in the trail. It was a five-hundred pound grizzly ten yards away with its ears waving back and forth and its nose wiggling. It was trying its best to figure out what I was. I'm sure it never heard me until it heard the click of the safety.

"We stood facing each other for what seemed like ten minutes but was probably more like ten seconds. Finally, my scent drifted to its nostrils and I could clearly see the guard hairs on its neck and shoulders rise. The grizzly's ears swiveled back out of sight and then flipped forward again. It was having trouble making up its mind whether to charge or run. Then its ears drew back and stayed, and its head slowly lowered about three to four inches. It was considering very seriously an all-out charge.

"Trying to keep my voice as low pitched as possible under the circumstances, I began to talk to the bear in what I hoped was a quiet, well-modulated tone. I could see its indecision reasserting itself. The animal's ears once again swung forward and its head raised [sic] to its original position. I said something like, 'Well, old boy, I sure didn't intend to make you mad. Just take it easy while I walk out of here.' I stepped to the right, a neutral area, because I didn't want to give the impression of retreating or advancing—either of which might have been an indication of fear or aggression. I saw the bear visibly relax, the hair on its neck lowering. It now seemed more curious than angry. It walked toward me three steps to get a better view with clearly no aggression intended. I moved fifteen yards into the timber and circled the bear's position until I felt I could once again safely resume the trail.

"I never saw the bear again."

One young woman used eye contact and her voice to confront a large black bear. Christianne Kearns was sunbathing between Forest Glen and Huron Estates when surprised by a bear's appearance. It sniffed around her, leaving and returning several times before she felt safe and rose to her knees. The bear jumped onto a boulder a yard from her and she said, at that point, "I kind of felt like I was an animal, like I was not a human. I was just trying to read the bear and get away from a predator. It was kind of like a magical moment, because I was talking to the bear and… crying, because I didn't know what to do! I was saying 'just leave me alone. I'm not going to hurt you, if you don't hurt me!' It's weird, because as soon as I said that, he kind of backed off from the rock and let me go."

As she stepped back, she found a large, pointed stick and picked it up to use as a weapon if necessary. The bear charged her direction half dozen times and she repeatedly showed the stick until she reached home. (Source: Wednesday, August 18, 2004, www.pabucks.com: Basking in the sun 18-year-old from *The Elliot Lake Standard* on July 29, 2004)

Reasoning with bears

It is interesting to note that people have attempted to "reason" with bears in their encounters. Marti Miller and Stephen Routh told their stories in *Some Bears Kill*. Of the predacious black that attacked Routh he said, "…I got turned toward him and I was staring him right in the eye. I tried to reason with him. Thinking it might calm him, I said, 'You don't want to do this.'" (Pg.109) But Stephen realized the bear was on a mission which did not include "reasoning."

Partner

Your safety could well depend upon a reliable partner. Do not go into the woods alone. I've lost contact with Al but am enclosing an Augusts 6, 2003, email I received from him:

Hi Larry,

I just finished your book *Danger Stalks the Land*. Thanks! It was really helpful to me.

I was just in Alaska with the family on a fun vacation that took us up the inside passage on a cruise ship. When we hit Juneau, I saw and bought your book.

When we got off the ship in Seward, we took the train up to Anchorage and rented an RV for two weeks of "camping" and touring.

We did a number of day hikes all over the state and the "adventures" outlined in your book were fresh in my mind each time I went out. It helped me keep my eyes open.

I am an avid hiker down here in California and much of what you wrote is appropriate here as well.

I think the #1 thing I am walking away with from your book is the importance of a hiking partner. The Bible says that two are better than one, if one falls the other can help him back up. The stories you presented where there were partners involved seemed to turn out for the better most of the time.

Also I never knew about the mudflats near Anchorage and their quicksand like bottoms.

Thanks again and God bless you.

Al

Electricity

Available information re: electrobraid (for campers, tenters, hunters, etc.) and audio…is there an instrument that can be attached to tents, bikes, packs that lets the bear know you're there (a sound people can't hear—not a siren, not bells)? All avenues of safety need be disclosed for the prospective consumer-outdoorsman.

Fight back

Until around 2000 experts suggested playing dead during a defensive bear attack and fighting the bear during a predatory attack. However over the past decade or so a different picture has evolved—play dead if it's a grizzly attack; fight if it's a black bear. If a bear makes contact with you, do everything within your power to stay on your feet—don't go to the ground.

Gary Shelton includes a good example of a man who refused to be a victim of a bear mauling. On September 5, 1991, Darin Brown and four partners worked an inventory cruise in the forest of British Columbia. At one point Darin heard a noise and thought it might be a moose. The noise grew closer and he heard teeth popping. Knowing he was defenseless, he climbed a tree with a large black bear hot on his heels. The bear bit into his right foot and he kicked it in the face with his left. Darin screamed at the bear and it retreated before climbing up and biting his right calf, pulling him down several feet, as he kicked it the entire time with his caulk boots.

For a second time the bear released its grip and climbed down the tree. Darin said, "I couldn't' quite believe it, but the bear came up the tree a third time. It stopped just below me and hit my right leg with its paw. My original horror had changed into a focused fight for life, and now I became enraged at this animal that was tormenting me so. Without thinking, I grabbed onto two limbs and jumped upward and landed on the bear's face with both feet and all my body weight. The bear was knocked from the tree, but I was also falling and grabbing at passing branches. I managed to grasp the trunk just before landing on the ground, but still in a fit of rage, I jumped down and ran up to the bear— we stood two feet apart for a moment, in a stalemate. I pulled the small hatchet from my belt, picked up a piece of wood, and started swinging them at the surprised animal. I chased the bear around the tree we'd been in, determined to win this battle." The animal ran off ten yards, Darin avoided further contact and reached the safety of his truck. (Pp. 154-155, *Bear Attacks II Myth and Reality*)

Later a conservation officer investigated the scene and told him it was an area where problem bears were transported and released and that his decision to fight the bear probably saved his life. (How much, if any, bear aggression toward man is attributable to tranquilizing, collaring and handling bears?)

Darin later acquired a permit for carrying a .44 Magnum and insists that having it along gives him confidence to "deal with an ever-increasing bear population." (pg 156, *Bear Attacks II*, James Gary Shelton.

Gene Moe told me, "I wasn't going to give my body up without a fight." (*Bear Tales for the Ages*) He fought for his life with a knife and won.

Consummate

Just because a bear charges, does not mean it will consummate the charge. Just because a bear consummates the charge and bites or mauls someone, doesn't mean the person will die. I used to think that should a bear come hell-bent, it was all over. Not so. A person can wave, shout, spray, look larger, fight, not give up or shoot…and live.

Aftermath

If you are unable to avoid a bear mauling and/or you need to address the necessity of getting (yourself or someone else) first aid and rescue, you must know first aid, have the necessary communication device to reach succor and the wherewithal to get out—you must know the way out and back if you have to go for help. One of the saddest tragedies I've heard of involved a hunter whose partner was mauled by a bear he'd wounded. When the shooter finally found help via a man with a CB, a helicopter was launched but the shooter couldn't remember where he'd left his partner, nor how to find him until it was too late.

Communication

Inform others about your plans and return information.

Sky Roberts suggests, "My advice for others going into the woods is to always expect the unexpected. You need to be prepared for any type of accident. Should something like that ever happen, you should be prepared to respond by carrying first aid supplies and a radio. Now I always carry a hand-held VHF and a personal ELT. The hand-held radio will reach any aircraft overhead." (*More Alaska Bear Tales*, Pg. 199)

Apprise others if you have a bear encounter by talking to proper authorities, posting a note at a trailhead

In the event of a mauling…How can you best assist in your "recovery"—are you able to signal with a mirror or flare or to light a fire? Do you have a cell phone, personal locator beacon, emergency locator transmitter or some other communicative device?

Hunting

Fine tune your senses—eyes, ears, nose. Carcasses and gut piles could harbor bears and birds. Listen for bear sounds and scavenger birds. These birds can warn of a downed animal; however they can also attract a bear to a kill site.

Numerous Wyoming hunters told me in November 2003 that rifle reports were bringing an alarming number of bears to their elk and deer kills around Yellowstone.

Bears equate hunters with food. As Bill Schneider (*Where the Grizzly Walks II*) points out, they have adjusted to hunting seasons as they have to the berry and salmon seasons. Kevin Frey of Montana's fish and game department said, "We did a project once…and we could see the distribution change. The bears moved right into the heavily hunted areas as soon as the hunting camps went up…even before the first elk went down. The bears knew that when the people started coming, it was dinnertime." (Pg. 224)

It's common in these bear areas to have a bear reach the wounded game before the hunter, making for some interesting events. It is wise to be on high alert while following a wounded animal.

To place a puny, unarmed man beside a wilderness predator his size or larger creates a no win situation for the man. To suggest that a man can take on a bear with equal or even chances of survival, is ludicrous (though a few examples of hand to hand with grizzlies exist). A single swat from a bear could easily disembowel man, break his neck or decapitate him.

After having read Montana outfitter Jack Rich's comments in Bill Schneider's *Where the Grizzly Walks II*), I looked up Jack on the Internet and he kindly responded to my query for his input on that subject.

"My family has been outfitting in the area for sixty years. We embrace management objectives that work to insure a healthy and sustainable population of all wildlife species. For over sixty years and three generations our family has made a living as guides and outfitters in Montana's grizzly bear country.

"During those nearly 10,000 days and nights in the backcountry we have seen many bears and experienced numerous close encounters, but have never been attacked by or had to kill a bear in self-defense. And I credit that mostly to the approach we take—in addition to a little luck.

"When we are in sensitive situations, like approaching an elk kill, we go in as a group (2 or more people) and try to make plenty of noise— talking loudly and even firing rifle shots. And we display bravado to give any bear ample time to figure it out and back away. When a bear hears, sees, or smells a human it should be his signal to skedaddle. A bear that is intimidated and afraid of man is destined to live a lot longer than one who isn't.

"We've always believed it's important to show the bear we're in charge. Don't give up your elk. If you do, you're telling the bear that he's tougher than you are, like the class bully. Backing down is a recipe for disaster. Standing your ground tells the bear it's your elk. I don't believe in acting submissive.

"When camping in bear country we use the 'small footprint' method.

In other words we have a compact campsite where we cook, eat, store our food and sleep. Bears are not welcome in that space. And if we leave the camp, then our food and any other attractants are stored in bear-proof containers.

"Some people—including government agencies—advocate a larger footprint,(i.e., campsite), in the shape of a triangle—with your cooking area, food storage and sleeping area all separated by 100 feet or more. In our experience the larger footprint is indefensible and provides opportunity for a bear to become comfortable around the sight, smell and sound of humans, especially during nighttime hours. And that habituation will more than likely lead to confrontations resulting in unnecessary risk for people and a premature death for the bear.

"In most cases we believe that passive behavior by man sends the wrong message to a bear. Encountering a sow with cubs is about the only time that it makes sense. As I've said before—it's similar to the class bully—once you back down it will just reinforce their bad conduct. It is our responsibility to condition bears the <u>right way</u>."

Rich has employed urination around an animal that they must leave till later. Rich also believes that hunters should not surrender game to a bear because they should not be rewarded with food, and it compounds the problem for future hunters.

Big game calling

Use EXTREME caution. When you use a big game call for moose, elk, deer or bear, remember the bear thinks that you're that animal. He's not expecting a dude in cammo sprinkled with deer urine with a deer call in his mouth. So you should be prepared for such an event by being in a position from which you can see in 360 degrees and be able to defend yourself from such an event. Preferably off the ground and/or have a partner watching your back. One Southeast Alaska hunter with his back to a tree was killed while blowing on a deer call (*More Alaska Bear Tales*).

Gunshots have been known to trigger a bear's investigation. In some areas where bears are conditioned to respond to the sound of a firearm with a food reward—Kodiak deer hunters lose deer to bears coming to the "dinner bell" reports of their rifles. The grizzly that killed Shane Fumerton and William Caspell in B.C. was probably such a bear, stalking them before its final rush.

Chuck Lewis told me that he had a brown bear come over a mile to his rifle shot on Kodiak. Bill Schneider talks about Molly in chapter 14 of *Where the Grizzly Walks*, a sow grizzly that staked out archers' tree stands. She was collared and for years regularly followed bow hunters to their tree stands, as if running a trap line. And he also talks about the dinner bell.

It's not uncommon for more than one bear to arrive, expecting food at the hint of a game call or firearms report.

Photographing - Filming from a distance—refrain from following a bear for the perfect close up!

Riding Whether on a bike, ATV or other vehicle, use extreme caution, remain constantly alert. Moving silently can result in a surprise encounter. Incorporate a noise maker on the bike.

Horseback is safer than walking

Tenting

Many experts believe a tent provides a safer night time sleeping quarters than a lean to or open air. The tent may confuse the bear should one approach.

Select the tent site and remove any vestige of garbage or anything else that might attract a bear. In the interests of those who follow you, leave a clean camp. Consider carefully your decision to camp where others have left food or attractants (like gut piles, salmon offal, etc.).

One of the major dangers involving possible bear attacks is what I refer to as the mystery camp…who has camped here before and/or conditioned bears toward people food, etc.? Activities bringing you into possible close contact with bears where others have left food items or attractants include float trips on rivers, fishing, campgrounds, an older hunting camp site. Avoid attracting bears with anything from discarded food or other such materials. (If you're in a camp area like Liard Hot Springs where black bears are prolific and a number of maulings and a few deaths have taken place, you might want to consider foregoing the experience and camping somewhere else!)

On a related note, if you are in a campground where officials are attempting to trap a problem bear, I strongly suggest you vacate that site for another, miles away. I refer you to Mary Patricia Mahoney who was dragged from her tent and killed September 23, 1976. She was tenting with four female companions. The night before her accident the girls and seven other groups of campers listened to and engaged in bear safety discussions with Ranger Fred Reese, who also informed them that there was a bear trap set in the west section of the campground which was closed to their use.

Your tent should be in a "defensible" location.

You might consider setting up your tent near climbable trees, but remember that bears climb. A few examples reveal bear's climbing as high as 35-feet to reach and pull down an intended human victim (*Bear Attacks: The Deadly Truth* chronicles a couple in the tree climbing section).

In order to avoid a fearsome night attack consider tent placement that provides visibility, electric fence, watchman (take turns keeping watch—one outside tent), fire for illumination, lantern for the same reason. Ideally a bear will NOT enter your tent.

A night time attack almost always indicates a predatory bear. This bear usually circles several times. Tent mates should each have accessible light, knife in sheath (preferably minimum 5-inch length fixed blade), pepper spray and/or firearm. The campers must have practiced safety procedures in the event of a bear attack—one (opens tent zipper or cuts through fabric) points light at bear's eyes, other sprays bear. If bear "opens" tent, tenters must react appropriately—get outside; keep light, spray and knife; spray bear; if that fails, use knife.

Common behavior for grizzlies in search of food is summarized by Gary Shelton in *Bear Attacks II*, "A grizzly enters a camp at night in its normal exploratory food search behavior. It becomes aware of something in a tent and starts to paw or bite the tent. Next it discovers an animal moving inside the tent, emitting high-pitched screams, and proceeds to bite and test it. Once the bear has blood in its mouth and the normal predatory instinct is aroused, it escalates the biting of the head and neck area until movement stops." (Pg. 85)

Know wind direction to avoid possibly attracting a bear with cooking odors.

Warning system around the tent are worth considering—like a trip wire with cans or other items like dried branches. (see deterrents above, such as Tom Hron's PackAlarm)

Pete Sainsbury (above) suggested a distant and closer early warning system of urine around the tent area—he never had a problem in thirty summers of working the Seward Peninsula of Alaska.

Some suggest urine and ammonia sprayed near the tent—which can be problematic because boars dislike the smell of human urine.

Some politically correct advice includes not cooking in the tent and not storing food in the tent as well as storing food 100 yards or so from camp. These words of wisdom must be interpreted by each camper based on his experience and his motivation or plans for the outing. For instance, what are the chances of being bushwhacked by a bear on your way to the stored food? What are the chances of losing your food if it is stored close by, as in your tent, where you can defend it? You must decide the risk and the benefits.

Work related (surveyors, camp workers)

Know area, bear nature, bear's habituation to it and be able to identify bear sign

Check area with helicopter fly over

Work with partner

Visually evaluate travel routes where possible with binoculars

Utilize bear bells and/or make constant noise (a danger: it could attract bears)

In your own yard

Does your environment require you to carry a weapon for your protection? Obviously if you live in states such as Montana or Colorado and your property abuts a timbered wilderness area, the chances of having a bear or cougar in your neighborhood are greater than if you live in downtown Tulsa, Dallas or Seattle. So, is bear protection even a consideration at your place? On the other hand if you live in Anchorage, Fairbanks or some other locale where your city has been plopped down in the middle of the wilderness like Lake Tahoe, what is the safest means of keeping you and your family or neighbors safe from a possible bear attack?

My friend and fellow wrestling coach, retired Anchorage school teacher Pete Aftreth, shared some bear problems they've had at their hillside home.

I was providing care for daughter Kjirsten's two children—our 4-year- old grandson Erik, while holding his 2-year-old sister Annika. I had applied a slate sealer on the front and back entryway slate floors and the odor was still quite strong when Kjirsten arrived with the two grandchildren. Wanting to keep her children "safe" from the petroleum fumes, she went around the house and opened up doors, windows and the sliding glass on the front and back storm/screen doors.

The next thing I hear is "there is a bear" from Kjirsten as she was opening the sliding glass door on the kitchen deck. It was June 2007 and I had not seen a bear since the previous fall. I walked through the kitchen to the back door while holding Annika and there was a 2-year-old black bear standing on its back legs with its front claws into the plastic screen (the sliding glass in the door was up). All that was between the bear and being inside the house was this flimsy plastic mesh screen.

Not wanting to deal with the bear inside the house, I set Annika down at the top of the back steps. She was crying at the unexpected behavior and I headed out the back door, grabbing a 4-prong garden rake.

When he saw me, he backed up a few feet so I hit it on top of the nose with the rake. The bear made no attempt to move away or leave so I went back inside and closed the door. Then I see it on top of the 6-foot chain link fence chewing on the Lexon greenhouse roof. I went back outside with my 4-prong garden rake where the bear continued chewing on the roof. Thinking I could push it off and outside the chain link fence, I gave it a shove in the chest. This time the bear snarled and came down on my side of the fence.

Kjirsten's telling me I'm scaring the kids and "please come into the house." I saw the bear climb over the 5-foot wood fence into the driveway and remembered the garage door was open. I was not sure the door from the garage into the lower rec room was latched closed. If it was not latched or closed tight, the bear could push it open and be in the house another way.

I ran back into the house through the rec room, opened the "unlatched" door and saw the bear in the garage looking like a mountain goat on top of a stack of studded snow tires. I grabbed a hiking boot and launched it at the bear which then left the garage.

We have had several bear interactions in the past thirty-seven years living in Stuckagain Heights. When we started building our house in 1975, we had lumber company delivery drivers refuse to drop off our building materials because there were bears in the yard close to the driveway. We have had a medium-sized black bear climb the vertical side of our wood house and over the railing on the deck to put its dirty front paws on the kitchen window over the stove.

Several bears have climbed over the 6-foot fence to steal food from our emu or break into the Emu food shed. Another large female black bear with three new cubs broke into our greenhouse looking for food to feed the cubs. We had a large male black bear climb into the yard and try to get our Emu. It was only a few feet from the Emu when we stepped out on the elevated back deck. The Emu seemed to know we were on her side and charged after the big male bear sending it on the run, looking for a place to get back over the fence. I have had my new Dodge Ram pickup truck scratched by a large black bear as it tried to climb over the back bed area of the truck.

About six years ago a large brown bear killed a 2 to 3-year-old moose in front of our house. Rick Sinnott (Fish and Game) came out to check out the kill site. In a neighborhood presentation he said we need to know there may be a few bear attacks or interactions in their Bear Management Plans. His message was "bears have FIRST priority. People have second."

While finalizing Pete's original stories in February 2014 I received the following email from him:

We had another large Grizzly bear climb over the six-foot chain link fence October 30, 2012. I measured its tracks in the fresh snow (backs were 15-17 inches long; fronts were 7-8 inches wide). I guessed 500 lbs plus. Although it walked past the outside metal auto dog (Emu) feeder (had turkey Grower feed in it) to the 6x8 Emu shed and pushed in the wood panel window (23x33 inches) and scared the daylights out of the Emu, I saw no hair on the lower window frame area.

I called Fish and game...talked to Mr. Battle who took over for Jesse Cultane when Rick Sinnott retired. I explained what I had observed and asked if he wanted to take care of the problem or if he wanted me to.

His reply, "Keep me advised."

My reply, "Sir, my next call will be 'come get your DEAD Bear,'"

I put up a chain link gate over the glass window and the pushed in wood window, stacked up 4 to 5 metal garbage cans for a warning alarm, slept with windows open and waited for the bear to return the next night. I had a medical vaccination for the bad bear. It never happened. Two weeks passed. Winter.

The following spring I learned from a neighbor that a big brown bear pushed in several windows on garage man doors the past November. He could have been inside several homes instead of the garages. He tore up several garage doors. He could have gotten into several homes. That was a VERY BAD BEAR

The homeowner reporting to fish and game was a recently retired state employee so he had more influence on the Fish and Game Department because they responded that night and set up the culvert bear trap baited with dog food, At 11 PM got the big bear. Shot it. Weight was 780 (not sure if actual wt or estimate).

I was GLAD that bear was no longer a problem to "People."

CHAPTER 9
WEAPONS—WHA-CHA-GOT?

What's the best advice for avoiding injury from a bear? Repeat. Best. Advice. Avoid. Injury.

What's your best advice?

Are you safer with a weapon or without one?

Throughout this book are numerous scenarios: people with weapons, those with "inadequate" weapons, some unusual methods of safety and people with no weapons.

No weapon

I find it tragic that so many have been injured because they carried no weapon. One such story involves an ill-informed couple. Patricia Van Tighem and her husband found themselves at the mercy of a bear (see Predatory Attacks). Patricia suffered emotionally until she took her own life.

They were hiking and their country's officials disallowed the use of firearms. What if they'd had pepper spray? A good dog? A flare gun? A firearm?

The park service and other agencies should not have the authority to dictate people's choices of safety in the forest.

Unusual Methods of Self-defense

It is idealistic—and perhaps not realistic—to keep both man and bear from injury. To dissuade a charging 100 pound or a 700 pound bear from damaging you is desirous, but how can this be accomplished?

Some successful "weapons" that have staved off bear maulings include feet, arm, mittens, knife, flame, flare, spear, bottle rocket, and stocking cap. Other unusual methods of self-defense against bears include one guy who chased off a bear by hitting it in the face with a tennis shoe.

In October 2015 Chase Dellwo, a Montana archer, surprised a sleeping grizzly at three feet. The animal immediately rushed him, knocking him down and biting his leg. When Chase recalled his grandmother's mention that large animals have a bad gag reflex, he thrust his right fist and arm into the bear's mouth. The 400-pound boar abruptly left.

I know a number of people who attributed their escapes or rapid healings to prayer or their calling upon the name of Jesus Christ.

When Larry Bond prayed and asked "Heavenly Father" to send the bear away, the bear left. (*Some Bears Kill*, Pg. 82+) Johnny McCoy and his partner prayed for strength and were supported later by the global Christian community. Gene Moe asked God for help and was supported by prayer. Bessie Meyers attacked a grizzly shouting "In name of Jesus" and the bear stopped mauling her father and left. (See Don Welty story in this volume, mysterious attack section)

Knife

(My other books include a few examples of men using knives— Robert Nichols, Hugh Glass, Gene Moe, etc.)

Tom Hron tells about Chris McClellan in his book *Fighting for Your Life*. While scouting farm land and deer hunting near Grand Prairie, Alberta, Chris inadvertently encountered a sow grizzly with three cubs. He immediately waved his arms and yelled but the old girl would have none of it. Here she comes!

Armed only with a camera and a knife with a foot-long blade, Chris faced the animals coming at him from a distance of 200 feet. After attempting to engage his camera's flash which would not cooperate, he pulled out his knife.

The sow hit him going full tilt, clamped his left forearm in her mouth and together they hit the ground. Chris repeatedly stabbed her in the neck and she released her grip to bite into his body and right arm. Suddenly the grizzly stopped her attack and walked away, allowing Chris to do the same.

Chris reached a farmer who called emergency and Chris took a ride in an ambulance to the hospital where he was treated for a broken left forearm and other injuries. The next day the bear was found dead with several wounds to her neck.

In September 1987 Jim Mariotte worked on a bull moose. While snow fell softly about him, bushes fluttered four feet away. Birds he figured. After two or three further "flutterings" with no sign of birds, he realized that there were no birds. He stood and discovered a grizzly with a penchant for moose meat. Perhaps the bear was more surprised than Jim as man rose above the moose to face bruin.

The bear wanted the moose and Jim stood in its way. During the ensuing fiasco Jim utilized a knife with a 3 ¾ inch fixed blade in his defense

He succeeded in stabbing the bear numerous times while being tossed about and bitten himself before the bear chose to leave. The last time Jim stabbed the brute, he lost track of the knife which may well have been imbedded in the beast.

Stan Price

My son Ben and I met Stan Price and had a great time learning more about this gentle and funny man. He lived on Admiralty Island at Pack Creek and oversaw the rearing of 82 brown bears in his time there. Many of the bears at Pack Creek knew Stan. We thought it was pretty cute that he referred to bears as rascals. Within a year of our meeting he arrived in Anchorage where I visited him at the Providence Hospital's Providence House and later at an extended care facility to which he's been transferred.

The actions of Stan Price which follow, quoted from *Of Bears and Man,* must be taken in context.

Electric fences

"I put those electric fences up to deter them. They'd plow right through any other fence, wire or wood. The shock from the electric fence will make them back off. They don't like it, and avoid it." Pg. 81

Disputing territory

"…I was digging potatoes in the garden…a sow with two cubs… charged right up and raised her paw as if she was going to bat at me. I guess I had a nervous reflex: I hit her in the face with the shovel (jabbed her). After I hit her, she ran out the gate…I wouldn't have had time to swing a shovel…I think she just heard me working in the garden when she was about fifteen or twenty feet away…she had no way of knowing that I wouldn't hurt her. I was just too close to her and her cubs." Pp. 81 and 82

Jabbing bears in the face

"I was down in a hole, knee deep, when this rascal came up to the edge of it. I just tapped him quickly in the face with the shovel, and he took off. They don't like to get hit on the nose." Pg. 83

Big bear charged Stan

"Gary [his nephew] was about seventy-five feet away and didn't know what was going on. The bear was on his side of the river, but it jumped in and came right across, charging at me. I had my stick with me, and when he put on the brakes—he really skidded to a stop—I was ready. I reached out with the stick and swatted him right on the tender end of the nose. He backed up and shook his head. I poked him in the face again with the stick. He backed up again and turned away. He just didn't want any more stick!" Pp. 83-84

"…the grizzly bear…backs down before an adversary of unquestioned courage. Stan's life with bears had shown him that they recognized dominant authority, and where there was nothing for them to prove or lose by attack, the best route for them was to retreat." Pg. 84

Rocks

In August 2003 two men escaped a grizzly sow on the Salmon River near Hyder, Alaska, (75 air miles northeast of Ketchikan on the Canadian border) when they tossed rocks at her. As Joel Barrett 22, and John Rowan, in his 30's, left the woods, they saw a mother and two large cubs advancing rapidly toward them from 50-plus yards. The men tried to escape down the stream but Rowan tripped and mama bit his legs. He rose and the bear turned her attention on his partner until Rowan fell again. Then she commenced biting his legs again. Barrett threw sand, gravel and rocks at her until a rock ended the affair and she walked away. Rowan was treated at the Stewart, B.C. hospital then flown to Ketchikan General Hospital where he was treated and released. (Source: "Man pelts bear with rocks, saves friend, Hyder: Pair was hiking when sow with cubs charged," The Associated Press, August 16, 2003)

Weapons known to kill

Men have killed bears with spears as well as bows and arrows. In addition to other unconventional weapons, men have also killed bears with large and small caliber firearms - .45-70, .416, .375, .338, .300, .30-06, .7mm, .270, .30-30, .220 (Jerry Austin tells of a friend who killed three full sized brownies in his cabin with three shots from his .243 rifle), .454 Casul, .44 mag, .357 mag, .9 mm, .22.

"Inadequate" weapons

I'm always amused by experts who know everything and tell others what works and what doesn't. Although the use of a pistol as adequate bear protection has long been disputed, some have employed it in their defense. Alaskan old timers have told pistol packing people they'd be better off filing off the front sight so they could more easily get the pistol into their mouths in the event of a bear attack. The following examples include pistols, "underpowered" calibers that WORKED.

Ben Moore saved his life with his .357 Magnum and his hands inside a grizzly's mouth when he fired. Likewise Louis Kis emptied his .357 into a Montana grizzly when it attacked after he released it from a culvert trap (perhaps you've seen the pictures traveling the internet as of 2008). My friend Wade Nolan killed a predatory black bear with his .41 Mag. A Russian River sow brownie was killed with a 9 mm using steel jacketed bullets. Lots of guys have killed grizzlies with .44 Mags.

In 1965 Jack Turner cruised up trail not far from his home packing a beat up old .30-30 lever action slung from his shoulder by a piece of nylon rope. Suddenly he came upon the largest grizzly he'd ever seen and it exploded toward him at the same instant. He un-slung the weapon, levered a round into the chamber, raised the .30-30 to his shoulder and touched off a cap when the bear was 3-feet from the end of the barrel. The 170 grain soft point bullet struck the grizzly between the eyes and jellied its brain before exiting the back of its skull. The beast dropped dead two steps from Jack. The bear's skull measured 26 10/16ths inches and was the world record for five years.

My friend Jack Muir killed a brown bear with his .44 Magnum; Dale Bagley staved off a brownie with his pistol.

One grizzly mauling victim, Steve Rose, declared, "I'll never venture into grizzly country again without a gun. If I can't take a gun, I won't go." (Source: *Bears*, Pg. 142)

Weapon of Choice

Which weapon provides the best margin of safety?

The current politically correct weapon of choice is pepper spray. Some who have had success with it are in cayenne Nirvana. Obviously, those who have seen it fail, aren't so inclined

Your choice of weapon could likely determine your safety in bear country

Numerous weapons are available for your safety, including audio (air horn, bells, whistle), fire, flare gun (Dick Griffin recommended a flare gun, *Alaska Bear Tales*, Pg. 222), highway flares, stick, club, rock, flashlight, handi-blaster, knife, pepper spray, pistol, shotgun, rifle.

There are some untested, or at least, undocumented weapons that might divert a bear's charge, like the handi-blaster. This butane filled mini-"flame thrower" which propels a 3-foot diameter ball of flame about fifteen feet was on the market for a brief time. However as of 2013 it seems to have been withdrawn from purchase. Is it worthy of self-protection? Does it have the potential to be as effective as pepper spray at about the same cost?

FIREARMS

Whether confronted by a thug or a band of brigands, do you use your personal charm and charismatic personality to sweet talk him or do you suggest that you are packing a firearm that could do them considerable harm if they don't let you pass on your way?

I suggest a firearm would work better than personal charm…IF you are prepared and qualified to engage it. Same thing applies to confronting bruin. Do you have the skills and is the weapon of a nature to stop the bear?

You can choose between a high-powered rifle or hand to hand…or somewhere in between.

My friend retired Alaska Department of Fish and Game biologist Lee Miller told me, "If you run into a bear, it's better to have a firearm that you don't need than to need a firearm that you don't have." (4/19/2006)

How practical is packing a firearm to stave off a bear attack? Not. For instance, in certain locales numerous everyday situations could involve a bear—you're working in your yard; you're on a bike trail in town or you're hiking on the outskirts of town. What are the chances that you'll see a bear? Or have to defend yourself against one? The reality is that, although the likelihood is nearly zero, if you encounter a bear, what kind of strategy do you have for escaping it safely?

It may be unrealistic to expect to see a bear. It may be impractical to lug a weapon. Nevertheless, what if someone encounters a determined bear of any size? What is the most effective means of dealing with it?

Is there a correlation between the size of the bear and the caliber in staving off a bear mauling? What size bear can be stopped with…a fist, stick, road flare, hatchet, small caliber firearm, pepper spray, dog?

Glenda Anne Bradley was mauled, killed and partially consumed by a 112 pound black bear. She may well have saved her life with a hatchet, road flare, stick or small caliber firearm. Whereas a person confronted by a grizzly of a thousand pounds may be under-gunned with a .30-06 rifle. An animal that can break the neck of a horse, steer or moose with one swat of a paw IS dangerous!

The Outdoorsdirectory.com carried an interesting illustration of success with bears via various weapons April 26, 2006:

      pistol   45% success

      shotgun 50 % success

      rifle   55% success

Ursus1 posted the following January 20, 2006:

For those who are a little slower, 45% of encounters where a person had a pistol ended favorably (that means 55% did not). then 50% of encounters where a person had a shotgun ended favorably (which means 50% did not). Also, 55% of encounters where a person had a rifle ended favorably (alas, 45% did not). so by my math,

    45+55=100

$$50+50=100$$

$$55+45=100$$

Some of the information I read about firearms continues to baffle me. For instance in *Mark of the Grizzly*, "That's when he decided guns weren't much good in a bear encounter, and he hasn't carried one since… (Pp. 4-5)…he doesn't believe that guns do much good in bear encounters, that attacks almost always happen too fast for most people to draw a weapon." (Pg. 8)

When I read such comments, I wonder what kind of experience led a person to such conclusions regarding firearms. Dozens of people were saved from further injury when they or a partner shot a bear off them. I can think of a few people whom I've interviewed who saved themselves from injury or reduced it when they shot a bear with a (little respected) pistol.

Because time is a key factor toward your survival, it is essential to consider your qualifications for carrying a firearm. Time fits right into the necessity of having visibility, enough to spot a bear from several dozen yards. Also here's where vigilance, readiness and anticipation come in. Were I to swim in a bayou with no thought of alligators, what could possibly be my plight?

Alaska guide for 30 years, Ralph W. Young expected his clients to be prepared, "One of the rules, which I expected to be followed to the letter, was that the hunter must never, never walk away from his rifle. More specifically, I insisted that any hunter must carry his rifle loaded, cocked, on safe, and in his hands at all times when actually hunting." (*Grizzlies Don't Come Easy*, Pg. 76)

In discussing the sensible way to approach bear country, veteran outdoorsman Mike Cramond commented on George Doerksen (see Predatory Attack section herein) who was killed and partially devoured by a grizzly at Liard Hot Springs, "I have learned that camping in the wilds is deliberately exposing oneself to attack by bears…I would no more go into bear country without a weapon than I would tour a high-crime area of a city in the dead of night unarmed and unaccompanied." (*Of Bears and Man*, Pg. 212)

Do your homework

What caliber, bullet and load do the experts suggest? Get the facts then improvise your own bear stopper "medicine."

So, here comes the bear. What do you do?

Generic advice is to shoot at center mass—point at the middle of the animal and fire. Hopefully you'll hit the skull or spine, decommissioning the bear. If all else fails, you can aim for a shoulder. Breaking down the bear will enhance your survival chances. Because the animal may still be able to maneuver with two pulverized shoulders, keep shooting until you've averted the danger.

Some debunk skull shots because of the ricochet factor. Alf Madsen allowed, "Popular belief has it that the bullet will ricochet off the bear's skull, but it won't. The skull isn't that thick. Near misses and grazing shots have brought that popular fallacy into being." (Pg. 283, *Alaska Bear Tales*)

Rifle

(Which caliber is most effective? Which model is more effective—pump, semi-auto, bolt action, lever?)

The experts who make their living in bear country—guides and old-time Alaskans—have a great deal to say about appropriate rifles. Most of them recommend a rifle of at least .30 caliber power. Kodiak guide Alf Madsen knew of a brownie that kept going although shot six times with a .375 and 300 grain loads. "The shocking power of the .375 is so great that a bullet placed near a vital organ such as the heart will kill the animal, though it does not actually touch the vital part…A shot in the shoulder or the big joints of the legs will completely pulverize the bones—but the bear will keep going unless hit in a vital spot." (*Alaska Bear Tales*, Pg. 282)

Even though a heart shot is usually fatal, a bear with its heart shot out can survive half a minute or longer…long enough to do some serious damage to the shooter if said bear can reach man.

Carl Williams moved to his Uncle Bill Duryea's residence in Alaska's Cottonwood Bay in 1934. The country at the head of the Alaska Peninsula where Bill had lived some fifty years was rich in brown bear and by the time he was done, Carl had lived there forty-plus years. Bill taught Carl how to live with bears.

"In my view, a rifle that is satisfactory for use on Alaska's brown bears must be at least .30 caliber and throw a bullet of at least 220 grains. The .270 I used to kill the charging bear in 1935, while fine for most other Alaskan big game, isn't enough rifle for the big bears. Good rifles that I have used include the .35 Newton (with which I used a 250-grain delayed expanding hollow-point bullet), the .450 Alaskan (a modified .348 Winchester) and the .375 H and H Magnum, especially with the 350-grain bullet. At close range I've had good results using the .405 Winchester with a 300 grain bullet.

"Perhaps the best big bear rifle I have used was the .450 with a 300 grain bullet. This bullet just keeps pushing when it hits a bear, and it doesn't blow up."

Carl had a close call with a charging brownie and "I sold the .300 Magnum soon after, having lost my confidence in it as a big bear rifle." (Source: My 40 years With Bears," *Outdoor Life*, February 1980, Carl Williams as told to Jim Rearden)

Probably from the 1940s through the 1970s or '80s most Alaska guides used the .375 Magnum as a backup weapon for stopping big bears. However new technology is availing a more potent piece of weaponry. The Alaska guide's lever action .45-70 loaded with 500 grain Garrett bullets has received high praise since around the early 1990's.

Keith N. Johnson of Anchorage, Alaska, wrote *Unpredictable Giants* and I told him I wanted to purchase the collector's edition because "it will be THE Alaska classic bear book, the only coffee table book written by a guide and including so many pictures." Keith and his guides recount numerous big bear kills, the caliber and the number of shots taken (not necessarily the number needed to kill, but the number needed to stop). I thought you'd be interested in seeing the following results:

Caliber	Number of shots	Bear size (squared/skull)	
.338	6	10' 2"	28 2/8
.375	4	9' 6"	
.30-06	3	10'	
.375 H&H (270 gr. Nosler Part.)			
	6	10' 2"	26 15/16
.270	1	8'	
.375 H&H (300 gr. Silvertip)			
	8	10' 4"	28 2/16
.375 (300 gr. Trophy Bonded)			
	6		
.300	22	9' 4"	

Guide Chris Kempf stated about this .300 shot bear…"He had lots of holes in him but only one in the right spot." (Pg. 156)

.375 Win Mag	4	10' 1"	27 9/16

Keith states on Pg. 147 that, "This caliber (.375) is the most popular and most recommended rifle for hunting brown bear."

Alaska bear guide Ralph Young stated in his book *Grizzlies Don't*

Come Easy, "Ordinarily, the best rifle to hunt with is the one the hunter likes best and shoots best. We hear a great deal concerning the comparative killing power of the .400 Ouch & Ouch, or the .500 Mangleum. Much of this discussion is strictly academic. No animal—field mouse or African elephant—can be killed by any rifle unless the animal is hit in a vital spot. What you hit 'em with is not as important as where you hit 'em." (Pg. 37)

Gary Shelton states in *Bear Encounter Survival Guide*, "In a normal bear defense situation, and excluding hunting of grizzlies at close-range, a person who is proficient with a large calibre rifle or pump 12-guage shotgun can reduce the risk of injury or death during a bear attack to about nil. Of course, the key point is firearms proficiency..." (Pg. 117)

"Any good-quality rifle that you are very familiar with and does not jam, that has .30-06 power and up, will do the job in all but the rarest of cases. High-quality ammunition with heavier thick-skinned bullets is needed—for example, Federal Premium with Nosler partition bullets, or Remington ammunition with Swift a-frame bullets. If you load your own, Barnes X are good bullets that will smash large bones without disrupting too badly." (Pg. 118)

John Holzworth (*Wild Grizzlies of Alaska*) tells of two bears that Alan Hassleborg encountered around 1908. Hassleborg ran into a sow and boar brownie when the boar attacked from 20 yards. Alan shot his .32 Winchester Special, hit it and the boar took off. The sow instantly rushed him. Not wanting to mess up her skull, he shot her in the body. The shot did not deter her so he shot for the skull, killing her instantly. He followed up the boar and shot it again before placing a final shot into its heart. Five shots and two dead brown bears, from a Winchester .32 Special.

On May 2, 2006 our farrier Joel Ringler told me that he had a friend who shot a charging brown bear with his .243 on Kodiak Island within the past couple of years. The bear was twenty feet away when the shooter dropped it in its tracks with a head shot.

Fred Mamaloff, a Kenai native, and his brother were often instructed by their father to "go get a bear." The boys took their rifles to the local dump and lay in the refuse until a bear showed up. Then they jumped up and roared. The bear invariably stood on hind legs and roared back, providing an open mouth as a target. The boys shot the bear in the back of the roof of the mouth which had a direct line to the brain. They never failed to kill bears with their .22 rifles.

Mike Cramond, author of *Of Bears and Man*, interviewed Lavern

Beier who told Mike about his .338 and his .45-70 rifles. Lavern's experience indicate the speed at which a brown/grizzly moves and the need for utilization of every second the person can call upon. Below I've summarized and partially quoted La Vern's comments of the three incidents.

La Vern hoped he'd not have to shoot a big grizzly that stalked him. In the end the bear gave him no choice because it charged, entering Vern's personal safety space—twenty feet. La Vern shot it with his Springfield .338 Magnum. "He didn't go down, but reared up on his hind legs and started to bat at his eye with his paw. He was shaking his head too. My second shot hit in the wrist, and he was spinning around in circles batting at it like a boxer. I shot again and then he was on the ground, biting at the earth. So I finished him off…The skull measured twenty-five and seven eighths inches." (Pg., 109)

On another occasion La Vern and a colleague were rushed by a sow grizzly… "Her eyes were glued right on Dick, and I hollered 'Shoot! Shoot!' He did, right over my shoulder when the sow was about eighteen feet away. She didn't even hesitate. The muzzle blast from Dick's .375 Magnum was right behind my ear as I slipped off my own rifle. There was a log about ten feet in front of me, and she jumped it with all her adrenaline up, headed right at Dick. She was in the air from the momentum of the jump, and I think she saw my gun come off my shoulder, and her right front leg stretched out with claws as long as my fingers, reaching for me as I leaned back to get out of the way. I could look right down her throat as I got my .338 up at my hip and pulled the trigger...

"The power from that big rifle completely changed her direction in midair. It blew her off the trail, over the bank, and into the stream…I jumped down the riverbank and into the stream, to make sure that the sow was out of commission…

"My own bullet went right into her mouth and blew out the back left side of her skull… There were powder burns on her muzzle." (Pg. 113)

As time went on La Vern purchased a .45-70 and had it customized… "The once highly polished, blued barrel was cut down to about eighteen inches, making the full length of the arm about twenty-eight inches instead of the almost standard forty-six inches common in most big-game rifles. It was, in effect, a very high-powered magnum pistol, which could be carried slung under one arm with little or the unwieldiness of a full-length big-game rifle. It was a gun entirely designed for its purpose: last-minute, close-up emergency self-defense." (Pg. 114)

La Vern became the "bear man" expert in the close confines of Southeast Alaska, often working with inexperienced men he encouraged to keep their guns loaded and handy when snaring bears. He has tagged roughly 1000 brown bears. He said, "You never know when someone may save your ass! I was carrying that .45-70 Mauser. We were working right along the bear trails, and sometimes it was fogged in. I was always the point man, out front. If it got 'beary,' I would flick off the safety, because I always kept a round in the chamber." (Pg. 115)

You might wonder if it is safe to have a round in the chamber. Mike Cramond defended the practice, suggesting to Beier, "If you were on bear trails and didn't have a shell in the chamber, you would be jeopardizing the lives of novice companions and your own life. I don't know a really experienced woodsman, trapper, or hunter who doesn't keep a gun on ready." (Pg. 115)

As a rule of thumb most Alaskan hunters hunt with an empty chamber until they're ready to shoot. However, if you don't have a bare minimum of 30 yards visibility, a chambered round makes a lot of sense because you have less than 2 seconds to react to a charging grizzly at that range. Maybe enough time to chamber a round and position the rifle. Maybe not. It's your choice. You'll notice that La Vern always had a round chambered in tight situations and that he barely had time to get off his shots. La Vern told me he had four close calls with bears, all from which he emerged victorious because he had a round in the chamber.

The April 1966 edition of *ALASKA SPORTSMAN* carried a piece by Wesley Blair in which he stated

"Even more important than the rifle is the choice of bullet. When hunting big bear it is necessary that the hunter choose a bullet with a heavy jacket that offers the maximum in penetration and still expands properly. Even the very fine .300 Weatherby Magnum is a poor bear gun with the wrong bullet selection. One guide reported that his client scored several hits in the chest area on a big grizzly with a .300 Weatherby and never knocked the animal off its feet. The guide had to stop a charge with a .375 Magnum. When they examined the bear they found the light woodchuck bullets had exploded under the skin of the bear in the fatty tissue.

"Hal Waugh suggests that the best bullet for the big bear in the .375 Magnum caliber is the 270 grain MGS bullet. Many of the guides highly recommend the 180 grain Silvertip bullet and the Remington Bronze Point in commercial loads and the 180 grain Nosler for handloading." (Pg. 283, *Alaska Bear Tales*)

Ralph W. Young wrote "Rifles for Brown Bears" for the February 1968 edition of *Outdoor Life*. He discusses both the need for adequate weaponry and ammunition. Recommending reduced punishment to the hunter from huge caliber recoil Young suggests:

"...the best rifle is a properly stocked, tuned-up, standard-make .30/06...this grand, all-purpose gun will kill with a single, well-placed shot the largest brownie that ever walked. No weapon, regardless of caliber, can do more. I used a custom-made '06 for years while guiding, and regardless of the situation, I never felt undergunned. My friend, the late Hosea Sarber, the best bear hunter that ever lived in Alaska, felt the same as I do about the .30/06." (Pg. 144)

As for bullets Young states, "Many experienced hunters rate the heavy-jacketed Barnes bullet as the best. Be that as it may, in my opinion no bullet on the market today gives the consistent, dependable performance in either the .300 Magnum or .30/06 that the 220-grain Core Lokt does." (Pg. 154)

In the summer of 1998 my son Ben and I were visiting Dan France at his Sterling, Alaska, home. His wife Mary invited us into their home and while awaiting his return we sat down at the kitchen table to visit with Mary. Ben picked up a pair of field glasses from among the several lining the window sill on the south side of the home. Instantly he pointed out two huge animals walking a stunted spruce flat across the Kenai River.

When I looked through the glasses, I saw a flash. My first thought was pickup truck, sun's flash from side mirror. Realizing that a pickup wouldn't be in the middle of a swamp, I instantly thought moose, because a bull's antlers would "flash" (white, post-velvet antlers reflecting the sun) in the fall.

It was the wrong time of the year for a bull's horns to flash. It only took a second to realize they were bears.

The first was blonde and the second was black. The flash was water falling from their hind paws as they crossed the swampy bog. I was amazed at their size and colors. I knew that there are brown bears varying from light brown to black, but I didn't expect to see a blonde one, much less on the Kenai Peninsula.

We watched the bears for some seven minutes. The black boar trailed the blonde sow as they slowly made their way across the three-quarter mile sloping terrain.

As they entered the distant timberline, I thought, "I need to get a cannon." I turned to Ben and asked, "How would you like to bump into those bears with your fly rod?"

Since that time I have given even greater thought than previously to the acquisition of a bona fide bear stopper. I've considered the ramifications of the bear's life or mine. I'm not comfortable with the idea of shooting bears. Even though I've traveled the outdoors of Alaska since 1966 and had some encounters with bears within twenty yards, the bears always moved out of the way for me.

Shotgun

The other long gun to consider is the shotgun.

U.S. Fish and Wildlife Service biologist B.J. Schmitz, 32-years-old, and her 60-year-old partner Johnson Moses worked from their tent camp near the south fork of the Koyuk River, some 35 miles from Bettles, Alaska, and approximately 85 miles northwest of Fairbanks.

They were six days into a wildlife reproduction research project in the Kanuti National Wildlife Refuge (I used to tell my students the refuge was named after me because "the Kanuti River is the outlet of Old Dummy Lake." They probably believed me). Their work consisted of trapping geese in live traps, banding their legs and releasing them. Their base camp was located on a willow studded island in the middle of a slough.

Schmitz and Moses were in their tent when honking geese roused her. Bored and wanting something to do, she took the opportunity to check the three wire mesh traps. She wondered whether she should grab her weapon. She'd seen a sow black bear with three cubs the previous evening and, though she felt a little silly—maybe overly cautious, she took her loaded 12 gauge pump shotgun with her.

A hundred yards from the tent in the night's cool air, she looked through her binoculars for the cause of the disturbance. Before long she lowered the glasses and looked to her left.

Not fifteen feet away stood a grizzly, where it had been digging for roots.

B.J. immediately knew that she was in trouble. As she stepped backward, the bear looked up. Then it started for her.

She tried to convince herself it was a bluff charge. However she knew otherwise. It was running too fast and had "that look" as it kept coming.

Although she'd been trained in the use of the shotgun, she did not consider herself an expert. She had heard that it was useless to shoot a charging bear in the head because of the likelihood that the bullet would ricochet off its thick skull.

She barely had time to rack a round. Not knowing where to aim and not having the strength to raise the weapon to her shoulder, she pointed the barrel at the bear from waist level. B.J. knew that she had time for only one shot. She squeezed the trigger, dropping the bear "like a sack of rocks." The bullet destroyed its right eye and entered the brain, killing it instantly.

It all happened so fast, maybe 15 seconds elapsed from spotting the animal until it lay dead ten feet away. No time to be scared. That's when she wondered…*what if I hadn't had my shotgun? What if the bear got up? What if I'd missed?*

She screamed for Moses who'd already exited the tent in a hurry—he left the shelter without opening the door. He reached her in an instant, shoeless. Moses shot the bear in the head to make sure it was dead.

They knew regulations required that they surrender the skull and hide. As they skinned it in the moonlight, they discovered that it had a healed but broken jaw, broken teeth, three broken ribs and a cut ear. It was skinny and appeared to be an angry bear that had lived a long, violent life. (Source: "Biologist kills charging grizzly bear," *Anchorage Times*, August 17, 1987. My efforts to contact BJ for her personal input failed.)

In his book *Bear Encounter Survival Guide* Gary Shelton recommends a specific shotgun and round—"The only shotgun that I would recommend, at this time, is the Remington 870 police model with a three-inch chamber. It must have a 20" barrel with rifle sights, and it must be shot accurately, just like a rifle.

"The secret is in the ammunition. Never use buckshot; it might kill a grizzly at 12 metres, and it might not. Federal 1-1/4 oz. magnum slugs are what you need, plus a shoulder pad that fits under your clothing." (Pg. 118)

Bud Helmericks and a friend were hunting ptarmigan when they encountered a grizzly on the tundra. The doc shot the grizzly at 50 feet with four rounds (reloading once) from a Browning over/under shotgun in 12 gauge, firing 00 buckshot (9 pea-sized pellets in each round). The bear trotted off as if on a summer picnic sojourn, showing no sign of the scatter gun's effect; and Bud followed with his .270 Weatherby to "herd" it back to the doc who planned to shoot it with a .30/30 carbine.

Bud followed the bruin three miles when it looked at him from 70 yards, just before igniting instantly into a full out attack. Bud dropped the bear with a shot to the spine at 15 feet.

After skinning the grizzly they found nearly all 36 pellets in or on the bear. The ones that penetrated the hide were just under the hide wrapped in a quarter-sized wad of fur. Several failed to penetrate the hide. Only a few had even drawn blood, being stuck in the fat layer. ("Of Terrible Courage," *Outdoor Life*, February 1956, Bud Helmericks)

During a phone conversation around April 9, 2001, my friend Chip

Church stated that he believed that "a 12 gauge shotgun with a 1 ounce slug is the best available weapon at close range."

Should your choice of weapons be a shotgun, it is important, again, that you select appropriate ammo. Some years back my friend Justin Giles suggested Dragon's Breath shells for effective bear medicine in a shotgun. Wikipedia states that Dragon's Breath often refers to a zirconium-based pyrotechnic round. When the round is fired, sparks and occasionally flames shoot out to about 48 feet—beyond that distance the round's already limited effectiveness is drastically reduced. This round is also illegal in some states. Numerous video clips are available on the Internet, as well as ammo suppliers' info.

If you choose to use a shotgun for protection in stopping a bear, research the best gauge, load and model. Engage firearms experts and examine their statistics and/or studies before choosing the weapon. Check out the latest in the way of shortened shotguns. Peruse the increasing types of shotgun shells and select the one(s) most effectively stopping a bear charge.

Pistol

Most bear maulings could be prevented or avoided with a large caliber pistol because a serious injury would stop most bears from continued mauling. Although most knowledgeable people do NOT recommend carrying a pistol as a primary weapon against a bear, how many people could have reduced their injury or saved their lives had they carried any caliber of handgun? Most bears are not of the huge variety and if wounded could likely be deterred with a medium caliber handgun. Since few people will ever encounter a monstrous brown bear, the need for a cannon-type weapon to stop them is unnecessary—unless, of course, they plan to hike the back country of Alaska. Isn't it logical, then, that a person carrying even a small caliber pistol could survive and/or avoid a Lower 48 run of the mill bear mauling?

Although I do not recommend a pistol as the best choice of weapon, bears being killed or injured with pistols include: **blacks** —Wade Nolan .41 Magnum; Vic Bruss .44 Magnum; W.M. Nutter .22 semi-automatic; **grizzlies**—Al Blalock and Ron Trumblee .44 mag; Maurice Goff and his friend Jack .45; Louis Kis .357 mag; Jerry Austin .38; and Ben Moore .357 Ruger single action.

Louis Kis shot a grizzly off him with his .357 and said, "Contrary to popular belief, grizzly bears can be killed with small-caliber pistols provided the bullet placemen is exact...poor placement of heavy, high-velocity slugs will not provide for an instant kill…" (*More Alaska Bear Tales*, Pg. 272) He also tells of additional pistol killings—a .357 shot-wounded grizzly that he trailed a mile and found dead; a Montanan shot a grizzly at 20-feet with a .41 Magnum, knocking it down before finishing it with the pistol; another man shot and killed a grizzly with an extremely under powered H&R .22 caliber pistol, saving himself from harm.

My friend Jerry Austin shared some valuable advice about a .44 Magnum encounter he had with a grizzly—it rushed him and he had time to put the barrel of the pistol into the bear's mouth and pull the trigger before its momentum took them both to the ground. Jerry rolled out of it prepared to shoot again but the 180 grain Nosler bullet had broken the bear's neck. Jerry said, "Almost every bear mauling I've heard of could have been prevented or at least been less serious if the person had a properly holstered .44. I can tell you it's pretty hard to hang on to a rifle when you're going head over heels." (*More Alaska Bear Tales*, Pg. 278)

W.M. Nutter used a pistol in the 1930's during a time when bears should have been in their winter dens. He encountered a black bear with a cub about 40-feet away. The sow got her cub up a tree then made for him. Fortunately, he had a .22 semi-automatic pistol with which he shot her.

Completing a month long photo mission near the Chickaloon River on Alaska's Kenai Peninsula in 1947 Cecil Rhodes got closer to a mother grizzly than he wished. She had three cubs; he had a .38 caliber pistol. She stared at him from 11 feet. He shot her off center of her skull with a 158-grain bullet. She slumped forward without leaving her feet, retreated, then came a second time. He fired a second shot into her skull and she slumped again without falling. She left with her cubs and he climbed a tree from which he shot her between the shoulders at 25 yards, rolling her down the knoll. She regained her feet and lumbered off with her cubs, trailing blood in the foot of snow. Even though he trailed her 2.5 miles without finding her and she may have survived, Cecil successfully defended himself with a pistol. (*Narrow Escapes*)

One remarkable pistol story includes a fishing group. What began as a dream vacation flavored with visions of tackle busting salmon slicing through icy water and making memories, ended in a nightmare, filling the mental screen with scary images of a camp invading brown bear.

Bob and Marietta Herron planned an August 1986 trip to the Tsiu River south of Cordova, Alaska, near the Bering Glacier. Anticipating a week of great fishing, the group of eight fisher people with high expectations exited the air taxi float plane that Sunday afternoon. The camp included seven paying guests—five men and two women—and consisted of four tents with wooden floors and plywood walls, with a fifth being constructed when the group arrived.

Wanting some protection in case of bear problems, before leaving on the trip both Herrons and friend Bill had practiced handgun use—the Herrons with .357 Colts and Bill with a .357 Smith & Wesson.

Sometime during their first night a coastal brown bear invaded camp, absconding with their six silver salmon cached in a plastic bag and staked under water near the tent. Even though the bear had done the deed within ten feet of the tent that Bob and Marietta shared with Bill, none of them had heard it.

Monday morning passed with more conversation about the bear than actual fishing. It seemed everyone was concerned that the behemoth would return, which wouldn't necessarily have been a problem as the guide had a .30-06 rifle. There was talk about the rifle power needed to stop a bear. Those armed with pistols hoped that it would not become necessary for their use. In spite of the guide's efforts to console the fisher people, they were anxious about the bear.

In the afternoon the outfitter dropped off more fishermen at the camp and the worried ones shared the bear's antics and their fears. One of the newcomers asked why they were packing pistols and scoffed, telling them that no .357 would stop a bear.

The fishermen decided to keep a night bear watch just in case the bear returned.

On Tuesday morning the bear appeared and campers hit the ground. The bear was within thirty yards of one tent before a total of nine pistol warning shots scared it away.

As Wednesday unfolded, people became more antsy and, even though some continued fishing, most spent the time awaiting the bear's return. If they'd had radio or phone communication, several would have called for an air taxi to come and get them.

From Sunday evening when the bear made its first appearance until Wednesday the animal's boldness intensified. The fishermen became more apprehensive knowing their arsenal included only a .30-06 rifle, one .44 Ruger Magnum and three .357 Magnum pistols.

Wednesday night during bear watch Bill spotted the bear a hundred and fifty yards across the slough and fired a warning shot which sent it on its way. Bob replaced Bill on watch around 1 AM and an hour later Bob saw the bear seventy yards distant. Since only fifteen yards of waist deep water separated the camp from the bear, Bob yelled and fired two shots to scare it. The bear ignored the noise and proceeded toward camp.

The fishermen exited their tents and watched the bear pacing back and forth in what appeared to be a making-up-his-mind mode at the stream's edge. The camp cook stood on a log holding a 6-cell flashlight on the animal and Bob stated that the time had come to stop firing warning shots and to shoot to kill.

The bear stood up, looked around then dropped to all fours and stepped off the knee high bank and into the water. Bill fired twice and Bob fired once. The guide's .30-06 misfired. Bill fired again when the bear turned broadside and the guide commanded the group to stop shooting.

Too late. Bob had just touched one off. He saw the bear in the flashlight's beam as it turned to quarter away. When he pulled the trigger, Bob saw the bear hunch up and its rear legs jerk. The cook held the light on the critter and some in the group saw it retreating, gobbled up by the darkness.

During the next few hours while awaiting daylight the group occasionally saw the bear moving in the distance. They wondered whether to trail it at daylight. Bill used his binoculars and eventually spotted an unfamiliar lump on the river flat.

He and the guide crossed the stream and followed bear scat to the dead bear. It had been hit twice with .357 pistol bullets: one bullet struck the rear leg; the killing shot entered the rib cage near the back rib and quartered forward through a lung and stopped beneath the skin between the front legs.

Obviously this bear was not highly charged on adrenalin and a .357 Magnum may not have stopped it under those conditions. However the caliber did kill the animal.

In July 1992 a 600-pound grizzly broke into a mining claim trailer near Central, Alaska. In the melee the bear was chased around the trailer, out a window and shot 7 times with a .357 Magnum pistol by Clint Reynolds, a 14-year-old. Three shots to the chest killed the bruin. (*Anchorage Daily News' We Alaskans*, Craig Medred, J-8, October 4, 1992)

After reading in the newspaper about Russell Gillespie's brush with a bear, I contacted him through another Gillespie in Seward, Alaska, and we emailed. His story follows. (Source: email received Tuesday May 22 10:18:19 PDT 2007)

It was July 2005, late afternoon. I'd observed fresh tracks/scat in the area for days (assuming it was black bears). Although I don't always take the gun (depending upon the situation), I carried a .44 revolver and pepper spray while hiking, making lots of noise. I hiked 45 minutes into the woods with my dog Thelma,

On the return trip Thelma growled and began backing up. I un-clipped the revolver from my waist holster. Two bears erupted from the brush near the side of the trail roaring like you wouldn't believe, heads down, hair on end, charging fast. I remember touching the can of spray, with the bears about 25-30 feet away, and then deciding against it.

I pulled my pistol and fired two shots into the ground in front of each bear, hoping the noise would drive them off. The smaller one backed off, the other didn't. When I realized it was not going to stop, I began firing at its head. It slowed down turned around and collapsed within about 10 to15 feet. I fired my last shot into her side/lungs

I was out of ammo at this time, and went back to my cabin a.s.a.p. and called it in. More than likely I invaded their space after doubling-back on the trail. They probably got off the trail once on my way in, but decided they'd had enough the second time. Warden (trooper Cloward) believed they may have been agitated from something earlier that day.

If I am going deep into the bush or if there is fresh bear-sign, I carry the gun (with two extra speed loaders now).

Dogs can be a mixed blessing. Bears don't like them. If the dog is well controlled (stays close, leashed, responds to commands, etc.), I believe they can save your life as well as weapons use/training.

Once again, I am not a sport hunter, but grew-up around guns and view them as a tool of last resort. I have had numerous bear encounters in Alaska, and this was definitely a fluke. I do believe that in this particular situation, my dog's extra senses, and my gun saved my life (or at least prevented one hell of a nasty mauling).

An advantage of handguns as opposed to long guns is that the pistol is on the person, not leaning against a tree on the fishing stream bank; not so cumbersome as a long rifle or shotgun.

Regarding the necessity of a pistol, my friend Dalton Carr wrote in his *Tales of a Bear Hunter*, "I never—never—go into the woods without my .45 Linebaugh or .44 Magnum Model 29 Smith & Wesson. Call me chicken if you like, but I will not be the victim of a bear attack without putting up a fight. A bear will almost always wind up with your hand in its mouth. You just need to make sure that the one it grabs has a pistol in it. I can think of six cases where the bear was killed instead of the hunter when at the last possible second the big pistol went off in its mouth.

"Personally, I never used a pistol as a primary weapon. I know how hard a bear can be to kill using a heavy-caliber rifle, and I do not believe that any pistol will accomplish what a rifle will in caliber .338, .375, or .416. I always carried a pistol when I hunted bear. I felt a real sense of added security knowing I had with me a large caliber handgun that I knew how to shoot." (Pg. 131).

My friend, Donald Hill of Ronan, Montana, discussed pistols in September 2007. He permitted me to include part of his email, which follows: (Source: Wed Sep 12, 2007, email)

"Larry,

"I practice shooting from all positions. Use both one and two hands. I was a police officer in South Idaho in my younger years and so most of my shooting is done in a combat stance using two hands. The Blackhawk that I carry has been in my possession since 1963. I also have other pistols that I like to shoot and one of them is a Ruger Redhawk .44 Mag. It is scoped. My groups are a little larger with it but still in the two inch range at 40 yds. I reload all my own ammo for target practice.

"To be a good pistol shot you have to put in many hours of target practice. When on the police force, I shot 1,000 rounds every week. Used the .38 special rounds for that. I have .22 caliber pistols that I shoot most of the time to keep my edge. Then every now and then shoot the bigger ones just to make sure that I still have it. Not everyone has the eye and hand coordination to be a good pistol shot, but practice makes perfect as they say.

"Just as everyone, that hunts, has a favorite rifle to shoot, so it is with pistols. That is one reason that I use the Blackhawk .357 mag. Have shot a deer with it and it is the only one that I have used to hunt with. Have put many ruff and blue grouse in the pot with it also. All head shots so there was something left to eat. Since I am comfortable shooting a pistol, I use it for protection. The key in this all is that you have to have confidence in your ability to protect yourself with your chosen weapon. Having seen the speed of a grizzly and also the size of the bear and his teeth, I know that in a time of an attack, I need to be as calm and confident as possible to stop him before he gets too close to use his equipment on me. To be protected, you have to have the utmost confidence in yourself and your weapon. That also means that you have to be able to get your weapon into play as quickly and smoothly as possible. That also takes practice.

"I have never had to face a charging grizzly and hope that I never do, but when you play in his backyard you had better be ready. Hope this answers all your questions.

"Sent you that story about the killing of the grizzly today in Idaho. Have spent quite a few years riding and hunting in the area where grizzly was killed and have seen grizzly tracks there for many years. Have reported it to the Fish and Game Department and had them come close to telling me that I was nuts. So many times people report things like this and they pass it off as some nut that does not know a grizzly track from a black bear track. Having spent a lot of time in Alaska, I know what I see when I see it and told them so. Spent many years muzzleloader hunting in an area that had a grizzly in it and was very careful there as one shot is all you have and trying to reload with a grizzly coming at you would be a tough thing to do. Even with a speed loader, you cannot reload quick enough."

Our family friend Russ Scribner sent me an amazing email story about a close call with a big bear and I subsequently tracked down Doug White who sent the story of him and his partner. He calls it "The Longest Minute" (Or was that twenty seconds),

Doug White, alaskadds@nushtel.net, January 29, 2007.

Many of us have heard reference made to or seen movies named after, The Longest Day, The Longest Yard, or "The Longest Mile." Well, I am going to tell you about "The Longest Minute" of my life.

Reed Thompson and I had been hunting hard for five days. The day was Thursday, September 7, 2006. The weather had turned from beautiful sunny skies to gale force winds and the blasting rain that comes with fall storms. Never has the weather dictated hunting time to us, so out we ventured into the Alaska bush. Not seeing a single bull moose for several days, we decided to hunt an area downstream that had always produced one. We left our base camp, located several miles above Portage Creek on the Nushagak River, early in the morning.

We were anticipating a great hunt, but just experiencing the unspoiled wilds of Alaska was priceless. Eight years ago, Reed arrived in Dillingham for a site visit. He was applying for a position as a Staff Dental Officer at the Kanakanak Hospital. After taking him for a boat-ride on Lake Aleknagik, I knew he was hooked when I saw his saucer-sized eyes observing the majesty of the water and mountains. Since that time we have survived many Alaska adventures together. I moved to Dillingham in August of 1997, expecting to fulfill a two-year commitment as the Chief Dental Officer of Bristol Bay Area Health Corporation. There must have been something in the water because now I'm addicted to bush Alaska.

Late in the evening, we were walking down a raised half-mile-long finger of ground that was full of grass and alders. This turf was slightly higher than the swampy tundra on either side of it. We had slogged across the swamp as quickly as possible during a sudden deluge to get

318

to the downwind point. Our hope was that our passage would not be observed with the abruptly amplified wind velocity and rain volume.

About halfway down the finger, Reed turned to me and said, "I think there is a moose up ahead. It looks like two white sticks in the grass. It would surprise me if it was not a moose." I glassed the area about one hundred yards ahead and to the left. With Reed's help, I zeroed in on the two white sticks and watched them for several minutes. With the slightest movement, the two sticks transformed into a white paddle and then back to the two sticks. The bull had moved his head ever so slightly.

I moved my scope out to ten-power and focused in on the two white sticks as Reed moved about ten yards farther down the high ground. Then, as Reed focused on the white points, I moved to his location for a better shot. Reed began moving toward our quarry as I watched for movement through the scope. With nothing solid or high enough to rest my rifle on, I was forced to aim free hand. When Reed had taken a few steps, I saw the horns rock to the right and then back to the left. The big boy then stood up and was looking directly our way. Even with the forty-mile-an-hour winds blowing directly at us, he sensed our presence.

I squeezed off a round from my Browning .338 and felt good about the shot, but the bull took two or three steps to my right and disappeared out of sight behind some alders. Reed could still see him and shouted, "Do you want me to shoot him?" I yelled back at him to go ahead because I did not want the bull running too far. I heard his shot as I was scrambling forward to get a better look. After a thirty-yard hustle, I was able to see the huge fellow still standing. I put another shot into him and watched him drop. We both hesitantly, but with great excitement, approached this giant and realized that he was dead. This was a mature bull with a beautiful rack and the biggest body mass I had ever seen. The fun was definitely over. Now, the real work would begin. After consulting the GPS, we noted that we were a half-mile from the slough and boat. We decided that both of us should return to the boat, discard unnecessary items, and return with the gear needed to prepare and pack out the meat. We placed red and blue handkerchiefs high in an alder bush so that the site could be located from the adjacent high ground. This was the easiest half-mile hike of the day. I was pumped up and excited beyond explanation.

At the boat, we left our heavy rifles. We gathered our pack frames, game bags, ropes, and knives. After Reed repositioned the boat to compensate for the upcoming low tide, I asked him with hand signals if he remembered to get the handguns. He did not understand my award-winning charade performance, but I let it pass after observing his revolver strapped to his chest.

Upon returning to the moose, we were hot, sweaty, and wet. The rain had abated for a while, so we removed our rain gear and hung it in a small tree about five yards perpendicular to the moose's belly. Reed removed his revolver, hung it from its holster on a branch opposite his jacket, and brought to my attention that it was there.

With darkness approaching, we decided to remove the top front and rear quarters, tie them to our pack frames, gut him out, and then roll the behemoth over to cool through the night. We would return in the morning to finish up. Two non-spoken traditions when hunting are: whoever pulls the trigger 1) does the gutting and 2) hauls the horns out of the woods. Having removed the two quarters, it was time to detach the internal organs. After cutting, tearing, and ripping, I had taken out all but the heart and part of the esophagus. Darkness was settling in pretty fast and I could barely move my arms.

At this point, Reed said that he would trade places with me. Instead of moving up behind the moose, I just scooted to the rear leg area and watched Reed crawl up inside the gut cavity. A couple cuts and the ordeal was over. As Reed pulled the heart out and tossed it behind us, a loud "HUFF" snapped us to our feet. Turning around, we saw a large, chocolate-brown grizzly bear standing before us on his hind legs.

The next minute seemed to last an eternity. The term surreal is so overused, but the next block of time was dreamlike, bizarre, fantastic, and unreal.

The bear was standing next to the tree where the pistol was hanging. We both started shouting and waving our arms back and forth as we moved somewhat to our right toward the tail end of the moose. The bear came down off his back legs onto all fours and started circling to his right—toward the head of the bull. My only thought was to get to the gun so that we could scare him off. I sensed that he charged at us from the head of the moose as I broke for the gun. Reed commented later that the bear vaulted over the moose's antlers and went straight for him.

Halfway to the tree, I tripped on a fallen log and went down on all fours. From my peripheral vision on my right, I saw the bear going after Reed, who had moved into the 5-foot tall grass. It appeared that the bear had knocked Reed down and was standing over him. My worst fear was that my friend was being mauled. I did not know if I could carry him back to the slough or if I could operate his boat to get him home for the care he would need.

As I stood up, I grabbed the holster but was unable to remove the revolver regardless of how hard I tugged. When I looked up, the bear was charging toward me. I started backing up as I continued screaming and hollering at the bear. I was frustrated that the pistol would not break free from the holster. With the bear almost on top of me, I backed into another log committing a classic backdrop. As I raised my legs to kick him away, I felt him swat or grab my left leg about mid-thigh, with his right paw. My rubber hip boots may have protected me from harm.

As he straddled my legs, his huge head hovered above my lap, just out of reach of my holstered club. I tried to hit him with the pistol but a crazy thought entered my mind—that I could scare him into thinking I was going to shoot by waving it back and forth. Unable to remove the pistol from the holster, I tried to shoot through it, but the strap held the hammer down on the single action revolver. Just when I thought all was lost, the bear rose up, pivoted 90 degrees to his left, and was gone.

The grizzly had charged back toward Reed when he jumped up and yelled once again. Later, Reed stated that he had seen the bear knock me down and it appeared as though I was being mauled. The thought entered his mind that he was toast. He was alone in the grass with no weapon. I was down and I had the gun. When the bear started moving toward him, Reed dropped back down into the low wallow area where he had fallen during the initial charge. In the blackness of night, Reed saw the bear's face about a foot from his own. He could hear the bear trying to sniff him out. At that point, the bear stood up, pivoted to his right, and charged back to me.

When Reed distracted the bear from its attack on me, I jumped up and had time to concentrate on the holster. I saw a buckle with a strap running through it. I could not figure out how it held the gun in place, so I grabbed the buckle and attempted to rip it off. To my surprise, the buckle was actually a snap and the strap peeled away. As I pulled the revolver out, a sudden calm came over me, and I knew everything would be fine. I looked in Reed's direction to once again see the bear rushing toward me. He was about ten feet away coming up and over the initial log that I had tripped over. I stood facing the bear with my shoulders squared.

It seemed like slow motion as I raised my right arm, thumbed back the hammer, pointed the revolver, and squeezed the trigger, firing at center mass. The .44 Magnum boomed in the night sending hardened lead and fire racing toward the boar. The 280 grain COR-BON bullet smashed into his chest killing him before the body slammed into the ground. His momentum carried him partially over the log, his head coming to rest three feet from where I stood. As he fell, the powerful jaws snapped shut crushing a mouthful of tundra.

I stood in a dumbfounded stupor. I had no expectation that the pistol would kill the bear. It was my hope that the flame and loud report from the pistol, and the shot impact from the bullet would scare him away. As his head sagged to the ground, I shot him three more times in the head as quickly as I could thumb the hammer and pull the trigger, out of fear and anger. I feel that the Lord's hand had more to do with the shot placement than my meager pistol experience.

My next sensation was hearing Reed's voice asking if the bear was dead. I responded with a "yes." He then yelled at me to save the rest of the rounds because we still had to walk out, and he did not have any more bullets with him. The minute was over. We hugged each other for a long time before packing out the two quarters.

The half-mile trek through the darkness was filled with trepidation and deep thought. The tiny LED lamps, strapped around our heads, did not light up nearly enough area as we marched out of the island's interior. The sensation emulated snorkeling in the ocean at night, unable to see anywhere except right in front of your eyes. It was one of the longest hikes I have ever taken.

Upon reaching the boat, we quickly realized that the bear encounter had delayed us long enough to prohibit our departure. The motor was out of the water and, hard as we pushed, the boat would not budge. The two of us had the joy of spending the night on the bank, next to the slough, in the worst storm of the year. Fortunately, we were prepared for such a possibility. Hunting on the lower Nushagak River necessitates dealing with twenty-five-foot tide swings.

After multiple attempts and two gallons of gas, we sat down next to a roaring fire that offered little heat through the rain. Our adrenaline rush exhausted, we mustered the energy to assemble the two-man tent, spread out our sleeping bags, and lay down out of the rain. There was no sleep that night. The tent-talk centered on the evening's events. We analyzed and re-analyzed everything we did and everything the bear did. We talked about what we did wrong and what the bear did wrong. We chatted about the bear's actions and our own actions. We discussed the outcomes of every scenario thinkable. We finally concluded that the manner in which the attack occurred was extremely fortunate for us. It could not have played out better had all the actions been choreographed months in advance. The placement of the revolver in the tree, the way we spread out when the bear attacked, the timing of our falls, the screaming and yelling by the different person when the bear was involved with the other, the way the bear came over the log just as I shot, and the distance between each of us, all worked out for our survival, or at least the freedom from terrible pain.

This incident occurred three days before bear season opened. Thus, we had to skin the bear, remove its head, pack it all out to the boat, and turn everything over to the Alaska Fish and Game Department. It was then that we learned a bear of the same size and coloring had raided two camps on the far side of the island the week before. He had taken at least a quarter of meat from one of the camps.

Many questions come to mind. It, however, is impossible to know the answers. I am convinced that bear experts will mull over this incident looking for blame, as well as answers to many of the questions. Did the bear hear the dinner bell when the shooting took place? With the severe wind, did the bear smell the dead moose and start zeroing in on it? Was the bear startled into action when the last entrails were tossed in his direction? Why was the bear not fearful of us? Why did he attack? Why did he charge Reed first when I was the one moving toward the gun? Why was he distracted between the two of us? Why didn't he put the hurt on each of us when he had us down? Would he have left us alone if we had pretended death? How did one shot kill such a beast? I do not have the answers and will not pretend to understand the encounter completely. I do know that we learned important lessons that will benefit us personally in the future. Some victims of bear attacks do not survive to learn from their experiences.

The following are some of those lessons:

1) Yes, a bear can attack you. Many of us who live, hunt, and subsist in Alaska have observed bears. Usually, they are seen running away as fast as their powerful legs can carry them. I have read information claiming that a grizzly bear can move forty-four feet in one second. With that kind of speed, it does not take many seconds for a bear to move great distances away from or toward a hunter or hiker.

2) While field-dressing an animal, always have a weapon within arm's reach. Fifteen feet away in a tree is much too far. An encounter can occur within seconds. Each hunter should have his or her own weapon, depending on personal preference, such as a long gun, a handgun, or pepper spray.

3) Be familiar with all the weapons (and holsters) present in the party. A situation may arise where a companion's weapon must be used. Practice with the weapons that will be available.

4) Do not get so involved with the task at hand that vigilance and alertness are forgotten. Keep all your senses on high alert—anticipate

trouble.

5) Bears can be as varied as people. They grow up in different environments, they have diverse growing experiences, they have dissimilar personalities, they get moody in various situations, and they have a huge desire to gorge themselves at various times of the year. Treat them with respect and give them a wide berth when possible. Bears are truly an awesome component of the miracle and beauty of nature. Beware; they have resided on top of the food chain for a very long time.

I wrote the first part of this adventure because my grown children requested it. I placed the story on the hospital intranet, along with four pictures, so the staff could see and somewhat feel the experience. Prior to writing the story, it seemed that every person who walked by the dental clinic stopped and asked about the bear incident. My workload did not allow me the time needed for re-telling the story. I was shocked at how fast the story spread out of Dillingham and into cyber space. There were reports that the story had spread throughout the country and beyond. Most people were amazed that we survived, while others scoffed.

What I have written is true. It was not an experience that we went looking for, nor would it be an experience either one of us would like to relive. I do thank my Father in Heaven every night that we both walked away that night. I have not had nightmares, nor do I jump at noises in the night, but I do think about the attack every day. I find myself trying to analyze why it happened and what we could have done differently. In trying to survive, did my mind shut down various sensations? I did not smell the awful stench others talk about. I do not remember any jaw or teeth popping. I do not remember hearing any growling or snarling. The first time the bear charged me, he was there in an instant. His head was down and angled to the right. When I toppled onto my back, I saw him snapping repeatedly in attempts to bite the holster as I swung it back and forth in his face, but I remember no sound.

I believe the reason bear tales are so captivating is that people share a primordial fear of the carnivore itself. It is a natural dread that resides deep in our human gene pool.

Many readers have inquired about the size of both animals. The moose had a rack that measured 63 inches across. Best of all, a large portion of a freezer was filled with wonderful-tasting meat. The bear measured 9 feet 2 inches from left front paw to right front paw, and 8 feet from nose to rump. When standing on his rear legs, as we initially saw him, this bear presented more then ten feet of spine-chilling terror. He was not a starving bear, for he was stuffed full of blueberries.

For some reason, I have developed a keen interest in reading about documented bear attacks. The more I read, the more I realize how extremely fortunate we were. After reading about our experience, I hope that you can glean from it tidbits that will make your outdoor experiences fun, long lasting, and safe. Enjoy the awesome beauty of the outdoor world, but stay alert and be prepared. There is no greater joy than returning home to loved ones followed closely by the ability to put into words the adventures and splendors of the wild country.

The local newspaper carried a piece about another hunter who was glad to be packing a *bona-fide* bear stopper.

A Kodiak rabbit hunter encountered a sow grizzly and she rushed him. He shot and killed her with his pistol from under fifty feet. He reported his activity to the officials who went to the scene and followed up the bear which was probably 25-years-old or older, 8-foot, 400 pounds and barely alive. She was killed as were her three cubs. (Source: Brown Bear Killed By Kodiak Bunny Hunter, KODIAK: The old sow's 3 cubs, which were too young to survive on their own, were also shot, www. ADN.com, MARY PEMBERTON, The Associated Press, January 1st, 2008)

I queried Alaska bear biologist Larry Van Daele about the Kodiak attack in hopes of getting information regarding the caliber and the hunter's experience. He emailed me Jan. 5, 2008:

Sorry, we cannot release the name of the person involved.

The sow and cubs had been hanging around that area for a few weeks. For the most part they were very tolerant of duck and hare hunters. One of the cubs (yearlings) came toward a duck hunter and his son the week before the shooting after they surprised the family while they were sleeping near the American River. I went out to investigate that morning with a couple partners and found the bears sleeping a couple hundred yards inland. When I got within about 10 yards they just raised their heads and watched us. We backed off and they went back to sleep.

This individual was hunting alone and came upon the family as they slept. He had a .22 for the hares and a .454 for bear protection. She came towards him, he fired his .22 in the air, waved his arms and yelled. She continued toward him, he got out his pistol and yelled again. She kept heading his way and he shot her. The distance was about 15 yds. After he shot her once with the pistol and wounded her, he backed off to call the Troopers with his cell phone.

We euthanized the cubs because they had little chance of surviving the winter and they were near a residence and a popular recreation area. They were also too old to be adopted by a zoo. Upon further investigation we found that the sow was probably over 25 years old (based on tooth wear) and she had little fat. Her age, the demands of her young family, and the poor berry crop we experienced this summer probably combined to keep her out of the den longer than usual. Her behavior was also characteristic of a bear that drastically slowing its body functions in preparation for winter. When bears are in this state they still have the ability to defend themselves if they feel threatened.

Hope this helps.

Larry

Even though many advise to practice over and over in order to develop muscle memory, how hard would it be to hit a bear that is within feet and/or chewing on you? What percentage of persons packing a pistol could successfully kill a bear that was below them in a tree swatting at their legs or trying to bite them? Or chewing on their arm or leg? In the past dozen years black bears assaulted at least two mothers—Susan Cenkus and Lisa Dunbar—who attempted to keep a family member from harm.

In spite of experts' and old timers' pooh-poohing a pistol's effectiveness as a bear stopper, numerous people have successfully stopped or killed bears with pistolas. At least four men since 2002 in the Anchorage Bowl relied upon handguns to save themselves during bear encounters.

A hiking trail in the Chugach foothills on Anchorage's east side generated a little excitement in September 2004. The popular "tank" trail crosses military land and sees much activity from civilian bikers, hikers, joggers and dog walkers.

When 57-year-old former helicopter pilot and retired maintenance chief Gary Boyd walked his 22-month old boxer pup Katie, they ran into a grizzly. He heard brush breaking behind him and thought it was a moose until he realized it was too low to the ground. The 750-pound boar grizzly boiled from the undergrowth within twenty feet of him, tearing up the soil in its rush to reach him. Boyd had just enough time to draw his .44 Magnum revolver and spin to face the bear.

Boyd fired a round at the bear's shoulder which didn't faze it. His second shot turned the animal. Three successive shots dropped the bear. Boyd was down to one round in his pistol and called Anchorage police with his cell phone then hiked to Klutina Street where he met Alaska State Trooper Kim Babcock.

The trooper and the ex-pilot returned to the site and found the disabled bear alive. Babcock shot it in the heart with a shotgun while Boyd shot into the bear's skull. Trooper Babcock defended Boyd's defensive shooting and she commended his pistol skills, "He didn't have a choice." Even though he hasn't hunted in three decades, Boyd carried a handgun and regularly practiced quick drawing.

He regretted having shot the bear but was "glad the instincts and the training paid off." A large number of unarmed people use the area. The dead bear had been defending a moose carcass near the trail. Within three minutes of the bear's death twelve high school cross-country runners cruised through the area.

Earlier in August Gabriel Wintters was rushed three times in the area. By early September three other grizzlies had been shot in Anchorage and four blacks killed in defense of life and property. (Source: Pistol-packing Hiker Kills Brown Bear in Sudden Chugach Foothills Attack, SELF-DEFENSE: Muldoon man credits reflexes, shooting practice with saving his life, DOUG O'HARRA, *Anchorage Daily News*, September 24, 2004)

A sow grizzly and cub approached Garen Brenner and a couple of friends as they packed up and prepared to leave the Russian River around 2:30 AM. As he backed into the water and tossed his shotgun at the animal, Garen's friend shouted "Bear!" Brenner looked down the bank at the bear which locked eyes on him and lunged toward him. He reacted by firing two steel jacketed bullets from his 9 millimeter semi-automatic pistol at the center of the animal which was within five feet of him. The 400-500 pound sow went down and Brenner administered three more shots to her head. The steel jacketed bullets provided penetration that likely would not have been effective with non-jacketed bullets in that caliber. There was some speculation that the bear may have been the same one which recently attacked Kathy Dunagan and her son three miles away on the Resurrection Trail. (Source: Fisherman shoots, kills grizzly, BEAR! BEAR! Man plugs lunging bruin with 9 mm pistol on Russian River, Zaz Hollander, *Anchorage Daily News*, August 18, 2002)

Having the most efficient bullet in the pistol could make a difference in the outcome of a bear encounter. If you choose to carry a handgun, research the ammo and the caliber and choose wisely.

When I asked Larry Jantz, a Washington State ballistics guy, to comment on pistols and bears, he kindly consented, titling his research "Pistols N Bears":

I'm 68 and have done a lot of ammunition and bullet testing for over fifty years. I've hunted the United States and Africa. While working for the Washington Department of Corrections I tested our .38 duty ammo and found it would not expand and the velocity was lower than published. I traveled to the state's capitol as a member of an ammunition and weapons committee. It was easy to convince the department to change from ammunition estimated to be 52% effective to 84%-93% one shot stops as per quoted statistics from Even Marshall's and Ed Sanow's book *Stopping Power*. The Washington state legislature approved $650,000 for the conversion; Department of Corrections personnel had semi-autos after that with quality ammo and written policies that came right out of my mouth during the committee meetings.

While researching information I found the effectiveness of pistols for bear defense to be a controversial challenge. This is emotional territory. After visiting hundreds of internet forums and threads, reading books and magazine articles, calling highly experienced bear guides and bullet and ammunition manufacturers, I came to the conclusion that pistols— as bear stoppers—should be a last weapon of choice. However, in the last 25 years I could find only two people killed using a pistol for bear defense.) A male outdoorsman/photographer was found with a cocked scoped .44 Ruger and a camera full of pictures of the grizzly sow and three cubs approaching. No shots fired. The second death (2018) of a male guide appears to have been caused by laying the weapon down out of reach with a back pack. Sadly, his client was not familiar with the Glock 10MM and the chamber was empty. The clients bear spray was in a back pack. No shots fired.

There was at least one incident where a pistol holster release mechanism prevented a draw. Saved by rifle fire. In 2016 Montana resident Todd Orr was attacked not once but twice by a sow grizzly with cubs. Bear spray was ineffective and his scoped pistol was ripped from his body and found 10 feet away Todd Orr todd@skybladeknives.com whom I befriended is an amazing outdoors-men and 32 year knife maker who has had more wild life experiences than men twice his age.

A significant amount of pistol saves (prevention of great bodily harm) came from civilians and law enforcement using their 9MM, 40 S & W or .45 auto side arms for wild bears and dangerous zoo animals on the loose.

After more than five years into this project my first thought has not changed—to recommend a double action .44 Magnum or a .45 Long Colt revolver with +P bear ammo for pack-able bear defense. If you cannot handle their recoil, it would be acceptable to use a .357 or .41 Magnum. Plenty of bears have been killed with all of these calibers. My S & W M629 6-inch BBL. .44 Magnum loaded with 300 grain bullets is a handful—255's reduced recoil and muzzle flip. The more powerful .454

Casull, .460 S & W, .475's, .480 or the 500 S & W— often recommended for hunting—pack more punch at both ends and may cause bloody hands, joint destruction as well as contribution to hearing loss. Shoot one before you buy. Shot placement is the number one stopping and killing factor.

Wayne at wwwfoggymountain.com reports numerous one shot kills with either the .41 mag or .44 mag. His bullet of choice for 25 years for black bears is a soft nosed jacketed bullet. Underwood Ammo, Double Tap, and Buffalo Bore produce ammo capable of penetrating deep/ through bears. The production manager of Double Tap Ammo said he stopped and killed an aggravated black bear pursued by hounds which charged by him. The hot loaded 200 grain hard cast flat point 10MM bullet traveled the length of the bear.

July 25, 2018, Bridger Petrini professional guide www. tristateoutfittersusa.com New Mexico needed more than 6 bullets (10) to eventually kill a cinnamon black bear. What started out as a training session for his hounds turned out to be a life and death struggle. The virtues and faults of a semi-auto came into play. At 20 feet the bear charged, and he fired His Glock M20 10MM at least 2 or 3 times before being hit by the bear. More shots were fired as they tumbled down a hill with large boulders. He kicked at the bear to keep him away from his upper body and head. The bear grabbed him and spun him around by the thigh and then grabbed his calf. Being careful not to shoot himself in the legs he fired a shot at the neck/spine which did not work so he tried for the brain and click. He racked the slide and watched in slow motion the live round ejected. One shot into the brain and the attack ended. Twenty seconds had passed, and the ordeal had just begun. One to two minutes for his wife Janelle to arrive. Then other family members. It took a half an hour before a game warden, his brother in law and other responders arrived. The 400-pound bears teeth were still clamped onto his right calf while he was stuffed and pinned into the brush and boulders upside down. His brother-in-law Brad cut off the bear's head an hour later, severing the jaw muscles in order to release his right calf which was turning grey.

Five adults could not separate the jaw without the saw and knife. A helicopter ride and 200 stitches. I thank Bridger and his wife Janelle for returning my phone calls. I Pray for a full recovery since Bridger is still wearing a brace 9 months after the attack. He had been on hundreds of bear pursuits prior to this one.

When I analyzed various penetration tests the Hornady Critical Duty 175 gr. he was using was at the head of the pack for penetration in its class. The click was most likely caused by shoving the muzzle against the head and moving the slide around 1/8"out of battery. Hair was in the slide also. The Glock did its job as designed.

One bear guide with over 300 bear kills was generally impressed with the performance of the 10MM on treed bears. With the 10MM keep in mind you might want to use a 22 pound guide rod spring. Read the comments from the manufactures about hard lead bullets and hot loads before you buy. I've seen a ruined spring on a Glock M20 Gen 4 and heard of another complete destruction. Caution! After what I just said I admit I had to go back to using the factory spring for reliability. Be sure to shoot at least two magazines of any new ammo through your auto to insure reliability using less than firm or ideal hand holds. In a test with a Glock M20 4.6" BBL. hot loaded 1280 FPS 10MM 180 FMJ versus the 6 "BBL. S & W .44 mag. Keith style 255 gr. SWC the .44 punched through several more layers of 1/2 inch sheet rock plus 5 dry magazines and still going.

All 10MM ammo is not equal. One manufactures 200 gr. ammo was advertised at 1250 feet per second and chronographed 1038-1042 FPS out of a 4.6" Barrel. Underwood 200 gr. hard lead 1150 FPS my test 4.6 BBL. Perfect and accurate. In 10% calibrated ballistic gelatin different lots of Winchester 175 grain Silvertips, have penetrated 16-17 inches. The 200 gr. Hornady XTP bullets go in about 19.5 inches and 180 gr. Speer Gold Dots 17.5" 200 gr. Gold Dot 19.7" Hornady Critical Duty 18.7-20.5". I like to see a minimum penetration of 18-24 inches. In 2014 Federal introduced a 1275 FPS 10MM 180 grain Trophy Bonded JSP designed for deeper penetration. The jury is still out on this one.

The standard for years has been a heavy for caliber (JSP) jacketed lead soft point or a hard cast semi-wad cutter. Now, the round nosed flat point is the norm. Heavy hard cast bullets are known for their ability to break through bones and completely penetrate through a large brown bear or polar bear. For large bears stay away from hollow points unless they are approved by the manufacturer for such a purpose. I say this because until recently not one major manufacturer recommended their hollow point bullets for bear which may require over 30 inches of penetration. To relate the point. The owner of Smiling Bear B&B Kodiak, Alaska Darlene is a retired Alaskan State Trooper Sergeant. While doing an autopsy (necropsy) of a poached brown bear she found where a 12 gauge Brenneke shotgun slug had penetrated a full 15 inches of fat plus hide and tissues from the flank before entering into the vital areas. The skull and hide weighed 350 pounds. Live weight estimated to be 1100-1200 pounds.

Suggested bullet weights: .357 mag. 158-200 grain; 10MM, 180-220 grain; .41 mag., 210-265 grain; .44 mag., 240-340 grain; .45 Long Colt, 250 gr. and up. Larger calibers manufacture's recommendations.

Most of the large caliber bullets are designed for large game. Check real close on the .460, some of those bullets may be designed for long range medium game. Any of the recommended bullets going over 1100-1300 feet per second will do the job. A well constructed controlled expansion bullet similar to the Swift A Frame has its place. You need to do your homework.

Some guides like hollow points for black bears in trees. Hollow points in .41mag and up are generally designed for at least medium game. Buffalo Bore Ammunition website had an article ("Stopping Bears with Handgun or Rifle Cartridges") wherein a professional guide associated with 1000 bear deaths, states a hit from any center fire pistol caliber will dissuade a black bear. It is likely wolves and cougars fall into the same category. I could not find fault with this statement after 5 years provided the black bears were not highly angered by hounds.

I assure you anyone who packs a pistol or a pistol with bear spray feels one heck of a lot safer. Predators come in four and two legs forms. Don't discount moose danger. While on a 28 day trip to Alaska in 1997 two people were attacked by moose and zero by bears. When you are attacked suddenly and knocked onto your back and lose your rifle or just run out of rifle ammo, or the bear spray can spits out only two weak blasts what are you going to do? A 279 bear attack study (1883-2009) done by the highly respected Tom Smith and Stephen Herro revealed long guns were 76% effective and pistols were effective 84% of the time. The effectiveness of pistols (37) in this study was a bit of a surprise. It goes to show you old timers packing those .45 long Colts for back up were wise.

I cannot stress enough to use a quality holster which retains your pistol under any circumstance with a release/thumb strap you can operate under violent conditions. Scoped pistols have proved to be a very poor choice.

April 2015 Bob (last name withheld) in the woods surrounding Joint Base Lewis-McCord Washington, near Seattle got attacked by a black bear for the second time in four years on the same trail as the first attack. Same dog led the aggravated bear to him. Forty bites and one hundred staples. His defense fist-feet-4-foot branch and a lot of bravery. The 300 pound bear was tracked by dogs and killed. Another reminder to have weapons/bear spray even in areas well traveled by other people.

By the end of 2016 it has been advised all members of a group of people have a bear spray can. For good reason (death 2018) guides should discuss the operational features of their weapons so in the event they are attacked/incapacitated/separated from their weapon the client has some operation knowledge.

During 2016-2018 more than an average number of bear attacks occurred. Some of those unarmed or not utilizing a firearm were injured or killed. In June 2017 one women was killed in Alaska by a black bear that had been thoroughly sprayed with bear spray by her and another female. Contrast this with Alaska Guide Phil Shoemakers Aug. 2016 experience. He defended his two fishing clients from a highly enraged grizzly bear which was within 3 feet of the husband and wife with a 8 shot S & W 9MM pistol loaded with Buffalo Bore hard cast 147gr. +P ammo. The first shot was aimed at the neck and the next 5 center of mass and the 7th at the rear hip at a distance of 6 to 8 feet while that bear was not standing still. Three of those flat nosed bullets went clean through the bear and exited. Seven shots and seven hits and the bear was dead 8 feet from where the last shot was fired. Absolute proof shot placement and good bullets are often more critical than caliber. The evidence people will anger bears by wounding them with a pistol and then be hurt worse is rare or subject to interpretation.

I talked to Buffalo Bore owner/president Tim Sundles about his pistol loads Oct 2016. He said His 9MM +P 147 grain load and his 255 grain .45 auto load is capable of penetrating 46 inches or more of 10% ordinance gelatin. His .40 S & W 200 gr. and 10MM 200-220 grain over 48 inches. Note, most rifle bullets designed for big game penetrate 20-24 inches. Even the highly regarded Barnes X bullets are designed for 28-33 inches. Alaska State troopers and other state agencies commonly use a Remington Model 870 12-gauge shotgun for dealing with problem bears and moose. The ammo is a 2 3/4 inch `12 ga. 1 oz. Brenneke slug. These slugs penetrate 34 or more inches of gelatin in FBI type tests. More than twice that of the common hollow point Foster type slugs. For comparison a .45 ACP auto 230 gr. FMJ penetrates 25-27".

Until recently the range of quoted firearm effectiveness has been from 50% (US Fish and Wildlife) to 76%-84%. Bear spray 87%-92%. One was 98%. Objective studies show attacking bears in the wilderness seem to overcome the effect of bear spray more often than those just being chased away at garbage dumps etc. Note: a 2018 study by Dean Weingarten link gunwatch ammoland.com listed 63 bear attacks where pistols had a 95% success rate. Either warning off or hits necessary to deter/end bear attacks. Key word used. Others and I have discovered more reports by credible witnesses and old published stories which Dean requests to add to his data base. This is the best study I have ever read since 1997 when I had an extreme interest. All these credible incidents back up my statements," you have a real good chance of survival using a pistol for defense from dangerous animals and humans. It can be reloaded. It can be used more than 10-30 feet away. It can be used to obtain food. Don't ever put your bear spray/pistol in a backpack".

One bear experience taught me this. Walking down a trail saying "hey bear", "hey bear" (making noise) does not guarantee a bear will run off before you are 13 paces away. I could draw an 8 3/8" barreled .44 Mag. underneath my rain poncho in around one second (three bear steps) when motivated. The borrowed pistol I packed up the 60 degree slope of Mt. Marathon above Seward, Alaska that day was worth more than its weight in gold.

I pass on my Grandpa Emil Jantz's saying: The Best is none too good.

You can do yourself a favor by reviewing the numerous You Tube clips regarding handguns versus bears.

Pepper spray

Is there a spray that works 100% of the time to deter a charging bear, leaving both man and bear unharmed?

The problem with pepper spray is the contents, delivery system and weather conditions. (see pepper spray section of book)

Miscellaneous pepper weaponry includes the JPX Pepper gun. There are other such options. (see next section)

Armed at home?

Even "tame" animals endanger people, raising the question, what is a person to do for personal protection, even in his home?

Around 4 PM January 26, 2001, Diane Whipple, 33-year-old women's lacrosse coach at St. Mary's College in Moraga, California, inserted her key into the door lock of her upscale sixth-floor apartment. How could the diminutive 5 feet 3-inch, 100 pound woman have known that two neighbors' Presa Canario dogs would attack her?

Marjorie Knoller and her husband Robert Noel owned Bane and Hera, weighing 123 and 112-pounds respectively. These dogs are a great mastiff and Canary Island cattle dog mix temperamentally loyal to owners but distrustful and aggressive with strangers. The breed's history includes being fierce fighters.

Because of Bane's and Hera's more than two dozen aggressive incidents, neighbors walked their dogs when they were least likely to encounter the two. Neighbors nicknamed Bane the Beast, Killer Dog and Dog of Death.

As Diane attempted to enter her apartment, Ms. Knoller was unable to restrain the leashed Bane which pulled her off her feet. Diane probably flashed back to an earlier experience when Bane had bitten her. She must have been terrified when she saw the dog bearing down on her. "Your dog jumped me!" (3) she shouted as Bane forced her against the wall. Unable to escape the biting brute, Diane fell to the floor and the animal bit her neck, ultimately ripping open her jugular vein while Hera tore at her clothes. Several minutes elapsed as Marjorie Knoller tried in vain to get between Diane and her dogs.

When police arrived, they witnessed clothes-less Diane trying to crawl to her apartment, bite wounds covering her entire body. The attack was so gruesome that responding police needed counseling. Whipple was rushed to San Francisco General Hospital but lost her battle on the operating table.

Both dogs were subsequently put down, their owners who had ignored warnings about their dogs' aggressive and vicious natures were convicted of negligence and sentenced to prison.

This story involves "tame" animals...inside a building. So, how do you protect yourself from a possible bear confrontation? (Sources:

1] www.igorilla.com, Franciscans Outraged as They Mourn Victim of Dog Attack, Tragedy: Many demand prosecution for owners of animal that mauled woman. Others fear new rules on pets. By MARIA L. La GANGA and JOHN M. GLIONNA, *LA Times* Staff Writers Times researcher Norma Kaufman contributed to this story.

2] Dog mauling verdict: Guilty on all counts, www.SFGate.com, San Francisco Chronicle, Jaxon Van Derbeken and Henry K. Lee, Chronicle Staff Writers; Associated Press, March, 21, 2002)

3] Dramatic start to mauling trial, Grisly photos, litany of attacks highlight scene in court, Jaxon Van Derbeken, Chronicle Staff Writer, www.SFGate.com, San Francisco Chronicle, Wednesday, February 20, 2002)

When you are deciding on whether or not to carry a weapon, do your homework. Research all available and the most up to date information on effective bear "medicine." Then make an informed decision.

With continual innovations coming to the market place, it's to your advantage to update yourself on different deterrents and/or weapons, how they work and safety advice on each.

CHAPTER 10
CONTROVERSY

Some topics surrounding bears that I consider controversial include pepper spray, playing dead, misinformation, bonding with wild animals, sensationalism, government agencies management issues and dogs.

SPRAYING AND PLAYING

A discomforting proposition in the arena of human safety in bear country is that of spraying and playing. If the pepper spray doesn't work, will playing dead suffice?

Pepper sprays as protection from bear attacks have been around going on half a century. Will pepper spray work against a charging bear? The answer is yes. However a more appropriate answer might be... sometimes. After several months' research I concluded that someone needs to take a bite out of the storied success of pepper spray during a bear attack. (APPENDIX 12)

In order to review the best advice experts provide outdoor users, I surfed the Internet for "bear safety" Friday, April 19, 2003. An even dozen sites offered advice but NOT one site mentioned the use of a firearm for personal protection.

The next day I decided to give the experts another chance and looked up thirty-eight sites. Virtually every site suggested pepper spray as the primary (and only) defensive weapon against a charging bear. Only two of the sites mentioned using a firearm for personal protection. The bulk of the sites were government agencies in either the United States or Canada.

The remainder represented, for the most part, touchy-feely groups intent on saving the great silvertip or its lesser cousin, Gentle Ben.

The sad commentary on the information on these web sites is that nearly all the "experts" advise outdoor users to 1) avoid eye contact with bears, 2) use pepper spray if the animal charges and 3) play dead in the event of physical contact.

I found that interesting in light of the fact that I had spent from 10 AM till 2 PM at my friend Keith N. Johnson's home, talking about his afore mentioned book *Unpredictable Giants* about mammoth brown bears and his 40-year career guiding and hunting them.

At one point he told me about a mating pair of brown bears wherein the boar killed the sow over a disagreement and in rage ate one of her shoulders before he calmed down. I asked Keith, "So, given that scene and I run into that boar just then, what are my chances of a safe encounter with my can of pepper spray?"

His instant and explosive response, "Minus 1!"

We were in total agreement that pepper spray works in some cases. The problem is, in which ones does it NOT work? More importantly, what are the statistics/chances of my encountering that specific situation when armed ONLY with my pepper spray?

Ann Quarterman and Christine Bialkowski were in British Columbia in 1994, when they were attacked by a grizzly from 330 yards. Ann sprayed it and it diverted to her friend Christine. Ann sprayed it while it chewed on Christine and the bear grabbed Ann who chose to play dead. Christine kicked at the bear until she kicked it on the tip of the nose. It bit Christine a final time and took off.

While surfing the internet February 16, 2007, I ran across two sites and the story of Julia Gerlach. (Sources: 1] Ironman Age-Group Champion Survives Bear Attack, Published on Tuesday, June 21, 2005, http://vnews.ironmanlive.com, Lisa Lynam at llynam@ironmanlive .com 2] Bear attack victim upbeat as she recalls ordeal, Fri. Jun. 10, 2005, Canadian Press, www.ctva.ca)

Julia Gerlach planted seedlings near Fort Nelson, British Columbia, on May 20, 2005. Immersed in her work she was unaware of the presence of a 200-pound black bear until it made its move. It gave her no warning, silently sneaking up on her, stalking in that traditional killer-takes-all thoroughness of its bruin clan.

Her only defense was a large can of pepper spray, which she sprayed as the bear attacked. She emptied the can then used it as a club, smacking the bear on the nose. Neither the pepper spray nor the empty can had any effect on the bear.

It pummeled her, tore off one ear and part of her scalp and inflicted puncture-bite wounds on her arms and legs.

Although conscious the entire time and gravely injured, she felt no pain. She was able to radio colleagues who arrived immediately. One frightened the bear off with a shotgun before radioing for additional support.

Julia reached medical help and a plastic surgeon worked for eleven hours reconstructing her head.

The bear was later tracked and killed by conservation officers.

Julia thinks it might be advantageous to have a dog along on wilderness outings. And considering another female athlete was killed a few days later in Canmore, Alberta, Julia feels very fortunate to have survived her encounter.

Following are some random examples involving pepper spray.

Person(s)	Bear type, time frame, locale, situation
Derrick Chapman	Sept. 1991 British Columbia; planting trees; grizzly rushed from 16 yards; Derrick emptied canister into bear's face; bear jumped on him-grabbed his left arm with its mouth-flung him into the air; Derrick played dead; bear left
Dan Baldwin	April 1992 British Columbia; engineer forestry work; predatory sow griz w. 2 large cubs; when Dan yelled she located him and came; he sprayed her within 3 feet and she split
Mark Matheny; Fred Bahnson	Sept. 1992 elk archery hunters; sow griz and 3 cubs on elk kill; knocked Mark down-mauled; Fred sprayed; she knocked him down and returned to Mark; Fred sprayed her again (emptied 4 oz. can); she knocked him down again and left
Wade Sjodin; Louie Van Gootel	August 1994 grizzly attacked B.C. forestry workers from 100-plus yards; men accessed their pepper spray and looked for climbing trees; bear stopped 3-feet from Louie-watched him try to remove canister's safety clip; bear shoved Louie to ground and he played dead; Wade yelled from his tree; bear mauled Louie and raked debris onto him then went for Wade (40-feet up tree); bear pulled him from tree and

	he sprayed its face from 2-feet; bear fled 40-feet wiping its face with its paws; Wade climbed again; bear climbed after him; Wade sprayed it a second time from a yard and it fled
Ann Quarterman; Christine Bialkowski	Oct. 1994 ladies spotted B.C. grizzly and cubs in full charge 100-300 yards distant; women retreated; Ann sprayed bear from 3-feet; it veered to Christine-bit-shook her by left arm; Ann attacked and sprayed it a second time-bear turned to Ann-she sprayed it a third time (emptied can); bear mauled Ann— Christine kicked it in the head; bear bit Christine and left
Alan Hobler	August 1995 B.C. grizzly charged hiker; Alan climbed tree; bear tried to shake him from tree; she climbed halfway to him-he sprayed her face; she froze then came on; he sprayed a second time and she fled, leaving cubs
Stan Thiessen	September 1995 B.C. black with cubs attacked archer from 50 yards; he sprayed her from 20 feet-she hit the spray at 10-feet and retreated; while leaving he looked back-saw her coughing and shaking her head
Brad Eddy	May 1996 working B.C. timber 165 yards from partner; black approached from 22 yards; Brad sprayed it from 8 yards, toward the paws turning the bear; as it moved away, he fired a second blast and the bear continued its departure
Young man	May 1996 B.C. engineer working alone in woods deters large black with hat while accessing his spray; bear pummels hat for 10 seconds then turns to man who deployed 3-second blast; bear backed up, coughing-shaking head-rubbing face in moss; man heads for truck with bear paralleling him-keeping its distance at 200-feet—apparently not wanting another dose
Sheldon Hillier	June 1996 black climbs tree after B.C. forest/logging worker; he sprayed the bear that dropped

to the ground only to return for a second helping at 5-feet; it backed down-rubbed its face-ripped into moss; bear came back for thirds and Sheldon emptied can; on its fourth trip Sheldon tossed his camera, ribbon and empty can…then sticks; he radioed for help, sawed limbs-tossed at the bear for 1 ½ hours as it periodically attacked the tree before the chopper scared it off

Chris Deile; Keith Benner	1996 Kenai Peninsula brown bear attacked. Chris yelled-sprayed; bear swiped his chest-knocking him down; bear growled-snarled in his face then left; Chris jumped up-bear returned, veering from Chris to Keith, knocking him against a tree before leaving
Wyoming hunter	September 27, 1998, grizzly rushed elk hunter from 25-yards; he discarded his high-powered rifle in favor of pepper spray and emptied it into her face before she blasted through it and mauled him severely; his partner intervened and shot-killed the 475-pound bear (the victim chose pepper spray in fear of prosecution for shooting a grizzly) (Author: my suggestion is for anyone in this situation to kill the bear and face the consequences rather than face the possibility of death —how many bears does North America need, anyway?)
Bruce D. Ohlson	August 1999 Teslin River, B.C. float trip, grizzly in camp; mauling-Phillippe Vermeyen sprayed by partner, bear stopped; victim escaped; bear resumed—sprayed again; bear choked-gasped; sprayed a 3rd and 4th time; bear didn't back off but stood on hind legs, looking. Bruce told it to leave and it gradually moved away.
June 2006	Yellowstone camp raiding black boar sprayed numerous times before it left on its own; trapped-euthanized.

You will notice that in eleven of the twelve samples bears left the victim(s) every time. However don't be misled for the reasons the bears left:

Chapman sprayed, bear mauled him but left only AFTER he played dead.

Baldwin experienced excellent results from the spray.

Matheny-Bahnson were both injured; the bear left AFTER the spray was exhausted.

Sjodin-Van Grootel's left only AFTER injuring both men.

Quarterman-Bialkowski's bear left AFTER their spray was exhausted

Hobler, Thiessen, Eddy and young man succeeded after a fashion.

Hillier persisted and bear left because of arriving cavalry.

Diele-Brenner's bear left of its own accord.

Ohlson-Vermeyen's bear left after several doses of spray.

Yellowstone bear probably would have repeated offense if not killed.

My question: how many bullets from a handgun would it have taken to kill these bears while they chewed or tried to access the victim?

While reading Shelton's books, I theorized that his emphasis upon the benefits of pepper spray was due to Canada's strict firearms laws, disallowing general use of firearms: "Pepper spray is not as effective as firearms for defense against bears, but it's the only alternative that has a high enough success rate to be considered a defense system." (James Gary Shelton, *Bear Attacks II*, Pg. 170) After Gary and I discussed that probability, he confirmed my suspicion.

If you rely on pepper spray as your first line of defense, I highly recommend that you also carry a powerful firearm in case the cayenne doesn't work. A firearm can stop a bear. Would you rather tickle a bear, deter one or kill one that wants to discombobulate you?

Do your homework. Research brands, containers and products…and test each in adverse weather conditions. Then find a cooperative bear which will let you test fire at him. If you choose pepper spray as your weapon of choice against a charging bear, hopefully it will not let you down.

Some people put their faith in pepper spray, but if I am responsible for my party's safe return from the woods, I'll be packing more than pepper spray in Alaska and beyond. I'm not going to refute pepper spray because I know it works. However, my question remains, am I willing to trust my life to it? Experts cannot assure effectiveness of deterring a bear with pepper spray 100% of the time. And what about playing dead? *Hmmmm.*

There is much empirical evidence that firearms are not 100% either.

I chose to write this book in part because I wanted to address the politically correct directive "spray and play." The clause "spray pepper then play dead" is clichéd to the point that people fail to consider its meaning. Do you realize what "play dead" implies? First, I'm going to present the spray, point it at the bear and trigger a burst of cayenne pepper at it. If that doesn't work, I'm to fall onto the ground in a fetal position, clasping my hands behind my neck. And then what?

"Play dead" tells the victim to lie on the ground in an inert, dormant, silent state, to actualize a corpse in a balled up position. While lying there, the victim waits…wondering, *will it bite me? How hard? What will it feel like? Will it kill me? What will be the extent of my injuries physically, financially, emotionally?*

Lie on the ground while an animal capable of ripping off my head bats me around? It's almost like proclaiming "golly gee, it's only a temporary inconvenience to have a bear maul me—just drop to the ground, protect myself, take a deep breath and take two Advil. It will be over in a jiffy." Giving advice to play dead sounds like a prelude to a box social—you pay the lovely maiden for the lunch and just before eating it, you allow a few moments for a bear to bite and claw you, then you sit down by the maiden and enjoy the lunch with her. (I refer you to Patricia Anne Van Tighem, who played dead along with her husband, and they were in the hospital for nearly three months and underwent ongoing surgeries for years).

In 2007 our family friend Charlotte Parent of Cottage Grove, Minnesota, asked me via telephone what I thought of the idea of playing dead as a solution to a bear encounter. I asked her, "When was the last time you thought about lying on the ground and letting your dog chew on you…and he loves you?"

Playing dead has two distinct facets: 1) non-contact and 2) contact. If you could guarantee that a bear would NOT contact you if you played dead, that would be great. But that's not the way it works.

Au contraire, mon ami! (for the non-Frenchie: On the contrary, my friend) A few of those who played dead, are DEAD. Others lost body parts and/or have emotional trauma. For instance, Harry Knackstead played dead with a brown/grizzly. Basically she chomped holes in him, leaving his brain exposed.

Why would anyone wish to go into an arena of danger unprepared to defend himself? Why would he put himself into a position wherein he could be maimed, blinded or killed...for life? What percentage of those who played dead survived the attack? How successful is playing dead as a safety action in bear country.

If you knew that a bear would sniff you and leave, playing dead is wonderful. However if a bear chewed, swatted or clawed you while you lay on the ground, what are the chances of serious injury? I refer you to Daniel Bigley. One bite took his face as he dived for protection in a "playing dead" effort on Alaska's Russian River, one of the world's most famous salmon streams. On July 15, 2003, around midnight he was jumped by a brown/grizzly with two cubs. His status went from critical condition to surviving...in the brief moment the sow blinded him forever.

Playing dead could be a precursor to the reality—death! Experts tout playing dead in a defensive attack, especially if the bear is a grizzly. Hold it! How many people can differentiate bears? And how do they know if it's a defensive attack? If people are cognizant that it is a defensive attack and that the bear will leave once it determines that you are not a threat, playing dead is a secondary option. However, if the animal is protecting a food source (other than its fishing grounds), and, especially, if it's a boar on a moose, elk or other game kill, you may be in for a long day of playing dead...I refer you to Forest Young—one of nastiest carcass defense maulings ever. While retrieving a moose hide from a tree cache, he was mauled repeatedly and figured he'd die. (*Alaska Bear Tales*).

However, playing dead has severe implications.

Cynthia Dusel-Bacon chose to "do the right thing" and played dead with a small black bear in the wilderness near Fairbanks, Alaska. It cost her both arms. Had her supervisor provided better information regarding weapons, it is 100% probable that she would have dispatched the bear at 20 feet and saved her arms. Partially as a result of Cynthia's accident, her government agency instituted firearms training and her friend and colleague Marti Miller had a mirror image experience with a black. She walked away from her encounter, shakily but alive (*Some Bears Kill*).

Another tragedy resulted when Paul and Christine Courtney played dead—they chose to adhere to faulty park information provided by a bear attack researcher-expert.

Because it's not uncommon for "playing dead" to become a contact "sport," it is in your best interest to glean the best information from the most qualified on the subject of human survival in a bear encounter. Those qualified would be guides with years in the field or other outdoorsmen who have witnessed bears in action. An easy place to start is the Internet.

You may wish to read accounts of those who played dead—some

survived with fairly minimal injuries; some sustained life altering and/or life ending injuries. If playing dead meant no contact from the bear, I'd suggest it every time. However most attacking bears do more than watch the victim—they chew and rip, usually until the victim lies motionless. So if you're into being batted about, clawed or bitten in the name of safety, God speed.

Canadian bear expert James Gary Shelton says it better than anyone I've heard so far (*Bear Attacks: The Deadly Truth*, Pp. 218-219):

"I took a strong stand against the play-dead/fight back strategy in 1992 and told people they must have a defence system (spray or firearm), because the types of attacks where this strategy doesn't work are increasing, and because my research regarding spray-use against bears indicated a very high success rate...Of the eight grizzly attacks (three deaths and five serious injuries), only one had clear evidence that the play-dead strategy worked. The three black bear attacks (resulting in one death) were all predatory, and in all three cases, the victims were unable to fight the bear off by themselves

"...when a person is attacked by a sow grizzly where the cubs run away, the play-dead concept works fairly well. But in an attack where first-year cubs go up a tree, or second-year cubs follow the sow, or if a person is attacked by a predatory grizzly or one defending a carcass, the play-dead strategy doesn't work worth a damn, and there have been many attacks since 1990 that clearly demonstrate this...

"Between 1992 and 1996 I warned people that they should not follow the bear attack guidelines in government pamphlets, they must carry a defense system and defend themselves vigorously. Many government officials were aware of what I was saying but ignored me because I was not part of the academic biological community. I knew that sooner or later a high profile case would come along that would prove me right." (Author: I also received criticism because I was not a biologist.)

After publishing *Bear Encounter Survival Guide*, Shelton wrote numerous outdoor magazines in hopes of seeing his playing dead/fighting back philosophy presented to hikers and campers. However in spite of his warnings, he was ignored. For instance, he wrote:

"On July 5th, 1996, a woman was killed by a grizzly bear in Yukon's Kluane National Park. When the woman and her husband were approached by a young grizzly on a trail, they moved off the trail, took their packs off, and put them on the ground. The grizzly ignored the packs, and as it kept up its approach, they both laid down and rolled into a protective ball (as suggested in many park pamphlets). Unfortunately, this strategy led to the woman's death. If these two people had stood their

343

ground with this curious young bear or had been carrying bear spray, the woman would most likely still be alive." (Pg. 219)   (See Courtney story herein)

On June 19, 2009, my friend Ken Wolter sent me the following e-mail:

I have a friend who is a receptionist in a church in a high risk area who was concerned about someone coming into the office on Monday to rob them when they were counting the collection. She asked the local police department about using pepper spray and they recommended to her that she get a can of wasp spray instead. The wasp spray, they told her, can shoot up to twenty feet away and is a lot more accurate, while with the pepper spray they have to get too close to you and could overpower you. The wasp spray temporarily blinds an attacker until they get to the hospital for an antidote. She keeps a can on her desk in the office and it doesn't attract attention from people like a can of pepper spray would. She also keeps one nearby at home for home protection. Thought this was interesting and might be of use.

Misinformation

Interestingly enough, Dave Smith, author of *Backcountry Bear Basics* (Pg. 85), states that a grizzly defensive attack "generally does not cause serious injury." On the contrary, I'm listing only a few victims of defensive grizzly attacks, people I've interviewed or to whose families I've spoken:

Name	Injury
Forest Young	mangled badly enough to consider suicide
T.J. Langley	severely injured in Yellowstone
Daniel Bigley	face bitten-torn off and blinded
Diane Nelson	major injuries (2000 stitches) and medical costs
Don Coverston	thousands of sutures to his head
Al Johnson	semi-scalped, arm damage
Ralph Borders	major injuries
Marcie Trent, Larry Waldron	both killed while jogging

344

So, the next time someone gives you the easy-to-give-never-been-there-myself advice of playing dead, may I suggest other alternatives?

Pepper vs. Firearm

A woman called me to query my opinion of pepper spray for a newspaper article she was writing and I've included it below: (*Seattle Times* story: author interviewed Larry Kaniut for some of it October 3, 1999, Lemhi County Today article from the *Seattle Times*, Florangela Davila: With Bears, Should You Spray -- Pepper or Bullets --The noise is the most horrifying detail of T.J. Langley's story: the pop when part of his pelvis was snapped off, the crunch of the jaws on his skull. Caught in the vise of a female grizzly in Yellowstone National Park last month, Langley, of Seattle, assumed he was going to die.)

His fingers had found the can of pepper spray held snug in his chest harness, but he couldn't get the safety before the bear reached him.

Recovering now at home - his forehead and scalp a tremendous web of stitches -Langley recounts the ordeal almost matter-of-factly. He will, he says, return to the back country he so loves. And he will carry pepper spray again.

But Langley's tale terrifies some who insist no aerosol spray can possibly deter an angry, 350-pound grizzly capable of breaking a bull moose's neck with one swat.

Hiker Chris Deile had been a lifelong pacifist, even after a grizzly assaulted him on the Kenai Peninsula in Alaska two years ago.

Deile said he shot a stream of bear pepper spray into the grizzly's throat, but it had no effect. The bear swatted his chest, rushed his hiking companion, then took off.

So with plans to hike the 3,000-mile Continental Divide trail next spring, Deile, even more impassioned after hearing Langley's story, will pack a gun.

"I can try to make noise. I can keep my food high away from my camp. I'd try to follow precautions so no bear attacks me. But I think if I'm going to have to save my life, then a gun is worth it," says the Seattle resident, acknowledging his opinion is likely in the minority.

Yellowstone park employees, federal and state wildlife agency employees, biologists and a nonprofit group that tracks the number of bear encounters all maintain that bear pepper spray can be effective.

Bear attacks in North America, either grizzly or black bear, are rare, according to the Center for Wildlife information in Missoula, Mont.

"Out of millions and millions of visitors, it might happen seven or eight times a year," said Chuck Bartlebaugh, the center's director. "And if you hike in groups of two or more during the day, and stay on the trail, the possibility is very small."

Among the precautions authorities recommend-like a good chorus of "Hey, bear; ho, bear" as you're hiking - bear pepper spray has worked extremely well in as many as 90 percent of bear encounters, according to the Interagency Grizzly Bear Committee, which is composed of federal and state officials from Montana, Wyoming and Washington.

Most bear spray, the outgrowth of Mace and other personal-protection sprays, is made from food-grade oleoresin capsicum, or the active ingredient in hot peppers. It attacks the mucous membranes of the animal's eyes, nose, ears and throat. But as more versions of the products have come out, the debate over their effective-ness has increased.

Last year, Tom Smith, a wildlife ecologist with the U.S. Geological Survey in Anchorage, noted some bears were attracted to pepper spray residue. A Missoula-based firm then began warning consumers about oil-based pepper spray products. It offered instead a new product that uses synthetic chemicals.

This spring, in the midst of the debate, the Interagency Grizzly Bear Committee published a position paper on bear pepper sprays.

The agency declared the sprays effective and said such products should only be used against an attacking bear and not applied to a tent and pack as a repellant. Smith agrees. He in fact carries the spray and says it works when used as intended. The committee also advised hikers to select a spray specifically designed for bear attacks, not the kind used on humans.

There are about 42,000 grizzlies in North America. Fewer than 1,000 of them live in the Lower 48, notably in the Yellowstone area and Bob Marshall Wilderness Glacier Park complex in Montana. An estimated 30 grizzlies live in Washington's North Cascades. There are more black bears in North America- about 600,000 - than all other seven bear species combined in the world. They roam throughout the forests of the Lower 48; about 20,000 live in Washington.

Black bears are generally less aggressive than grizzlies, the larger of the two species, which can weigh between 300 and 500 pounds. It is illegal to carry a gun into a national park, and in the national forests where guns are permissible, you cannot shoot a grizzly, a threatened species in the lower 48, unless it's in self-defense. But even a gun might not be effective, says Tim Eicher, a federal game warden with the U.S. Fish and Wildlife Service.

"A shot might be a killing shot, but there's still a chance the bear will be able to maul you," he said.

Moreover, small guns, which might be preferable for a backpacker, aren't powerful enough to kill a bear.

"You might just injure the bear and further aggravate it," said Chris Servheen, the grizzly-bear-recovery coordinator for the federal wildlife service agency. "I used to carry a firearm, but I don't anymore," said Servheen, who always carries bear spray.

Langley, 32, a theater actor and apartment-building manager, each year plans a two- to three-week hiking vacation. A cousin in Bozeman urged him to carry bear spray "just in case." Langley had practiced taking the safety off the can.

While hiking the Black Butte trail, he came upon two bears, likely yearlings, foraging on white-pine bark authorities said. Their mother was up the hillside, out of view, when she suddenly charged.

"It's a really rare occurrence, and I think I would be really, really unlucky if it were to happen again," he says. Next time, he'll hike with someone else and not let his guard down.

And yet Deile says there are others, people he's found on the Internet or in casual conversation, who agree a gun is the only defense. "All my idealism about wanting to be peaceful ..." he says. "Now I'm realistic. If it happens again, pepper spray will not work." He will take either a rifle or a .45 Long Colt revolver. When he hikes, he'll skirt national parks.

In the great grizzly state of Alaska, Larry Kaniut of Anchorage doesn't think Deile is wrong.

"If I'm somewhat remotely concerned about bear or cougar, I just won't depend on my knife," says the English teacher-turned-author, who has written two books on bears.

On a recent hike with his daughter and some of her friends above timber line in the Chugach Mountains, he took his rifle.

"Bears are interested in two things - food and sex - and we're not one of them," says Kaniut, who buries his firearm under a shirt so as not to scare anyone he might come across.

"But if I have to depend on my safety or the safety of anyone else with me, in bear country, I won't rely on pepper spray."

Ned Rozell wrote a piece about pepper spray. (ALASKA SCIENCE FORUM, Pepper Spray Works, But Don't Bet Your Life On It, Article #1245, by Ned Rozell, July 27, 1995. This column is provided as a public service by the Geophysical Institute, University of Alaska Fairbanks, in cooperation with the UAF research community. Ned Rozell, is a science writer at the institute.

My eyes water when I remember my introduction to bear-deterrent pepper spray. During Park Service bear spray training, the instructor wet a finger to the breeze, walked upwind of our group, and let go with a short, orange burst of pepper spray. The few particles that wafted our way inspired us to kill him--lucky for him, we couldn't open our sizzling eyes long enough to see where he was.

We learned that day pepper spray works on humans, but is it effective on discontent 700-pound bears moving rapidly toward you?

Stephen Herrero said yes, it is, but don't bet your life on it. Herrero, a researcher with the University of Calgary, presented results of a pepper spray study in Fairbanks recently during the Tenth International Conference on Bear Research and Management. He and Andrew Higgins combed North America for 66 examples of what happened in the field when bears were hit with a snout full of pepper spray.

Their study included black bears and brown (grizzly) bears in a variety of pre-spray moods that ranged from curious to aggressive. All of the bears had been sprayed with the type of pepper sprays found at sporting goods stores--a tubular canister containing propellant and 10 percent capsaicin, a toxic chemical extracted from red peppers that acts as a powerful irritant to respiratory systems and eyes.

Because pepper spray can be aimed and shot several body lengths away, it gives people a skunk-like ability to ward off aggressors such as other people and snarling dogs. But the spray's effectiveness on bears in the wild hadn't been evaluated until the recent study.

In the 16 cases Herrero and Higgins looked at in which pepper spray was used against brown bears in sudden encounters, 15 brown bears turned away after receiving a direct blast to the eyes and nose. Three of the sprayed brown bears ended up attacking and injuring the sprayer anyway, but Herrero said it didn't appear a face full of pepper made the bears any more aggressive than they normally would have been.

Of 20 brown bears sprayed while searching for human food, garbage, or just appearing overly curious, Herrero and Higgins found all 20 stopped what they were doing, and 18 left (only two of those 18 came back later).

Blasted black bears didn't seem as affected by the spray, especially those with a taste for garbage. Nineteen of 26 black bears sprayed while acting curious or searching for human food and garbage stopped what they were doing, and 14 of 26 bears left the area. But six of those 14 came back.

"The spray appears ineffective as a means of deterring black bears that are strongly conditioned to human foods and garbage," Herrero said.

Pepper spray also didn't send black bears running in the four cases where people sprayed them after aggressive sudden encounters. Although it stopped the black bears' aggressive behavior in all four cases, none of them left the area. Herrero said although their sample size of their study was too small for bombproof conclusions, black bears seem to be more resistant to the physiological effects of pepper spray than brown bears.

Herrero, author of the 1985 book *Bear Attacks: Their Causes and Avoidance*, has studied bears since long before pepper sprays became popular in the 1980's. He said he raised his eyebrows at some of the study results, such as how consistently pepper spray turned back brown bears. But he also pointed out the sprays can become useless or even debilitating to the user in a strong wind. Rain and thick brush also cause delivery problems.

He said to rely only on the spray as protection while ignoring other bear country essentials--such as storing food out of reach of bears or in bear-proof containers and making noise in thick brush--is just plain stupid. "This stuff isn't brains in a can," he said.

If you choose to utilize pepper spray as your first or second line of defense, I suggest you consider at least five factors regarding your choice: ingredients, delivery system, propellant, atmospheric-environmental conditions and the targeted animal.

First, what quality are the ingredients? Is there sufficient oleoresin capsicum to ward off the bear? Many pepper sprays contain diluted—thus ineffective—products. Pepper spray comes in a variety of "packages." Some work; some don't. Make sure the brand you choose is the best.

Second, what is the quality of the delivery system? Pepper spray comes in an aerosol canister with a spray nozzle. How functional is the nozzle? When triggered, how many containers fizzle foam from the outlet?

Third, will the aerosol provide the needed power to deliver the product to the intended target? How far will your chosen spray propel toward its target?

Fourth, what weather conditions could affect the efficient delivery of the product? How far away is the target? What effect will a wind or heavy drizzle have on the product's concentration and trajectory? What if the wind is blowing from the direction of the bear to you—what amount of spray will reach the bear? What amount will reach you? Will any existing foliage negate the spray's travel?

If any one of these factors fail to provide 100% results, your safety is compromised.

And fifth, even if the first four factors prove effective, how will the spray affect any given bear? What percent of the time does it work? With black, grizzly and polar bears? Different bears react differently to pepper spray. Has it been tested with all bear natures—docile, aggressive, determined (predatory, bad attitude boar), young/old, black/grizzly, wild/ habituated, etc. Bears that have been sprayed tend to be conditioned to it and often walk around the spray to get closer to the person spraying.

James Gary Shelton discusses pepper spray in his *Bear Attacks II*, "Firearms are successful against bears about 95 percent of the time (not including grizzly attacks on hunters), and sprays about 75 percent of the time. You must have a defense system when exposed to bears if you want a fighting chance of surviving an attack." (Pg. 75)

At least one author recommends pepper spray over firearms as the way to deal with problem bears (his book looms as a 200-plus page commercial for pepper spray). My question, if you're lost and need to kill an animal for food, will pepper spray produce food? A firearm can kill your food source.

Dr. Tom Smith, former Anchorage U.S. Government employee and Boy Scout leader, has amassed an extensive data base (incorporating his own work, that of Steve Herrero, Alaska state epidemiologist John Middaugh and my research). Before leaving his job with the government and taking a job with the Brigham Young University, Tom conducted many studies with bears. After reading my *Some Bears Kill*, he gave me a heads up and we periodically compared notes (see Dedication of this book).

In January 1998 he called and talked about pepper spray. His studies include discovering that brown bears on the Alaska Peninsula like pepper spray and that they are undeterred by bells. He stated, "If you have a can of pepper spray in your tent, you don't need to worry about being mauled…you need to be concerned about being crushed. Bears love it!" Tom equated pepper spray to having an open jar of salsa in your tent. He spoke with me about his pepper spray study, "The impetus for my study came when I observed a bear rolling vigorously in beach gravel that had been inadvertently sprayed with the spray five days prior."

Tom went on to say that "pepper spray may be an effective deterrent." However in this particular study of Dr. Smith's, the spray proved an attractant. Red pepper residues attracted non-aggressive bears and in no case was a bear deterred. Of course, as Tom indicated, the pepper was latent and not sprayed at the bears.

Tom uses pepper spray only as a last resort. If the bear is upwind or temperatures are low, the propellant is adversely affected —the 25-30 foot projection of the spray is reduced to 8 feet or so.

He said, "Serious consideration is needed in usage. Because many outdoors people carry pepper spray, it is important to advise that it's a potential attractant. It is necessary to remove all residue from the nozzle after use."

Tom told me that he tested four products. After spraying nine sites with 10-15% concentrations of oleoresin capsicum he found those sprays attracted brown bears in Katmai National Park in late October 1997. Twenty bears approached the sites 40 times, 37% exhibiting moderate to high interest which included pawing, licking, rubbing heads and rolling in the sprayed sites.

He shared anecdotes demonstrating the bear's affinity for the pepper spray: the spray around an Alaska Peninsula tent served as a salt lick, attracting bears from all around; bears flattened a sprayed outhouse; another bear chewed the pepper sprayed rubber bumpers from the floats of a float equipped private aircraft.

Later in a different study related to spraying bears directly Dr. Tom Smith catalogued different results (www.absc.usgs.gov/research/brownbears/pepperspray). His data base indicates that spray has been effective in 87% of the cases he's studied. I'm wondering how a person would handle the other 13%, especially with a determined bear.

On a different note, statistics for pepper spray's successfully deterring a bear range between 87% and 90%. If you like statistics, check this out. You're one of 10 to 13% of persons for which pepper spray was unsuccessful. Or…you're one of the infinitesimally small percent of those mauled by a bear…or worse, you're the ONE person whom each year a bear in North America kills! How do you like those statistics!

Mark Matheny is the founder and developer of UDAP (bear spray). I met him around 1995, heard his story and pumped him for information about pepper spray and its effectiveness against bears. In all our conversations he has always affirmed his confidence in it—during a February 23, 2004, phone call he said, "I've never had anybody call me without success with our product. It's a lack of confidence that people don't know how to use it."

Mark was more than generous and provided me some of his magnum spray. I was pleasantly surprised when I sprayed a bear and the noise—spray did not reach it—triggered its running gear…accelerating him from our yard.

In 2007 I watched a UDAP Discovery video. The documentary, written and produced by Gordon Forbes III, showed 17 minutes of pepper spray information. Play dead ONLY as a last resort. Do NOT climb a tree, it's a sign of submission. Not once was a firearm for defense mentioned—all spray and blame man for his ignorance in bear habitat. I'm wondering, would you rather be submissive and alive or dominant and dead? If you're able to out climb a grizzly or have a weapon, why not be submissive? *Hmmmm.*

Pepper spray results run the gamut from immediate success to miserable failure. Gary Shelton states, "...if you stopped the bear but did not get a real good dose on its face, the bear may come back. Leave the area immediately...some of the problem black bears along the Alaskan Highway that have been repeatedly sprayed by C.O.s or Parks staff become somewhat resistant to spray, and return to the area quickly." (*Bear Encounter Survival Guide*, Pg. 116) (Ironically and sadly, it is common for people north of Fort Nelson on the Alaska Highway to feed bears)

Gary details how a park ranger continued to spray pepper into a black bear's face while it approached a garbage dumpster devoid of garbage near where a man lay beneath his car attempting mechanical work. After numerous sprayings and over a half hour of cat and mouse, the ranger shot and killed the troublesome bear. (*Bear Encounter Survival Guide*, Pp. 168-169)

Shelton discusses numerous other pepper spray failures in his books.

On another note the Internet website Alaska Outdoors Directory has a forum on pepper spray in which most of the posters choose firearms over spray. A couple of long time game workers comment on defective spray canisters—not all are functional.

Bear spray will probably deter a bear 90-95 % of the times it's used—especially in the Continental US. It's easy to advise the use of pepper spray for bears in the Lower 48 states, but when you throw into the mix a thousand pound brown bear hell bent to make a believer out of you or determined to turn you into an immobile first aid experiment, the advice gets more difficult. Some bears ignore the spray and keep coming. Some are of a mood that nothing but a young howitzer or an F-22 Raptor would deter.

For instance, brown bears fight for the ardor of their intended mate. Let's say you observe Old Buster fight a newcomer for Susie's attention and Old Buster loses. These two bears, weighing over a thousand pounds each, are capable of breaking the other's jaw or dislocating a shoulder. Old Buster leaves the battle, bleeding and with a chip on his shoulder. You encounter him on the trail with your pepper spray. And you think your can of cayenne will stop him?

Pepper spray, partners, bike

Wyoming mountain bikers learned a ton from their confrontation with a grizzly, mostly about proper protocol, pepper spray and using a bicycle as a deterrent.

Lured by mountain grandeur and prime weather the mountain biking trio anticipated a great day riding in the Shoshone National Forest. Their playground lay close to Wyoming's Teton and Washakie wilderness areas around 9,500 feet elevation. They planned to traverse a couple of passes including Togwotee beneath the Pinnacle Peaks in the Kissinger Lakes and Brooks Lake area.

On August 29, 2004, Kirk Speckhals, Tom Foley and Mark Wolling set out near Brooks Lake. A ski patroller working with Evans construction, Speckhals had never carried pepper spray, though he'd biked the loop numerous times. Foley offered his extra canister of spray and Wolling figured if they had a problem he'd be most likely to need it since he had his dog Sir Charles Winston VI.

They enjoyed their first leg to Kissinger Lakes without incident. Because they were in the Yellowstone ecosystem and grizzly country, they made noises to announce their presence and to warn bears. Climbing the second pass and ringing his bicycle bell, Speckhals put distance between himself and his companions. And he rang his bell less frequently. As he crested a rise, Speckhals heard a sound and saw a grizzly 300-feet away charging him at full speed.

Given the choice of playing dead or facing the bear, Speckhals dismounted his bike and placed it as a shield between himself and the bear. He yelled "bear!" to alert his companions.

From the distance Foley heard Speckhals' dramatic and scary shouts; and he increased his speed in order to assist. Meanwhile Wolling brought up the rear.

As he neared Speckhals, Foley heard grunts and realized that the combatants were engaged in physical contact.

Spekhals used his bike as a battering ram, thrusting it at the bear. The game of cat and mouse—man thrusts; bear backs up—continued, the bear charging half dozen times. Every time the bear showed aggression, the thrust bike stopped him.

At one point the bear jerked the bicycle from Speckhals' hands and pounced on it with its front paws, bending the wheel and popping the tire.

While the bear was engaged with the bike, Speckhals sneaked away. But the grizzly had none of it. The bear rose up and placed its forepaws on him. It took him to the ground where Speckhals twisted to his chest.

When Foley reached his partner at the Basin Creek Meadows, things seemed calm and he spotted the bear sitting on his friend. Feeling no fear, Foley approached the grizzly with his pepper spray, blasting the bear from fifteen feet.

The bear reacted by walking off Speckhals and circling Foley who continued spraying into the bear's face. Although the bear's huge eyes were full of pepper spray, the animal didn't even blink. As his can emptied, Foley yelled for Wolling. The bear continued circling him.

Thinking he was going to see a bloody mess as he zipped around the corner, Wolling reached the mayhem and searched his pack for his pepper spray, knowing that Foley's can was almost empty.

What he saw surprised him. The bear was standing and Foley in retreat. About that time Sir Charles Winston VI appeared, barked twice and fled back down the trail.

With about a second's worth of spray left, Foley yelled at the bear. That's when Foley noticed a change in the bear's demeanor and that its eyes changed. The bear turned and departed.

Speckhals escaped injury, merely receiving four dirt marks on his forearm.

The guys agreed that Foley likely saved Speckhals' life by arriving when he did with the pepper spray. They felt that they should have made more noise, carried more pepper spray and stayed closer together.

Speckhals straightened out his wheel and patched his flat, enabling him to ride the few miles to the end of the loop. (Sources: 1] HelendIR. com, Independent Record, The Associated Press, 9/06/04; 2] Jackson Hole News & Guide.com, Bikers battle grizzly bear, Rider fends off repeated charges with bike before friend fires pepper spray in nick of time, By Angus M. Thuermer Jr.)

Hunter

While Vic Workman, a Montana Fish, Wildlife and Parks Commission employee, and hunting partner Eric Paine stopped to discuss options during their Thanksgiving weekend hunt north of Whitefish Lake, a large grizzly erupted from the brush. Vic only had time to raise his rifle to his hip and fire, hitting the bear in the chest. After the bear swerved off and fled, the men searched the area discovering a whitetail buck buried nearby.

Workman stated that the bear was so close and so fast that, "If I hadn't had my rifle ready at my hip, he would've got me...These people who think that they're safe with bear spray, I'm here to tell them it's a false sense of security.

"It's too fast. Way too fast."

Workman and officers with the FWP returned but found no sign of the bear; but the deer had been moved across the creek and eaten.

(Source: Missoulian.com article Nov. 27, 2007, Shot from the hip deters bear's charge, by Michael Jamison of the Missoulian [demonstrates determination of bear, its speed, need for bear stopper and questionable employment of pepper spray])

A week after Workman's bear scare, the Missoulian carried another on-line piece, addressing his hastiness and "reckless" comments regarding pepper spray and bear numbers.

(Source: "Spray vs. gun bear deterrent debate rages," Monday, Dec. 3, 2007, By John Cramer of the *Missoulian*)

Critics did not like the fact that Workman stated that the thriving numbers of grizzlies should qualify for their removal from the endangered species list. Nor did they like the idea that he preferred spraying lead instead of spraying pepper.

And yet another allusion to grizzlies, pepper spray and common sense from the *Missoulian* on line, December 12, 2007, by John Cramer, "Man mauled by bear believes spray wouldn't have deterred charge." Brian Grand was mauled by a grizzly while he hunted pheasants October 15, 2007, adjacent Dupuyer Creek near the Blackfeet Indian Reservation. The bear was captured and relocated.

Although Grand and his hunting partners did everything right, including having bells on their dogs and making lots of noise, the bear still mauled him. He agrees with Vic Workman (above) who believes that bear spray provides a false sense of security and that firearms are probably more effective in staving off a grizzly. Grand also espouses the idea that grizzly numbers warrant their being delisted from the endangered species list and hunted in limited numbers. And he thinks those that attack humans should be removed from the gene pool because they are given precedence over human beings and their safety.

Examples or illustrations can be cited for just about any topic, therefore one can argue for or against that topic. However it is in your best interests to do your homework to determine how effective pepper spray and playing dead are, how much preparation is necessary to hike-camp in bear country for a few days, what does it take to defend yourself against a bear attack?

You can skew this information about bear spray and playing dead any way you wish to suit your personal beliefs. Before you decide to either utilize pepper spray or play dead, consider the ramifications of both.

And remember, the important factor remains, what is the most effective means of self protection?

BONDING, STUDYING

For whatever reason, people fall under the spell of bears. Many think that they can bond with the animals or tame them or be their friends. I've selected two examples of some men who spent a great deal of time with bears, but the bears weren't sufficiently persuaded to bond with these men.

Some people approach bear-man relations as though they'd gone to college with ursus and were frat brothers or sorority sisters. It's almost like the people think they can reason with the beast, *I won't bother you and you won't bother me.* That's fine and dandy, but the bears don't know man's philosophy or his rules. And the sad part is that most people don't know the bear's.

James Gary Shelton makes the point (*Bear Encounter Survival Guide*, Pg. 48) that "...grizzly bears cannot distinguish the level of danger an intruder poses...They do not know whether you want to end their life or wish them well."

So, where does man fit into this scenario?

Some men with good intentions have studied and photographed bears but in the end these men were destroyed by the animal they studied.

Vitaly Nikolayenko

A double tragedy resulted in one man's bear research. First, his passion led to his death. Second, his passion became his widow's loss.

Long time Russian bear researcher Vitaly Nikolayenko, 66-years-old, failed to return from the field at the end of December. His love of the giant Kamchatka Peninsula brown bears lured him to their grounds. Though small in stature the self-educated researcher and photographer walked their river valleys over 600 miles a year, returning to his one room hut on the Tikhaya River. There he compiled his exhaustive research into hundreds of journals by kerosene lamp at night, documenting 800 bear contacts annually.

But the love of his life became the loss of his wife's as she voiced her lament, "I loved him dearly, and he loved me, too. But he had this other passion in his life which was watching bears, and this passion took him away from me.

"Most of the time, he was out there in the woods. But I knew he would come back, and all my life I was waiting for him."

Wanting to celebrate New Year's with him, his wife Tatiana had tried several times the final week of December 2003 to find a helicopter flight to bring him home.

When a helicopter arrived to pick him up and found no sign of him, a search was launched. His friend Victor Rebrikov was with the search team that found Vitaly's body and said it appeared that Nikolayenko had followed a large male bear attempting to get closer for better photos. Vitaly's footprints indicated that he had worked his way through the trees within three and a half yards of where the bear had rested.

Searchers found Vitaly's partially devoured remains less than a mile from his hut. Beside his body were an average-sized male bear's 6 ½-inch paw print, Vitaly's bloodied and broken camera, an unfired flare gun and an empty canister of pepper spray—a large area nearby was covered with orange residue from the pepper canister.

(Source: www.seattletimesnwsource.com, "Bear kills well-known Russian researcher," Kim Murphy, LA Times, Wednesday, December 31, 2003, *L.A. Times* staff writer Sergei L. Loiko in Moscow contributed to this report)

Michio Hoshino

The good news was that they were filming bears. The bad news was that the salmon run was weak and that there were only a couple of bears at the lake. It would be another two weeks before the salmon showed up in enticing numbers for Russia's giant bears of Kurilskoya Lake, a remote brown bear refuge in southern Kamchatka Peninsula. Further compounding the bad news was a problem bear that had broken into the Grassy Cape cabin two days earlier, ransacking it just before the party's arrival. The damage included the bear's telltale claw marks on the outside walls and a broken window which they covered with a board before moving in.

The party consisted of seven men: two Alaskan photographers—Michio Hoshino and Curtis Hight, a three-man Japanese television crew and their two Russian guides. The guides were brothers Andrei and Igor Revenko, a veteran bear biologist.

Because the television crew stored their gear in the dwelling, there was not enough room for Hight or Michio. They would sleep separately in their tents.

Both Alaskan photographers looked forward to getting some great bear shots. The 43-year-old Michio was known around the world, his portfolio including spreads of Alaskan moose and grizzlies, *National Geograhpic* work and star status in his Japanese homeland.

Though he did not share Michio's credentials, Hight hoped to add substantially to his film portfolio.

Other outbuildings at the camp included a sturdy food cache, an outhouse and an observation tower overlooking the mouth of the nearby Khakeetsin River. It was a clean camp where occupants burned edible trash and placed other items between the cabin and the outhouse in a hole provided for the purpose.

When Hight arrived at the lake Saturday, July 27, shortly after noon, he wondered how the other clients would react to his dropping in. Andrei approached him and helped with his gear and Hoshino walked over to welcome him. Hight learned that in addition to assisting the film crew with a Japanese TV program "Amazing Animals," Hoshino was photographing brown bears for his own purposes as well. He planned to remain there about three weeks.

By 10:30 it was dark and both American photographers prepared for the night in their tents as rain misted. Hight had staked his tent twelve feet from Hoshino's yellow and gray nylon tent—both tents were within ten yards of the cabin door.

Before turning in, Hoshino told Hight to wake him if a bear showed up.

Awakened by a loud noise six hours later, Hight wondered if he were dreaming. As the noise continued, Hight investigated by slipping from his tent and creeping toward the food cache 40-feet distant. When he circled the cabin, he noticed a large brown bear jumping on the metal roof of the food shed in an effort to break in.

The man yelled and clapped his hands. The bear looked at him.

Hight yelled again and the bear moved away, circling behind Hoshino's tent.

Hight yelled to Hoshino, who stuck his head out the flap. "There's a bear—about 10 feet behind your tent!"

"Where?" Hoshino asked, squinting into the darkness.

"Right there!" Hight said. "Should I get Igor?"

"Yes, get Igor," Hoshino said.

Hight found the cabin locked and banged on the door, alerting the occupants about the bear.

Moments later Revenko stepped outside with a can of pepper spray.

Because no guns were allowed in camp, Revenko, Hoshino and

Hight tried ineffectively to chase the bear away by yelling and banging pans. Finally, Revenko pulled out his bear spray, approached within five yards and fired.

The white jet of atomized pepper shot through the air and balled up just short of the bear's nose. The spray settled to the ground. Leaning forward, the brown bear sniffed it in the grass. The 600-700-pound animal with a distinct wound on its head was unfazed. The bear played cat and mouse with the men for half an hour—it moved up the hill then came back—before finally leaving on its own accord. The bear would prove more problematic in the days ahead.

Camping in tents had not previously posed a threat. The summer before veteran bear researcher George Schaller and an REI group had done so. Michio Hoshino nearly always slept outdoors—he preferred it.

Hight wasn't so comfortable in a tent at ground level. Although he'd be further from the others, he moved his quarters to the observation tower which would give him some twenty feet of protection above the ground about a third of a mile down the lakeshore at the mouth of the Khakeetsin River. Igor warned him that a large bear slept at the tower's base, meaning Hight would want to be in the tower before dark. A ladder ran up one side of the tower where a vertical door secured the interior. Another door opened onto a balcony overlooking Kurilskoya Lake.

During Michio's first week numerous visitors dropped in for brief stays before departing.

The problem bear continued to harass the camp and campers. One morning a visiting Russian camerman videoed the big bear eating from a can of food he'd left along the shoreline near the tower. The Russian had also left open food inside his helicopter, inviting the large boar's discovery and demolition of cockpit windows. As the bear grew bolder, it became dangerously indifferent to their threats.

The second night the large boar menaced Hoshino's camp Igor had to drive it off with pepper spray.

After a few days of storms the sun reappeared August third. That day visitors who had engulfed the camp for the past days departed and a kind of normalcy returned to Kurilskoya, bringing more bears.

Rain fell in torrents on the fourth and Hight remained inside the tower.

The big boar continued to hound the camp, night after night. Because the upstream run of red salmon was so late and the Kurilskoya bears were hungry, there was no let up from the boar's visits.

On August 6, a new sow with cubs arrived near the mouth of the river, venturing within fifty feet of the large boar.

That night, the boar approached Hoshino's tent once more. For the third time the Revenko brothers shot it with pepper spray. Later, Igor said, he urged Hoshino to move inside the cabin. But Hoshino still preferred sleeping outside.

On Aug. 7, the fish finally arrived en masse. The large boar was there, too, fishing with occasional success.

Sometime after 5 the next morning, Hight awoke to the sound of motorboats. One of them pulled near the tower. He heard Andrei Revenko call out, "Can you come down?"

Hight knew that something serious was wrong.

Then Andrei shouted, "Someone was killed by a bear in camp!"

Because of Andrei's broken English, Hight wondered if meant their camp or the fish camp across the lake.

Andrei called that the victim was "Michio."

Around 4 AM Igor Revenko awoke when a Japanese cameraman alerted the camp about a bear at the tent. The Revenkos and the Japanese film crew exited the cabin within moments and heard Michio's cry and the bear's growl. They shone flashlights onto Michio's collapsed tent and spotted the bear eleven yards away in the grass.

They immediately yelled but the bear ignored them. Igor grabbed a shovel and metal bucket and banged the two together within five yards of the bear. Nonchalantly the bear raised its head briefly before taking Michio's body in its mouth and disappearing into the darkness.

Activities were chaotic after that. Igor Revenko motored the Japanese TV crew across the lake to the science station. One man radioed for help before the party returned to the camp with guns. At daylight they searched the area near the cabin and learned that the bear had taken Hoshino's body into a thick forest.

At noon, a helicopter carrying a professional hunter and special forces officer arrived. Revenko boarded the chopper which lifted off and he quickly pointed out the large boar. When the pilot flushed it from the trees, it ran toward camp. The helicopter followed and veered in front of the bear to turn it. From the hovering chopper the special forces officer and the hunter shot it several times from a distance of thirty to forty feet.

As the helicopter touched down, the bear stood up and ran full speed toward the forest, resulting in immediate chase. The chopper quickly swept over the bear, the special forces officer fired and knocked the bear down. They landed and the hunter stepped out and shot the bear a final time. (Source: We Alaskans 10/13/1996, Copyright *Anchorage Daily News*, "The Last Days of Michio Hoshino," By George Bryson)

SENSATIONALISM

Many events are sensational—amazing, unbelievable, stunning. The event and the facts are sensational. When the sensational event is exploited or exaggerated, sensationalism results. The difference between sensational and SENSATIONALISM is that one indicates unbelievably amazing while the other represents EXTREME PRESENTATION.

When a person is attacked by a bear and the event is reported in the media, the coverage is nearly always labeled sensationalism. Just because someone writes about a bear attack does not relegate the story to sensationalism. Sensationalism should be determined by the context of the story. There is no ethical reason to exploit a bear mauling. However it is important to discuss the event in an effort to inform others in hopes of curbing a repeat of a mauling and to avoid similar encounters.

Stating the facts is NOT sensationalism. Describing injuries to depict the awesome powers of a bear's repertoire of weapons is NOT sensationalism. Enumerating the quantity of stitches to demonstrate the extent of injury and the need to reduce the same result for another adventurer is NOT sensationalism.

Sensationalism is exploiting a person, his experience or his story. Sensationalism is overreaching ethical body language at the expense of the bear(s) or the person(s). All too often the vivid portrayal of a bear mauling IS sensational because the explicit graphics are the focal point of the piece.

One author stated, "…exaggerated publicity about the ferociousness of bears will result in a prejudice against bears, casting them as ruthless killers." (Pg. 139, *Bear vs. Man*, Garfield)

"Exaggerated publicity" may be the same as sensationalism, and could prejudice people against bears. However if you detail the facts, the facts remain. If a bear slightly injures a person and is factually presented in media, the bear slightly injured someone. If a bear rips someone's face off, that doesn't make the bear a ruthless killer.

Some people accuse my books of sensationalizing bear attacks. One Internet site owner wrote me that he thought my book covers were too sensational therefore he chose not to market my books. What about the content of the book? Can you judge a book by its cover? (besides, when it comes to covers and formatting, most publishers do not allow a whole lot of input from authors).

Out of respect and to avoid sensationalizing the story, I have striven to minimize graphic depictions in order to lessen pain to the victim and/or his family. I have purposely omitted materials that were an infringement upon the victim or the victim's family. I have gratefully declined to incorporate pictures that might be offensive.

My recommendation to the reader is to read the book, collect the information that is most effective and incorporate it into practice for personal safety. Focus on the message, not the messenger.

Furthermore, if you're reading this book in order to avoid injury from a bear, because there's so much information, I suggest you highlight, note or underline what is relevant to your needs...that will allow you to condense-collect the most useful information for yourself.

PATTI REED MCCONNEL (from Predatory chapter)

Little did I know when I interviewed Will Atkinson about his Liard Hot Springs fist fight with a black bear (*Some Bears Kill*), that I'd be writing about other Liard bear encounters.

Following a horrific bear attack at Liard, my initial efforts to interview participants to this event resulted in locating a single article. A reference librarian at Loussac Library in Anchorage kindly spent several minutes looking for the *Reader's Digest* article from April 1999 involving this incident and emailed the following: "Thank goodness the Americans had a gun," by Derek De Cloet, Alberta Report/ Newsmagazine; Western Report, 09/01/97, Vol. 24 Issue 38, p25; 2. Periodical Writers Assoc. of Canada, Victoria Chapter, http://www. islandnet.com/pwacvic/hancoc04. html.

I re-wrote the story from that article and, wanting to provide more salient information, I Googled Duane Eggebroten, Lynn Hancock and Ingrid Bailey. Both Lynn and Ingrid responded with emails. Until then I was unaware of Lynn's *Reader's Digest* story "Rogue Bear on the Rampage." My failed efforts to contact Duane Eggebroten reminded and saddened me that some people actually said, "the bear should have lived."

Although I've listed my source for this event, there may be inaccuracies since I was unable to interview participants. The known facts include the date, venue and a black bear is attacking four people and killing two. After I wrote the following story, I learned it was a fabrication and a prime example of sensationalism.

Liard Hot Springs Provincial Park, 196 miles north of Fort Nelson, British Columbia at Mile 497 on the Alaska Highway, encompasses several heavily wooded acres and consists of two lodges with visitor accommodations (fuel and some rooms), 25 RV sites, 53 camp sites, picnic tables, toilets, drinking water and two hot pools—Alpha and

Beta—whose temperatures stay between 105-110 year around. Wooden decks partially surround each pool and each boasts its own changing room close to the water.

From the parking lot a boardwalk traverses a few feet above the ground where the visitor first encounters Alpha pool. Since the Beta pool involves a longer walk of perhaps a half mile, fewer people sample its waters. Between the two pools is a side trip to the Hanging Gardens, a series of terraces with lush vegetation.

When Patti Reed McConnell, her son and daughter stopped at Liard Hot Springs en route from Paris, Texas, to Anchorage, Alaska, how could she have known what awaited them that fateful August 14, 1997? After parking, she and her two children—Kelly, 13, and Kristen, 7—headed up the boardwalk toward the refreshing pools.

Dozens of people were at the site that day and included Fort Nelson trucker Ray Kitchen; naturalist and author Lyn Hancock; Frank Hedingham; California firefighter Ingrid Bailey; Calgary, Alberta college student Arie-Jan van Velden and Duane Eggebroten of Anchorage, Alaska.

After some time in the Alpha pool Patti and her children got out. Having made friends with another family the two families continued on the boardwalk to view the rest of the park.

After leaving the Beta pool the group headed back toward the parking lot. When they reached the boardwalk to the Hanging Gardens, Kristen continued with the other family who planned to eat lunch. Still clad in swimming attire, Patti and Kelly walked to the first viewing platform of the Hanging Gardens.

In a short time mother and son decided to return to the parking lot for lunch, Patty in the lead. They spotted a black bear half dozen yards distant beneath the boardwalk sitting on its haunches and chewing on a branch. The bear woofed when it saw them. They planned to ease past it and Kelly suggested that they play dead if the bear approached.

As they tried to pass the animal, it woofed again and jumped onto the boardwalk knocking Patti off her feet. It bit into her chest, picked her up in its jaws and began shaking her from side to side. Her son intervened, yelling for her to "play dead." Wanting badly to protect his mother, Kelly kicked the bear in the head once. His efforts had no effect on the animal and it continued mauling his mother. Within seconds the brute had punctured Patti's lungs and other internal organs in its savage attack and she lay on the boardwalk bleeding profusely and mortally wounded.

Continuously yelling for help, Kelly grabbed a stick and attacked the bear with it, hitting it on the nose and drawing blood. It backed off

363

then leaped at him, raking him with its claws before knocking him down. The animal pinned him to the boardwalk with a front paw and bit the back of his neck several times. It picked him up by the chest in its mouth and shook him, smacking his head against the handrail then tossing him aside. Kelly attempted to crawl to his motionless mother but the bear tore chunks of flesh from his body.

Most of those enjoying the park's hot spring pools ran away, but a few brave souls arrived to help. One of those was Ray Kitchen who had brought his 11-year-old daughter Joline and her friend Sarah to the springs for a swim. When he heard female screams, the 57-year old veteran hunter lunged toward the sounds, in the direction of the Hanging Garden area. Numerous others followed him.

As Kitchen neared the mayhem, he picked up a limb and slammed it against the handrail and boardwalk in an effort to deter the bear's assault on Kelly. He yelled and raced toward the sounds. Then it bit Kelly's neck and twisted its head and Kelly heard bones crunch before he lost consciousness.

Kitchen raced onward, up some wooden steps and stopped at the sight of a large bear astraddle of a boy next to a non-moving woman, covered in blood. Yelling for help, Ray picked up a large stick and stabbed the bear in the side with it. That got its attention. But after a momentary pause, it lunged for Ray, its impact toppling man and bear from the boardwalk five feet to the ground. The bear grabbed Ray by the abdomen in its jaws and tossed him violently. Wearing only swim trunks, Ray scrambled on his knees toward a tree and covered his head with his hands. It was all for naught. The killer bear bit his neck, tearing the carotid artery before twisting its head and breaking Ray's neck. The brute then spun around, sat on his chest and head while ripping chunks of flesh from his groin and right thigh and ingesting them.

Relaxing near the lower pool, Frank Hedingham heard shouts and assumed kids were being kids until he distinguished "Bear! Get a gun!" He immediately sprinted in the direction of the screams.

By now people in the area had heard the disturbing cries for help. One of those was Ingrid Bailey, a smokejumper/paramedic from Felton, California. Her friend Brad Westervelt was with her. She knew bears and did not fear them. She, Westervelt and Hedingham converged on the melee, gathering weapons in the form of sticks and wood chunks as they ran.

The disturbing view of two bodies on the walkway greeted them as they reached the mauling scene. More disturbing was the sight of Kitchen on the ground clinging to life, the bear mercilessly ripping at him.

Several dozen people stood aghast, yelling and throwing objects at the bear. Ingrid screamed and stomped on the boardwalk while smacking the railing with a stick, periodically chucking wood at the bear. Her efforts were useless.

Her companions grabbed a chunk of tree and when they moved it into place Ingrid joined Hedingham and Westervelt, driving it against the bear. Another useless effort.

People wondered where a park ranger was and wished for a weapon that would stop the brute.

Westervelt released the tree trunk and sped off, informing those present that he was going after a ranger.

The bear bit Kitchen's neck and tossed him into the air. When he hit the ground, soaked in his own blood, he was dead.

People continued throwing rocks and towels at the bear until it retreated under the boardwalk.

Realizing that they could do nothing for the dead truck driver, Ingrid and Hedingham, Lyn Hancock's assistant from Vancouver Island, turned their attention to Kelly and his mother, in hopes of saving them. Blood covered the boardwalk where the McConnell's lay face down. Ingrid instructed several people to retrieve first aid equipment from the park headquarters.

Ingrid began CPR on Patti while Hedingham consoled Kelly, instructing him in breathing and telling him that they were doing all they could. He pulled a handkerchief from his coat to clean Kelly's worst wounds.

By then men arrived. One had a towel and helped Hedingham with the boy's wounds while another performed chest compressions on Patti while Ingrid breathed into her mouth.

Moments later the bear's head popped up next to Kelly and it tried to bite his arm but Ingrid pulled Kelly away and Frank delivered a shattering blow to the bear's nose with a kick. Frank grabbed a fallen 5-inch log and fought the bear off until it lost interest in him and wandered down a boardwalk towards another group of people.

When Hedingham turned his attention to Kelly, the lad was attempting to crawl to his mother. Hedingham knew of the need to get the McConnells to the hospital and stated that he was going for help. He reached the parking lot and he ran up to Dave Webb, a Fairbanks, Alaska businessman who had just pulled into the campground. With blood on his head Hedingham shouted, "You've got to do something. There's a bear up there!"

Webb rushed to his motor home, grabbed two rifles—a .223 Remington and a .30-30 Winchester—and asked Hegingham if he knew how to use a rifle.

Bystander Duane Eggebroten stated that he could manage a .30-30. They loaded the rifles and sped to the attack site.

As the bear retreated toward the main boardwalk, someone ran toward the Alpha pool screaming "Run for your life!"

Arie-Jan van Velden, a 28-year old Calgary, Alberta citizen, had rested in the Beta Pool with several others when they heard screaming before a lady stopped to warn them that a person was trying to scare a bear away. Unaware that two people were already mortally wounded, Arie and friends hopped from the pool and ran toward the melee to try to help the victims.

As they neared the action, someone shouted, "The bear is coming your way, run for your lives!"

They saw the bear and fled. Because his boots were not tied, Arie lost his balance and fell. At this point the black lowered its belly and head to the boardwalk and went into its cat-like stalking mode, approaching Arie who lay on his back.

When Arie was within its reach, the bear bit his legs. Arie kicked at it in self-defense. The bear repeated its "going for the neck" maneuver and chewed from his legs to his neck at which point man and beast tumbled from the boardwalk and onto the ground below. Even though Arie struggled to keep away from the bear below the boardwalk, the animal proved too strong and pulled him from beneath it. The bear then bit his back and shoulder briefly before returning to the neck of the defenseless man.

By now Duane Eggebroten arrived at the scene and heard low groans coming from below the boardwalk. The bear repeated the same maneuver it had on Ray Kitchen, spun around, sat on Arie's chest and head and began ripping at his pelvic area.

Eggebroten aimed carefully for the back of the bear's neck and fired. At the rifle's report, the bear sagged off its victim. Although confident that it was dead, Eggebroten fired twice more to be sure.

Moments later Hedingham arrived. Eggebroten stood guard as Patti, Kelly and Arie were evacuated to the lodge's helio pad on the other side of the highway. Kristen McConnell had arrived at the parking lot without knowing of her family's encounter with the bear. She watched as her brother and mother were taken through the parking area and noticed that her brother was conscious and breathing but her mother was unmoving as people administered CPR to her.

The 225 pound male black bear was devoid of distinguishing garbage dump marks such as a garbage odor, singed hair, cuts on its tongue or feet. Its stomach contained only natural foods. The only dump in the area had been closed two years previously. The beast had not been collared nor studied as it had all of its teeth and in all likelihood entered the park just prior to the attack.

Ironically, the Alaskan shooter was technically in violation of the B.C. Park Act. Outside of hunting season it is illegal to carry a firearm in a park; however, parks officers can authorize individuals to carry guns and it is not illegal to store a rifle in a vehicle. Royal Canadian Mounted Police officer Corporal Morrison stated, "If he hadn't done what he did, there quite likely would have been another death, and maybe more." Assistant deputy minister of Environment Lands and Parks Lynn Kennedy indicated that Parks officials do not intend to pursue charges. She said, "This man is a hero."

Over the years since the event and my original story, Ingrid Bailey kindly responded to my request for information. As you will read, most of my "information" was inaccurate.

Ingrid indicated she wanted to retain the copyright to her account… to which I heartily agree. After reading her comments on the event, I was reminded that the facts are often lost for miscellaneous reasons. I thanked her for correcting my mistakes. I think you'll agree that facts are of greater value than a "good story." AND that the writer (in this case I) is NOT always right. I am truly grateful and forever indebted to Ingrid for her candid input. Thank you, Ingrid for responding and for your following factual account.

Dear Larry-

I think of the incident at Liard as an excellent opportunity to study both human and bear behavior. If the story hasn't jelled for you, it's probably because there is a lot of misinformation out there, most of it generated by Lyn Hancock and Frank Headingham, who were there that day, but didn't do anything to help the victims of the bear attack. Any first-hand knowledge that these two claim regarding the bear attack are complete flights of fancy, born of greed and vanity. More on that later.

I was on my way to Fairbanks to visit a dear friend, Craig LaBare, who worked as a firefighting Airtanker Pilot, with another friend, Brad Westervelt, along for the trip. Brad and I are both fans of the undeveloped hot springs on the east slope of the Sierra Nevada mountain range, so we were both a bit leery of these more developed pools at the most popular Canadian Provincial Park on the Alaska Highway. We walked in to take a look, and the "Beta" pool looked inviting, so we went back for our suits, stopping to take in the "Hanging Garden" area on the way.

As we made our way back to the springs, we started hearing talk of a bear attack from the folks urgently leaving the area. I picked up my pace, glancing back to confirm that Brad was right behind me. As we approached the Hanging Garden, I started gathering sticks and chunks of wood to use as weapons. The paths in this park are on boardwalks over muskeg, and have warm water hidden between and below large clumps of bog plants. We could see two injured people, a woman and a boy, laid out on the boardwalk and a third off the edge, a man leaning up against the butt of a tree, covering his face and neck, but no longer able to fight the bear. I screamed angrily "Bear! Bear!," smacked the railing with a stick and threw what I had gathered, taking care to miss the man, but the bear ignored my efforts.

I then helped Brad and another mystery man who had just arrived, (who was too short to have been Frank Headingham), to maneuver a slim but wolfy spuce tree over the railing. We did our best to jab the bear in the head with the cumbersome tree, to no effect. Brad and I quickly conferred, and agreed that a gun was necessary and that he should be the person to go after one, since I had first aid training to help the others. Brad left for the parking lot.

As the situation grew more desperate, I sized up the other rescuer, but decided that he was too small and too old to suggest that we try to jump the bear together. Then, the bear took the man, who was prone on the ground now, by the neck lifting his head and shoulders up off the ground, and shook his head. The man fell back with fatal injuries. That was enough for the other rescuer. He shook his hands in front of his face, mumbled something I couldn't understand, and left.

I was briefly alone when I lost hope for the man and began CPR on the woman, while the bear began to eat the man 15 feet away. Fairly quickly, other rescuers began to arrive, and I coached them in CPR and how to treat the boy's sucking chest wounds. As we were working, someone said, "Here comes the bear!" I looked up to see the bear's nose inches from the woman's feet, which were hanging 10 or 12 inches off of the edge of the boardwalk. I scooped her up under her arms and pulled her onto the walkway, while I roared my best roar at the bear. The bear took off through the woods, I think because by then, we were a group of five of six. Strength in numbers, people. Stick together!

The bear then caught up with a group of college students who foolishly ran. One of the students slipped and fell on the boardwalk, which was wet with light rain, and became the bear's fourth victim. I never saw this person or the bear again.

Brad ran to the parking lot where he found a man with a hunting rifle. The gun owner briefly claimed to have shot the bear, but there is photographic evidence that he handed his gun over to a more experienced Alaskan hunter who shot the bear. I remember hearing the first shot and yelling, "Shoot him again." The delay before the second shot was because the bear was attacking the student when it was killed.

No one from the Provincial Park ever showed up to help. I sent people to the springs to look for medical equipment and a backboard so we could carry the victims to where the helicopter lands while we continued CPR. When Brad returned, I asked him to go back to the parking lot for my first aid kit. It was after this point that Lyn Hancock arrived with Frank Headingham in tow, frantically instructing him to photograph poor Mr. Kitchen. This was their only contribution that day. I yelled at them to "Get out of here!", and continued doing CPR.

It took a long time for people to return with a disassembled bike rack to use as a stretcher. I sent the boy out to the parking lot first, where a Basic Life Support (BLS) equipped ambulance had arrived. We used a pickup truck to transport the woman to the field across the highway where the helispot is. We had achieved our goal but too much time had passed. I asked the Canadians what the law is there regarding discontinuing life saving efforts. Then, two hours after I had initiated CPR, the first of two helicopters arrived and, without assessing the patient, told us we could stop.

A young man who worked for the park concessionaire appeared and asked me and Brad to give statements. This person informed us that a Royal Canadian Mounted Police officer would arrive the next day and relayed a request that we remain in the area.

I've heard, but not personally confirmed, that after the attack, Lyn Hancock and Frank Headingham visited several Mounty offices under the guise of seeking Critical Incident Stress Debriefing, where they gleaned information and inserted themselves into the event. Hancock managed to acquire a copy of the official report that she promised she would send me, but never did. They used me, too, as they did their research.

Hancock called me at my home in the Santa Cruz Mountains not too long after the attack, told me that she was there that day, that she had someone with her that I would want to talk to, and she put Headingham on the line. He proceeded to butter me up, telling me how very brave I was that day, that he saw me running toward the commotion, and that he was "damned if he was going to let a woman take the bear on alone." I should have called him on it right then and there, because I checked and saw Brad right behind me, but I wasn't as suspicious a person then as I am now, and I hadn't looked that hard at the third helper to arrive. Hancock said that she was an author, and planning to write about the incident, and asked if they could come for a visit.

At my home, they asked a lot of questions without offering much in return except a few photos. Hancock asked me to draw a map of the walkways. My map wasn't very good. Hancock remarked to Headingham, "See Frank. No one will remember." I remember well, that this comment struck me as very strange at the time. When "Rogue Bear on a Rampage" came out, I scarcely recognized the story. When I saw Hancock in Quebec City when we received our "Bravery Decorations" from the Governor General of Canada, she very apologetically claimed that the *Reader's Digest* editors had rewritten the facts.

After the story took on a life of its own, Headingham's family initially sought to distance themselves. It seems that Headingham had a long history as a hustler and charlatan. It was only at Hancock's post-mortem insistence, that they came to believe that their father had finally done the right thing. Now, I am left in the uncomfortable position of calling a dead man a liar. It bothers me that Hancock's well publicized, grossly inaccurate version of this event seems to be what has gone down in history.

Brad and I continued on our trip to Alaska without seeking recognition. Hancock and Headingham were more than happy to fill the vacuum. I regret that I didn't turn them in for filing false police reports as soon as I figured out what they were up to. Now the statute of limitations makes that impossible. Hancock even had the temerity to suggest that the stress of what Headingham had witnessed at Liard had likely hastened his death from a heart condition. Feel free to forward this email to Hancock. She should know that the cat is out of the bag. I have a budget for an attorney to defend the truth about what did and didn't happen at Liard.

There are numerous events inconsistent with my experience in your narrative:

1. There were never several dozen people throwing things and yelling at the bear, just Brad and I and the mystery man, who wasn't there for long. The people who arrived later helped with the victims. They didn't try to fight the bear.

2. Bear never "threw him" (the man, Mr. Kitchen) "into the air." The bear grabbed the prone Mr. Kitchen by the neck, lifted his torso off of the ground and shook him, tearing his neck open.

3.   Kelly, the boy, and Patti, his mother, were never "covered in blood." I don't know about Mr. Kitchen, as I never looked at him again after I started CPR on Patti.

4.   Brad didn't suddenly "run off" after a Ranger. He went after a gun, after we discussed the need for one and how he might get it.

5.   Headingham never provided any medical assistance to Kelly. This is a complete lie and the most elaborate version I've heard yet, "instructing him in breathing" and cleaning Kelly's worst wounds with a handkerchief. 100% false.

6.   It was Patti that I pulled up onto the boardwalk, not Kelly. If you would like confirmation of this: when we were in Quebec City, Harvey Smerychynski, a retired Canadian military officer, told my father that this was the bravest act that he had ever witnessed.

7.   Frank didn't kick the bear. He wasn't even there.

8.   The McConnells were face up on the boardwalk, not face down.

9.   Kelly never tried to crawl towards his mother after we arrived. He stayed in the same place that we first found him, not saying much, struggling to breathe. I don't believe for a moment that Headingham was procured or the bear was shot. It also would have been impossible for Headingham to have both helped Kelly and obtained a gun in the distant parking lot.

10. I wouldn't go so far as to say that I was "unafraid" of a bear that had already attacked three people. It was painfully obvious that these people needed help. That was my motivation.

There are so many inaccuracies in "Rogue Bear on a Rampage." I'll just touch on a few:

1.   While I have served previously as a Smokejumper, at the time of the bear attack, I was employed as a municipal Firefighter for the city of Berkeley, California. I was an Emergency Medical Technician (EMT), not a Paramedic. I've never claimed to be a Paramedic. This is another of Lyn's inaccuracies/exaggerations. There is a big difference between an EMT and a Paramedic. Please don't perpetuate this.

2.   Headingham never kicked the bear or drove him away with a stick. He wasn't even there. Headingham and Hancock arrived after the bear had left the area. Complete B.S. I suspect that they were at home listening to a police scanner when the bear attacked.

371

3.   I certainly never said "What we really need are towels to act as compresses and two more pairs of hands for CPR." All Hancock fabrications. I can only guess that her version of Kelly's efforts on his Mom's behalf before Brad and I arrived, are just as inaccurate as everything else she's put out there.

Feel free to contact me further if you have more questions. I don't have a problem talking about what happened. One witnesses a lot of tragedies working as a Firefighter. I know that I did everything I could for Mr. Kitchen and the McConnells at Liard.

Sincerely,

Ingrid S. Bailey

(from the author: It is with humility and heartfelt gratitude that I accept Ingrid's candid comments, which go a long way in correcting my misinformation of the story. And, it is always wonderful to get the truth of an event…not sensational speculation.).

(Author aside on black bears: In November 2017 I received digital manuscripts from Ted Gorsline, *Man-eating Black Bears*, which are forthcoming. He addresses the Patty Reed McConnel story using four sources—not the one I used, and Lyn's "Rampage" story. You'll want to read his outstanding books.)

I believe that in a park comprising but a few acres in size with a known bear population (which is a risk for human safety), why in the world isn't there a park ranger present/on duty with a means of protecting people? Had a ranger been within hailing distance armed with pepper spray, a taser or a firearm, probably two lives would have been saved and, in all probability, only one person mauled.

This incident begs the question, how can we be safe in parks?

What kind of advice can we give those in similar circumstances? How can you back away slowly from an animal that jumps onto your body? I love the "the attack will usually last less than two minutes." Kind of like saying, "While your nails are drying you can read a magazine." Or, "It's okay to play dead when a bear grabs you, it will probably only chew and rip into you for a couple of minutes." And how long did it take this animal to break two person's necks—under 2 minutes each, I'm sure.

I found it quite interesting reading about the governmental bureaucracy involved in management of Liard's bears and include the following from the 2000 Legislative Session: Parliament.

HANSARD (WWW.LEG.BC.CA/HANSARD/36TH4TH/H00613. HTM#16542), Official Report of DEBATES OF THE LEGISLATIVE ASSEMBLY, TUESDAY, JUNE 13, 2000, Afternoon Sitting, Volume 20, Number 11.

A. Sanders: ...Two years ago I asked the then minister for a copy of a report on the review of the black bear incident at Liard Hot Springs. I have yet to receive that report. Has that report been done, and if so, may I have a copy of it?

Hon. J. Sawicki: I'm advised that the coroner's report about that incident did actually come out long before I was minister. If the member didn't get a copy of that report as was promised, then we will make sure that you promptly receive one.

A. Sanders: I did get a copy of the coroner's report. I had wondered whether there had been an internal investigation following the coroner's report to look at the problems that have been cited with respect to the park—the access to emergency supplies and other things—and whether there had been some internal document to look at that for the future, to make sure that we didn't see such an incident again.

Hon. J. Sawicki: There's no report that would have come out of our ministry on this. But clearly anytime a tragedy like this happens within a provincial park, our ministry does try to analyze if there is anything that could have been done to minimize that impact.

As the hon. member knows, many of our parks. . . . If they were not established for habitat and wildlife values primarily, they certainly have them. While British Columbians recreate within provincial parks and we always try hard to educate people about wildlife and minimize that point of conflict, when a tragedy like this happens, one cannot guarantee that any number of reports would have avoided it.

A. Sanders: I don't want to go all the way back through that, but there were a number of very good, solid recommendations put forward by some of the people who had been at Liard Hot Springs. There were suggestions—for example, an alternate route down, other than where the bear was killing people on the causeway, to be instituted so that there was an alternate escape route. Those things were part of what I was anticipating might occur with internal reflection of that tragedy.

Author: interpretation of the last paragraph re: the Liard Hot Springs bear management is that the animals have more value than people—leave the bears there, leave them alone, just provide an escape route for people that the bears attack!

After reading numerous posts on the World Wide Web, I'm wondering if ANY changes have been implemented in the Liard Hot Springs facility. One site I read purported that the year after Patti McConnell's fatal encounter, her mother visited the hot springs and said there were as many bears as ever. (Source: Persistent link to this record: http://search.epnet.com/login.aspx?direct=true&db=f5h&an=9709300029)

GUV'MENT AGENCIES

One of my major concerns regards the value outdoor users pose to the agencies that control outdoor use. Many federal and state agencies seem to place the bear's future above that of humans (and within the last few decades, private property versus BLM takeover). People should have the right to carry legal, personal protection of their choice into the forest. Because government agencies establish rules that have proved both injurious and fatal for park visitors, these rules should be seriously considered, altered and/or disobeyed.

TRIED BY TWELVE

It is paramount that the woods traveler have the option of returning unharmed and a choice of weapons. Is it safer to go into the woods with bear bells and/or pepper spray (or another deterrent); or is it safer to do so with a firearm?

When government agencies forbid the carrying of firearms into national parks and other venues, the backwoods traveler has at least three options: 1) obey the law, 2) break the law or 3) get the law changed.

While I researched this book and for years previous, it was illegal to carry a firearm in America's national parks. The bulk of my reporting addressed government restrictions of U.S. citizens to protect themselves in parks. The Canadian government disallows firearms carry except during hunting season or unless the weapons carrier pursued government paperwork.

While surfing the Internet December 18, 2007, I noted www.helenair. com which carried a piece by Noelle Straub, "Senators want changes in national park gun restrictions." Noelle states that a number of U.S. Senators are "pushing to allow gun owners to carry their firearms into all national parks and wildlife refuges." Forty-seven senators signed the letter led by Sen. Mike Crapo, Idaho Republican. One can spend hours perusing internet sites and/or blogs speaking for and against the need for packing firearms in proximity with dangerous critters, or the opposite… those who see no need to arm people.

Voila! As of February 2010, the U.S. Congress passed a weapons bill. Beginning the last Monday of February 2010, firearms WILL BE PERMITTED in all U.S. national parks. "Visitors now can pack heat in any national park from Gates of the Arctic to Everglades, provided they comply with the firearms laws of the park's home state, according to the new law that was passed…" The law passed Congress in May and reverses 94 years of National Park Service policy. (NEWS FLASH—3/1/2010

"Guns are now permitted –but not necessarily welcomed—in national parks," articles.latimes.com, February 22, 2010, by Julie Cart.)

Before entering bear country choose to defend yourself or to be at the mercy of another. In an area where firearms are disallowed, you can choose to be tried by twelve for breaking the law, or carried by six—in your coffin—for being killed by a bear. I'm in favor of twelve vs. six. Every time! It's your choice.

Granted, there are those who are unfamiliar with firearms and/or their proper usage. That in itself should send a message to them about self-education on the benefits of carrying a firearm, or at least learning about firearms (or an equally strong deterrent) as a safety factor if approached by a "bad guy."

UNARMED VICTIM

Ben East told about three fishermen who were attacked by a grizzly in Alberta's Jasper National Park in 1968 ("Death Came Running," *Danger*). One of the men, Steve Rose, commented about their lack of a firearm:

"I can understand officials, either in this country or Canada, not wanting tourists running around the national parks with guns. But a sidearm would have saved us. Even with a .22 I could have killed the bear when she had me by the leg in the tree or was chewing my back.

"I feel strongly that side arms should be allowed in the back country or certain parks for the sake of safety. The wardens in Jasper carry rifles for their own protection. Why should visitors be denied the same right? A man is entitled to protect his life, in a national park as well as anywhere else…"At the very least, I believe licensed guides should be allowed to carry guns in such parks, to protect the members of the party they are guiding. "I can make one guarantee. Any time I go into grizzly country from now on I'll have a short-barreled .44 Magnum along, laws or no laws." (Pg. 200)

NIGHT OF THE GRIZZLIES

Because the U.S. Park Service did not permit visitors to carry firearms within the boundaries of specific parks prior to 2010, many people died because they had either no personal protection or it was limited by park regulations. The classic case in point is the tragic story of two college girls that my friend Jack Olsen told so well in his unforgettable *Night of the Grizzlies*, a chilling and scathing exposé about two young ladies who died unnecessarily in Glacier National Park on the same night several miles apart, the victims of two grizzly bears. Both young women were ripped from their sleeping bags and dragged into the night.

One of these bear culprits spent an entire summer scaring and harassing people in or near camp grounds before she ultimately dragged a helpless young lady to her death. The other bear was one of half dozen that fed regularly at the trash pit of one of the park's chalets. In both cases the bears were conditioned by man and allowed to run their turf without so much as a threat of harm from man to either of these animals. These bears were unquestionably habituated to man—along with the carcass defending bear, the habituated bear represents one of the most dangerous situations.

The women's tragic deaths could have been prevented but for two major factors:

First, the National Park Service did little, if anything, to prevent the deaths of these women. On the contrary they were party to the deaths in that one bear was allowed free license for the summer to do whatever it wanted.

Second, the understanding or knowledge of bears, their behavior and nature by would-be rescuers was either non-existent or seriously mistaken. Had the panicked group at Granite Park Chalet known that no bear has ever attacked a group of more than five people (excepting a few on record), they could have rumbled after the bear with their fire, chanting, safe in numbers and found the bear's victim within a half hour of her disappearance instead of waiting two hours before finding her— grasping to the thread of life which was later extinguished by her injuries and blood loss.

The following quotes from *Night of the Grizzlies* highlight the problem that summer and the National Park Service's position:

"I told him that they should destroy that bear, because it was too bold and the fear of man had gone from it. I said if you don't, the federal government is liable to have one of the darndest lawsuits that they ever had if this bear kills...I told him I thought the park spends too much time thinking about the preservation of the species and to hell with the preservation of the people." (Pg. 38, A 40-year visitor to the park and critic of their policies, Jim Hindle's advice went unheeded by the park people.)

"The rules of the National Park Service specify clearly that such a bear must be shot, but somehow the skinny animal managed to remain alive through June and July." (Pg. 46)

"A ranger...said that the bear had been bothering people all summer and that he was planning to do something about it...A few days later an official report appeared in park records. It read…No action taken." (Pg. 49, "no action taken" regarding problem bears was quoted at least three times in the book—Pp. 38, 49, 170)

"The park people are so dedicated to preserving the wildlife that they aren't even protecting the people. Why, a bear could have gone berserk and massacred everyone there!" (Pg. 69)

"…rangers exterminated a few bears that had lost their fear of man." (Pg. 98)

"The order had been out for a month to shoot the animal…Landa could not rid himself of the feeling that the order to kill the bear was merely a formality that park officialdom hoped would not be carried out." (Pg. 130)

"High park officials would deny that so much as a single scrap of food was being put out for wild animals anywhere in the park." (Pg. 60)

"'Oh, they come to eat the garbage that we put out,' the other young girl replied." (Pg. 98, She was an employee at the chalet which dumped garbage each night. The garbage subsequently attracted several bears to the site.)

MISINFORMATION/LACK OF CORRECT BEAR KNOWLEDGE

"They had all been informed over and over that wild bears in this wild park could be counted upon to run from humans…" (Pg. 44, hiker-campers)

"…the boy and his family had listened to an orientation lecture by a park ranger, and about all Paul remembered from the talk was the information that a grizzly will not attack you if you do not attack it, and if you see one, just climb a tree." (Pg. 93) "If there was one thing that was drummed into us, it was that bears wouldn't bother us if we didn't bother them. And we certainly weren't going to bother them!" (Pg. 95)

Tom Hamilton choked back a rising sense of panic and moved just behind Bunney, expecting the bear to come charging out of the brush at any second and knock them all to the ground before the ranger could get off a shot." (Pg. 122, group of several would-be rescuers)

"…Walton remembers saying, '…There could be fifty of us going down there, and the bear could gobble us all up.'" (Pg. 113)

"Grizzlies had never killed in the park: therefore they never would kill in the park." (Pg. 171)

BEN EAST

When Ben East, writing for *Outdoor Life*, contacted park officials, "Park officials were completely uncooperative, probably because they faced the almost certain likelihood of costly damage suits brought by the families of the victims. Park personnel clammed up, and in a telephone interview the superintendent of Glacier offered me the astonishing excuse that lightning, which had started several fires in the park that evening, had enraged the bears and caused them to attack. I was told later that his superiors in Washington complimented him for the originality of that ridiculous alibi. Actually, both bears were park bums, used to feeding on garbage or scraps and lacking all normal fear of humans." (Pg. 138)

In 1975 I addressed the search for Alan Lee Precup in *Alaska Bear Tales*. My friend Bob Brown of the Alaska State Troopers Fish and Game division showed me a picture of his remains that I have refused to use in any of my books. During Precup's absence four Seattle area hikers were within shouting distance of his remains at Thunder Bay in Glacier Bay, Alaska. While playing cat and mouse with a coastal brown bear they tried a number of means of getting away from him. They were faced with the dilemma of having virtually nothing but what lay on the ground for defense since the Park Service did not allow the carrying of a firearm (even though the Forest Service topography map that they had advised firearms as a weapon in the wilderness)—but Forest Service employees carry firearms!

(Author: for years government agency personnel carried .375 Magnum rifles with shortened barrels; and, yes, the D-2 land proposal added more park lands in Alaska)

PARK SERVICE SUED

Law suits against government agencies continue. *Field and Stream* carried "Park Sued Over Bear Attack" by Don "Rouanzion in October 2001, on page 18 which I've copied verbatim:

"The Great Smoky Mountains National Park has been sued by the family of a woman killed there last year by a female black bear and her cub. The attorney who filed the $3.5 million suit claims to have proof that park officials knew of the aggressive nature of the female bear before the attack occurred on May 21, 2000, and yet took no action to warn or protect their visitors from being mauled. The attorney added that there is some doubt that park rangers acted quickly enough to kill the bears after they arrived and found the bears standing over the victim, Glenda Ann Bradley, a schoolteacher from nearby Cosby, Tennessee.

"Park Service officials in Gatlinburg have admitted to receiving an aggressive bear report from at least one park visitor; however, they claim the report wasn't received until after the attack occurred.

"Sidney Gilreath, the attorney who filed the lawsuit, countered that eight to ten park visitors filed reports about aggressive bears up to two weeks before Bradley was mauled."

SOLUTION

It is expedient that park providers have competent people in the field, those who have been trained and can carry the responsibility of prompt, result-getting action. Training needs to be conducted in order for an expeditious rescue.

The Park needs to provide necessary lights and medical supplies for such emergencies. A firearm must be available at ranger facilities and park accommodations (Had a firearm been available at Granite Park Chalet, more than likely a life would have been saved). Park rangers in areas with lots of bears—like Liard Hot Springs in British Columbia, where the bulk of the people are within a few acres—should be required to have firearms on site or a ranger packing a bear stopper (the four people mauled—2 killed in 1997 would likely have been reduced to 1 or 2 mauled, 0 killed if an armed ranger or guard were present). (Author note: As of July 2015, the Hanging Gardens and boardwalk at Liard Hot Springs were closed to significant bear activity)

Park visitors should be allowed to carry a firearm even if it requires passing a qualifying firearms test. Hikers must be given the choice of carrying a bear-stopper weapon that will immobilize an attacking bear.

The removal of a problem-causing bear is paramount.

Many people defend saving the noble silver-tip grizzly, but they refuse to raise a single finger in defense of their co-humans who visit bear country…as if the person is the trespasser in the bear's domain and deserves injury or death by the big bears as trespassers. Some say that the best way to avoid injury is to stay out of bear country.

And how many people care not a wit regarding the taking of an innocent life via abortion but clamor to the rooftop at the death of a bear!

CRAIGHEAD

Beginning in 1959 Frank and John Craighead conducted exhaustive studies on park grizzlies in Yellowstone National Park. Their statistics indicated that closing the garbage dumps would result in more human-bear conflict and in time their fears were realized. They agreed that the dumps should be closed, but not in the one to two year time frame targeted by the parks. They wanted the dumps closed over a period of years that would enable the bears to wean themselves away from people garbage.

In Yellowstone a camper was killed June 25, 1972. The 25-year-old man Harry Walker and a friend Phillip Bradberry camped in the Old Faithful area. While returning with the aid of a flashlight around midnight, Walker was attacked by a "large, toothless grizzly" that "hauled him off and crushed his larynx, not even breaking the skin. Thirty-six hours later the suspect bear was caught in a snare and shot.

"Walker's death is the more tragic in that it might perhaps have been avoided had park personnel been more diligent in investigating an incident that had occurred nearly two years earlier." (*Track of the Grizzly* by Craighead, Pg. 212)

On September 16, 1970, Eugene, Oregon, resident Dan Bean reported to park officials at Old Faithful station that an abandoned camp had been ransacked by a bear on the Firehole River, half-mile south of the new highway bridge. The camper never returned.

As a result of a lawsuit in which the National Park Service was sued for negligence by the estate of Harry Walker in Los Angeles in 1975, Frank Craighead accessed the records at the Federal District Court. "No evidence in the logs suggested that any attempt was made to locate relatives of the victim, if there was one. I found no evidence that any warnings were issued to the public that there had been a man-grizzly incident perhaps resulting in a fatality. The Park Service's handling of this situation so disturbed Ranger Jerry Schroeder that when an opportunity arose, on October 10, 1972, he introduced himself and told me about it. In doing so he knowingly risked his job and perhaps future employment. His job was 'eliminated' the following year, he claimed later, and he left the park...

"...the overall reaction of the Park Service to the attack left much to be desired. A key function of this government agency is to provide the public with professional services in the areas under its jurisdiction, including information affecting visitor safety. In failing to remove to a safe distance from a heavily visited area a bear that ought to have been presumed hazardous, and in neglecting to alert visitors to the presence of such a bear or bears in the vicinity, the Park Service certainly did not perform the function. Now, rather than immediately taking steps to prevent further incidents and to alert the public, the agency first undertook to protect its own image. Denying the possibility of its own negligence, the Park Service attempted to shift the blame onto the Walker and Bradberry boys, giving out the impression that they had a dirty camp and were camping illegally, thus inviting a confrontation with a bear. Careful investigation in federal court later showed that the boys were not at fault, that they in fact camped well and conducted themselves in a manner above reproach. One of Judge Andrew Hauk's findings of fact was that 'the decedent was not contributorily negligent, and did not directly or indirectly contribute to the cause of his own death.'

"Judge Hauk...found the Park Service negligent in that it willfully and intentionally failed to provide warnings and place signs of danger from grizzlies, and that it was negligent to discontinue radio and visual monitoring of bears at the time it undertook the extra hazard of closing down the garbage dumps. He found that the defendant (Park Service) had failed to exercise due care toward decedent in five respects, and concluded: 'As a sole, direct, and proximate result of each of the negligent acts and omissions of defendant, taken individually and together, including and as a direct and proximate result of the activity of abrupt closing of garbage dumps, and as a direct and proximate result of defendant's failure to avert an attack on the decedent by prudent control action on the grizzly bear which killed decedent, and as a direct and proximate result of the failure of the defendant and its employees to warn decedent of danger known to them but unknown to him, to wit, the danger of grizzly bears in Yellowstone National Park, and particularly in the Old Faithful Subdistrict and Old Faithful Village area of Yellowstone National Park, Harry Eugene Walker's death was caused.'" (*Track of the Grizzly*, Pg. 214)

LEGALLY OR ILLEGALLY?

Over forty years ago my friend Jay Massey wrote a piece in the *Anchorage Times* entitled "On Bears, Bearing Arms And Breaking Laws," Saturday, October 2, 1976. I've included it below in its entirety:

If you were hiking through rattlesnake country, would you carry a snakebite kit? If you were swimming in shark-infested waters, wouldn't you like to have a spear gun with you for protection? Let's suppose that you, like many other Alaskans, often camp out in country inhabited by bears. Do you carry a gun? If you're one who doesn't, chances are you've never had any trouble with them.

Many Alaskans, however, have had bear trouble. Some who have been killed or mauled could have been helped by a gun.

The problem is that you can't carry a gun everywhere there are bears in Alaska. Federal law prohibits carrying guns in our national parks such as McKinley, Katmai and Glacier Bay. It was in Glacier Bay National Park where the hiker from Illinois was recently killed and eaten by a bear. Another party was harassed for several hours in the same area by a bear, believed to be the same man-eater.

I hate to encourage people to break the law. But there are times when breaking the law may be preferable to another alternative.

One might argue that a person's chances of being mauled or killed by a bear in Alaska are remote. But are they really? I have two friends who have been mauled, and I know of at least a dozen other maulings and killings during the past few years. Your chances of being attacked may be only one in a thousand, but those odds are small consolation while you're being chewed on by a grizzly or even a black bear.

Park Service officials say firearms are prohibited in national parks in order to protect bears from humans. Some have even stated that a person is actually safer without a gun because, without it, he is not so quick to overreact to a potentially dangerous situation. Many bears will "false charge" and stop a few yards away from the intruder without actually attacking.

The no-gun-is-safer argument makes one valid point: many people are ignorant of the true power of a gun, especially handguns. Some people have actually put themselves in danger by the indiscriminate use of firearms. But Al Johnson, a biologist who was attacked three years ago by a grizzly in McKinley National Park, says he could easily have killed the bear with a pistol as it attacked him.

The argument that guns are prohibited to protect bears is a weak one. During the past 12 years, thousands of people have visited the McNeil River State Game Sanctuary, one of the best places in the world to photograph brown bears. Most of these visitors carried guns, but during that time only two bears were shot in defense of life.

The McNeil River area is managed by the State of Alaska, not by the federal government. Many people feel that while Park Service regulations such as the no-guns rule may be necessary in national parks Outside, they do not apply to Alaska. Here, national parks are essentially wilderness areas, with few roads, no traffic congestion with people feeding bears, and no open dumps which cause bears to lose their natural fear of man. When a visitor is hiking through national park in Alaska, he is on his own. He cannot call on a park ranger for help; he has to rely on his own resources.

Frankly, I would not even consider camping out in prime bear country, national park included, without some sort of bear protection. But then, I have experienced the hair-curling thrill of being chased and treed by a bear. Some folks may like this "thrill", but once was enough for me.

I am not advocating that we all carry .375 Winchester Magnums. But I do feel that if National Park Service officials were less dogmatic and more sympathetic to the needs of Alaskan, they might allow some sort of limited range firearms. For example, the regulations might allow visitors to carry one shotgun with slugs or buckshot or one handgun for each party of visitors without endangering bear populations.

These bear-human problems are just developing. If Congress approves the D-2 proposal and we add several more national parks with an additional 40 or 50 million acres, we had better start looking for solutions.

FIREARMS IN NATIONAL PARKS

I say that I have a right to carry a firearm to defend myself from animals intent on doing me harm, whether they live in the pine clad forest or the asphalt jungle. Every man hiking into bear country has the same right. If national or state agency policies preclude citizens from carrying firearms in park jurisdiction, consider contacting your legislator at the national or state level to have those agencies' policies changed.

Since the parks became a national institution, something like 37 people have died to black bear attack. One of the most recent black attacks was in Tennessee in 2006 where a lady and her children were recreating and a bear assaulted the family. What are the chances that the lady would be alive today had she carried a .22 caliber pistol? Or some larger caliber weapon? And what are the chances that she would be alive had the park personnel removed the bear which had exhibited problematic behavior the previous couple of weeks?

Although I do not advocate the use of a pistol as adequate medicine to stop an adrenaline pumping brownie of the monster size, I venture to say that any number of smaller bears could and would be turned with a round or two from a pistol.

MORE GOVERNMENT LUNACY

June 22, 2007, Paul Harvey discussed a black bear incident in Georgia. It represents both an unusual means of killing a bear and the official's "punishment" of a camper. While former Marine Chris Everhart camped, a black bear snagged the family cooler and in the process of making off with the goods, Chris' 6-year-old son hucked a shovel at the 300-pound bruin. The shovel got the bear's attention and it turned toward the boy. Meanwhile Chris grabbed a chunk of firewood and hurled it at the approaching bear—protecting his son as any manly father would do. The wood hit the bear in the head and killed it, nevertheless Everhart was cited for not properly securing his campsite. (Source: "Ex-marine kills bear with log, gets ticketed," www.woodtv.com, Associated Press - June 22, 2007, HELEN, Ga.)

It baffles those with common sense that innocent people are being prosecuted. Why are they? The following might shed some light on the subject, "Getting mauled while going by the book," William P. Pendley, Nov. 19, 1998, *Voice of the Times, Anchorage Daily News*. I summarized the piece:

Montana rancher John Shuler heard a ruckus with his sheep and stepped outside with his rifle in September 1989. He discovered three grizzlies attacking his sheep and fired shots over them to scare them off. Turning toward his house he was surprised by a grizzly standing on its hind legs, pawing the air and roaring only 10-yards away. Taking time only to consider the consequences, he dropped the bruin and was accused by the U.S. Fish and Wildlife Service, charging him with violation of the Endangered Species Act. The FWS brought the charge despite the fact that the ESA contains a "self-defense" exception.

According to the agency, John should not have protected his property. And even worse, he should not have gone into his yard where his dog and he provoked the bear.

Excuse me! Since when is a man not allowed to protect his property or himself?

Answer: since the government agencies got too big for their britches! Many administrators of these agencies lack the common sense to address issues with realistic solutions.

For nearly nine years Shuler fought to clear his name and avoid the $7,000 fine the Fish and Wildlife Service sought. His legal fees would have been excessive had he been forced to pay them himself. Mountain States Legal Foundation supported Shuler or he would have had to come up with more than $225,000 for killing a bear that was attacking his livestock.

Because of this incident William Pendley, president of the Mountain States Legal Foundation in Denver, predicted that some person in the future "facing the most deadly killing machine in North America would think about what happened to John Shuler, would hesitate and would pay an awful price." And he was right.

About the time the smoke cleared for Shuler, nine years later, to the month, in neighboring Wyoming an elk hunter tried to move away from a sow grizzly charging from 25 yards. The hunter carried a high power rifle which he dropped, grabbed and emptied his can of pepper spray into the bear's face and got his butt kicked as a thank you. He used the pepper spray instead of his rifle because he said, "I didn't want to go to jail and lose my hunting privileges."

Who was it who said the government "is here to help"?

Dogs

Many "experts" recommend leaving fido at home, because the dog could easily become a "retriever"—bringing the bear back to the dog's best friend. I say, that's an arguable "absolute." Many a dog has saved his master. There are dogs that are capable of deterring a bear…of alerting the master, of chasing the bear away. Maybe you'd like to have a good bear dog, one that does not fear a bear…that will keep you posted as to the presence of wild animals.

It may benefit you to investigate the Karelian bear dogs. On the other hand… maybe not. In September 2002, a Karelian bear dog did little for its master, Larry Miller of Wasilla, Alaska, who was hunting with his wife Brinda. Larry, a veteran hunter and bear slayer, shot and wounded a grizzly near the Denali Highway and took up its track the next day, assuming from the blood trail and body parts that it was long since dead. After some time searching they reconsidered their situation and that's when their Russian bear dog roared back to them, closely pursued by the grizzly.

The bear knocked Larry down and he kicked at it while trying to release the safety on his .458 rifle. While the bear bit his leg, Larry shouted for Brinda to shoot the bear. She pumped three rounds from her .338 rifle into the beast from half dozen feet before it gave up the fight. The punishment that it took was amazing. (Injured grizzly attacks hunter, *Anchorage Daily News*, Peter Porco, September 14, 2002)

Another dog-bear had a different ending. When a grizzly made for his master, a dog named Shadow saved him. Don Mobley gathered firewood on a sandbar on the Nakochna River northwest of Skwentna, Alaska. His dog was in the bushes in the vicinity when Don discovered to his discomfort and dismay that the grizzly sow with a cub growled and charged the man who fled.

The sow was hot on his heels and closing within ten feet when his 3-year-old German Shepherd mix Shadow, bounded from the woods barking at the bear. Shadow chased the bear and her cub into the brush.

Mobley is convinced that his dog saved him. The Los Angeles chapter of the Society for the Prevention of Cruelty to Animals was impressed also as they awarded Shadow their National Hero Dog Award.

Travel, lodging and food was provided by Pedigree, the pet food company sponsoring the award. (Source: Dog who took on charging grizzly earns national heroism award, Shadow the German shepherd mix saved owner from a mauling, By LIZ RUSKIN, *Anchorage Daily News*, September 16, 2003)

Commenting on dogs (and Tanya De Groot's dog), Gary Shelton (*Bear Attacks II Myth & Reality*) states, "I've met many young women in B.C., like Tanya, who use dogs in the field when working. Most of these women work in forestry-related jobs. They all tell me that there is no way in hell they're going to be exposed to bears without their dogs along, no matter what policies a ministry or company may have regarding dog use." (Pg. 136)

After being attacked by a black bear and rescued by her dog Keela, Tanya De Groot of British Columbia told Gary Shelton, "I still pick mushrooms in the same area, but pack more protection than bear spray, and, of course, I always have my trusted Keela with me." (*Bear Attacks II Myth & Reality*), Pp. 135-136)

The *Anchorage Daily News* internet site (www.adn.com) carried a piece by Beth Bragg ("Jogger survives bear by seat of her pants"), October 27, 2007, stating some significant information for a person's minimizing injury inflicted by a bear. A brown bear sow interrupted Anchorage nurse Sarah Wallner's jog up Eagle River valley, biting her and departing. Sarah was fortunate in that her injuries were not life threatening, her husky-German Shepherd dog intercepted the bear which chased the bear. Paul Hanis arrived and helped Sarah. She did not carry her normal pepper spray because she thought the bears would be hibernating…but even then, she didn't think she would have had time to use it.

Before deciding about your dog in the woods, ascertain whether it might be helpful or harmful. It might be worth your while to consider other domestic animals as woods partners because of their heightened senses that could alert you of danger—animals such as horses, llamas, goats. A trusty pet might save your bacon.

CHAPTER 11
MISCELLANEOUS

From *Anchorage Daily News*, April 15, 2009 blog re: bear sightings
After reading about a man-bear encounter a couple of miles from our home October 2008, I looked up Dave Rand in the phone book, called and asked his wife if he had an encounter last fall with a brownie. She said she'd have him call me—he's working late preparatory to trip Outside. The following is his e mailed story:

I had a large, brown bear aggressively charge me near my home on Friday afternoon. I was mountain biking with my dog on Moen trail; Barley and I have had many run-ins with bears this year but this was very different.

We were going downhill on Moen Trail. This trail connects Goldenview just south of Bluebell with Potter Valley Drive near the bridge. We were going slow downhill and making lots of noise as this is a "bear-y" area and the trail was sloppy from all of the recent rain. Barley, a Goldendoodle, was out in front by about 20 feet and was wearing a bear-bell. I was yelling out so I wouldn't surprise a bear.

I was about ¾ of a mile down the trail when I heard a ruckus up ahead: grunting/growling and crunching branches. I was expecting an ornery moose that have been prevalent lately. What I got was a 1000 pound, angry, charging, brown-bear.

I was at a full stop and yelling when the bear came out of the alders roaring at me. I was straddling my bike going for my pepper spray that was strapped to my cross-bar. But the bear was literally in my face before I could get the spray out.

I didn't know if I should I punch it in the nose or continue to go for my pepper spray. Instead I did neither. I stood my ground and yelled at it for all I was worth. Which was quite easy to do since I was scared silly and I really couldn't go anywhere.

And just as quickly that it was in my face, it turned and ran off down the trail.

It all happened within seconds and inches.

Barley, who has chased off lots of black bears for me this summer, wasn't as effective against a big brown. He apparently had doubled-back around me; as the bear turned off and ran down the trail Barley came from behind me and gave a couple of half-hearted barks and slowly trotted after the bear.

And that was the end of it.

The interesting thing was that I didn't startle or surprise this bear. It heard me well before it saw me. Yet it still aggressively came at me. Rick Sinnott, the AF&G biologist thinks it was defending a moose kill which makes sense to me.

I don't know what the lesson is here. I think more than anything I was lucky. But I did hold my ground. I will however, practice going for my bear-spray and be quicker on the draw. I did get the spray out as soon as it turned away from me, but I decided not to spray it in the ass; it was already retreating.

Have that pepper spray readily available and practice your quick draw!

-Dave

An Alaskan brown bear hunt can be an adventure. Many have ended badly for the trophy, the hunter or both. Tim Hunt's represents one such hunt.

"MY ONE AND ONLY BEAR"

Although I had no luck, my first Alaska brown bear hunt taught me to pack lighter, leave the .454 Casul back up pistol behind (since it felt as if it weighed more than the .375 H&H I was carrying) and to get into better physical condition, even though I work out twice a day. I dreamed more about my next hunt that took place on Hinchinbrook Island.

It started with a boat ride from Whittier on May 4, 2005. Jeff and another co-worker who owned the boat, Morrill Mahan, kindly escorted me on this hunt. Those two never had to be asked twice to go hunting. I think they both had their hunting gear next to their front doors awaiting a hunting invitation. The boat trip was long but enjoyable, seeing whales and otters throughout the trip. We passed many small islands, their cliffs white with sea birds. There were so many birds you could hear their loud cries over the roar of the boat engines. The water was like glass which Morrill said was rare in those waters.

When we arrived at Hinchinbrook, the sun was just starting to go down. We looked forward to arriving at the Forest Service cabin that I had reserved and lucked out, catching the tide at the correct time. Because the water was shallow en route to the cabin, it took nearly an hour to reach the cabin at Double Bay. It was a typical Forest Service cabin having two bunks and two stoves. The shelter was well hidden unless the tide permitted entrance to the area.

Jeff cooked every meal on this trip and, believe me, nothing was left on anyone's plate. He could always quit his day job and become a cook. As the sun was still visible on the snow covered mountain peaks, we glassed the mountain side from the porch of the cabin. Spotted four or five bears up in the snow at the top of the mountains. A couple of them looked worthy but they were out of reach. So we bedded down for the first night dreaming of the bears we would be seeing the next day.

Got up early to another great meal and then took Morill's boat along the shoreline around the island, stopping to fish a little and enjoy the nice weather. We spotted some smaller bears not far from the beach, but nothing large enough to shoot. We also saw a ton of deer. Since the hunting season was not open and we did not want to go to jail for dropping one, we shouted to scare them away.

That night we glassed from the boat and spotted another big bear on the ridge. His tracks in the snow led into and out of his den and indicated that he never left that area.

The bear seemed close and we guessed at the distance. Morill is about ten years younger than Jeff and I, and asked how long it would take to reach the bear. Jeff said calmly, "About two hours, an hour and a half to skin it and we'll be off the mountain in less than three hours." That sounded simple enough. As things turned out, I wish I would have asked Jeff which day he expected this to happen.

The next morning we started after the bear. Just before leaving the boat, I asked Jeff where his gun was. He said, "Not going to bring one. Just gonna bring this here camera and video you getting your first bear." He's reconsidered since then.

We started walking and I thought, *this is much easier walking than my Afognak hunt*. Then it dawned on me that the mountain—or should I say mountains?—had just begun. It was an easy hike until we reached the snow where we sank six-inches with every step and the terrain steepened quickly. We still had about four miles to go, including a waterfall we used as a short cut. The waterfall was a small gulley cut in the rock of the mountainside. Would have been easier if it was not mostly ice and snow but it did save time. In the back of my mind I thought, *if I fell it would not be good*, considering the waterfall was around seventy-five feet high.

When we reached the area we had glassed from the cabin, we discovered to our dismay that a large, impassable stream and cliff separated us from our quarry on the adjoining mountain. Doesn't take old construction workers long to figure stuff out now does it? That's when something caught my attention moving higher on another ridge to my right. It was a large bear walking through the snow in no big hurry… in fact, it lay down to take a nap. Although it was around a mile away, its dark coat showed up easily in the snow. We agreed that this bear was easier to get at and also as big as, or bigger than the first one we sought. When Morril asked what I thought, I said, "The hunt is on."

So the climbing and falling through the snow continued. I made a mental note to buy some snowshoes before my next hunting trip. It was one of those days with no noise whatsoever and every little branch or crunch of snow thundered like a freight train. The closer we got to the bear, the more my hair stood up. The old bear stories are accurate when stating that getting close to bears increases your heart rate, your hair stands up and you start sweating no matter how cold the weather.

About this time I stepped into a patch of snow near the bottom of a tree trunk. My left foot sank into the snow up to my crotch and I heard a pop in my knee. I knew without a doctor's evaluation that I'd injured my knee. Adrenaline must have taken over because after prying myself out of the hole, I never thought much of it until later.

Of course falling through the snow did not help the stealth hunt we had planned. Jeff's video caught his audio telling Morill how loud I was. We finally rested and huddled for the final game plan.

Since I'm 6-foot 5-inches tall and my partners are less than 6-feet, Jeff told me to stand up and see where the bear was so that I'd have an idea where he would be coming from. I had seen the bear and knew that we were close enough to almost hear it snoring. Jeff whispered about moving towards my left side. I knew that was not gonna happen since the bear was closer than thirty yards from us. We stood dangerously close to the avalanche chute that we were stupid enough to climb.

About ten seconds after I started moving forward with Morill, I heard Jeff say, "OH!" That's when I saw the bear stand up on its hind legs, sniff and look right at us.

The monster took a step up the hill and to my scared surprise spun around right towards us. I pulled up the .338 rifle and looked through the scope. Flaring, high speed nostrils greeted me. I truly remember thinking we are so screwed. About the same time I pulled the trigger, thankfully, Morill did likewise.

My first shot hit the bear in the jaw which turned it down hill away from us, averting us from backing over the edge of the avalanche chute.

Instinct and muscle memory took charge, resulting in a succession of loading and firing. By this time Jeff had become quite the little cheerleader, trying to figuring out how he will shoot this bear with his only weapon, the video camera. He shouted, "Shoot!" and "Don't shoot!" in the same sentence. At one time he told me to shoot again but my frantic fingers fumbled shells into the snow.

As Jeff yelled that we were shooting over his head, Morill shouted that "the bear's dead." (In the video you can hear Morill say four times after four shots, "He's dead." Weird because I still saw him running.) Jeff yelled one last time, "Shoot, Tim!"

I aimed and hit the bear which just dropped like a lead weight. That's when Jeff said, "Good shot, Tim" followed by his murmur, "OH, OH."

The bear dropped alright. It dropped straight down an avalanche chute—something resembling a huge water slide. Even though the hunt was somewhat compounded, we high fived and celebrated joyously, first for killing the critter and second for being alive.

From the time the bear stood to look at us until it began sliding down the slope, maybe thirty seconds elapsed. For fifteen minutes we yelled, talked about how it charged and how stupid we were, laughed, got serious about almost getting killed then laughed again. Every couple of seconds Jeff would get real serious and whisper, "That was way too close," at which time Morill asked him about carrying a gun next time. Jeff kept repeating the idea that we were way too close and that he was glad that we had shot.

We then looked over the edge the bear had slid down. This animal was crawling out of a six or seven foot trench (just a narrow area where water ran through under the snow). I didn't dare shoot because we were still in the avalanche area ourselves. Now I see what people mean that it's not easy to kill a bear.

We descended a short distance to a small grove of trees. I took the final shot to put the awesome animal down for good. We realized later that if the bear had died in the trench, we would not have been able to get the huge creature out. I also did not realize how un-macho I was until I went down alone to see if he was really dead. After checking to make sure one was in the chamber three or four times, I turned around with knees shaking.

As Jeff and Morill took pictures, I asked Morrill if he was going to back me up with his rifle; and they both laughed and said, "You have the gun. We're taking pictures." I thought I would have enjoyed the moment more if we KNEW the bear was dead before expressing all the humor.

With my swollen knee I knelt down and edged close enough to poke the bear. Your mind does funny things during this scary time. I was sure that the bear moved so I lunged backwards into the snow trying to get away from it. If it would have been alive, I would have been lunch. It had not moved (but every time people watch the video they get a chuckle of the brave bear hunter I had become). My hunting partners also saw great humor in the moment my life flashed before me when falling back.

We were very impressed not only by the size of the bear, which squared 10' 2", but also by the color of the dark chocolate rub-free fur. Jeff and Morill skinned the bear since I feared wrecking the hide.

The first shot during the charge hit the bear in the lower jaw. There were also two lung shots, one shoulder and a hit to the back leg. Five of the six shots had hit the bear.

By now my knee tightened up, which was mild compared to getting the hide on my back pack. Good knee or bad, I could not lift it off the snow. This caused another good laugh from my friends. So Morill and I started up the opposite side of the steep ridge carrying the back pack between us. I say carry which translates into one, two, three lift. Each "carry" got us about a foot up the hill each time (the "hill" being the mountain cliff). We would grab a branch, limb or anything to get a better grip between each little lift.

Finally after making it to the top of the first-of-many-tops, my mouth opened and I said, "I will carry it from here." Stupid remark. Jeff carried the skull in his back pack so he already had a good enough load to carry. They lifted the full hide back onto my back and I started hiking down through the snow. Of course with the additional 100 to 150 pounds on my back, I sank a lot deeper into the snow. After covering what I thought was two miles, I stopped to rest. My lungs, knees and back screamed for a little break, so I flopped onto the snow. That's when I turned around to see that I had traveled maybe fifty yards and wanted to trade loads with Jeff.

Morill—bless his heart—took over and made it a little farther than I had. We all had enough sense to realize that we would not make it off the mountain before dark with the hide, let alone get back to the cabin if the tide was wrong for the boat. Although leaving the hide on the mountain overnight about killed me, we decided that was the thing to do. I imagined every animal known to man eating my prized bear hide in one night. That was the first of two difficult decisions with the hide.

When we finally reached the cabin, Jeff and Morrill decided it would be best to cut the hide in half so it could be carried by two people. I said some words like "no way" with some strong construction lingo thrown in to make sure they understood.

While I took off my bibs, I noticed my left knee was twice as big as it was supposed to be. The panic started to set in that no matter what, even if it meant crawling back up the mountain to retrieve my possession the next day, I was going.

I tossed and turned trying to get comfortable on the bunk when all of a sudden I heard screaming from the bunk area below. I already had teased Jeff and Morrill that the bear we got was big enough to crawl through the window and kill us so I thought one of them had a bad dream. When I looked over the edge of the top bunk, I saw Jeff standing in the middle of the cabin screaming. He was not having bear dream attacks, but Charlie horses in both legs at once. Between the laughing and arguing with Morrill about what is better for Jeff's Charlie horses, bananas or Gatorade, Jeff's screams subsided.

The next morning, I did not hop off the top bunk, but gingerly rolled down. The knee was as big as the night before and twice as stiff. I went outside the cabin and walked around, until it loosened up. I already knew that Morrill and I would retrieve the hide. Since we agreed to head to Whittier when we got the hide to the boat, we packed up the cabin. Jeff stayed in the boat after we told him how old he was and other mean things. He had the last laugh because we found out he just kicked back and fished while we tramped back up the mountain.

We took the same route Morrill had been smart enough to mark on his GPS from the previous day. Unfortunately that included the ice filled waterfall. Every step I thought if I mess up my knee or damage the other one, I'm going to fall to my death. As we climbed, we noticed numerous fresh bear tracks along the trail that kept us both very awake. We made good time to where we stashed the bear hide and discovered, to my amazement, that it had not been disturbed. Not even a track in the snow around it. We rolled the hide out flat and cut it in half just behind the front legs, or arm pits. I could already imagine the taxidermist wondering what was going through our minds—to cut a bear hide in half. We finished and separately rolled up our halves to put onto our packs. (I wish I had had a camera because the head of the hide was perfectly centered with that big snout pointing out making a great picture of its size.)

We started down through knee deep snow. Every step I prayed my swollen leg would keep working. When we got to the area of the water fall, my companion said he had a great idea. Morill said in his energetic voice, "Instead of chancing going down the water fall, let's just sit down on our butts with the packs still on our backs and slide down this big honking avalanche chute."

My mind was saying don't listen to this person; he's gone crazy. My leg was saying listen to this person because we're not going down the waterfall with the extra weight. He said, "It will be easy. We'll just put our heels down when we need to go slower." Morrill made my decision when he took off down the chute. I felt like one of those lemmings following the others jumping off the cliff. Morrill was yelling and laughing the whole trip and I was screaming and grabbing any branch I could find to slow me down. Because the weather had been warm, I wore a short sleeved shirt. My arms were shredded from shoulders to fingers. By the time I made it to the bottom, Morill was sitting back and watching the cheap entertainment at my expense. Makes it pretty tough swearing at a person who brought me in his boat, backed me up when the bear charged and was kind enough to go up the mountain the second day to help bring the hide down. So my thoughts of accidentally shooting him passed pretty fast.

The rest of the trip down was pretty much uneventful and was pure joy when I saw the boat out in the bay. When we finally reached the water, I felt like a person who had walked across the desert and finally found water. We took the small raft we had used to get to shore, loaded the hide into it and finally got it out and into the boat. We headed for Whittier, which was a good thing as it would get us home for Mother's Day.

We were lucky enough not to wear out the video before we got it home. We had made a promise of only making three videos of this hunt—one for each of us, period. We must have meant three a day for a year because there are still people asking for it. They have been sent from New York to Florida and every place in between. To this day when someone is watching it and I hear laughing, I know it is the part where I fall over backwards after jabbing the dead bear with my gun barrel.

The bear made the three year Boone and Crockett Club for North American Big Game at a score of 26-15/16 points. The beautiful full mount of the bear on all fours graces my living room thanks to Wayne Desoro, my taxidermist who worked his magic of making the hide whole again, my lovely wife Lisa who demanded it needed to be in the living room and to the two people who took me on this hunt.

This bear has brought both great joy and some sorrow. The joy is seeing others' faces light up watching the video and seeing the bear in the living room each day. The sorrow is taking an animal that was not bothering anyone and still was in its prime. People reading this may laugh but I still look into that bears eyes and tell it thank you and also ask it to forgive me. My wife sees this in me and she knows this will be the last bear I will want to shoot. Yes, I know every year bears attack fisherman in Alaska, but this was not one of those bears. This bear was just one of God's creatures wanting to live out its own dreams of being free to roam in a majestic place called Hinchinbrook Island.

The camaraderie, the challenge and the great memories of the hunt will stay with me forever.

CHAPTER 12
ADVICE

There is no dearth of advice for safety in bear country. The magnitude of information found in "bear safety" books and their enormity of "rules" burdens a person with so much advice that he might choose to forgo the outing. For instance, various books discuss a pulley system for raising your food or gear to a safe elevation away from bears, bathing at the end of the day, bringing along enough changes of clothing so that you don't sleep in the clothes you cook in, burning all garbage, hauling your food 300 yards from camp.

Many of these precautions may be necessary in park settings; however when I go afield in Alaska, I practice none of them. In fact were it necessary to follow all of these type suggestions, I'd stay home.

Sheep hunters are subjected to grueling terrain and pack their camps on their backs. A successful hunter has his gear as well as a minimum weight of 100 pounds of boned out meat, horns and cape to pack out. The only sheep hunting I know of is above timberline with no "hoisting" mechanism for the harvested game. Therefore when I hunt sheep, I go light—I wear good boots, pants and quilted shirt. My pack contains vest, rain poncho, extra socks and undies. No extra clothes. If the bear wants me or my food, he's going to have to earn it the old fashioned way…as in "come and get it."

Because bears can smell food from 12-50 miles distant, move ghostlike in predatory mode, run 35-40 mph and defy fire power once aroused, bear safety advice is essential.

Is it possible to be safe in bear country? As suggested earlier, is it safe in your own home? Mike Cramond, outdoorsman and reporter-author of bear books says, "There is no single method or manner in which a human can be sure of surviving in bear country, with or without a gun, even a gun that is actually loaded, cocked, and ready to be fired in an instant." (Pg. 122, *Killer Bears*)

In response and in keeping with the theme of this book, although I agree with Cramond to a great degree, I still believe that if a person has twenty yards visibility, a bona-fide bear stopper and is qualified to properly use it, he will put down the attacking bear. I refer you to La Verne Beier—he had a chambered round in a large caliber rifle (later in this section).

Let the reader be warned. The three North American bears—black, grizzly and polar—come in all sizes. It is easier to defend yourself against some than others. It doesn't take a brain surgeon to know that fighting a 100 pound bear is easier than taking on a 500-plus pound bruin. The same is true of a self-defense weapon—a small caliber weapon would stop a smaller animal easier than it would a large animal. (One consideration is adrenaline in the bear—a few examples exist of brown/grizzlies pressing their attacks until they had exterminated their tormentors, although the bears' hearts were blown away. It is extremely difficult to stop an alarmed brown/grizzly unless its central nervous system is affected.)

Even though I can advise people about safety in bear country, there is no guarantee they will comply…for a number of reasons. First of all, many people would not comport with the wilderness. It's likely that they couldn't enact some of the advice. For instance, how many people visit national parks and try to get a picture with their baby next to or on a bear? Could these people overcome their misunderstanding of bears, viewing them as a wild and dangerous animal?

How many of these people are capable of developing a bearing of confidence? We've been told that criminals look at their victims for signs of weakness…that one of the best ways to avoid trouble with an assailant is to carry yourself with a confident manner, making eye contact, having a good posture, walking purposefully—not looking at the ground like a victim, stoop shouldered and shuffling along. And being ever alert—knowing what's going on around you and anticipating saving yourself.

In order to avoid problems with bears a person needs an air of confidence and an "attitude." Carry yourself in a manner that demonstrates confidence and a lack of fear. Can this attitude be taught, coached, interjected into a person who can't be taught? No, it can't!

The same applies to providing general information. Some people are incapable of carrying, let alone, discharging a firearm. Or there are those who could not hit the back end of a bull with a base fiddle at point blank range. So, what kind of disclaimer is necessary in producing a book such as this?

Safety Formula

You CAN escape injury from bears at ground zero…if you follow the formula.

Providing a fool proof formula for safety from bear injury is a daunting assignment, one that seems almost ludicrous because of the variables such as personalities of people, experience in bear quarters, attitudes towards bears and physical and/or emotional disparities. Let's say, for instance, that we plop a city slicker into bear country on any given day of busy bear activity. This guy has never seen a bear. He is unarmed. He's never held a firearm and, in fact, doesn't see their value. What do you tell him regarding his personal safety in bear country?

On the other hand, take a long-time outdoorsman—hunter, fisherman, cowboy— from Wyoming, Colorado or Montana who has seen grizzlies in action—watched them rip across terrain, knows and respects their power. He's armed with a can of pepper spray, a pistol or a rifle and his knife. Plop him in front of a grizzly that means business. What do you think his chances of avoiding injury are compared with the city slicker's?

You can see that providing advice for injury avoidance is monumental. Although guaranteeing safety from injury is desirable, that prospect is easier said than done. How many people are physically capable of getting around quickly or at a normal human rate of expectancy? How many could take on a brown bear with a knife as a last resort?

A safety guarantee is not easy because most people stray from the formula. Too many become complacent.

Most outdoorsmen know about tenting away from game trails or salmon streams, keeping a clean camp, not cooking in your tent and storing food a hundred yards from camp and staying alert to a bear's presence—sensing "signs"; however other advice may benefit.

My formula for staying out of a bear's mouth places **attitude** and **visibility** at the top. Enter the outdoors as the Boss of the Woods—your body language is all important. You must be able to see 30 yards in order to respond to an attacking bear. A reliable **partner** is essential—even partners have been ambushed and killed. Use a **bear stopper** that your **experience** and **practice** enable you to execute. A **chambered round** avails instant access. Know your **personal capabilities**—assets and liabilities.

Other considerations include 1) the advisability of urinating around your camp; 2) portable electric fences have proved effective and 3) other camp deterrents include the Pack Alarm.

ATTITUDE

The key to safety in bear country is attitude. Develop the attitude that you are the Boss of the Woods that sends a message to bears that you're the biggest, baddest banana there! Stand up to the bear. Wear the shield of bad hombre. This attitude will enable you to exude confidence in your body language and voice. Display an aura of confidence just shy of arrogance. You own the woods. The analogy is the same as that of a victim walking through a dicey neighborhood where he might be confronted by bad guys. Announce to the bear that you're not afraid but that he'd better be—because you are the Boss of the Woods.

Let the bear know that you own him and his environment. Don't be a wimp. Stephen Routh (*Some Bears Kill*) determined to kill a black bear with a switch—he demonstrated an attitude! As did the lady marine who fought off a black bear, using her brain and a club (see Christianne Kearns above).

Show the bear who's boss…but be able to back up your bluff! Gary Shelton talks about eye contact, "Scott kept facing the bear, and the bear never quite got the confidence to press the attack." (*Bear Encounter Survival Guide*, Pg. 61). Eye contact is strongly recommended to diminish cougar encounters also.

It may be that a predatory grizzly would be undeterred by your macho attitude nevertheless it pays dividends to know that you are the king of beasts and that you project that demeanor in the woods.

Take no crap.

ANTICIPATION

One of the greatest characteristics of a champion athlete is his anticipation. During any serious training the trainee is instructed to anticipate things in order to prepare for their eventuality. Anticipate different things. Practice thinking that there IS a bear behind the bush that you are approaching, or on the opposite side of your vehicle. That way when it happens, you've anticipated it and know how to deal with it.

Bear country visitors who anticipate a bear encounter and are prepared for one, have a greater chance of departing bear country intact. Be thinking all the time. What if this or that? Expect and know how to handle various situations. Anticipate a bear's presence at any moment.

Being alert is important; however being vigilant is imperative. Although *American Heritage Dictionary*, 1970 defines these words almost synonymously: alert—"vigilantly attentive; watchful"; vigilant— "on the alert, watchful," I emphasize vigilance as an almost cunning appraisal of all that is in the air. Just like a person is "on alert" in a life threatening situation, a person needs to be vigilant. Have your "bear" peepers, listeners and smeller working.

There is a difference between anticipation-alertness and paranoia. Americans have mastered the art of living in fear—especially expert are we in the fear of the unknown. We have a fear of bears (as well as strangers, certain races, etc.). No reason to be bearanoid! Rather, be pre-beared.

In a nut shell, the best advice for avoiding a bear injury is <u>PAPP—prepare and practice for performance</u>. To enter the backlands without preparation and without practicing activities that will keep one safe is foolhardy. There are entirely too many people in the woods with no outdoor experience or with insufficient experience to match their challenges. How often do we hear about park visitors' feeding bears from their vehicles, departing same vehicle to follow and photograph bruin—even putting baby nearby so papa can video Mr. Bear and Baby together?

In the Event of a Bear Encounter

Even though you will not likely encounter a bear in a non-hunting situation, what if you do? Have sufficient information and training to return safely from the woods. If you're not prepared to go into the woods, if your philosophy disallows your killing a bear or you will not risk loss of life or limb, perhaps you should forego the experience. You owe it to yourself, your family and/or your companions to opt for their safety.

Make noise in order to apprise the bear of your presence. Let him know that you are man— "Whoa, bear! I'm man. I'm moving away." Talk to the bear in a calm but firm voice. Do NOT run. You can NOT outrun a bear (unless some convenient shelter is very close). Bears will bully you if you let them. Boss bears rule by aggression. So, you decide. As for me, I'm going to be the boss bear and make that eye contact.

Minimize bear conflict by NOT wearing headphones (CD players, radio, etc.)— listen for natural noises.

Raise your weapon and prepare to use it.

Consider water escapes.

Having a tree at your back protects your back side.

Be aware of bears that appear in winter (we've had bears in our Anchorage neighborhood in January after weeks of below zero weather).

Horseback is generally safer.

If, by some chance, you sustain injury and get out of the woods, you still may not be "out of the woods." You'll need the best of medical care and special attention to any possible infection from the wounds.

QUESTIONABLE ADVICE

Perhaps there should be two sets of directions—one for Lower 48 park-campground bears and one for freelance outdoors people who may not visit parks.

Authors of bear books recommend that you learn bear body language—flat ears, stomping forelegs, huffing or chomping—in order to act accordingly. They describe page after page of bear behavior—is it a grizzly? Is it a defensive attack?

How do you know it's a grizzly? What constitutes a defensive attack?

Most people don't know the difference between a grizzly and a Chihuahua. Therefore I'll simplify the information for them. I have a different rule of thumb which has nothing to do with the bear's ears, nose, fur color, whether it's flipping pancakes or eating a banana split. It doesn't matter whether the animal is wearing a Ralph Loren suit, smells like oil of Olay, wears a war bonnet or winks its right eye.

My rule of thumb is whether the bear's in MY personal space!

I've been within inches of a grizzly—awakened from my sleeping bag, left the windowless cabin in the dark planning to fetch firewood from the woodpile where a partner shone a flashlight exposing two green grizzly eyes—that we chased off unhurt. I've also been within 20 yards of a grizzly that I advised, while making solid eye contact, that "you'd better be on your way if you don't want to get hurt." He complied with a surly look over his shoulder while I passed with rifle shouldered. I've thrown rocks at black bears in our yard and tapped on our window while one walked hurriedly across our deck. And I've thrown rocks at grizzlies.

In 50 years' hunting-fishing-outing in Alaska I've never had to kill a bear and I hope that never changes.

We can talk avoidance, making yourself bigger and so on, but, again, your primary concern is how close the bear is to you. Your secondary concern is what you're prepared to do about it. And I'm not talking kissy-huggy hoopla…I'm talking protecting yourself *chutzpa*!

If a threatening bear comes within 20 yards of me, he will have my full attention. And very possibly some lead directed his way.

Know your personal safety space. How close will you permit a bear before you take action? My friend Norwegian explorer-adventurer Lars

Monsen suggests 7 yards. That is pretty similar to the personal space that La Vern Beier suggests, twenty feet...enough room to allow the bear to stop, and enough space to allow for one disabling shot from an adequate firearm.

In a word, know what's in your surroundings and prepare to defend yourself against it.

BEAR STOPPER

If you don't want to be on a bear's dance card or on his menu, you'd better carry a proven bear stopper. When I enter bear country, my preference is to return from the outing...uninjured and alive! Therefore I prepare, practice and carry a bear stopper. And I recommend that you do the same.

A bear stopper is a weapon that produces enough juice or "medicine" to dispatch a bear. One that STOPS him. Not one that tickles but one that produces a cadaver, as in *kaput, fini*, done, *au revoir*, kill it and grill it!

The word *bear* conjures different images depending upon one's experience and his geographic location. Different areas, different animals. To put things into perspective, a person in black bear country could expect to see a bear of varying colors and sizes, from cinnamon to black and from a 20-pound cub to a 200 to 300-pound (or larger) adult. The person in grizzly country—especially in the national parks which they inhabit—could see bears from light blonde to dark brown, even black, ranging in size from dozens of pounds to hundreds. A person in polar bear country who sees nanook, will observe a crème colored animal of the size of the grizzly (and, just to let you know, in some areas grizzlies and polar bears coexist).

Because different areas produce different bears of varying sizes, it is hard to generalize in the use of the word bear. When I think of a bear attack and an adequate weapon to keep the animal from grievously injuring a companion or me, I invariably think BIG, brown bear, rarely considering the smaller black. That's because I'm anticipating the worst case scenario. It is important to relate the principles of personal protection as they apply to the appropriate animal.

For instance, if you hike Texas, where you could encounter a black bear, your personal protection weapon could be a much lighter caliber than one used to stop an enraged, adrenaline pumped 1000-pound brown bear.

Bear medicine: what is the best way to stop a determined bear? First, what is the animal's value as juxtaposed to man's life? (which is more valuable, the bear or the man?) Second, if man's life is placed at a higher value than the bear's, why should man be afraid to stop a determined animal? Third, what currently recommended remedies have limited results if they work at all?

To stop a bear immediately requires a central nervous system shot—to the brain or spine. To slow it down and increase your chances of escape a shoulder shot is recommended, breaking the animal down. You have three options for stopping or slowing it—skull, spine or shoulder (but they can travel rapidly on three legs!). The charging bear normally comes with head low thus there is a line from nose to tail aligning his skull and spine.

SUMMARY

If you don't know your expert, do the research. What's the best solution to man-bear encounters of a very close kind?

I recommend when you enter bear country to be fully armed—know about bruin, practice proper bear etiquette, be prepared to deal with various situations (especially have practiced of the techniques that could save your life), have first aid training and equipment as well as a communication device (like cellular phone or PLB) and always carry a bona fide bear stopper.

Next time you're in your tent wrestling that boulder, sleep on these ideas. And be "beary" careful out there.

Additional tips exist in APPENDIX 13.

APPENDICES
APPENDIX 1
DISTANT CHARGES

Most attacks are within 50 yards, probably 20 or closer. However, the following information taken from only 3 of roughly 100 bear books in my collection shows at least 10 people who experienced bear attacks from 50 yards or more:

PERSON	SOURCE	TYPE	DISTANCE	BEHAVIOR
Cal Pappas	*Some Bears Kill*	grizzly	50 yards	protect cub
Marti Miller	*Some Bears Kill*	black	70 yards	predatory stalk
Bill Gonce	*Some Bears Kill*	grizzly	60-80 yards	cubs
Forest Young	*Some Bears Kill*	brown	100 yards	protect kill
Tom Jesiolowski	*Some Bears Kill*	brown	100-plus yards	belligerent
Jerry Austin	*Some Bears Kill*	grizzly	500 feet	belligerent
Jim Magowan	*More ABT*	grizzly	200-300 yards	cubs/Denali
Chuck Lewis	*More ABT*	brown	400-500 feet	cubs
Ann Quarterman & Christine Bialkowski	Track / Grizzly	grizzly	330 yards	cubs
Chuck Lewis (from November Mike Snowden & Jeff Ostrin)	*Some Bears Kill* *Alaska Dispatch News*	brown brown	1 mile Nov. 6, 2014 500 yards	dinner bell smelled carcass

APPENDIX 2
NINNY

Dave Smith in *Backcountry Bear Basics* suggests that "The chances of being charged by a black bear are zilch unless you're a biologist working closely with bears or a ninny feeding roadside bears in a national park." (Pg. 58) If I knew nothing about bears, I'd feel safe anywhere bears reside because I'm not going to feed them nor am I a biologist.

However, I do know something about bears. It just so happens that I know of a few black bears that not only charged but also mauled and/or ate their victims—none of whom worked as biologists nor was a roadside ninny. It would be unfair of me to pile on Dave but I must apprise the reader that just because something is in print doesn't make it so.

For instance, I've studied a number of people who were attacked by blacks, over a dozen below occurred prior to publication of Smith's book—more than a dozen other black attacks fill my books (some stories below are in this volume).

NAME	DATE	ACTION MY BOOKS*	SOURCE
W. M. Nutter	1936	chased up a tree, shot-killed bear with .22 pistol	MABT
Art LeGault	1961	toe to toe with sow in Michigan, stabbed her w. knife	BTA
C. Wayne Majors	1963	asleep when bear bit his head, yelled, friend scared bear off -killed it	ABT
Jim Heine	1975	stalked hunter, stabs with arrow until she left tree	
Robert L. MacGregor	1976	bear stalked-killed and fed upon victim	ABT
Cynthia Dusel-Bacon	1977	USGS worker taking rock samples, bear mauled-began eating her alive, she radioed for help, was rescued	ABT
George Halfkenny, Jr. Mark Halfkenny	1978	attacked-killed all three (partially eating two of the boys)	

NAME	DATE	ACTION MY BOOKS*	SOURCE
William Rhindress			SAFE
Stephen Routh	1980	tying plane to lake beach, bear mauled, Stephen fought, his wife started plane engine, bear fled	SBK
Darcy Staver	1993	killed-partially eaten by bear outside her cabin	SBK
Will Atkinson	1994	swimming at Liard Hot Springs, punched bear, others rescued Will	SBK

Marti Miller	pre-95	stalked Marti over a half mile, she shot-killed bear	SBK
Sven Satre	1996	rancher stalked on horseback, killed and partially devoured	SAFE
Ian Dunbar	1996	mother tries to pull son from bear's jaws, bear kills boy	SAFE
Patti Reed McConnell Ray Kitchen Arie-Jan van Velden	1997	bear mauled-killed Patti and Ray, son Kelly mauled Kelly and Arie	SAFE
In fairness to Dave Smith,		the following attacks transpired after publication of *Backcountry Bear Basics* in 1997	
Glenda Anne Bradley	2000	Tennessee hiker, killed and partially eaten by sow and cub	SAFE
Adelia Maestas Trujillo	2001	attacks-kills woman in her home	SAFE
Kristy L. Abbott	2002	stalked over an hour, fought with sticks, air horn, bear left	
Luke Cenkus	2006	bear mauls all three, kills 6-year-old Susan Cenkus	SAFE
Elora Petrasek	2006	black killed	SAFE

*ABT	*Alaska Bear Tales*
*MABT	*More Alaska Bear Tales*
*SBK	*Some Bears Kill*
*BTA	*Bear Tales for the Ages*
*SAFE	*Stay Alive From Encounters*

APPENDIX 3
WIKIPEDIA NORTH AMERICAN
FATALITY LIST

Wikipedia fatalities (as of Nov. 2014, partial list, condensed, * author supplied info)

Name, gender, age	Date	Species, Location, Comments

2010s

Name, gender, age	Date	Species, Location, Comments
Erin Johnson, 27 yr. old female	June 29, 2017	Pogo Mine, Alaska, contract employee Johnson collected soil samples, black bear was shot-killed by mine personnel
Patrick Cooper	June 18, 2017	competing in Bird Ridge mountain race at Indian, Alaska, attacked-killed by black bear which officials later killed
Daniel Ward O'Connor 27 yr. old male	5/10/15	killed during the night at his campsite near Mackenzie, BC, his fiancé discovered his body the next day, officials killed bear
Claudia Huber female, 42	10/18/2014	grizzly, husband investigates disturbance outside near Wild Crossing, Yukon, returns to house, bear enters, husband-wife flee outside, bear mauls wife as he shoots it dead, rushed wife to medical help but she expired
Darsh Patel male, 22	9/21/2014	black near West Milford, NJ bear followed 5 friends, they fled, Patel later found with bear
Ken Novotny male, 53	9/17/2014	grizzly, hunter attending moose kill when bear kills him near Norman Wells, NWT
Adam T. Stewart male, 31	9/2014	grizzly? solo hiking went missing, found dead
Rick Cross male, 54	9/7/2014	grizzly sow protecting cub and deer carcass, Kananaskis Country, Alberta
Name, gender, age	**Date**	**Species, Location, Comments**
Lorna Weafer female, 36	5/7/2014	black, walking from washhouse to oil mine job site
Robert Weaver male, 64	6/6/2013	black, attacked near his cabin, wife escapes inside George Lake near Delta Jct., Alaska

Thomas Puerta male, 54	10/2012	brown attacked on his Chichagof Is. camp in Alaska
Richard White male, 49	8/24/2012	grizzly photographer in Denali Ntl. Park got too close
John Wallace male, 59	8/24/2011	grizzly, "expert" refused Yellowstone Park advice, attacked while eating snack
Lana Hollingsworth female, 61	7/25/2011	black, walking dog at country club, died a month later from injuries
Brian Matayoshi male, 57	7/6/2011	grizzly, hiking Yellowstone with wife, he fled, wife hid
Bernice Adolph female, 72	6/2011	black, First Nation lady reported missing, bears tried to enter home, 5 killed—one was killer
Brent Kandra male 24	8/19/2010	black, captive bear free of cage at Columbia Station, OH, attacked caretaker
Kevin Kammer male, 48	7/28/2010	grizzly, sow pulls him from tent, 2 other campers attacked, officials trapped-killed bear
Erwin F. Evert male, 70	6/17/2010	grizzly, encountered trapped-tagged that day bear, it was killed 2 days later

2000s

Kelly Ann Walz female, 37	10/4/2009	black, cleaning pet bear's cage near Ross Township, PA, neighbor shot-killed bear
Donna Munson female, 74	8/6/2009	black, feeding bears at home, dominant male killed-ate her, Ouray, CO
Cecile Lavoie female, 70	5/30/2008	black, missing on fishing trip, husband found bear dragging her into woods La Sarre, Quebec
Robin Kochorek	7/20/2007	black, missing mt. biker, found next day with bear
Samuel E. Ives	6/17/2007	black, pulled from tent at night in Uinta Ntl. Forest, UT
Elora Petrasek, female, 6	4/13/2006	black killed; her mother and 2-yr.-old brother seriously injured in Cherokee Ntl. Forest, TN
Arthur Louie, male, 60	Sept. 20, 2005	grizzly sow killed as he returned to his mining camp after his car had flat tire, Bowron River, B.C.
Jacqueline Perry, female, 30	Sept. 6, 2005	black predatory attack Missinaibi Lake Prov. Park, Ontario Canada; husband seriously injured

Name, gender, age	Date	Species, Location, Comments
Harvey Robinson male, 69	8/26/2005	black, picking plumbs in Selkirk Mts., Manitoba
Richard Huffman, 61 Kathy, 58	June 23, 2005	grizzly, tent site Hulahula River, Kaktovik, and AK Arctic National Wildlife Refuge
Merlyn Carter, male, 71	6/14/2005	black, son found him dead at fish camp cabin 186 miles northeast Ft. Smith, NWT, Canada
Isabelle Dube female, 35	June 5, 2005	grizzly, jogging w. 2 friends, Bench Trail, Canmore, Alberta
Timothy Treadwell, male, 46 and Amie Hugenard female, 37	Oct. 2003	brown, tent site, both partially devoured, bear killed by authorities
Forestry worker	April 17, 2003	black, predatory, partially consumed, Waswanipi, Quebec
Maurice Malefant male, 77	9/29/2002	black attacked at camp Saint-Zenon-du-Lac-Humqui, Quebec
Christopher Bayduza male, 31	9/1/2002	black, went for walk near Ft. Nelson, BC trailer at oil rig site
male hunter	Sept. 2002	black, campsite, Gaspe, northern Quebec
Ester Schwimmer, female, 5 months	Aug. 2002	black, pulled from stroller on porch at home, Fallsburg, N.Y.
Adelia Maestras Trujillo, female, 93	8/18/2001	black, killed inside New Mexico home
Kyle Harry male, 18	6/3/2001	black, a group at campsite, 14 miles east Yellowknife, NWT
George Tullow, male, 41	July 14, 2000	grizzly, Run Amuk campground, Hyder, AK
Mary-Beth Miller, female, 24	7/2/2000	black, training run, Quebec, Canada, bear trapped-killed 4 days later
Glena Ann Bradley, female, 50	5/21/2000	black, 112-pound sow and 40-pound cub partially devour, Smokey Mts. Campground, Gatlinburg, TN

1990s

Ned Rasmussen, male	Nov. 1999	grizzly, found 2 days after deer hunt disappearance, Uganik Island, Alaska

Name, gender, age	Date	Species,	Location,	Comments
Ken Cates, male, 53	May 25, 1999	grizzly, hiking Funny River Trail, Soldotna, AK, Cates wounded unfound bear		
Craig Dahl, male, 26	May 17, 1998	grizzly, partially consumed hiker, Glacier Ntl. Park, USA		
Audelio Luis male, 40	Feb. 8, 1998	grizzly, seismic worker, blow to head, Swanson River, Cortes, Kenai, AK		
Marcie Trent, 77, female; son Larry Waldron, 45	July 1, 1995	grizzly, bear defends moose carcass, McHugh Creek, Anchorage, AK		
Male	Aug. 10,	unknown, WAGH Mountain, CO, USA		
John Petranyi, male	Oct. 3, 1992	grizzly sow w. 2 cubs; Loop Trail, Upper McDonald Valley, Glacier Ntl. Park, USA		
(*Darcy Staver) female	July 8, 1992	unknown, west of Glennallen, AK (*black)		
Male geologist	June 14, 1992	black, on field assignment, Cochrane, ONT		
Female and male	Oct. 11, 1991	black, Opeongo Lake, Algonquin Prov. Pk., Ontario, Can. camper		
Male camper	May 26, 1991	unknown, Martin River Campground, Aberta, Canada		

1980s

Gary Goeden,	9/1/1987	grizzly, partially consumed, Natahki Lk., Many Glacier		
male, missing	7/28	Valley, Glacier Ntl. Pk, USA		
Charles Gibbs male, 40	April 25, 1987	grizzly, filming sow, Elk Mountain, Glacier Ntl. Park U.S.A.		
Photographer	Oct. 1986	grizzly, too close to sow, Hayden Valley, Yellowstone		
Hiker	July 1984	grizzly, campsite White Lake, Yellowstone Ntl. Park		
Camper	June 1983	grizzly, Rainbow Point campground, Gallatin Ntl. Forest		
Laurence Gordon, male	Sept. 30, 1980	grizzly, Elizabeth Lake campsite, Glacier Ntl. Park		
Male and Female	Aug. 17,	unknown, Zama, Alberta, Canada		

Name, gender, age	Date	Species, Location, Comments
Jane Ammerman, Female; Kim Eberly,	July 24, 1980	grizzly, Divide Creek, Glacier Ntl. Park
Male	July 18, 1980	unknown, Leo Creek, B.C., Canada

1970s

Male	June 19, 1978	black, Porcupine Mts. State Park, MI
3 young men George and Mark Halfkenny; friend William Rhindress	May 13, 1978	black, Radiant Lk., Algonquin Prov. Pk., Ontario, Canada
Mary Pat Mahoney, female, 22	Sept. 23, 1976	grizzly, dragged from tent, Many Glacier campground, Glacier Ntl. Park
Male	June 1972	grizzly feeding on left out food, Yellowstone

1960s

Male	Oct. 1, 1968	black, Atikokan, Ontario, Canada
Julie Helgeson, USA, 19, female	Aug. 13, 1967	grizzly, Granite Park campsite, Glacier Ntl. Park, companion Roy Ducat companion severely mauled
Michelle Koons, 19 female	Aug. 13, 1967	grizzly, Trout Lake campsite, Glacier Ntl. Park, USA

1940s

	Aug. 1942	unknown, Old Faithful campground, Yellowstone Ntl. Park

1910s

Man	1916	grizzly, roadside camp, Yellowstone Ntl. Park

Russian Tragedy—www.express.co.uk

World News

BEAR'S EATING ME, GIRL TOLD MUM IN CALL

Wednesday August 17, 2011

By Will Stewart in Moscow

A DISTRAUGHT mother listened on a mobile phone as her teenage daughter was eaten alive by a brown bear and its three cubs.

Olga Moskalyova, 19, gave an horrific hour-long running commentary on her own death in three separate calls as the wild animals killed her.

She screamed: "Mum, the bear is eating me! Mum, it's such agony. Mum, help!'"

Her mother Tatiana said that at first thought she was joking. "But then I heard the real horror and pain in Olga's voice, and the sounds of a bear growling and chewing."

She added: "I could have died then and there from shock."

Unknown to Tatiana, the bear had already killed her husband Igor Tsyganenkov – Olga's stepfather – by overpowering him, breaking his neck and smashing his skull. Olga, a trainee psychologist, saw the ¬attack on her stepfather in tall grass and reeds by a river in Russia and fled for 70 yards before the mother bear grabbed her leg.

As the creature toyed with her, she managed to call Tatiana several times during the prolonged attack. Tatiana rang her husband – not knowing he was ¬already dead – but got no answer.

She alerted the police and relatives in the village of Termalniy, near Petropavlovsk Kamchatskiy, in the extreme east of Siberia.

She begged them to rush to the river where the pair had gone to retrieve a fishing rod that Igor had left.

In a second call, a weak Olga gasped: "Mum, the bears are back. She came back and brought her three babies. They're...eating me."

Finally, in her last call – almost an hour after the first – Olga sensed she was on the verge of death.

With the bears having apparently left her to die, she said: "Mum, it's not hurting anymore. I don't feel the pain. Forgive me for everything, I love you so much."

The call cut off and that was the last Tatiana heard from her ¬daughter. Half an hour later, Igor's brother Andrei arrived with police to find the mother bear still devouring his body. Badly mauled Olga was also dead. Six hunters were sent in by the emergency services to kill the mother bear and her three cubs.

The double killing is the latest in a spate of bear attacks across ¬Russia, as the hungry animals seek food in areas where people have ¬encroached and settled on their former habitat.

A weeping Tatiana said that Olga had everything to look forward to, and was happy with her life and boyfriend Stepan.

"My daughter was such fun. She was so cheerful, friendly, and warm," said Tatiana.

"She had graduated from music school, and just days before the bear attack she got her driving license."

Her husband and daughter are due to be buried today.

North American Children fatalities

Children or youth killed by bears in North America (most fatalities attributable to black bears)

Samuel Evan Ives, 11	June 2007	black grabbed from tent
Elora Petrasek 6	April 2006	fled in fear, black later found guarding her body.
Ester Schwimmer,	Aug. 2002	black, pulled from stroller on porch at home, female, 5 months, Fallsburg, N.Y
		4-yr.-old son Ian Dunbar black in their back yard 1996
Anton Bear, 6	July 1992	near King Cove, AK refuse dump, brownie, chase instinct
James Waddell, 12	May 1991	lesser Slave Lake, Alberta, dragged from tent
Juan Perez, 11	May 1987	climbed fence in Brooklyn zoo
Allan Russell Baines, 10	July 1980	Leo Creek, BC fishing with two other friends
3 young teenage men George 16 Mark Halfkenny 12, friend William Rhindress, 15	May 13, 1978	black, Radiant Lk., Algonquin Prov. Pk., Ontario, Canada
Allison Muser, 5	July 1977	Waterton Lakes while playing in creek with sister
Susan Duckitt, 11	August 1967	Okanagan Landing, BC playing with friend, black

Continued - Children or youth killed by bears in North America (most fatalities attributable to black bears)

Phyllis Tremper, 3	Sept. 1966	Prescott, AZ pet bear dragged her into its cage
Barbara Coates, 7	Aug. 1958	Jasper Nt. Pk. black chased her while she picked berries
Girl	1950s?	Nabesna, wounded by woman's husband grizzly in village
Carol Ann Pomeranky,	July 1948	Marquette Nt. Forest, Michigan black dragged her 3-years-old from fire tower steps
Richard Strand, 8	Sept. 1945	pet bear, Seattle, WA
Grant Taylor, 11	Oct. 1933	Brookhaven, NY child fed tethered bear
Peter Matthew Ryan, 5	Oct. 1932	Albion, NY tethered pet bear
2 native boys	1910	trailed wounded brownie
Baby Laird, 1	Oct. 1908	Tucson, AZ bear escaped from park
Henry 7, Willie 5	May 1901	Job, West VA children gathering flowers, bear and
Mary 3,		Porterfield killed

APPENDIX 4
HETRICK

The following is from emails received from Kenny Hetrick.

School children love coming here. It's a free animal sanctuary where donations are accepted.

Only my wife and I take care of all the animals, we do lots of butchering. The bears love road killed deer, and horse meat, along with donuts, bread and whatever is sweet. We go broke all the time over these animals. We never get enough butcher calls or road kills. I have to travel 450 miles to buy food for them. I usually bring back 10,000 pounds on a trailer, all fresh turkey meat, no bones. They love it, and it's good for them.

When I was 20-years-old and right out of the service (Viet Nam paratrooper), I trained both of my older boys to fight and they were both national champions. I've got a very large collection of vintage boxing gloves, dozens of pairs. I used to be a boxing coach, training the kids, had a few champions.

I have been a policeman for ten years. I'm also an Ottawa County Deputy Sheriff. I worked in a prison for a year, that was interesting, never had one problem with the prisoners.

I got into the mountain man thing, have all the buckskin suits, throwing knives, tomahawks, tepee. Nobody can beat my wife at throwing a knife—she sticks it every time from 20 feet. Used to do re-enactments, lots of fun. Never get time any more to do these things.

I love to read. I've read most of your books which I own. I have all the good bear books.

When I was a safety inspector at Chrysler, I read five to six hours a day. I like Custer, Crazy Horse, Circus cat trainers, bear books, Jim Corbett—I have all his books. Frank Buck, all of his, Gunfighters, And I love Mountie books. Sled dog stories, survival stories, nothing that is fiction. I don't have much time to read any more, but right now I'm in the middle of three different books. I go to book fairs, antique malls and old forgotten about book stores. I've got some real valuable books that are almost impossible to find. I bet I have a very hard to find book you would love to read. It's the true life story of John Clayton Adams (the real Grizzly Adams). The bear on the California Flag is Lady Washington, Grizzly Adams female grizzly bear. He was just a small man, but he did some unbelievable things with his bears. His big male finally killed him, fractured his skull. He lived for a year but you could see part of his brain.

He was buried in PT Barnum's beaver skin coat. The only known picture of him.

A few years ago after feeding my tigers, I walked by them while they were eating. Boy, did I get bit good, broke my leg, two big holes in my leg. I grabbed the chain link fence and got out of there. Luckily a nurse just happened to be looking at the animals. She got the bleeding slowed down till I got to the hospital. I limped around for a long time.

Probably my worst injury was from being bitten on the hand and arm by a monkey. I had to have plastic surgery, got blood poisoning, and a staph infection at the same time. Was in the hospital a couple of weeks and almost died. This was a tame monkey.

My wife was hand feeding a big tiger and he took her hand with the meat—left her hand hanging by a thread. They sewed her back together.

Then the big powerful meat saw got her, almost lost her hand again.

I read in the paper about this guy who got into trouble with his tiger, in Erie, Pennsylvania. It was just what I wanted—a big beautiful Siberian female. He said he hasn't been in the cage with her in years. We got her loaded into my van. I'm going down the Ohio Turnpike with this tiger right behind me. Somehow, she got the cage open and started licking my neck. I almost had a heart attack! I pulled over real slow and got out of the van. Quick!

Luckily, I had a baggie with some chicken in it. I opened the back door and threw the chicken into the cage. She walked into the cage and I tied the door extra good and secure. She turned out to be a wonderful animal.

Another time I was bringing a pair of adult jaguars in the back of my pickup in a super strong cage from a zoo in New Jersey. I had a Fiberglas cap over the cage. As I rolled into Scranton, Pennsylvania, I looked in my rear-view mirror and the huge jaguar had his head sticking out of the cage through a hole he had torn open.

I took the first exit and started making phone calls. The local vets wanted nothing to do with me. I saw a group of guys talking in a plaza parking lot, pulled up and told them I had a problem. One guy said, "Follow me, my brother is the chief of police."

On the way to my truck the chief told his brother that he didn't believe this scenario. But when he saw the situation, I got a police escort into this big trucking garage. They shut all the doors. Cops were standing around with machine guns, just in case.

They called this guy who put both cats to sleep, pulled them out of the cage, welded it back together. The cats were still sleeping when I pulled into my driveway hours later.

A few hours after that the phone rang—a friend from Akron said that I was headlines in the newspaper, that was scary.

One more good story…a lady in Montana who owned a zoo called and wanted a baby tiger cub. She had a nice, captive born grizzly to trade me for the baby tiger cub. Because I didn't have any, I contacted a friend in Minnesota who did. He said I could have one. That was a long drive 2100 miles in a beat up 1987 Ford pickup.

Early Sunday morning I was coming into Devils Lake, North Dakota. I noticed the little tiger wasn't acting right, getting real weak. I asked this cop for help, told him I was a cop in Ohio. He thought for a moment and said, "Follow me."

He took us to the Devils Lake Hospital. I'm thinking, I can't take this tiger in here this is a people hospital. Any way I walked in with the tiger. What a response. They gave the little tiger a badly needed IV and wrapped it in a warm blanket. Three nurses cared for him. When I left the hospital, the little tiger was like new. They saved his life. Made the trade and brought the bear home, without incident.

APPENDIX 5
BRENT HUGHES

For each of the previous three years, I had spent nearly the entire summer at a cabin across from the Matanuska River, near the glacier by the same name. There was never a soul over there except me. It was always a blissful sojourn. I even relished the routine of hauling water up the steep hillside from the rivulet (which allowed the silt to settle out) jutting out from the river streaming down below the cabin in the neighboring valley. I had never had a bear encounter and I cast about, carefree, typically without a shirt or a care in the world, sawing wood, squirrel-proofing this or that unintended portal of entry for these, my principal companions. A favorite "chore" was my weekly baking of bread in my Dutch oven inside the wood stove. The scent was heavenly and bread baking was one of my principal delights throughout those memorable summers.

To get on with the account, it was a rainy, lazy day that June 19th, 2002, that found me sleeping in late, listening to the deeply soothing hours-long patter of rain on the cabin's back porch overlooking a steep drop into the valley below, when I suddenly heard a sound so incongruous to anything I had heard in the summers previous that for a moment I felt teleported back to "civilization" and simply assumed (for the moment) that a large dog had ambled on up onto the deck below the loft where I was lying.

I quickly came to my senses as to where I was, that such a sound "just couldn't be possible" there, and, deeply curious, I rolled over onto my side and peered out the small loft window and down onto the back porch. What I saw first caused a real shock of amazement: a big, black-fur covered "3-wheeler." A black bear! How fantastic! I watched with surreal fascination. Then some primal instinct nudged me to make a move: I opened the loft window, and looking down on the bear spoke calmly (almost endearingly) "Hey, you're not supposed to be here." At that, the bear jerked it's head up, then tore off down over the bluff, never to be seen again (or so I assumed).

Weeks passed and I was preparing for a 4-day exploratory trip half way up the glacier (about 9 miles) to an abandoned hut rumored to be at the far end of an unusual, almost pasture-like recess in the mountain side, roughly at the fork of a glacier system. I was excited. The night before the early morning departure on my adventure up glacier I was sitting in the most comfortable make-shift wicker chair I'll ever know, looking down on the beaver ponds below, cradled by sheer cliffs below and jagged cliffs above. As the "midnight sun" lowered, spreading fingers of pine-shadows across the sleepy valley below, my eye caught sight of a striking figure standing in the middle of one of the lower beaver dams: a moose was grazing apparently leisurely drinking and grazing on underwater shoots—a crowning cinematic moment of yet another spectacular Alaskan summer "sunset."

As I prepared to stand up and head for the cabin, I noticed a sudden agitation in the moose's behavior far down below me: it kept looking back over its shoulder toward the nearby woods. There was a large stand of trees nearby the pond, but I could not detect any obvious motion in the woods. Soon the moose continued its browsing and seemed no longer distracted. I gave the episode no further thought. Another beautiful night—one of many such nights I have experienced over the years thanks due to my friends who own this remote setting in paradise.

I got up early the following morning, having eagerly packed the night before, and headed out to make the always adrenaline charged "dance" (the importance of whose rhythmic timing cannot possibly be underestimated) from rocky terrain to icy glacier terrain underfoot for the nine mile journey to an abandoned hut, the location of which, I wasn't sure, but I had my trusty ultra-light, ultra-tough Stephenson tent whose debut performed marvelously two years earlier on a one-day push the full 18 miles up the glacier to yet another hut. But I had spoken to a good friend of mine, legendary in his exploits all over the Chugach Mountains and his meticulous description of the location of the 9-mile hut (the objective of this first leg of my adventure) was every bit as detailed as his description two years earlier of the 18-mile hut's location (after 12 hours of negotiating crevasses—solo, and my first time on a glacier— was mercifully accurate—thanks Richard!). So my spirits were buoyed with exhilarating confidence as I bounded out of the cabin's front door, "securely" bear proofing the front door with several figure 8 wraps of string, and I was gone!

It was a predictably thrilling journey and late that evening, as the setting sun cast shadows out across the glacier from which I had just disembarked, I cast my eyes to the farthest reaches of the pastoral plateau I was told to expect, and with a sudden shot of adrenaline I excitedly stole into the gathering shadows, conscious that I was now well within the dominion of larger creatures than accustomed back in "civilization." The slightest tinge of anxiety made for a perfectly thrilling finality as I burst through the last thick patch of alders—and there it was! A much smaller than anticipated, but brilliantly shiny, silver hut—I found it!

After taking a moment to attempt to comprehend the magnanimity of the total panoramic majesty of jutting peaks, webbed together since time immemorial with the ever pervasive branching glacier systems, I slowly, purposefully, examined every aspect of the hut's exterior. It appeared to be of very tight, solid aluminum siding construction but both the front and back plastic windows had been shattered. As I twisted the door's metal locking apparatus and entered, my heart sank at the horrific trashing of the interior, the floor being covered with three inches of assorted shards of plastic, wood and insulation.

Thick walled aluminum pots had been pierced by impressive sets of teeth. Nearly all of the insulation had been ripped from the walls and roof. I decided that the entire following day would be devoted to cleaning up the mess and doing what I could to "bear proof" the hut upon departure.

First things first: Find tools and materials to "bear proof "the windows. I was relieved to find a hammer—and visitors log! —tucked safely far under what cabinetry remained intact (only five other parties had logged in since the hut's construction—the most recent, two years since the previous visitors).

Outside and stowed under the back of the hut, I found enough scraps to enable me to retrieve enough old nails and collect enough wood (running a reverse pattern of nails) to effect a makeshift deterrent over the windows. Satisfied that, despite my inevitable deep sleep, I would be roused long before any critter could make its way in uninvited, I fixed a quick meal, thoroughly washed all scent away in the nearby stream, and I was set for the night. I stepped outside the doorway and took in the surreal moment that seemed to focus into one instant, the day's twelve hours of constant, intense primal physical and mental demands. As I gazed at the mountainside, no more than 300 yards away I noticed, about 100 yards up the side, three large black bears—about 50 yards apart from each other—apparently feeding. I was transfixed. I had received unmistakable assurance that I indeed was a very solitary traveler in a very different land. This was no dream! And it was electrifying!

The following morning was brilliantly sunny and as I sat with my back to the wall in the deepest trance of serenity, I heard the increasingly audible sound of a rhythmic "woofing" approaching the wall at my back. I immediately imagined the swaying of a bear's head from side to side as it approached. Not really alarmed but definitely "thrilled" with primal alert, I unpassionately called out, "Hey, Griz." And the woofing ceased, followed by an absolute silence. The bear was gone!

Exhilarated at the triumph of finding the hut, and pleased to have been able to restore the hut to as "bear proof" a state as I thought was possible, I set off on my next leg of the adventure -- up over the ridge a few thousand feet further up the mountain, planning to exit the next valley the following day. After about a half hour of climbing, I turned to catch my breath and take in the view. The glacier system, forking several hundred feet below, was a glistening broad shimmering ribbon in the brilliant morning sun. It was glorious! At that moment I noticed a few hundred feet below, on the other side of the gulley, was a large black bear, foraging about in the brush. In an odd moment of invincibility and euphoria at being one with this timeless moment in the wild, and supposing it possibly prudent to alert the bear to my presence as not typical prey, I called out my standard bear call to identify my location, "Hey, Griz."

The large bear immediately looked up from below, and promptly began ambling toward my side of the ravine, and appeared to gain elevation in the process. I at once concluded my nonchalant, rather high spirited vocalization rather foolish, and with my .44 Magnum Smith and Wesson holstered across my chest, under my jacket, I sat down to prepare to deal with whatever development I had just precipitated, resolving to never commit such a pointlessly foolhardy act ever again.

I arrived at the ridge late as the sun was setting, having spent five hours in a bizarre, near-epochal dilemma staged in the middle of a patch of waist-deep snow, resting on an ice layer in a relatively narrow, steep chute. I attempted to ascend the rocky border of the snow/ice patch only to find that the rock at that elevation simply crumbled, having undergone yearly freeze-thaw cycles for millennia.

I decided that I needed to sacrifice my crampons' sharp points and using an ice axe so light it bordered on being a "toy" and using the only carabiner I had (a key chain variety with the words "Not for Climbing" stamped into its side) (I had excavated all snow under and around me in the simple act of trying, defiantly, to avoid sliding backward, off the small cliff and down the steep incline into the next ravine 100 feet below and I managed to drive the axe tip into the 1-inch of ice, then clip the key chain carabiner through it and then holding on with one hand, my other hand finally removed my pack and temporarily clipped it into the "toy axe/key chain carabiner" combination upon which now my fate rested. To keep the whole system from sailing down the mountain, I pressed my knee against the back of the pack to minimize strain on the axe while I used my free hand to eventually remove my crampons from the pack. Wedging my crampons against my other knee, I unclipped my pack and slung it onto my back. Somehow, with only my one free hand, I managed to untie my crampons from each other and hook one on to my axe, while I attempted to raise my first foot into the first crampon.

No sooner had I positioned my foot into the crampon than I experienced my characteristically intense leg cramps, the pain of which drove me to instantly remove my foot again to stretch my leg out. Were it not for the potentially-epochal dilemma in which I found myself, I might well have fully enjoyed the comical predicament played out (unbelievably, for hours, it turned out) in the rhythmic raising of my leg, arduously positioning my foot into the crampon, getting the first strap positioned just right—only to have to yank my foot back out as paroxysmal bolts of pain shot through my leg, cramped yet again. Hours past, and I eventually got both crampons on sufficiently securely to allow me to "crampon" through the crumbling rock, eventually making it to the ridge.

I had spent five hours in a stretch of gully I would have anticipated would have taken no more than twenty minutes. At the ridge's peak, 4000 feet above the glacier, I took the obligatory sequence of self-portrait photos of the titanic colossus of rock and ice from horizon to horizon in the background, and wasted no time heading on down the next valley with the resolve to get as far down into the valley as possible to pitch my tent in a relatively wind-free lower altitude.

Not surprisingly I slept well.

The following morning again was brilliantly sunny. For a fleeting moment of triumphant euphoria, I fancied myself on a Ulyssesian odyssey of my own. I was just effervescent! Taking my time I methodically released my tent anchors and began to stretch out my tent in preparation for folding it up when I happened to swing my gaze upward, and I was dumbfounded to look straight into the eyes of a black bear, no more than 40 yards away—sitting on its haunches, just watching my every move, intently. It was an eerie moment to realize the bear surely had been watching me for at least several minutes, and so close! I was most impressed with what (in retrospect, comically!) appeared to be a white bib, as if prepared for a "claws on" breakfast. Hmmmm!

Again, having logged a couple of "encounters" with black bears without any threatening incident, I had no precedent for anxiety and, having been my custom in every instance, I simply called out, calmly: "Hey, Griz." This bear, rather than take off, began zigzagging more or less straight for me in small loping lurches—which was not according to my expectation. I reflexively found myself reaching in for my silent partners, Smith and Wesson, and with an uneasy initiative again called out, but gone was the "teddy bear" endearment for this ursus. I well remember waving my arms, crisscrossingly, while speaking now in a very stern, determined voice. The bear immediately halted, and with my gratitude, turned around and raced out of sight, a cute little black furry cub bursting into view, bounding away, just above grass level until both were out of sight, never to be seen again. What a thrill to have experienced! What a relief to have ended.

Late that night, more exhausted than at any time in my life, I stumbled into my base cabin, and removing only my pack I made my way up to the loft and noting the time was 8:00 PM I instantly plummeted into sleep. When I awoke with boots still on, it was 8:00 PM. For the first time in my life I had actually slept 24 hours straight! To this day I am amazed.

APPENDIX 6
MYTH AND MISINFORMATION

I'm not sure how many e-mails I have received regarding the 20-foot man-killer brown bear. It ate three guys and took 20-plus rounds and several reloadings to bring it down (later the instrument of its destruction became a machine gun. Before long it will probably require a Sherman tank or two and an F-22 Raptor). The animal weighed around a ton. This was definitely NOT your garden variety brown bear. It measured 20 feet from paw to shoulder on 4 legs. Although this critter started out a normal life, it grew way beyond normalcy on the Internet.

The facts digress from the myth.

After responding to so many emails, I decided to summarize the event (taken from the Outdoor section of the *Anchorage Daily News*, Dec. 16, 2001—it's just out of arm's reach from my computer).

Theodore Winnen, a 22-year-old airman with the 18th Fighter Squadron at Eielson Air Force Base near Fairbanks, hunted deer with three buddies. They'd been dropped off on Hinchinbrook Island in Alaska's Prince William Sound October 14, 2001. Winnen and Staff Sgt. Jim Urban walked along a stream, carrying a .338 Win-Mag and a .300 Win-Mag respectively. As they continued upstream, they spotted a brown bear looking for salmon 40 yards distant.

They momentarily lost sight of the bear and it appeared 10 yards away moving toward them. All Winnen saw in his scope was head when he fired. The bullet entered its brain and knocked it backward. Winnen fired two more rounds into the bear's vitals and three more for good measure, a total of six shots…though the first did its job.

Each front paw, festooned with 3 to 4-inch claws, was nearly as wide as Winnen's chest. The skull's raw score was 28 8/16 inches, a combination of the length and width of the skull (Alaska's record brown bear skull measured 30 12/16 and was killed on Kodiak Island in 1952). Its hide measured 10-foot 6-inches from nose to tail and the animal's live weight was likely 1,000-1,200 pounds.

Enter Round 2. In June 2003 my friend Cas Gadomski sent me an email picture of a male corpse in a verdant glade. Squatting to the left is a person in a dark suit, extending a right latex gloved hand (possibly a coroner) above the corpse's crossed arms. It was a ghastly photo, the nastiest I've seen re: bear-man encounters, the other being one of the Glacier Bay fatality in September 1975.

Upon further query and review, I was informed to study the foliage. Note the pointy "leaves" in the foreground. Could this pix be from India and involve a cat (as in tiger)? I've not taken the time to research but someone out there probably could find the corpse picture and trace its origins.

On to Round 3. A few months later I began receiving pictures of the Winnen bear (along with the outlandish explanation of the renegade bear's size and demeanor) AND the corpse picture with the explanation that Winnen was the victim of the bear. Yawn.

NO. Winnen, his bear and the corpse pictures are NOT linked.

The *Anchorage Daily News* story includes two pictures—one of Winnen lifting the bear's right forepaw with both his hands in front of his chest and one of Winnen behind the bear carcass. Would not a newspaper that covered the nasty, renegade bear include a picture of the corpse also?

APPENDIX 7
R.C. HARROP

Captain Morgan:

RE: Bear Attack, Yukon River, Yukon Territory, Canada, 29 June 2001

On June 29, around 2215, one of the children noticed a moose and a calf being chased by a grizzly bear. The bear chased them onto an adjacent island from the one that we had already set up camp. The moose went straight through the adjacent island and jumped into the Yukon River. The calf was not behind it and neither was the bear. We then heard the bear running through the bush toward the island we were on. James Dishman yelled to RC Harrop and Joe Nash to get the guns, in fear that the bear may have smelled our dinner that had just been served. James Dishman and myself (Brent Morgan) then picked up some driftwood for defense and proceeded to get in front of the children. The bear came out of the brush and onto the point of the island, less than 100 feet from the group of children, hesitated, then charged toward the group. A few of the children started to run backwards away from the bear. We both yelled at them to "stop" and "don't run." James and I started to yell and wave the driftwood at the bear in hopes of discouraging it. The bear stood up on it's hind legs and sniffed the air and then made a charge at James who was about 10 feet from me and 30 feet in front of the children. The bear charged again, stopping around 10 to 15 feet away, when James charged back at it causing to back off. Once again the bear stood up on its hind legs. It was at this time that RC Harrop fired a warning shot into the air, in hopes that the bear would be scared off. It seemed to work at first when the bear turned around and moved away 30 feet before circling around to the left of us. The bear came back toward the group about 20 to 25 feet of where the first and second charges took place. RC tried to fire a second warning shot into the air but it misfired. RC then dropped to his knee and started to reload the firearm. The bear started its third charge toward James and myself. James and I both moved toward the bear waving our arms and yelling to keep its attention on us and not the rest of the group. The bear backed off for the third time. James moved back to the right to stay between the group and the bear. The bear turned around and started to charge for the fourth time. This time the bear had its head down and was moving a bit faster. The bear moved forward 15 to 20 feet then slowed. I noticed Joe Nash move in on the far right side with his weapon. The bear never stopped this time and kept coming toward us, picking up speed. The first shot from Joe hit the bear in the upper left side of the chest. This shot hit the bear about 15 feet from us. The second shot hit the bear mid-chest about 7 to 10 feet from us. The bear then swerved from its path and started to turn when the third shot hit him in the side. The bear then turned fully around and headed into the brush. I ran to RC's raft to get extra rounds for the weapons and gave them to RC. I got the rest of the group started packing after RC, Joe, and James told me to get them packed up and ready to leave the island. The group packed the gear while RC, Joe and James formed a perimeter to protect us in the event the bear returned. The group had packed the gear up and was ready to push off in fifteen minutes. It was at that time RC, Joe, and James pushed off the rafts and boarded the last one. We floated the river for about two miles before stopping for the night. RC and Joe got the whole group together and had a discussion on what just happened. This was to ensure the children were all right and allow them to express their feelings and concerns. With this done, RC and Joe performed a sweep of the new island then came back to set up camp and got the children in bed.

Having led these trips for over five years, including many encounters with both black and grizzly bears in the Alaskan wilderness, I have never experienced so aggressive a bear. Based on my experience as a U.S. Army Special Forces NCO, I know the armed forces recognizes bravery above and beyond the call. In the Army, for this type of action, a Soldiers Medal would have seemed appropriate to me. I would like to recommend that TSgt James Dishman be formally recognized by the Air Force for heroism for his actions. Unlike RC, Joe Nash, and myself, James was not a group leader on this trip, but stepped in anyway, risking his own life, unarmed (driftwood doesn't count against a grizzly) and unafraid, to help safeguard the lives of the 22 children and the other adults. James stepped right up with me and took decisive action that resulted in our averting a catastrophe in the wilderness, over 10 river hours from the nearest town.

Brent D. Morgan
Assistant Director,
Youth Enrichment & Outdoor Adventure Program
Fort Richardson, Alaska
CAPTAIN MULLIN:
    DEPARTMENT OF THE AIR FORCE
    PACIFIC AIR FORCES
MEMORANDUM FOR RECORD
FROM: 962 AACS/MA
SUBJECT: Bear Attack, Yukon River, Yukon Territory, Canada

1. While participating in a Ft Richardson Youth Services Outdoor Adventure Club outing on the Fortymile and Yukon rivers, we were attacked by a grizzly bear. The attack came on 29 June while encamped on the northeastern shore of the Yukon River, in the Yukon Territory, Canada. We had just finished cooking dinner, having set up a field kitchen about 100 yards from the campsite, and were playing Ultimate Frisbee on the beach when a bear chased a moose calf across the river and a grizzly bear burst through the brush on an adjacent islet, crossing a stream and arriving on our islet about 15 yards from our group of 22 kids and 13 adults. The bear charged several times and eventually had to be shot. Two individuals with our group, Brent Morgan, from Youth Services, and TSgt James Dishman, from the 19th Fighter Squadron, stood out for exemplary courage at the risk of their lives during this incident.

2. Mr. Morgan and TSgt Dishman responded immediately when the bear emerged from the brush by picking up driftwood and positioning themselves between the bear and the kids, yelling at the bear and waving the driftwood attempting to drive it away. TSgt Dishman directed the kids not to run when he saw a few of them running back toward the camp (as it would just further excite the bear). I was positioned to the left and behind TSgt Dishman, between him and the kids, keeping them back and under control and backing up TSgt Dishman and Mr. Morgan.

3. TSgt Dishman stood his ground through several charges and actually charged the bear back on two occasions. This bought the group valuable time needed for the weapons to be unpacked, loaded, and brought up to the line. Mr. Harrop, the group leader and guide, fired a shot into the air in an unsuccessful attempt to scare the bear off. When he attempted another warning shot, his gun misfired. As he did so the bear moved closer to him and TSgt Dishman charged toward the bear, making it pause, and allowing Mr. Harrop to reload his weapon. The bear continued to maneuver, stand up on its hind legs, and circle the group.

4. When the bear charged for the last time, it came within only a few feet of contact with Mr. Morgan and had to be shot by Mr. Joe Nash. The bear was shot a total of seven, and amidst the shooting the bear recoiled and charged again, finally turning back after the 6th shot. The bear took four 12 gauge sabot rounds and three .44 Magnum rounds. Once the bear retreated into the brush on our islet, TSgt Dishman, Mr. Morgan, Mr. Harrop, and Mr. Nash set up a perimeter. Of the four standing guard for the kids, only Mr. Harrop and Mr. Nash had firearms. The other adults directed the kids to pack their gear and bug-out. After arriving at our next destination, about two miles down river, we set up and Mr.

Harrop and Mr. Nash performed a sweep of the islet. Mr Harrop then led the kids through a group discussion so they could "air out" their thoughts and try to get over what had just happened. Most of the kids were still pretty shaken up over the incident. We arrived in the town of Eagle the afternoon of the next day and reported the incident to the U.S. Customs agent there. He told us he would notify the appropriate Canadian authorities. Mr. Harrop gave him contact numbers in the event further information was needed.

5. I recommend TSgt Dishman for the award for the Airmans Medal for heroism at the risk of his own life to save the lives of others. TSgt Dishman was under no obligation to put his life on the line, and many of the adults who participated did not place themselves in the unique position of risk that he did. This bear was hungry and exceptionally aggressive. TSgt Dishman's initiative in stepping to the front and challenging the bear prevented a mauling of one or more of our kids. In my experience as a former emergency medical technician, a bear attack on any member of the party while still a days paddle from the nearest town and outside radio or cell phone range could have easily been life threatening. The only rescue available was self-rescue. With the extent of injury typically associated with grizzly bear attacks, the likelihood of a successful attack from this bear resulting in a death was very real. TSgt Dishman placed the lives and safety of the kids above his own. He was an inspirational example of Service Before Self and a compelling example of heroism. He deserves the recognition commensurate with these qualities and his actions.

JAMES F. MULLIN III, Capt, USAF

Squadron Maintenance Officer
CAPTAIN MULLIN EMAILS:
Mr. Kaniut,
Sir,

I'm sure you're very busy, but I was hoping you could give me some feedback on the bear attack story related by Mr. Harrop (ref: the email below). One of the men who helped defend the kids from the bear attack is a U.S. Air Force sergeant for whom I am trying to submit a decoration for bravery. Just to refresh, we had a group of about 35 (22 kids, 13 adults) and the grizzly bear had chased a moose calf across the Yukon (in Canada, just a few miles east of the border) and ended up on our island facing a very large group of humans. The bear charged a few times, most of the time apparently turned back by Mr. Dishman, but on the last charge he had to be shot because we didn't think he'd stop. Jim Dishman was one of the two men who stood out in front of the crowd fending off the bear through its early charges with a piece of driftwood. The types of questions I need answered are (based on the info you have):

1. Was he at risk of his life?

2. Was the bear likely to attack?

3. Was there anything unusual about this bear incident?

4. What would have been the impact, had the bear attacked successfully

(i.e., we had not had time to get and load weapons)?

Again, I appreciate your time and if you need any further information I'd be glad to send you R.C.'s statement we're using for the submission of the medal for bravery for Mr. Dishman. My intent is to use your reply as an expert on bear attacks to support the submission for the medal.
Thank you very much,
James Mullin
Captain, US Air Force
(907) 753-0244

From: Larry Kaniut [mailto:kaniut@alaska.net]
Sent: Monday, December 03, 2001 11:47 PM
To: Jim and Laurie Mullin
Subject: Re: R.C. Harrop's Bear Attack story from the Yukon, June 2001
Captain Mullin,

I'm flattered that you'd want my input. I'll answer your four questions and attach a simulated bear attack which I'm developing for a bear mauling book (it demonstrates the quickness and tenacity of a charging grizzly, even though I believe the one that attacked the group was NOT a sow with cubs but rather an adolescent or young bear, which either didn't know better or had had success in charging groups in the past).

1. Was he at risk of his life?

All of the 35 were at risk. Once a bear makes up its mind and attacks, it is pretty much stop the bear or suffer the consequences. These men were not only responsible for those in their care but also very brave. How easy is it to stand in the way of a charging grizzly, with little ammo and take the full charge?

2. Was the bear likely to attack?

This was a very unusual animal. Either it was man-ignorant or had had some success scaring off groups in the past, because a wild grizzly will usually avoid humans. This animal was determined as it kept coming back, not swatting the ground and huffing or blowing from its mouth, but actually running more than once full speed towards the group, and even detouring away from one to another.

3. Was there anything unusual about this bear incident?

In the hundreds of bear attacks--black, grizzly and polar—that I've studied, I've never heard of a bear charging or attacking more than 5 people in a group. The most unusual thing about this bear that I've discovered is the size of the group and that the numbers did NOT deter it.

4. What would have been the impact, had the bear attacked successfully (i.e., we had not had time to get and load weapons)?

This bear had the time and power to seriously injure or kill several of the group. It is to the credit of the shooters that they kept the attention of the animal as it attacked them and not the kids. There are cases of grizzlies killing all in a party. A few years ago two experienced hunters were gutting a bull elk in British Columbia and a grizzly killed them both, even though their rifles were nearby and they held skinning knives. I believe serious injury or death would have befallen one or more of the group had the men not been adequately armed. It is obvious that more than one weapon was beneficial if not crucial to the safety and lack of injury to the party. Even though the presence of pepper spray and/or its use is unknown, the best "bear stopper" available was employed. As much as one hates to destroy a bear, better the bruin than the human. I commend the group for its "state of mind", the leaders for the preparatory teaching of the kids and the men for having the presence of mind and training to keep the group safe by dispatching the bear. I'm happy to provide more information if necessary. Please advise.

Congratulations for your efforts to reward their actions.

Respectfully,

Larry Kaniut

From Capt Jim Mullin, USAF
Squadron Maintenance Officer
962d Airborne Air Control Squadron
14410 30th St. Elmendorf AFB AK 99506-3980
Phone: (907) 552-3082 [DSN 317-552-3082]
Fax: (907) 552-1501 [DSN 317-552-1501]
james.mullin@elmendorf.af.mil

Mr. Kaniut,

Sir, thanks for the quick response--I'm sure it will be a big help. Just a note: The guys who held off the attack through the first charges were armed only with sticks and courage. The guns were packed in boats and tents over 100 yards away and had to be retrieved, loaded, and brought up to the front of the group. The guy I'm writing the medal for stood off the bear and actually charged him back--with nothing but a piece of driftwood in his hands. I was about 10 yards behind him.

Jim Mullin

From: "Jim and Laurie Mullin" <mullinf@worldnet.att.net>
  To: "'Larry Kaniut'" <kaniut@alaska.net>
  Cc: "'Mullin James III Capt 962AACS/MA'" <James.Mullin@ELMENDORF.af.mil>;
  "'Harrop, R.C. [.mil]'" <royal.harrop@richardson.army.mil>
  Sent: Monday, December 03, 2001 10:11 PM
  Subject: RE: R.C. Harrop's Bear Attack story from the Yukon, June 2001
Larry,

I'd be glad to keep you in the loop. I attached your email response, attack scenario, and the cover Pg. of your web site to the decoration package. The award we are going to is called the Airmans Medal (in the Army it is called the Soldiers Medal). It is an award for bravery at the risk of your own life to save the lives of others when your failure to act would not result in any sanction (i.e., Firemen can't get the medal for rushing into a burning building, but an aircraft mechanic might). The approval process goes all the way to the Secretary of the Air Force. A board of colonels in Washington D.C. reviews the statements and the incident and makes a decision. This is a very significant award, and the most prestigious award given to members of the Air Force in peace time.

I appreciate your response and have attached the statements of myself, Brent Morgan, and R.C. Harrop that we are using to support the award. Of course, as you'd expect they differ a bit ("fog of war" - ha ha), but I hope they help you capture the sense of the event. Brent Morgan and Jim Dishman stood in front of the group with nothing but driftwood and fended off a grizzly bear through three charges to allow the others to get their guns and eventually and, unfortunately, shoot the bear. It is that courage we are trying to recognize for Jim Dishman. Unfortunately, the Army (Brent's employer) does not have a similar award for people in Brent's employment category. If it did, we'd be pushing for that as well.

Thanks again for the "expert testimony," and I'll keep you posted on the status of the decoration. I hope to read our story in print some day in the future!

Jim Mullin

From: Larry Kaniut [mailto:kaniut@alaska.net]
Sent: Tuesday, December 04, 2001 8:41 AM
To: Mullin James III Capt 962AACS/MA
Subject: Re: R.C. Harrop's Bear Attack story from the Yukon, June 2001
Capt. Mullin,

In the interests of expediency, I did not re-read the piece that Harrop sent me. He told me the story this summer, and I told him I'd never heard of even a bear charging as many as 35 people, let along attacking the group. Extremely commendable action.

Perhaps you could remember me in your ongoing efforts as it would be great to encapsulate your efforts in this medal awarding and bear attack...as well as some of the kids, etc. I hope to carry Harrop's version to the end by incorporating others' comments to illustrate the need to be prepared AND practiced in bear country.

Thank you.

Larry

APPENDIX 8

ENDANGERED SPECIES

(My July 19, 2003, email response from Don assured my use of this piece)

The Morality of the Grizzly Hunt
by
Don H. Meredith
First Place
Magazine Feature (Hunting)
Outdoor Writers of Canada
2000 National Communications Award

(first published in the April/May 1999 Alberta Outdoorsmen and subsequently published in the book, Voices in the Wind, B. Grinder et al. (ed.), © 2000, The Waterton Natural History Association.)

If you ever wonder how important wildlife and wild places are to people, just mention the phrase "endangered species" and watch the emotions take flight. As an information officer for Alberta Environment, I receive countless inquiries about threatened and endangered wildlife from school children and teachers throughout the province. It's a hot topic in the school curriculum that can trigger a wide range of emotional responses in both children and adults. **How can we allow a fellow species to become extinct?**

Now, add to this legitimate concern the hunting of a high profile species that's perceived to be endangered, and you have a very hot issue indeed. Such is the plight of grizzly bear hunting in Alberta and British Columbia.

Before I go much further, I want to make two things clear. 1) I am not a bear hunter, either grizzly or black bear. Although I hunt big game, bears are just not on my list of desired game animals. I can understand why others hunt them, but I don't. 2) Although I am an employee of the Government of Alberta, I am not representing government here, and the opinions I express are my own. However, I do believe my position with government and as a non-bear hunter does provide me with a unique view of the issue.

The Facts

The grizzly bear is not endangered in either Alberta or British Columbia. Yes, it is classified as endangered in the United States, outside of Alaska. But in British Columbia the population is very healthy indeed. Here in Alberta the species is on the Blue List of wildlife species at risk (see Alberta Environment's Status of Wildlife report). Blue List species are those that may be at risk in Alberta (Red List species are at risk, Yellow and Green List Species are not at risk). Blue List species require special management to ensure they do not become threatened or endangered. But why is the grizzly bear on the Blue List?

Of the two bear species that inhabit Alberta (black and grizzly), the grizzly is the least tolerant of human habitation. Like the wolf, it was exterminated from large tracts of North America as human settlement expanded from east to west. Ranchers and farmers did not abide a predator that threatened their livelihoods and their lives. Now, the bear is restricted to a few of the remaining wilderness areas on the continent, mostly in Montana, western Canada and Alaska. These are areas where either development is just getting underway or wilderness areas and parks have been established to conserve these remaining wild places and the animals that live in them.

Here in Alberta, we are on the eastern edge of modern grizzly bear range which runs in a strip roughly down the western third of the province from the extreme northwest corner through the Peace River region and the Swan Hills to the foothills and Rocky Mountains of central and southern Alberta. In the south, the range is limited on the east by agriculture, industry and urban development. These limits are absolute. The bear will not expand east from where it is now.

In the north, however, the grizzly has been expanding its range in recent years, moving out of the Rocky Mountain foothills into the boreal forest. Annual population assessments conducted by Alberta Environment indicate the grizzly bear is slowly moving into areas it hasn't occupied since the early years of the 20th century.

In 1987, biologists estimated the provincial population — outside the national parks — to be between 520 and 575 bears. (These are not absolute figures because it is difficult to count most big game species, especially grizzly bears. But they are the best estimates we have based on scientific survey techniques, that include capture and marking studies, and relating the results to known grizzly habitat throughout the province.) By 1995, similar studies indicated as many of 750 bears occupied the province. Today, the estimate is closer to 800 bears outside the national parks (the three mountain parks are home to 125 to 150 grizzlies). This is steady progress towards Alberta Environment's provincial population objective of 1,000 animals — the theoretical number of grizzlies this province is capable of supporting.

Although Alberta is on the margin of grizzly bear range, the bears are doing well here. Some might argue too well.

Why are the bears increasing in numbers and expanding into new range in the north? The answer to this question lies in the close relationship we have with the grizzly centering around the hunt. As with most relationships, it is a two-way street.

The Hunt

There is a long tradition of hunting grizzlies in this province. In the early years, much of the hunting was unrestricted. In 1927, the government sought to control the hunt by requiring grizzlies be hunted under licence. However, the bear population continued to decline in southern Alberta. In 1969, the government closed the season in the south to protect the population there. In 1971, it restricted grizzly hunting to the spring throughout the province, eliminating the killing of bears incidental to the hunting of other big game in the fall.

In 1982, the season was reopened in selected Wildlife Management Units (WMUs) in the south where grizzlies were again becoming a nuisance. However, the number of hunters in each WMU was controlled through the introduction of limited-entry draw hunts. These hunts were expanded to all grizzly hunting by 1989.

The result of these restrictions has been that fewer grizzlies are killed and more bears survive to reproduce. As the densities of bears increase, more individuals disperse into new habitat to find enough food and escape from aggressive males. Fortunately for the dispersing bears in the north, there is habitat to occupy.

However, there is a cost for this success. As our human population increases and more people enter grizzly habitat to exploit resources or just enjoy wild landscapes, they encounter an increasing number of grizzlies. The number of reported incidents of grizzly bears causing problems to the public in the 1970s averaged 25 per year. From 1988 to 1990, that average increased to 117 per year; and by 1993 to 1995, 303 per year.

Likewise, the number of so-called "nuisance" grizzlies handled by Alberta Environment (those requiring transplantation to remote areas or indeed killing because of public safety concerns) increased from about 6 per year in the mid 1980s to 26 per year in 1997. Many of the bear-human encounters that led to the removal of the bears were life threatening, some ending in maulings or death. The grizzly bear is a large predator that needs a lot of space. Fortunately, the bear avoids encounters with people when it can. But with more people in the bush, more encounters are unavoidable.

This give and take relationship with the grizzly is one reason why the government allows the hunting of this Blue List species. Alberta Environment justifies the hunt for the following reasons:

1. There is a small annual surplus of male bears available to support the season.

2. Because Alberta Environment requires that hunters not kill bears that are found in groups of two or more individuals, mostly male bears are killed in the spring. Males kill and eat grizzly cubs. By reducing the number of the surplus males, the population has a better chance of growing.

3. Hunting reduces the number of problem bears by killing many of those that are least wary of humans.

4. A hunted bear is a wary bear, and less likely to cause problems with people.

5. Because each grizzly killed must be registered with Alberta Environment, the harvested bears provide important information about the bear population, such as distribution and age of individuals.

6. Grizzly bear hunters are people who learn much about the bears and, as a result, are strong advocates for programs that conserve the species in Alberta.

(A complete discussion of grizzly bear management can be found at Alberta Environment's Hunting in Alberta; go to "Management Issues and Programs.")

The limitations placed on the grizzly bear hunt has not deterred hunters. On average, about 1,200 residents apply each year for 160 licences. That means it takes an average of about seven years to obtain a licence in the draw, depending upon where you apply (it takes longer in the south and shorter in the north).

Getting a licence does not ensure success in the field. On average 12 grizzlies are harvested each year, with the harvest in some years being as low as five and as high as 20.

What's the Fuss About?

If the taking of 12 mostly male bears each year is not affecting the population growth of grizzlies, then what is? The real culprit that threatens our grizzly bears is human encroachment on grizzly habitat. If you want to protect this species so that it doesn't regress from an animal that may be at risk to one that is endangered, then you'd better protect where it lives. In order to do that, you're going to have to convince people that unlimited economic growth in this province and grizzly bears do not mix. You can't have one with the other. If you want the grizzlies and a strong economy, then you must fit the bear and its habitat into the economic/environment equation.

In the last few years we have done remarkably well with the grizzly bear. Despite significant growth in human population and the economy, the grizzly population has also grown and expanded. But the accompanying increase in number of problem bear incidents shows us that there is a limit to the number of grizzlies that will be tolerated.

If habitat destruction is the main threat to grizzly bears, then why are grizzly bear hunters being singled out as scapegoats by some so-called environmentalists? Aren't we all in this together — we who want to conserve this noble symbol of our wilderness? The reason is grizzly bear hunters are easy targets for a frustrated environmental movement. Grizzly hunters hunt a high profile species more for its trophy value than its meat. By attacking them, protesters can take public attention away from their own inability to make a difference on the habitat protection front.

But what the hunt protesters do not understand is that by attacking one of the bear's allies, they are attacking the bear. While we argue over the killing of 12 bears per year, others are making irrevocable decisions about grizzly habitat that will ultimately seal the fate of the animal.

Must we hold to our ideologies so strongly that we have to sacrifice a species to prove we are each right? Perhaps we would do more for the bear if we all agree that fighting among ourselves does not solve the problem. By putting aside our differences for the animal's sake, perhaps we can learn a little bit from each other about how important this animal is to the heart and soul of the province, and work together to keep it here.

To me, the grizzly is a symbol of the quality of wilderness we still have in Alberta — true wilderness where I am not in complete control of what might happen, where I must take calculated risks in order to truly enjoy it. Experiencing such wilderness forces me to come to grips with my own mortality, and shapes my view of the world and my place in it.

If the possibility of seeing a grizzly was removed from that experience, I would lose an important part of who I am and why I live in Alberta.

Is the grizzly bear hunt moral? Questions of morality are personal issues, although governments legislate morals all the time. But if hunting an animal causes someone to know and understand that animal better, and contributes to its conservation, then who am I to question the morality of the hunter? Instead, perhaps I should try to better understand that hunter, and rejoice in the fact the grizzly bear population in this province is healthy enough to support a limited hunt.

APPENDIX 9

PUBLIC SAFETY

Our family friend reported her Girdwood bear problem to ADFG some years past and was told "we're not here to protect people but to protect bears."

Not all members of the Alaska Department of Fish and Game are locked into rubbing shoulders with bruin in town. Some ardently oppose the idea but have been out-voted by colleagues. It seems the ADFG is PC and wants to let the city dwellers allow dangerous animals in their yards—a prime example of ADFG's managing people rather than animals. The citizenry of Alaska needs to speak up with a loud voice demanding public safety in public as well as private spaces.

My friend Lee Miller, former ADFG biologist in charge of defense of life and property, told me the 35 or so bears killed in Anchorage in 2018 was prohibitive, more like statewide numbers at the end of the season and "something needs to be done about the bears in town."

Another ADFG biologist friend told me the "new guys think they know it all and don't listen to or respect the veterans."

Regarding reducing bear numbers in town and trying to discern proper protocol, I wrote three ADFG personnel (including the commissioner) during the summer-fall of 2018. I found it somewhat amusing that their ability to manage people rather than animals resulted in the commissioner's delegating his south-central regional supervisor to respond. His email, copying my two letters to area biologists, told me not to bother his biologists any more with similar messages.

I also wrote all seven members of the ADFG game board and had ZERO responses. In January 2019 I wrote the new governor hoping he'd selected a commissioner who wasn't PC and going to poll the public about their desires for wildlife in our yards. It would be nice to see legal reduction of bears. We'll see what develops.

Since bears are gaining a stronger foothold in our cities, why not use leg hold snares? A simple and safe solution for removing innumerable bears is the 5-gallon bucket trap used so effectively in Canada, eh?

APPENDIX 10
GAME BOARD LETTER

January 5, 2009
Alaska Board of Fisheries/Game
POB 115526
Juneau, AK 99811-5526
Dear Board,

Having resided in Anchorage since 1966 it has become apparent to me that it's time to thin the herd. We have more moose and bears and more humans being injured by them than in Anchorage's history. From 1970 to 2000 (30 years) my wife and I had 2 bear sightings (Author update: should have been 3 bears) within a mile of our home. From 2000-2007 we saw 2-5 every day in our yard. Last summer a juvenile delinquent black was in our chicken run until I sprayed him with pepper (I reported it to ADFG anticipating killing it if it returned).

In the interests of public safety we request a reduction of 10% of Anchorage bears in 2009. This could be accomplished by way of an archery season (certified archers only) or asking for qualified volunteers who could be tested at the range (to shoot bears with weapons that would not endanger humans).

We propose manageable fish weirs on salmon streams downstream from human use areas (such as hiking, biking, skiing trails) which should minimize bears' presence. Any bear down stream of the weir has a death penalty. Other habituated bears would be harvested by certified archers or designated ADFG "harvesters." Hides could be retained by hunters or turned over to ADFG; same with meat.

Reducing bear numbers will be enhanced by reducing attractants. Because moose calves are the bears' primary attractant to Anchorage, we request at least 20 animals be harvested by archers before December 2009 (and that number be repeated or increased in 2010). OR that these animals be transferred to Alaska Moose Federation for removal to more sparsely populated moose areas.

The people in the group that I represent (B.E.A.R.S.—Bear Elimination And Related Strategies) agree that it's time to thin the numbers and hope that the Board initiates a doable program for doing so. Thank you.

Larry Kaniut
4800 Natrona
Anchorage, AK 99516
kaniut@alaska.net

P.S. It's possible that Hunter Education would benefit by selecting-allowing young people to observe this community problem as future problem-solving citizens.

APPENDIX 11
THIN THE HERD NEWSPAPER PIECE

I would be the first to admit that some people will take issue to this satire as well as this book. However, in the interests of public safety and the safe-good health of our fellow travelers, I submit it in the hopes that people will gain the necessary information to remain safe with bears. If one person is saved from a mauling or a life altering or ending experience, I will be grateful.

In April 2009 disgusted with the inaction of Anchorage wildlife managers I wrote a satire for the Anchorage Daily News titled "Thin the Herd":

This piece is addressed to the fairy dust sniffers of Anchorage (and elsewhere) and to those who have lived here long enough to understand reality.

Craig Medred covered a lot of territory in his piece Sunday, August 3, 2008 seemingly in search of a leader in addressing the bear confusion in Anchorage. I particularly enjoyed three highlights to the article. First the information about salmon in our streams. Second, the concept that if you reduce bear numbers, "others will come." Third, Craig's frustration-dilemma over finding a leader to confront the confusion.

I've followed Anchorage bear numbers since 1966 and have become increasingly amused the past few years by the city's response, more specifically the "inaction" of those given authority to "manage" fish and big, wild life. We lived in the same domicile from 1970-2000 during which time we saw 2 bears [should be 3; author notation] between our house and the New Seward Highway 1.5 miles distant; from 2000-2005 we saw 2-5 bears each summer in our yard; in 2006 we saw 7 around our house. Are there more bears in Anchorage? Is there a way of dealing with them?

The answer to both questions is YES.

I'll address Medred's points and the bear numbers in reverse order.

Third, appoint or elect me to the management position of overseeing bears in Anchorage. Here's what you'll get. With the help of my volunteer BEARS organization we will return Los Anchorage to its original Anchorage. Before statehood a yard bear likely ended up on the table. Ditto that in 2009 (after I'm appointed) and beyond.

Any bear reported in a neighborhood will be promptly removed. Edible portions will be donated to charity. Skull, hide and/or claws will be auctioned.

Contemplate a spring bear hunt along the hillside—rifles allowed no closer than 1 mile from a permanent residence. Qualified archery hunters are required to hunt within 100 yards of garbage cans. Contemplate an annual moose hunt within the Anchorage Bowl beginning this fall—trophy bulls will be "sold" to the highest bidder (monies go to further thinning the herd and anticipated litigation against parties responsible for "management"—mayor, assembly, ADFG, Public Safety). If moose are to be hunted in a residential area, archery gear is required; on the hillside the same firearms regulations exist as for bears.

Contemplate a thorough house cleaning within the department. I'll hire biologists who manage game, not biologists who manage people. I'll rid the department of spineless people who fear criticism from fairy dust sniffers. I'll hire only biologists who prefer public safety over **big, wild life**.

Second, if you kill them, others will come. Okay. So would you rather have 10 bears in town or 5? Hello. The reason that we have bears now as opposed to twenty years ago is because they are not hunted, they are not adversely conditioned and we doltish humans "tolerate" them.

If we kill them and others come, we reduce them to a manageable number. We also send them a message that they don't dictate our living conditions. Many of my neighbor women fear going into their yards—the operative word here is THEIR...not bears' yards.

First, salmon numbers attract bears and if we reduce salmon numbers in our streams, that will reduce bears in town. Say, WHAT!

Initially Fish and Feathers wanted us to eliminate dog food. Then it was bird feeders. Next they frown upon livestock and blame people for having attractants such as chickens, ducks, peacocks, goats, llamas and horses. Based on Medred's article we can now add salmon to their list.

So if we rid our yards of attractants such as small children and slow moving seniors and our streams of salmon, we will reduce the bear numbers in Anchorage?

Wrong.

The number one attractant to bears in Anchorage is the cute, chocolate colored, 4-legged, furry bear magnet called moose calf. How many moose calves have been "harvested" by bears in the Anchorage bowl this summer?

Might I suggest that instead of reducing slow moving seniors, children, bird feeders, dog food, pets, livestock, raspberry and strawberry patches from our yards and salmon from our streams...that it would be much simpler, more cost effective and psychologically healthy for all those who fear leaving the confines of their homes (not to mention those

444

who have killed bears within their homes) to reduce bear numbers. And moose. And, of course, reevaluating the salmon runs up Campbell and Rabbit creeks…maybe installing weirs way downstream.

It is not necessary to live in a city that is overrun with big, wild life. After all it is a city.

My leadership plan calls for a like-minded volunteers who see this issue as one of public safety rather than a tourist attracting, tree and bunny hugger la la land. We will implement BEARS—Bear Elimination and Related Strategies (AKA Bear Busters United).

If you wish to join my BEARS organization, call me at (907) bye bear.

If you're a fairy dust sniffer, don't bother applying.

By the way Craigo, I've found the leader. And he is I.

P.S. I don't need some sniveling tree hugger, bunny saver or fairy dust sniffer to tell me to move elsewhere if I don't like the animals. I love bears, but not in my yard or house. Nor do I need you to tell me that the bears were here before I was. Trust me, there ain't a bear in Alaska that was here before I was. His grandpap may have been but he wasn't! Thank you very much.

And, yes, I'm the bear tales guy Larry Kaniut—the one who doesn't want to read about you, your spouse, your children, grandchildren or pets being savaged by a bear, in town or out. Have a BEARY nice day.

As you might expect, the critics came out of the woodwork, like so many termites. Either they do not understand satire or they do not share my concept of putting bears in their proper place. I've listed a few selected letters to the editor from the *Anchorage Daily News*:

RESPONSES TO KANIUT:(I've included some responses showing strong emotions from both sides of the satire)

Letters to the editor (4/22/09)   Published: April 21st, 2009 07:44 PM

Bear hunts are a necessity

Finally a letter I agree with, Larry Kaniut! (" 'Los Anchorage' is too soft on bears," April 20).

I lived in Anchorage from 1978-91 and saw one bear the entire time. I moved to Funny River and didn't see any bears until June of '98 and that was a sow brown and her two cubs on the chase to kill a newborn moose.

I knew for years she was around, but she always kept her cubs away from my cabin. She has been gone for two years and my freezer has been broken into, my dog had a face-to-face with a young brown and the neighborhood has been terrorized by young bears. A cub from Russian River with a tag on was finally killed for being a bad bear.

Granted, I live in a subdivision in the woods but people are moving here and game control has to become an issue.

We need a hunt to clean out the bad bears and put the fear of man in the others. The Kenai Refuge is just a couple of miles away, and the smart ones will go there.

I don't hunt, except with a camera. Now I have shotguns with slugs at every door.

--Scott Millen, Funny River

Let's control bears, moose

I have new hero, Larry Kaniut.

I too am sick and tired of Rick Sinnott wandering around Anchorage like a society doctor. Offering up little nuances of animal behavior so we can live in Shangri-La holding hands with animals. The problem is these animals, particularly moose, have a brain the size of a walnut ... OK, the size of a fist. The point is the moose do not know they are related to Bullwinkle and the bears to Smokey, consequently people get trampled, killed and/or eaten. I grew up in Anchorage and in the '50s we would shoot moose during the second season where Indian Hills and Shady Lane are now and around Boniface Lake, now called Cheney Lake.

Why the second season? That is when deep snow drove them down out of the hills. Having moose and bears wandering around town is ludicrous and anyone who doesn't think so is an idiot.

-- Jim Miller, Anchorage

Marry me, but bring a rifle

I would like to know if Mr. Kaniut would like to get married and live in Bird Creek. Bring rifle to protect slow-moving senior.

-- Joan Daniels, Bird Creek

Letters to the editor (4/23/09)

Published: April 22nd, 2009 06:31 PM **Kaniut's bear solution ridiculous**

I was deeply disturbed by Larry Kaniut's cavalier attitude toward killing bears and moose within Anchorage, expressed in his article "Los Anchorage" printed in Monday's paper. Most of the article was a pointed critique of Rick Sinnott's handling of wildlife within Anchorage. Rick seeks to find a way for Anchorage residents to cohabitate with the wildlife that they will inherently encounter. Kaniut proposes an easy solution, by simply shooting all the bears in Anchorage.

Kaniut's comment about "cleaning house" at Fish and Game only highlights his ignorance of the situation at hand. Rick Sinnott is one of the hardest-working people I know. Rick has done a great job so far and the insinuation that someone else could do better is absurd, the idea that it would be Kaniut himself, laughable.

One of the joys of living in Anchorage, as opposed to other cities this size, is the wildlife, and although I agree that last year's rash of bear encounters is concerning, I don't agree with Kaniut's gun-happy brand of management.

— Erin Remley, Anchorage

Writer's ideas are frightening

I thank all the spineless, fairy-dust sniffers out there that Larry Kaniut is just a "harmless writer" and not a staff biologist with the state or federal government.

His vitriolic writing ("Los Anchorage' too soft on bears," ADN 4/20) and the ideas he expresses are much more frightening to me than encountering the occasional moose or bear in the Anchorage Bowl.

Mr. Kaniut, I suggest you try a sniff of that fairy dust; it's not as bad as you might think.

— Mark Miner, Anchorage

Letters to the editor (4/29/09)   Published: April 28th, 2009 08:49 PM

Bear control is common sense

I'd love a return to the common sense practice of putting people's safety over bears as advocated by Larry Kaniut (" 'Los Anchorage' is too soft on bears," April 20). And I have similar anecdotal evidence.

Bear sightings have increased dramatically and dangerously in the neighborhood that lies one-third of a mile from the Seward Highway where I've lived since the 1960s. Please get rid of some of the bears and some of the moose that attract them.

-- Kathy Burgoyne, Anchorage

APPENDIX 12
PEPPER SPRAY

Missoulian online Wednesday, December 12, 2007; Grizzly bear committee to examine spray claim; By JOHN CRAMER of the Missoulian

The Interagency Grizzly Bear Committee voted Tuesday to look into whether it is unintentionally endorsing one brand of bear spray in its public education materials.

The committee, a coalition of federal and state agencies that oversees the endangered bear in the lower 48 states, also decided to review whether its spray guidelines were needed since the Environmental Protection Agency already regulates the product.

The committee, which met in Missoula, took the action at the request of Mark Matheny, president of UDAP Industries of Bozeman, which makes Pepper Power bear spray.

Matheny said the committee was using tax dollars to unfairly endorse one of his competitors, Bushwacker Backpack and Supply Co. of Kalispell, which makes Counter Assault bear spray.

Counter Assault is the only spray mentioned in the IGBC's education materials, which include brochures, posters, videos and Web sites.

The materials are produced for the IGBC by the Center for Wildlife Information, a nonprofit group in Missoula.

Chuck Bartlebaugh, the center's director, said Counter Assault deserved to be mentioned in the materials because it is the only EPA-approved spray that also meets the IGBC's guidelines for spray duration and distance.

"It's a public safety issue," he said.

He said Counter Assault also deserves to be mentioned because Bushwacker is the only spray manufacturer that makes donations to help pay for the IGBC's education materials.

Bartlebaugh said he would include the other three EPA-approved sprays if their manufacturers helped to pay for the materials.

Under a partnership created last year, the IGBC gave the Center for Wildlife Information $38,000 to produce education materials, training programs and other services as part of the government's bear awareness campaign. The center is slated to receive $60,000 from the IGBC next year.

Matheny and Tim Lynch, UDAP's general manager, praised the IGBC and the Center for Wildlife Information for its bear awareness campaign.

But they said they have been trying for years to convince the IGBC to stop including Counter Assault in its education materials.

They also challenged the IGBC's spray guidelines, which were adopted in 1998 after several companies marketed pepper sprays that were of questionable effectiveness.

The IGBC's guidelines include a minimum percentage of capsaicin, a spray duration of six seconds and a spray distance of 25 feet.

The EPA's regulations, which were adopted in 1999, do not include spray duration and distance standards.

Matheny questioned the basis for the IGBC guidelines - which only his competitor Counter Assault meets - but committee members said they didn't know where the guidelines originated.

Bartlebaugh said the guidelines came from recommendations from bear biologist Chuck Jonkel, who led studies in Missoula in the 1990s using various bear sprays on captured bears.

But Matheny said the guidelines came from Bartlebaugh and Pride Johnson, president of Bushwacker Backpack, who devised the guidelines to promote Johnson's product.

Johnson could not be reached for comment.

Bear spray is a red pepper-based chemical aerosol that is designed to deter a charging bear by temporarily irritating its eyes, nose and throat.

Chris Smith, the IGBC's chairman, said the group's education materials do appear to promote Counter Assault.

The IGBC voted to appoint a task force to review its spray guidelines and to submit a report by March 1.

The group also voted to remove any information from its education materials and Web site that appear to endorse any brand of bear spray.

Matheny said his company would consider legal action against the IGBC if it didn't remove the references to Counter Assault.

Bartlebaugh said he did not think the materials favored Counter Assault.

He said he expected Bushwacker to withdraw its donations if Counter Assault was not mentioned in the IGBC's education materials.

The company has donated about $3,000 annually for the past five years toward the materials, he said.

Bartlebaugh said losing Bushwacker's donations would make it more difficult to promote bear awareness, including tips for living and recreating safely in bear country.

Reporter John Cramer can be reached at 523-5259 or at JohnCramer@ missoulian.com

APPENDIX 13

TIPS

Attacks I've studied from my books

Victim	Lesson
Coverston	had no partner nor bear stopper; sow left after he stopped moving
Diane Nelson	sow & 2 cubs; lots of noise w. chainsaws and helicopter didn't phase bear; partner shot bear off; effects in medical costs and feeling safe in woods again
Roberts-Mc Cracken	followed wounded brownie too soon; partner shot off; didn't know area or where they were; lost companion in effort to return; no communicative device
Chuck Lewis	brownie came to gunshot/dinner bell—from great distance (maybe 1 mile)
Greg Brown	fought bear—punched brownie with fist and kicked in groin; kept away from its jaws by pulling himself below its chest downhill
Marti Miller	agency training protected her from predatory black; she felt badly for killing it
Will Atkinson	punched out black at Liard Hot Springs
Larry Bond	prayer saved/brownie unusual; no bad dreams four years later
Trent-Waldron	visibility? No weapon. Brownie/surprise near moose kill. No reaction time.
Routh	plane noise. Was black bear predatory or people conditioned? Told me he chose to kill bear. Steve

turned defense into offense switching bear's eyes w. branch. It left him and rushed wife, swam out to him. Plane starting saved Routh. He radioed.

Austin	Griz bear ambush—dug hole in tundra in minutes. Bears not always bothered by noise. Friend shoots 3 griz in cabin with 3 .243 shots! Importance of practice.
Helmuth Port	solo tent-hunting, griz into tent, he screams shrilly into its ear and it leaves after biting his arm
Bruce Brown	reliable partner, brown bear
Ellie Florance	dozen-plus tents, adolescent brown bear enters her tent, colleague shoots w. .44, kills w. shotgun
Jesiolowski	partner shot brown bear off him. Later charged by other brown—hound dog nose to ground on their scent trail
Carl Stalker	couple in Pt. Lay, 4:30 AM encounter polar, she flees into sister's cabin, he keeps going around cabin, bear kills him—armed with knife. Most polar bear villages have polar bear watches/warnings.
Jack Muir	solo archery hunting, shoots charging brown sow w. cubs w. .44 Magnum at 8 feet.
Al Thompson	Al punched brown, bear carried-dropped him under foreleg, played dead, bear left, first aid
Guy George	strikes grizzly with ice ax—instinct from practice
Al Johnson	Griz bear climbed 15-feet up tree, pulled him out, immobile on ground, bear left
Moerlein-MacInnes	sling shot and stick—shot at and hit bear; grizzly bear fled w. Scott on ground
Craig Sharp	tracked wounded brownie, partner shot bear off him
Dick Jensen	toe to toe/hand to hand, brown sow left when he went immobile
Knut Peterson	immobile = griz bear left
Forest Young	brownie carcass defense, partner found and left shotgun and gear
Rod Darnell	partner shot brown bear off

Jay BL Reeves	eaten by brownie
Alan Lee Precup	eaten by brownie
Thayer	surprised/awakened brown that killed him
Pennington	griz "ambushed" see Austin and some native kids pre-1920 MABT list
Caposella	grizzly protecting moose kill, partner shot off too late
John Patrick	Slate Creek fatality to black, shot when cache protecting black attacked
Alexie Pitka	approaching wounded black; knife saved him
Cynthia	no weapon whatsoever/mis-information from supervisor; played dead w. black; USGS (other agencies) instituted shooting safety
Hagemeier	surprise brownie, mauled, immobile, left
Wade Nolan	shot camp black w. .41 mag
Ben Moore	hands and .357 in grizzly's mouth when he fired, left
Louis Kis	shot grizzly w. .357, killing it
Rollin Braden	played dead w. two adolescent browns w. something to prove/learning how to live w/o mom—beat him up and left
Dale Bagley	approached kill site, mauled, shot .44 until empty up/into brown, no partner, wasted round from -06
Harley Seivenpiper	solo, deer call, visibility, no time, brownie
1910	2 native boys wounded brown, followed, struck from behind by 2nd bear
1939	Chignik man killed brown w. knife
man	runs around alder patch three times while brownie chases before leaving

Park-agency advisories means to being scarred and scared—misinformation about playing dead. Why not allow visitors firearm?

Improvise	arm in mouth, stall then shoot

Thermos bottle saved Carlsons-brown sow knocked him down, dragged wife, he hit with Thermos, bear left.

Whacked brownie with rifle butt and it left

2 men chase grizzly from mauled woman in Denali

Solo hunters	killed—no partner to help
Effects	Hagemeier and Bigley blinded; Cynthia lost arms
	Some mauling victims have shot themselves after a mauling
	8/1921 two prospectors mauled by sow, one later went insane from tooth wound that penetrated his skull
Unusual	Eskimo lady jammed mittened fist into polar's mouth, suffocated it
1950's	Swede miner near Nome hurled kerosene lantern at polar and ran, she didn't follow
	one Eskimo played dead as polar sniffed him, went to partner-killed-ate
	Bill Martin hazed brownie sow from moose kill to save Joe Delia
	Ray Machen urinated from tree onto black that fled
	Shouting scares griz (MABT list 150)
	Firecrackers scare black away (MABT list, scouts)
	Harry Boyden beats grizzly with stocking cap to face

Killed black with .22 pistol; Eskimo killed 11 griz w. .22 rifle single shot

Dan Gillis c. 1949 switched and dissuaded black with knife

Many kicked-diverted bear (Leo Beeks slugged, kicked & brown sow left)

Dogs	saved many

Got to be a way for people to set up for protection—hunters who don't get off a shot

Vigilance	Fumerton and partner in B.C., griz bear stalked w/in 15 feet—importance of visibility

Danger following wounded bear solo OR w. partner—Forrest McCracken and others

SOURCE NOTES

BOOKS

American Heritage Dictionary, 1970

Carr, Dalton, *Tales of a Bear Hunter*, Safari Press, Inc., Long Beach, CA, 2001

Craighead, Jr., Frank C., *Track of the Grizzly*, Sierra Book Club, San Francisco, CA, 1979

Cramond, Mike, *Killer Bears*, Outdoor Life Books, Times Mirror Magazines, Inc., NY, NY, 1981

Cramond, Mike, *Of Bears and Man*, University of Oklahoma Press, Norman, OK, London, 1986

Domico, Terry, *Bears of the World*, Facts On File, New York, Oxford, 1988

Edwards, Hugh, *Crocodile Attacks*, Avon Books, New York, 1990

East, Ben, *Bears*, Outdoor Life Crown Publishers, New York, 1977

East, Ben, *Narrow Escapes*, E.P. Dutton & Co., Inc., NY, 1960

East, Ben, *Danger*, Outdoor Life-E.P. Dutton & Co., NY, 1970

Eddy, John W., *Hunting the Alaska Brown Bear*, G.P. Putnam's Sons, NY and London, 1930

Feazel, Charles T., *White Bear*, Henry Hold and Company, New York, 1990

Fish, Chet (Editor), *The Outdoor Life Bear Book*, Outdoor Life Books, NY, 1983

Garfield, Brad, *Bear vs. Man*, Willow Creek, Minocqua, WI, 2001

Holzworth, John M., *The Wild Grizzlies of Alaska*, G. P. Putnams Sons, Inc., NY, London, 1930

Howe, John R., *Bear Man of Admiralty Island*, University of Alaska Press, Fairbanks, AK, 1996

Hron, Tom, *Fighting for Your Life*, Proman Inc., Fountain Hills, AZ, 2009

Hubbard, W.P., *Notorious Grizzly Bears*, W.P. Hubbard, Sage Books, Denver, 1960

Johnson, Keith, *Unpredictable Giants*, Gran Farnum Printing and Publishing, Glennwood Springs, CO, 2001

Kaniut, Larry, *Alaska Bear Tales*, Alaska Northwest Books, Seattle, WA, 1983

Kaniut, Larry, *More Alaska Bear Tales*, Alaska Northwest Books, Seattle, WA, 1983

Kaniut, Larry, *Some Bears Kill*, Safari Press, Huntington Beach, CA, 1997

Kaniut, Larry, *Bear Tales for the Ages*, Paper Talk, Anchorage, AK, 2001

Kaniut, Larry, *Danger Stalks the Land*, St. Martin's Griffin, NY, 1999

McMillion, Scott, *Mark of the Grizzly*, Falcon, Helena, MT, 1998

O'Connor, Jack, *The Big Game Animals of North America*, Outdoor Life, 1961

Olsen, Jack, *Night of the Grizzlies*, G.P. Putnam's Sons, NY, 1969

Prodgers, Jeanette, *The Only Good Bear is a Dead Bear*, Falcon Press, Helena and Billings, MT, 1986

Samson, Jack, *The Grizzly Book*, The Amwell Press, Clinton, NJ, 1981

Schneider, Bill, *Be Bear Aware*, Globe Pequot, Guilford, CT, 2004

Schneider, Bill, *Where the Grizzly Walks II*, Falcon, Helena, MT, 2004

Shelton, James Gary, *Bear Encounter Survival Guide*, James Gary Shelton, Hagensborg, B.C., Canada, 1994

Shelton, James Gary, *Bear Attacks: The Deadly Truth*, James Gary Shelton, Hagensborg, B.C., Canada, 1998

Shelton, James Gary, *Bear Attacks II Myth & Reality*, Pallister Publishing, Hagensborg, B.C., Canada, 2001

Smith, Dave, *Backcountry Bear Basics*, The Mountaineers, Seattle, WA, 1997

Van Tighem, Patricia, *The Bear's Embrace*, Anchor Books, NY, 2003

Young, Ralph W., *Grizzlies Don't Come Easy*, Winchester Press, Tulsa, OK, 1981

PERSONAL EMAILS, CORRESPONDENCE AND CONVERSATIONS: cited in text

MAGAZINES, NEWPAPERS, WEBSITES: cited in text

INTERVIEWEES:

Lavern Beier

Daniel Bigley

Dalton Carr

Sig Casiano

Don Chaffin

Kathy Dunagan

Tara Edwards

John Graybill

RC Harrop

Kenny Hetrick

Brent Hughes

Tim Hunt

Joe Huston

Larry Jantz

Keith N. Johnson

Benjamin Kaniut

Jill Kaniut

Brian Knowlton

TJ Langley

Johnny McCoy

Ken Radach

Dave Rand

Ginger Risch

Jennifer Schrage

Guy Sines

Ted Spraker

Stephany Thomas

Gary Titus

Gordon Van Tighem

Don Welty

Good Bear Safety Books

James Gary Shelton is the best. I can't recommend Gary's books highly enough

Bear Encounter Survival Guide
Bear Attacks: The Deadly Truth
Bear Attacks II Myth and Reality

Bear books by Gary Shelton are now available on his website in an electronic format.

James Gary Shelton
Pallister Publishing
Armstrong, B.C. Canada
bearattacksurvival.com

Mike Cramond

Killer Bears
Of Bears and Man

Ted Gorsline

Man-eating Black Bears trilogy

Tom Hron

Fighting for your Life (Man-eater Bears)

Jeannette Prodgers

The Only Good Bear is a Dead Bear

Dalton Carr, born in 1935 in Colorado Springs, Colorado, hunted since the age of 10. He worked bears as a predator control agent on the Yakima Indian Reservation in Washington and has hunted them a lifetime as a sport hunter in Colorado and Wyoming. He published his *Tales of a Bear Hunter* in 2001 at the age of 66.

Larry Kaniut - LarryKaniut@gmail.com

Alaska Bear Tales
More Alaska Bear Tales
Some Bears Kill
Bear Tales for the Ages
SAFE with Bears (Stay Alive From Encounters)
Alaska's Fun Bears
Cheating Death
Danger Stalks the Land
Alaska Air Tales
Brachan
Instant Sourdough
Trapped

Kaniut Titles

Alaska Bear Tales

Comprehensive research about man-bear encounters includes victim, rescuer, family and medical comments—from false charges to fatalities.

I was lucky enough to have Mr. Kaniut as an English Teacher around 1980. During that time he read us stories from *Alaska Bear Tales*. As a struggling student he made me want to read and write. Mr. Kaniut does a great job in pulling the reader into the story. His ability to get people to share the most horrific details of their encounters with bears keeps you wanting more.

Anyone looking to read real life drama this is the book to start with. You will not want to put the book down.

Amazon reader, Daniel Bird, Seattle, WA, November 12, 2000.

More Alaska Bear Tales

Many bear stories with greater emphasis upon humor than original book.

Great Book and Fast Read. Spine tingling reading full of chills, thrills, and even some laughs. Do not pass this book up but be prepared to not be able to put this book down!

Reviewer from San Luis Obispo, CA August 12, 1999

An eye opener…much more than a blood and guts thriller. It affords the reader an open minded look at the attacks and as you read you find yourself second guessing the victims. Larry has put forth alot of effort in his research I enjoyed the book and hope that there is a book three in the works...--Reviewer: jdmiles@worldnet.att.net from Arizona October 28, 1998

Cheating Death

Eighteen stories of outdoor mishap in Alaska.

"I was not able to put it down."   --P.K. Willis

"I have enjoyed *Cheating Death*; the story about Mike Harbaugh is terrific, reminding me of my close calls in similar flying conditions. All your stories are good reading."

--Lowell Thomas, Jr., former Lieutenant Governor, State of Alaska

After my 2 trips to Alaska (3 months RV, and then a cruise) I really enjoyed reading this book and discovering even deeper the wild and dangerous side of Alaska. Kept me reading, and was hard to put down.

I finished reading the book in 2 days and shared it with my neighbors. I actually went on the Boat Adventure from Talkeetna, AK, as we were in the class 4 rapids - the owner went further - as it describes in the book, and after meeting him, this inspired me to buy the book.

5.0 out of 5 stars Amazon reader, Loretta Savary, January 12, 2010

…"one savors the triumph and giddiness of survival when survival seems out of the question." --General Aviation News & Flyer

Some Bears Kill

Thirty-eight stories involving men struggling against the hairy, four-legged beast known as bear.

Three of the best known writers about Alaska are Rex Beach, Jack London, and Robert Service…All of those authors are from a period, early in this century, when Alaska was a vast, unknown territory. Their stories and poetry helped in formulating a vision, often inaccurate, of Alaska that continues to this day in the minds of armchair adventurers. Larry Kaniut is destined to join Beach, London, and Service as one of the best of Alaskan writers. --Wayne Ross

Danger Stalks the Land

Forty-two stories ranging from saltwater to mountaintop…pitting man against the nasty elements dished out by Mother Alaska.

Good book for city slicker youth, say 14 years old and up. As opposed to video games or TV, reality just oozes from every Pg. Not a bad thing to hammer home the actions/consequences theme in a young'un, Lord knows Darwin isn't welcome in modern society.

Amazon reader Michael Eckhardt, 5.0 out of 5 stars Amazing stories, March 11, 2010, (Douglas, AK)
Mind numbing true adventure! 5 stars

This is easily the best collection of true adventure tales ever assembled. I was blown away by the courage, danger, and pure adrenaline running through these stories. My advice: run to your nearest bookstore and BUY THIS BOOK!
--Jim Walters (jimwalters@regency.org) Washington State,11/19/99

From *Publishers Weekly*

A pair of youthful newlyweds embarks on a gold-panning outing, but only one returns alive. Twelve climbers, roped together in groups of four, plunge down a mountainside, landing in a twisted heap of mangled bodies. A geologist on a mapping expedition radios to her superiors: "I'm being eaten by a bear!" These are just some of the vividly rendered disasters and close calls Alaskan writer Kaniut details in this collection of true life adventures. Stretching from the mid-19th century to the recent past, the 43 pieces are plenty scary, but Kaniut, a former high school teacher who has lived in Alaska since 1966, also uses the stories to teach valuable lessons about character, loyalty and courage. In some cases, the difference between survival and death is no more than happenstance. But in others, disaster is due to inexperience or the failure to recognize a dangerous situation. Short introductions and brief teasers leading to the next story help move the reader through the book, and an appendix contains valuable information on what it takes to have a chance of survival in the Alaskan wilderness.

Your book has jumped to the front of my reading list, the other twenty books under the bed will have to wait a couple of days til "danger" is finished. One day into the book and half of it read already. Eagerly awaiting your next book. Cheers Andy

Kaniut.com email, Andy Millard, South Wales, UK, November 11, 1999

THE ULTIMATE HUMAN TRIUMPHS AND TRAGEDIES   5 stars

READING THESE REAL LIFE ACCOUNTS WILL LEAVE YOU MARVELING AT THE POWER OF THE HUMAN SPIRIT AND THE WILL POWER SOME MEN HAVE TO LIVE. YOU WILL SEE HOW TRAGEDY CAN STRIKE EVEN THE WELL PREPARED AND HOW NATURE CAN PUSH MAN TO UNTHINKABLE LIMITS. BY FAR, LARRY KANIUT'S BEST BOOK.

--ernest w. hedrick, Collegeville, PA, March 12, 2000

Mr. Kaniut.   Thank you for your publication *Danger Stalks the Land*. There are several things I appreciated most, 1-The articles and stories were more recent, 2-The bystanders and survivors were able to look back and capture what they might have done differently 'next time.' As an active Board Member and active field member of Pacific Northwest Search and Rescue and a Survival Instructor at (NWSOS) Northwest School of Survival, I am always looking for examples, results, and follow-up on searches and rescues. I am also the editor of our SAR groups monthly newsletter. I hope you don't mind, but I took the liberty of recommending your book to our group! Thank you! If you are ever in Clackamas County, feel free to stop by one of our monthly meetings. We'd love to hear your experiences. Thanks you for this opportunity
Kate Brackin, Oregon   Kaniut.com email April 4, 2000

Hello and thank you for doing such a great job with my dad's story which you included in the last chapter of Danger Stalks The Land. Once again I thank you for doing such a good job of putting my dad, C.D. Tuggle into print. He deserved something like that and you were the one to do it! Natalee Roe erbberoeb@aol.com, New Mexico

Kaniut.com email August 8, 2000

Norwegian adventurer and explorer Lars Monsen emailed me: I really enjoyed *Danger Stalks the Land*. I shook my head over and over. Everyone interested in survival should read this. Great job?

Bear Tales for the Ages

…Larry Kaniut's seventh adventure packed book of outdoor danger; bear attacks, and outdoor lore. It's a can't-put-it-down white knuckle read from page one to the end…28 stories of bear attacks from 1816 to 1999. These were mostly gleaned from his extensive collection of out of print bear books, and rewritten here to introduce a new generation to the wonder of this tenacious animal, and the indomitable spirit of man.

A grizzly bear in Montana ambushes a sheepherder, then there was the man who mounted a "set-gun" to kill a grizzly…bear and bull fights, and a bear and Bull Moose fight in the wild.

Since I, too, live in Alaska, this book has certainly increased my respect for the big bears. They are beautiful animals, but they do not interact well with people. Kaniut's writing is very exciting; he is a premier storyteller, and the action is nonstop.

You can feel the author's anguish when man loses the battle, but the bears are portrayed with respect, awe, and a merged love and fear. Plan to stay up all night to finish this book. You just as well…you are not going to sleep.

© MyShelf.Com. All Rights Reserved; Reviewed by Beverly J. Rowe

Alaska's Fun Bears

Ninety-four fun packed pages for adult-child interaction—designed for adult-child engagement with activities, coloring and information… instead of relegating the younger to Game Boy and another room. Over forty bears dressed and engaged in human outdoor activities—such as—snowboarding, skiing, curling and clamming in Alaska. The book includes alphabet, maze, matching, coloring and tons of questions for the adult to share with the child.

Alaska Air Tales

If you're looking for insight into the world of Alaskan bush pilots you will enjoy this book. It's packed with personal accounts of real experiences written in a page turning way. The mountains, winds, and wilds of Alaska can be very unforgiving for those ill prepared. It's not just a book of machismo moments of thrill seekers. Dr. Bobbie Hemry writes, "After several seconds, a searing pain began in my left shoulder and crescendoed to an intensity that finally made me realize I had been struck by the airplane propeller. Being a physician, my mind made a rapid assessment. Was the blow fatal?" And so the stories go. Paul Claus, with over 28,000 logged hours, gives remarkable insight into unique aspects of mountain flying in Alaska. The book is an excellent addition to anyone's Alaskan aviation library that might already include such books as *Wager with the Wind*: The Don Sheldon Story and *Glacier Pilot*.

Amazon reader Alaska Guy, 5 stars, August 3, 2016

Instant Sourdough

Humorous definitions of Alaska terminology, most of which goes over the head of Cheechakoes (or newcomers)…words like Spenard divorce and bear insurance.

Brachan

A Roman soldier, selected to monitor John the Baptist as a threat to the Empire, finds more than one "threat." On his mission Brachan discovers way more than he'd anticipated.

I absolutely love Brachan. You have something very special here. I am amazed. I had no idea you could write like this.

--Randy Mc Kenzie, Bookmasters, email 10-13-15

I often judge a book by the emotions it takes me through. I laughed, I cried a bit, I felt like I was there in the city, on the road with the dust and dirt, there in the temple, your description of the whip, and for the good of Rome, you nailed it, I can't say enough, this is big time to me. I felt like I was there. Your descriptions are very good.

--Randy Mc Kenzie, Bookmasters, email, October 2015

I read Brachan in cold, snowy December and found it so engaging that it lifted me out of the winter doldrums. Brachan, which means called of God, is a story narrated from the point of view of a Roman soldier who was sent to keep an eye on Jesus lest there be a potential plot brewing to overthrow the Roman empire.

Brachan's accounting of his experience observing the famous Nazarene is so remarkable that the reader actually feels like a back-seat participant in the narrative. This story flows on seamlessly without judgment. While the chronicle regales the last few years of life of Jesus, it does so sans a preachy tone.

Some of the vivid, detailed descriptions in the book show meticulous research into the era and place where Jesus walked. And the reader gets a good glimpse of the Roman worldview too.

It is a great read and I would recommend it for all audiences—those who enjoy non-fiction as well as those who just like a good plot and story. Brachan is a natural storyteller and once the reader begins, he or she will be hooked to the end.

Amazon reader, 5 stars, Jeanette Prodgers, Dillon, MT, March 19, 2016

Great book!! Larry Kaniut is a wonderful writer in the sense that he can transport his readers to the place and events in the story. You feel as if you are there --hearing the sounds, seeing the action, and even smelling the atmosphere! It is a wonderful, different approach to the events in the life of Jesus Christ. I would recommend this book to anyone- believers as well as nonbelievers.

Amazon reader, Janice Eckard, 5 stars, March 9, 2016

A wonderful read. I just finished your book and had to write you a quick note to tell you how moving and wonderful it was. I am an avid reader, usually spending at least two hours each day reading. A good book is often described as one you can't put down. This often implies that you want to get to the end. Your book was different. I read each page and then often went back and reread sections of the page to fully digest it. I wasn't happy just reading it. I wanted to immerse myself in the details. It is a terrific book Larry. I am so glad that the story doesn't end. I just can't say enough about how really good it is!!!

Amazon reader, August 14, 2016

Trapped!

Gabrielle wasn't attempting to save the world but she thought she'd have a chance on her return to New York to shed light on the rights of animals with a photo-journalist piece. What she didn't realize was that her return would be a question and concern.

www.ingramcontent.com/pod-product-compliance
Lightning Source LLC
Chambersburg PA
CBHW070033030426
42335CB00017B/2406